UNDER THE GUN:

Weapons, Crime, and Violence in America

UNDER THE GUN:

Weapons, Crime, and Violence in America

James D. Wright, Peter H. Rossi, Kathleen Daly

with the assistance of Eleanor Weber-Burdin

Aldine de Gruyter
New York

About the Authors

James D. Wright is Professor of Sociology at the University of Massachusetts, Amherst and Director of the Social and Demographic Research Institute. He is the author of many ground-breaking books including: *Victims of the Environment, The Handbook of Survey Research, The State of the Masses,* and *Armed and Considered Dangerous* (with Peter H. Rossi).

Peter H. Rossi is Professor of Sociology at the University of Massachusetts, Amherst, Director of Research at the Social and Demographic Research Institute, and Past President of the American Sociological Association. Widely regarded as among the most eminent of American social scientists, Dr. Rossi has authored over 20 books including *Reforming Public Welfare, Measuring Social Judgments, Natural Hazards and Public Choice,* and *Armed and Considered Dangerous* (with James D. Wright).

Kathleen Daly is a member of the faculty of the department of sociology, Yale University. Her research has recently focused on the effects of gender in court proceedings and case disposition.

Aldine de Gruyter
A Division of Walter de Gruyter, Inc.
200 Saw Mill River Road
Hawthorne, New York 10532

ISBN 0-202-30306-3 paperbound
       0-202-30305-5 clothbound

Library of Congress Cataloging in Publication Data

Wright, James D.
    Under the gun.

    Bibliography: p.
    Includes index.
    1. Violent crimes—United States. 2 Firearms—
Government policy—United States. I. Rossi,
Peter Henry, 1921–   . II. Daly, Kathleen
(Kathleen M.) III. Title.
HV6791.W74   1983   363.3'3   83-2615

Printed in the United States of America
10   9   8   7   6   5

Table of Contents

Preface   xi

Acknowledgments   xvii

ONE

Weapons, Crime, and Violence: An Overview of Themes and Findings

Text   1

Part I: Weapons

TWO

How Many Guns in Private Hands?

Text   25

THREE

Recent Trends in Weapons Ownership: I. Sport and Recreational Demand

The Trend in Weapons Supply   45

Household Increase   50

Sport and Recreation Demand   53

Summary   63

FOUR

Recent Trends in Weapons Ownership: II. The Police Demand for Armament

The Personnel Trend   66

The Armaments Policy Trend   72

FIVE

Recent Trends in Weapons Ownership: III. "Fear and Loathing" and the Mass Demand for Defensive Weapons

Survey Data on the Weapons Trend   84

Empirical Studies of "Fear and Loathing"   93

SIX

Characteristics of Private Weapons Owners

Locational Variables: Region and City Size   104

Social Status: Class, Religion, Race, and Sex   107

The Southern Subculture   109

Socialization   112

Personality Characteristics   120

Conclusions: The "Typical" Gun Owner   121

SEVEN

On Crime and Private Weapons

Is Crime a Cause of Private Weaponry?   128

Is Private Weaponry a Cause of Crime?   129

Does Private Weaponry Deter Crime?   138

Part II: Crime and Violence

EIGHT

How Much Crime? How Much Violence?

Longitudinal Trends in Violent Crime: UCR Statistics   154

Trends in Violent Crime from Victimization Surveys   160

Trends in Accidental and Self-Inflicted Death and Injury   166

Police Homicide and Deaths and Assaults of Police Officers 170

Summary and Estimates of Violence   172

NINE

The Firearms Used in Crime

Magnitude of Crime Guns Confiscated: The NBS Survey   176

ATF Project Identification   177

ATF Project 300   181

ATF Project Cue   182

Burr's Study of Florida Citizens and Convicted Felons   183

Summary   187

TEN

On the Matter of Criminal Motivations

Text   189

Part III: Weapons and Their Control

ELEVEN

Public Opinion and Gun Control

Technical Comparisons   217

Comparisons of Substantive Findings   221

Conclusions: Weapons and Their Control   240

TWELVE

Regulating Firearms: An Overview of Federal, State, and Local Practices

Federal Legislation   245

State and Local Regulations   247

Coverage of Existing Firearms Regulations   269

Implementation of Gun Control Laws   270

Conclusion   272

THIRTEEN

Weapons Control Legislation and Effects on Violent Crime

Issues in Assessing the Impact of Gun Control Legislation   273

Landmark Evaluations of Gun Control Effects 282

On the Effectiveness of Gun Control Legislation 307

FOURTEEN

Some Policy Implications

The Civilian Firearms Policy Issues 310

The Role of Firearms in American Life 311

Violence and Guns 313

The Circulation of Weapons in the United States 315

An Assessment of Gun Control Measures 316

A Concluding Polemic 319

Bibliography 325
Index 335

SOCIAL INSTITUTIONS AND SOCIAL CHANGE

An Aldine de Gruyter Series of Texts and Monographs

EDITED BY

Michael Useem • James D. Wright

Mary Ellen Colten and Susan Gore (eds.), **Adolescent Stress: Causes and Consequences**

Paul Diesing, **Science and Ideology in the Policy Sciences**

G. William Domhoff, **The Power Elite and the State: How Policy is Made in America**

Glen H. Elder, Jr. and Rand D. Conger, **Families in a Changing Society: Hard Times in Rural America**

Paula S. England, **Comparable Worth**

Paula S. England, **Theory on Gender/Feminism on Theory**

Paula S. England and George Farkas, **Households, Employment, and Gender: A Social, Economic, and Demographic View**

George Farkas, Robert P. Grobe, and Daniel Sheehan, **Human Capital or Cultural Capital?**

F. G. Gosling (ed.), **Risk and Responsibility**

Richard F. Hamilton and James D. Wright, **The State of the Masses**

Gary Kleck, **Point Blank: Guns and Violence in America**

James R. Kluegel and Eliot R. Smith, **Beliefs About Inequality: Americans' Views of What Is and What Ought to Be**

David Knoke, **Organizing for Collective Action: The Political Economies of Associations**

Dean Knudsen and JoAnn L. Miller (eds.), **Abused and Battered: Social and Legal Responses to Family Violence**

Robert C. Liebman and Robert Wuthnow (eds.), **The New Christian Right: Mobilization and Legitimation**

Theodore R. Marmor, **The Politics of Medicare** (*Second Edition*)

Clark McPhail, **The Myth of the Madding Crowd**

Clark McPhail, **Acting Together: The Organization of Crowds**

John Mirowsky and Catherine E. Ross, **Social Causes of Psychological Distress**

Carolyn C. and Robert Perrucci, Dena B. and Harry R. Targ, **Plant Closings: International Context and Social Costs**

Robert Perrucci and Harry R. Potter (eds.), **Networks of Power: Organizational Actors at the National, Corporate, and Community Levels**

David Popenoe, **Disturbing the Nest: Family Change and Decline in Modern Societies**

James T. Richardson, Joel Best, and David G. Bromley (eds.), **The Satanism Scare**

Bernard C. Rosen, **The Industrial Connection: Achievement and the Family in Developing Societies**

Alice S. Rossi and Peter H. Rossi, **Of Human Bonding: Parent-Child Relations Across the Life Course**

Roberta G. Simmons and Dale A. Blyth, **Moving into Adolescence: The Impact of Pubertal Change and School Context**

David G. Smith, **Paying for Medicare: The Politics of Reform**

Walter L. Wallace, **Principles of Scientific Sociology**

Martin King Whyte, **Dating, Mating, and Marriage**

James D. Wright, **Address Unknown: The Homeless in America**

James D. Wright and Peter H. Rossi, **Armed and Considered Dangerous: A Survey of Felons and Their Firearms**

James D. Wright, Peter H. Rossi, and Kathleen Daly, **Under the Gun: Weapons, Crime, and Violence in America**

Preface

In 1978, the Social and Demographic Research Institute of the University of Massachusetts, Amherst, received a grant from the National Institute of Justice to undertake a comprehensive review of the literature on weapons, crime, and violence in the United States. The purpose of the project is best described as a "sifting and winnowing" of the claims and counterclaims from both sides of the Great American Gun War—the perennial struggle in American political life over what to do, if anything, about guns, about violence, and about crime. The review and analysis of the available studies consumed the better part of three years; the results of this work are contained in this volume.

The intention of any review is to take stock of the available fund of knowledge in some topical area. *Under the Gun* is no different: our goal has been to glean from the volumes of previous studies those facts that, in our view, seem firmly and certainly established; those hypotheses that seem adequately supported by, or at least approximately consistent with, the best available research evidence; and those areas or topics about which, it seems, we need to know a lot more than we do. One of our major conclusions can be stated in advance: despite the large number of studies that have been done, many critically important questions have not been adequately researched, and some of them have not been examined at all.

Much of the available research in the area of weapons and crime has been done by advocates for one or another policy position. As a consequence, the manifest intent of many "studies" is to persuade rather than to inform. We have tried to approach the topic from a purely agnostic point of view, treating as an open question what policies should be enacted with regard to gun, or crime, control. Thus, we have tried to judge each study on its own merits, on the basis of the routine standards normally applied to social-scientific research, and not on the basis of how effectively it argues for a particular policy direction. It would, of course, be presumptuous to claim that we have set aside all our own biases in conducting this study. Whether or not our treatment is fair and objective is clearly something for the reader, and not us, to decide.

With a few relatively unimportant exceptions, the work reported here does not add new evidence or data to this field of academic criminology. Our goal was not to strike out in new and innovative research directions, but to compile and assess the research work of others. The value of this undertaking lies in the wide coverage and critical assessment we have given to the topic of weapons and criminal violence in the United States.

We have defined the topic of the study in the broadest possible terms. Thus, we touch down frequently on issues that are only peripherally related to the more narrow question of the uses of weaponry in the commission of violent criminal acts. Exhaustive details on some technical points are thus sacrificed for wider coverage of relevant topics and, for this reason, we are certain to have overlooked at least some of the important literature. Indeed, the current version of the book includes discussions of, or citations to, a number of studies that were omitted in earlier versions. We do think, however, that all major studies are covered here—at least all major studies published as of early 1982.

Most of our criticisms of other studies are methodological in nature. We sought to determine if samples were drawn correctly, variables measured adequately, analyses performed competently, and so on. We fully recognize that standards of research are intrinsically relative in nature: if one adopts absolute standards of the pristine variety, then *any* piece of research can be dismissed. Dr. Johnson once remarked that patriotism is the last refuge of a scoundrel. Methodology may well be the first. This notwithstanding, although we have held the literature to high standards, we have not held it to unattainable standards, and have attempted to be realistic about the capabilities and limitations of current research methods in the social sciences.

Given the nature of our assessments, many of our conclusions are essentially methodological rather than substantive. Thus, we often conclude that "there is no compelling evidence that . . ." or "there are few data to suggest that. . . ." A critical but often overlooked methodological point must, therefore, be stressed in advance: *the absence of evidence is not the same as evidence of absence.* For example, one of our conclusions is that there is no compelling evidence that the private ownership of firearms among the general population is, per se, an important cause of criminal violence. This is *not* to conclude that guns are not a cause of crime, but rather that no one has yet persuasively demonstrated this to be the case. The unproved hypothesis is just that: *unproved,* not necessarily true or false.

The point is perhaps best made by example. At one stage in the history of human thought, it would have been perfectly true and in order for someone to conclude that "there is no compelling evidence to demonstrate that the earth is round." Indeed, the very notion of a spherical earth would have, at one time, been grossly inconsistent with a mass of direct visual evidence. The absence of compelling evidence for the round earth hypothesis, however, does not make the flat earth hypothesis true! The skeptic whose conclusion is quoted above, in other words, did *not* conclude that the earth was flat, only that no one had yet demonstrated it conclusively not to be. To mistake the one conclusion for the other is an analytic error of the most basic sort.

Many of the conclusions reported in this volume turn on the rather thorny issues of inference and proof in the social (or, more generally, nonexperimental) sciences. We have made every effort to explain these issues in straightforward and nontechnical ways. Readers who are highly sophisticated in the methods of social research will find many of these discussions pedantic. However, our intent has been to write a book that is readily accessible to those without advanced methodological training. If the price of so doing is tedium among our more sophisticated colleagues, then we have struck an acceptable bargain.

Under the Gun enjoyed a previous incarnation as a research report published by the National Institute of Justice, entitled *Weapons, Crime and Violence in America: A Literature Review and Research Agenda.* There are only minor differences between the earlier and present versions: we have added new literature where appropriate, greatly condensed some of the original chapters, and added a new final chapter in which the policy implications of our findings are discussed. Also, to the extent possible, we have corrected all the factual errors that were brought to our attention by readers of the earlier draft. But the general themes, approach, and structure of the two versions are the same.

The importance of reliable information and valid insight about weapons, crime, and violence cannot be overstated. In one or another way, all of us are *"under the gun."* Although estimates vary widely (see Chapter 2), there are currently at least 100 million firearms in private hands in the United States—the true figure may well be several tens of millions higher. In any recent year picked at random, approximately a million of these firearms will have been involved in some sort of unfortunate incident—in a chargeable crime, a successful or attempted firearms suicide, a gun accident, and so on (see Chapter 8). In recent years, the annual domestic death toll from firearms has been on the order of 30,000 (combining gun homicides, gun suicides, and fatal gun accidents). Directly or indirectly, firearms violence threatens the quality of life in the society as a whole.

In any major American city, the fear of crime and violence is palpable. People walk the streets on the defensive. Recent poll data (reviewed in Chapter 7) suggest that as many as 7% of the nation's adults—about 1 adult in 14—carry a handgun with them while outside the home. In the 1980 General Social Survey (conducted by the National Opinion Research Center), 43% of the adult population reported that there are areas around their homes where they are afraid to walk alone at night; in the same survey just under 10% reported that their home had been broken into in the previous year. Sooner or later, the American crime rate touches everybody and degrades the quality of our collective existence.

Because of the seriousness of the problem of firearms violence, the Congress, too, is *under the gun.* What to do about crime and what to do about the weaponry with which it is committed are perennial issues on the policy agenda of the nation. New proposals on how to deal with the problem arise in nearly every session of Congress, and on state and local political agendas as well. Both sides of the Great American Gun War are organized for the battle, although the pro-gun forces apparently enjoy a distinct advantage: the last major Federal gun law was passed in 1968. Thus, several new proposals are currently pending before Congress, but the prospects for their enactment do not seem bright. As we emphasize in the concluding chapter of this book, many of the proposals that periodically surface are based more on half-baked hunches and wishful thinking than on hard, scientific facts. History has already taught us the folly of trying to solve problems before we completely understand them, and the problem of gun violence is one that we do not understand very well. Indeed, to anticipate a major theme of this book, there is a virtually complete absence of sound, nationally generalizable evidence on most of the important issues involved in the matter of firearms and crime. Important policy decisions, affecting the lives of vast segments of the American population, are being made in what amounts to an information vacuum.

It is for precisely this reason that the social sciences are also *under the gun.* Violent crime amounts to a *social* problem of the purest sort; nobody expects some technological or engineering breakthrough to solve it. If we are going to solve the problem at all, it will be through influencing the behaviors of individuals and groups, and assuredly not through some cheap or convenient technological "fix." Yet, the sociology and psychology of the acquisition and use of firearms are rudimentary at best. In our view, it is not the role of the social sciences to advise on matters of public policy, but rather to provide a reliable information base on which policy decisions can be made. Toward this end, the first step must clearly be some assessment of the reliability of the information presently in hand. It perhaps goes without saying that such is the purpose of this book.

James D. Wright
Peter H. Rossi
Kathleen Daly

Acknowledgments

Earlier versions of *Under the Gun* have been reviewed and commented upon by a large number of people—some prominently identified with the pro-gun forces, others prominently identified with the pro-control forces, and still others of a more neutral persuasion. When it was issued, the initial research report was widely covered by the press, and this in turn occasioned several scores of letters from people from all over the United States. Interest in the topic of firearms and crime is evidently quite widespread! All these letters were entertaining and informative, and called our attention to materials or perspectives that we had overlooked. It is not possible to thank each of the individuals, but we are grateful for their interest and the insights they provided.

Others have had a more sustained and direct involvement in the project. Our first debt and highest gratitude must, of course, go to the National Institute of Justice for funding the project and for continuing to fund the violent crime research program of the Social and Demographic Research Institute. Although NIJ financed this study, neither the Institute, nor the Department of Justice, nor the Federal government is responsible for the analyses, interpretations, opinions, and conclusions expressed here, all of which, for better or worse, remain our own.

Our Project Manager at NIJ was Dr. Lois Mock of the Community Crime Prevention Program, and we extend our deep gratitude to her for the many valuable insights and for her patience with the rhythms (and the blues) of University life. We also thank her for insulating us from the various political struggles that are endemic to the Federal bureaucracy, particularly in the late stages of the project. We would like to thank the staff at NIJ for contributing many valuable comments and criticisms of the larger study during a policy briefing in which the major findings and their implications were aired.

We are grateful for the time and advice given us by our Advisory Committee: Dr. Alan Lizotte, Indiana University; Dr. Philip Cook, Duke University; Dr.

Ilene Nagel, Indiana University; Dr. David Bordua, University of Illinois; Dr. James Short, Washington State University; and Dr. Marvin Wolfgang, University of Pennsylvania.

Several research assistants worked with us on various parts of the project and are owed a special note of thanks for service well beyond the going rate of pay. We acknowledge in particular the work of Huey Chen and Joseph Pereira. We were also blessed by a capable and cheerful secretarial staff; we thank Ms. Cindy Coffman, Ms. Jeanne Reinle, Mrs. Laura Martin, and Ms. Nancy Sturge.

Finally, we acknowledge the assistance of the following individuals who read and reacted to one or another part of this report in earlier versions: Mr. Paul Blackman, Mr. Nelson Shields, Mr. Donald Kates, and various of our colleagues at the University of Massachusetts.

Research reported in this volume was conducted under a grant (No. 78-NI-AX-0120) from the National Institute of Justice, United States Department of Justice, Washington, D.C.

ONE

WEAPONS, CRIME, AND VIOLENCE:
An Overview of Themes and Findings

The United States stands out among the contemporary industrialized democracies of the world on at least two counts relevant to the topics of this book. First, there are more privately owned firearms, both absolutely and proportionally, in the United States than in most other western societies. Evidence from several sources confirms that at least one half of the households in the country possess a firearm and that the total weaponry in private hands probably numbers somewhere in the vicinity of 120,000,000 guns. There are a few nations (such as Switzerland, Israel, and Norway) where, through the force of special circumstances and the existence of an armed reserve militia, the proportional prevalence of small arms among households rivals that of the United States, but as far as a discretionary weapons arsenal among the private citizenry is concerned, the United States is certainly at or near the top.

The general prevalence and ready availability of small arms, America's frontier past, and the omnipresence of guns and gun imagery in our popular culture and myth have led at least one noted historian, Richard Hofstadter, to depict "America as a Gun Culture"—a culture where The Gun plays a central symbolic role, and quite possibly, the only such culture on the planet today. One might properly quarrel with many of the details of Hofstadter's (1970) depiction, but its general thrust seems plausible enough. Where else but in the United States, for example, would one expect to find surplus military submachine guns being marketed, in all apparent seriousness, as "The Perfect Father's Day Gift" (Sherrill, 1973)? Or .45-caliber semiautomatic carbines being advertised as "Life Insurance—Regardless of Age an Adult Can Buy This Kind of Protection—Paid Up for Life for $179.00" (Smith, 1979)? Less sensational, and rather more meaningful evidence on the unique role of the gun in American culture can be had from Hollywood movies, American fictional literature, or the typical contents of any evening's prime-time television

1

programming. The Gun may not constitute the very heart of American culture and civilization, but it is assuredly an important component. Whether for sport or self-defense or illicit criminal purposes, the United States is, without any reasonable doubt, among the more heavily armed private populations in the world.

A second American "distinction," rather a dubious one, to be sure, is that the incidence of violent crime, and of violence in general, is also higher in the United States than in most other places. Unfortunately, as is well known, crime statistics in the United States are not especially reliable, and outside the United States they are even less so. Therefore, it is difficult to state in precise quantitative terms just how unusual the American experience is in this regard. But there are several fragments of evidence, some quantitative, some episodic, to suggest at least the approximate magnitude.

Newton and Zimring (1969) have compiled gun homicide and gun robbery data for the United States and for England and Wales. The comparison suggests that the gun homicide rate in the United States may be as much as 40 times the rate in the United Kingdom, and the gun robbery rate as much as 60 times higher (1969: 124).

In the same vein, a writer for the *Montreal Star* (April 8, 1971 issue) compared the homicide rate in Detroit with that of Windsor, Ontario, a "sister city" just across the Detroit River. The Detroit rate exceeded the Windsor rate by roughly 100 to 3.

Bakal (1966) reports that there were 9250 murder victims in the United States in 1964, of whom 55% were slain by firearms; at present, the numbers of homicides and gun homicides per year are about twice or more the 1964 figures, and the proportion of homicides committed with firearms appears to be increasing. In sharp contrast, in the same year, Japan had 37 gun homicides from a total of 1469 (3%); Britain, 29 of 309 (9%); Canada, 92 of 266 (35%); Belgium, 9 of 53 (17%); Denmark, 6 of 23 (26%); Sweden, 5 of 86 (6%); The Netherlands, strikingly, had no firearms homicides at all over a 3-year period. More recent compilations of international comparative data (e.g., Curtis, 1974) show essentially the same results. The idea of putting one's fellow citizens to death, and using firearms to do it, seems rather more widespread and firmly established in the United States than in any other advanced industrial civilization.

More recently, a well-known pro-gun-control pamphlet entitled *A Shooting Gallery Called America* observes, "The United States has more gun deaths every year than any other country in the world. In fact, the total number of gun deaths in all other nations is exceeded by the number of gun deaths in the United States alone. Furthermore, not only does the rate of American homicides and accidents by firearms far surpass that of every Western European nation, but it is also higher than those of the 'frontier' countries of

Canada and Australia" (Massachusetts Council on Crime and Correction, 1974).

To be sure, none of these international comparisons can be taken strictly at face value. Aside from differences in the completeness and reliability of the crime data, the nations being compared also differ in history, culture, and tradition; in ethnic and socioeconomic composition; in the rates of private weapons ownership and the legislation that governs such ownership; in the customary patterns of sentencing for people committing gun crimes; and in hundreds of other ways that make straight nation-to-nation comparisons misleading. However, the general lesson to be drawn from such comparisons is much less ambiguous and is generally unassailable. As Newton and Zimring (1969: 123) summarize, "most industrially developed Western nations experience far lower rates of gun crime than the United States."

What is the relationship, if any, between these two "distinctions" or, in other words, between the general availability of small arms and the rates of crime and violence in the United States? This question has been the object of much intense political debate and speculation, most of it white-hot. It has also been the object of at least some credible empirical research, although it must be confessed that the debators and speculators are several times more numerous than the researchers. Such research as has been done on weapons, crime, and violence in the United States constitutes the subject of this volume.

In general, one would be ill-advised to point to the academic literature on weapons and crime as an example of the scientific objectivity that is discussed in introductory methods textbooks. Both "guns" and "crime" are emotionally laden symbols that evoke strongly held and not always rational feelings, anxieties, and concerns, and researchers are not exempt from such evocations. Further, what to do about guns and how to deal with crime are hardy perennials on the nation's political agenda, and thus something of potentially overriding importance for policy is at stake in every piece of research on these topics. Almost everyone has some opinion about guns and crime and, certainly, the people who spend their professional lives researching guns and crime are no exception. Thus, many (perhaps all) researchers in this area bring with them to the research task a set of personal beliefs and political ideologies, which, if they do not destroy outright the credibility of the research, at least sometimes interfere with sound research judgments.

When we first undertook this literature review, our intention was to avoid as much as possible the polemical literature and deal only with serious, credible, objective research. What we have found is that virtually all of the literature on these topics is polemical to some extent, if not by intention then certainly in effect. As in Harlan County, "there are no neutrals here."

What accounts for the generally polemical tone that one finds in this literature? There are a number of sources, not all of them entirely avoidable. First, here as in all other areas of scholarship, people are drawn to particular research topics because they have some personal stake in them. These personal stakes influence what aspects of the topic are selected for study, which pieces of the assembled evidence get more or less emphasis, and what policy implications are drawn out of the results. To cite one obvious example, there are at least 100 million firearms in private hands in the United States today. Depending on one's outlook, this fact demonstrates quite conclusively either (1) that there is an obvious, self-evident, and immediate need for some sort of control over this vast supply of arms, or (2) that the vast supply of arms already in private hands renders futile any efforts at governmental control. Thus, proponents of stricter controls can cite the sheer numbers of guns as evidence that "something *must* be done," and opponents can cite the same numbers as evidence that "nothing *can* be done." Which of these conclusions is the "right" one, of course, does not depend at all on the numbers themselves but on the implications one is willing to draw from them, and the implications one is willing to draw seem as much the result of a priori beliefs as anything else.

Also, even when the producers of knowledge are relatively neutral and objective, the consumers and users of that knowledge typically are not. In the "Great American Gun War," as Bruce-Biggs (1976) has described the American firearms policy debate, the lines of battle are sharply drawn and no love is lost among the contestants. Leading the anti-control faction is the Institute for Legislative Action, principal lobbying arm of the National Rifle Association, which is often described, not without some justification, as the most powerful political lobby in Washington today. From the pro-gun point of view, the advocates of stricter gun control are seen as mostly bleeding-heart liberals and pointy-headed bureaucrats whose intelligence, manhood, and respect for citizens' rights are all open to some question. The pro-control faction is rather more dispersed and consists of perhaps a score or more of organizations working for some aspect of stricter gun control. From their point of view, the pro-gun organizations and the private gun owners they represent are demented and blood-thirsty psychopaths whose concept of fun is to rain death upon innocent creatures, both human and otherwise. Polarization at the extremes, of course, has made it difficult for a responsible center to form. The extremists on either side are always willing (and, more often than not, able) to append a polemical interpretation to a research finding, even when the researchers themselves have not. Thus, researchers often find themselves aligned on one or the other side of the issue, regardless of whether they have intended to take a stand.

Then, too, proper national policy with respect to firearms and crime has long been an open political question, and no capable researcher in the area could possibly fail to notice the potential policy implications of his or her research, most of all in an era of declining research monies in which it has come to be expected that research generate "policy-relevant" results. In the haste to say something of relevance to policy, the bounds of good science, as well as good taste, can be quickly exceeded.

Yet another problem, possibly more tractable than those just discussed, is that there is very little in the weapons, violence, and crime literature that would qualify as hard empirical fact. Solid, nationally representative evidence on any relevant topic is rare or nonexistent. Rather, the literature is dominated by small-scale state and local studies, with the ensuing unavoidable disarray of contradictory findings and results. At present, we do not know the total number of privately owned firearms in the United States except to the nearest few tens of millions, and we have even less knowledge of the kinds of firearms in private hands (except for the rough distribution between handguns and shoulder weapons), how they are used, why they are owned, or how long they last. Such fragments of knowledge as we do have on these topics are typically derived from studies in a single community or occasionally a single state, and their implications for the nation as a whole are therefore uncertain.

In the same vein, our knowledge of crime and violence is substantially less than ideal. Here too, small-scale state and local studies predominate, and the national data that do exist are beset with various problems. For example, we do not know for certain just how many violent crimes are committed in the United States in any given year. From the FBI's *Uniform Crime Reports,* we can get the approximate numbers of violent crimes known to the police, but we also know from surveys of criminal victimization that crimes reported to the police are only a fraction of all crimes actually committed. The proportion of these crimes committed with firearms and other weaponry, the proportion committed by previous weapons offenders, the proportion planned and premeditated versus the proportion unplanned and spontaneous, even the fate of people convicted of weapons crimes in the courts—none of these matters is known with any certainty for the United States as a whole. The smaller-scale state and local studies that have been done often report sharply contradictory findings.

The disarray of single-city or single-state studies has an immediate, if obvious, implication: namely, with a sufficiently diligent search, the committed advocate can always locate at least one study with a finding consistent with his or her point of view. To a lay observer, this might imply that researchers only "find" what they want to find. In truth, all it implies is that what is true in, say, Detroit is not necessarily true in Washington or St. Louis or Los Angeles, much less true of the nation as a whole.

And, of course, even when there is some consensus on the facts themselves, there is typically little or no agreement on their meaning, significance, or correct interpretation. To cite an example considered in great detail later in this volume (see Chapter 10), it is an agreed-upon fact that attacks with a firearm lead to the death of the victim more frequently than attacks with another weapon such as a knife. There is some disagreement on the magnitude of the lethality differential; depending on the study, gun attacks are reported to be between 1.8 and 6 times more lethal than knife attacks. But what does this difference mean? To what conclusion does it lead?

One possibility, favored by the pro-control faction, is that the gun is *intrinsically* the more lethal weapon, that many victims die not so much because anyone intended them to but rather because the weapon at hand, a gun, is an efficient killer whereas alternative weaponry is less so. If this is the correct interpretation, then the implication is obvious: if there were fewer guns, there would be fewer homicides.

The alternative possibility is that murderers choose guns precisely because they are determined to bring death to the victim, and that assaulters choose knives or other weaponry precisely because they do not *intend* to kill, but only to injure. The lethality difference across weapons is, in this view, a result of underlying differences in intention or motivation; or, in short, the truly determined and earnest killers choose guns. An implication of this view, then, is that the lethality differential is not a property of the weapon but is inherent in characteristics of the offenders, and that the people who currently kill with firearms would, given their intent, find other ways to accomplish the same end if no guns were available to them. If this is the correct interpretation, the implication is again obvious: reducing the availability of firearms would leave the homicide rate largely unaffected.

Similarly, hardly any responsible observer would want to quarrel with the two observations made at the beginning of this chapter: that there are more guns and more gun crimes in the United States than in most other advanced societies. But what implication can be drawn from these observations? One popular interpretation is that there is a very obvious causal connection here, that we have more gun crimes precisely *because* we have more guns, and that if fewer guns were available, fewer crimes would be committed with them. By the same token, however, the proportion of privately owned firearms that are involved in any sort of criminal activity in any given year is on the order of a fraction of 1% of the total, so it is certainly possible that outright confiscation of 99% of all private firearms in the country would still leave the rate of gun crime unaffected, especially were one to assume, not unreasonably, that the criminally abused 1% would be the last weapons affected by any gun policy. Thus, one can note and accept that the United States is among the world leaders both in weapons owned and in crimes committed with firearms and, on that basis alone, conclude either (1) that the need for stricter weapons control is self-evident and that such a policy would reduce the rate of violent crime, or (2) that trying to solve the problem of violent crime through restricting the general ownership and use of firearms would be ridiculous—equivalent in all important respects to trying to solve the problem of accidental drownings by legislation to prohibit swimming.

To be sure, neither of these conclusions is at all self-evident. For example, that the number of guns greatly exceeds the number of gun crimes does not, in itself, rule out the possibility that the general availability of guns is an important cause of gun crime, any more than the fact that there are many more smokers than lung cancer cases rules out smoking as a cause of cancer. At the same time, that there are more guns and more gun crimes in the United States than elsewhere does *not* prove that guns are an important cause of crime (or that crime is a cause of gun ownership); in fact, the correlation itself has no direct causal implication at all, since the United States might rank high on gun ownership for one reason and high on criminal violence for entirely different reasons. To cite the evidence on numbers of guns owned and numbers of violent crimes committed with guns in support of *either* conclusion is to affirm only that one was committed to a conclusion before the research began.

Given the uncertainties of the facts themselves and the inherent ambiguities of their meaning or interpretation, it follows that much research on weapons, violence, and crime leads to the construction of images favorable to one or another point of view. There is, first, the imagery associated with "the criminal." One prominent image, typically identified with liberal or progressive theories of crime, is of the criminal as *victim,* forced to commit criminal acts by the racial and social injustices of the larger society and driven to violence not because of inherent meanness or innate brutality but simply because, in a moment of passion or desperation, the instruments of violence were at hand. Given this imagery, the solution to criminality is obvious: in the long run, one must solve the injustices that give rise to crime; in the short run, one rehabilitates the offender (thus compensating for the social injustice) and, to the extent possible, reduces the availability of the means by which violence is perpetrated.

An alternative image, associated with more traditional or conservative theories of crime, depicts the criminal as a *rational economic actor,* one who commits criminal acts primarily for economic gain. In this view, weapons are just tools of the trade; one is a more efficient criminal when armed than when not; violence is committed only because it increases the daily take. A corollary is that the person intent on arming himself or herself for criminal gain will always find a way to do so; as many have pointed out, a serviceable firearm can be made from nothing more than a piece of pipe, a block of wood, a nail, and a box of rubber bands. The inevitable implication of this image, of course, is that reducing the general availability of private weaponry would have little effect either way on the incidence of violent crime. Indeed, in one version, reducing private armament would deprive the citizenry of an effective and potent crime deterrent.

So, too, with images of "the gun." In the minds of many, the gun symbolizes all that is wrong in American culture: it symbolizes male dominance, sexual frustration, aggression, violence, and a host of other pathologies that are offensive to a civilized society. In this view, the gun is blood lust incarnate. But in the minds of many others, the same gun symbolizes all that is right in the culture: it symbolizes manliness, independence, self-sufficiency, out-doorsmanship, and a willingness to die for one's beliefs. In this view, the gun is the virtual embodiment of traditional American values.

This sort of starkly opposed imagery is rife throughout the literature reviewed in the following pages. In many accounts, for example, weaponry is seen as an important *stimulus* to the commission of violent acts, whereas in other accounts, private weaponry is seen as an important *deterrent* to much of the violence that would otherwise take place. Some studies argue that gun crime is a very substantial part of the total crime problem in the United States; others argue that gun crime is effectively trivial. In some accounts, the "typical" private gun owner is depicted as a virtual psychopath, and in others, as an upstanding and respectable middle-class citizen. To some people, the various shooting sports are at worst harmless diversions and at best affirmations of man's relationship to nature, whereas for others, these same activities represent an acting out of our most regressive, infantile, and violent fantasies.

The emotive imagery and strong ideological predilections common to the weapons and crime literature imply that the many scholarly and policy issues inherent in this topic are not going to be put to rest through any sort of empirical research, no matter how sound or well conducted. Too much of what is at issue involves total world-views; relatively little involves factual matters that could be adjudicated through research. It would thus be foolish to think that one might go through this literature refereeing among the various contenders, doling out penalties for fouls against scholarly standards, and announcing a winner at the end of the contest, and such is not our purpose here. Our hope, rather, has been to sift through the competing claims and assertions, noting those that have been (or could be) researched, and gleaning from the material those few facts and relationships that appear to have been solidly established. We are quite confident that this review will *not* put any end to the weapons and crime debates, or should it; but we do hope that it elevates the whole discussion to a somewhat higher empirical plane.

Our review begins with an assessment of what is presently known about the existing stock of private armament among the United States population. Chapter 2, "How Many Guns in Private Hands?," compiles the existing empirical estimates of the total firearms supply and attempts to reconcile the apparent contradictions among them. In general, two methods have been used to estimate the total firearms supply: compilations of production and import data, and estimates generated from national surveys containing a weapons ownership question. Both methods are intrinsically problematic for one or another reason. The first method, for example, requires that we know the rate at which firearms are removed from use, and no source provides any firm evidence on this rate. The second, likewise, is hobbled by all the usual infirmities of survey research, plus a possibly large response bias resulting from the unwillingness of respondents to admit to owning weapons.

Although much is made in the literature of the apparent disparity in estimates generated by each method, by reconsidering the several assumptions that go into each estimate and making the appropriate recalculations, one can show that both methods tend to converge on common values for the total number of weapons possessed. We estimate that in 1968 there were roughly 80 ± 20 million guns in private hands and that by 1978 the figure was roughly 120 ± 20 million guns. In both years, handguns accounted for 25 to 30% of the total firearms, and shoulder weapons for the remainder.

The estimates of Chapter 2 thus confirm a common speculation in the literature that the total number of weapons in private hands has sharply increased over the last one or more decades. In Chapters 3 to 5, we consider several possible sources of this trend.

Given about 80 million guns in 1968 and about 120 million in 1978, our best estimate of the total increase in weapons is on the order of 40 million guns, although because of the large uncertainties in the estimates for both years, the true increase could fall anywhere between zero and 80 million. The proportional increase in *handguns* was distinctly sharper than the increase in shoulder weapons.

Chapter 3, on "Sport and Recreational Demand," refines the estimates of the trend and corrects the trend figures for simple growth in the numbers of U.S. households. In 1968, there were about 60 million households in the United States, and in 1978, about 75 million—a 25% increase. Calculations undertaken in Chapter 3 show that this increase in the number of households *alone* accounts for approximately one-half the total increase in weapons owned. Thus, after this factor has been considered, there remain some 20 million "new" weapons to be accounted for by other factors. Additional calculations suggest that about 10 of these 20 million are handguns, and the rest are rifles and shotguns.

Chapter 3 then considers what proportion of the remaining "new" guns can be ascribed to enhanced sporting and recreational demand for firearms. Although the data are rather spotty at best, our estimates suggest that, at the outer limit of plausibility, growth in sport and recreational firearms demand accounts for *all* the remaining new weapons, handguns and long guns alike. Rather less liberal assumptions about the rate at which new hunters and other shooting sportspersons arm themselves suggest, as a more likely possibility, that the growth in demand for sport and recreational firearms accounts for all (or nearly all) of the increase in shoulder weaponry, and roughly one-third to one-half of the increase in handguns. The chapter thus compiles some evidence *against* the common claim that handguns have "no legitimate sport or recreational" use. Contrasting with that claim, some of the evidence presented in the chapter suggests that handguns are as likely to be owned for sport and recreation as they are to be owned for protection or self-defense.

Chapter 4 considers another possible source of enhanced arms demand, one that has received little or no attention in the literature, namely, growth in "The Police Demand for Armament." Again, the data are spotty and inconclusive, but evidence from several sources suggests a rather large increase in the total number of armed public servants over the period 1968–1978, possibly amounting to as many as a quarter-million new police officers. There has apparently been a parallel increase in private security forces as well. In addition to these trends in the number of armed personnel, there is much fragmentary and episodic evidence to suggest considerable police department experimentation with new small arms policies in the decade. The trends in both personnel and arms policy pose the possibility of a sharp increase in small arms purchases by police over the decade. The evidence and speculations contained in the chapter suggest that the total police demand for new arms in the decade amounted to perhaps 2 to 3 million handguns and an unknown number of shoulder weapons. Subtracting these figures from the numbers of unexplained guns remaining at the end of Chapter 3, we are left with no more than about 5 million handguns, and essentially no shoulder arms, to be accounted for by other factors.

In Chapter 5, we assess the most commonly offered explanation for the private arms build-up: that it has resulted from "fear of crime, violence, and civil disorder" (Newton and Zimring, 1969: 21). There are several compelling reasons to believe, despite many claims to the contrary, that "fear and loathing" have actually been the underlying motives in only a relatively small fraction of all recent firearms acquisitions. First, after household increase, new sport and recreational demand, and enhanced arms demand among the police have been taken into account, few or no excess weapons remain to be explained. Second, an analysis of available survey data on *handgun* ownership from 1959 to 1976 shows that the increase in proportional handgun ownership was concentrated mainly in middle-sized cities, whereas the surges of "crime, violence, and civil disorder" were mainly big-city phenomena. Other considerations advanced in the chapter suggest that much (perhaps all) of the domestic arms build-up has resulted from additional weapons purchases among families already owning one or more guns (rather than first-time purchases by previously unarmed families). In other words, there has quite possibly been an increase in the average number of weapons owned among households that already owned at least one of them.

Several studies have inquired directly into "fear and loathing" as sources of the recent arms trend. None of them demonstrates a clear or decisive "fear and loathing" effect. Some studies *claim* to provide evidence for this effect, but the assembled data are consistent with equally plausible alternative explanations; and most studies, especially the methodologically more sophisticated ones, show little or no support for fear as a factor in the trend. For example, one time-series analysis concludes, "the strong upward trend in handgun sales cannot be explained by . . . rising violent crime rates" (Clotfelter, 1977: 13).

Altogether, the analyses in Chapters 3 to 5 suggest little support for the idea that the recent domestic arms build-up has been in reaction to crime, violence, or civil disorder, and considerable reason to believe that the trend has had other sources entirely, most relatively benign from the larger societal viewpoint.

Chapter 6 reviews the available evidence on "Characteristics of Private Weapons Owners." By far the largest share of private firearms is owned primarily for sport and recreational uses; evidence from several sources suggests that sport and recreational guns outnumber protection guns by about 3 to 1. Weapons ownership varies sharply by region and city size, being higher in the South and West than in other regions, and sharply higher in rural than in urban areas. Contrary to a common speculation, gun ownership also tends to *increase* with social status and is more prevalent in the higher income categories. Also, for reasons that have not been adequately explained, Protestants are much more likely to own a gun than either Catholics or Jews. Men are, of course, much more likely to own a gun than women. There does not appear to be any consistent racial variance in weapons ownership.

Some authors have ascribed the higher rate of weapons ownership in the South to a presumed "regional subculture of violence." A review of several relevant studies provides no compelling empirical support for the "subculture of violence" hypothesis.

There is substantial evidence from several sources that early parental socialization is an important factor (possibly the most important factor) in weapons ownership among adults. In all studies to have inquired into the matter, whether one's father owned a gun is the single best predictor of whether the respondent owns a gun. This finding strongly suggests that the modal or typical adult firearms owner has had experience in the use of small arms stretching back well into childhood.

One study based on data for Illinois (Lizotte and Bordua, 1980) allows for a differentiation between sport and defensive weapons owners. Their data suggest that these owners are of *qualitatively* different types. Sport ownership is largely a function of early socialization, a suggested above. Other than income and sex, the only strong predictors of sport ownership are parents' gun ownership and the age at which the respondent first acquired a gun. Ownership of a gun for protection, however, is entirely different; the only significant predictor is the violent crime rate in the county where the respondent resides.

Only a few studies have examined personality differences between owners and nonowners; none show gun owners to be an especially distinctive group.

In general, the review contained in Chapter 6 supports the notion that the "average" gun owner is a small-town or rural middle-class Protestant male who owns a gun primarily for sport and whose interest in and familiarity with firearms result from early childhood socialization.

Chapter 7, "On Crime and Private Weapons," considers whether there is any demonstrable causal relationship between private weapons ownership and the rates of criminal violence. Three hypotheses are considered: (1) private firearms as a *cause* of crime, (2) private firearms as an *effect* of crime, and (3) private firearms as a *deterrent* to crime. The chapter also reviews some recent survey evidence on the actual uses of private firearms in self-defense.

The existing research on all three hypotheses is highly inconclusive. There are serious logical and methodological barriers that, in essence, prevent any decisive test; these issues are reviewed in the beginning of the chapter.

There is some, but not much, evidence to suggest that at least a fraction of private firearms is purchased in reaction to crime. Most firearms are purchased for entirely different reasons, and at least some of the weapons purchased for defense are used to defend against animals rather than people. Evidence from several sources confirms that the criminally victimized are *not* any more likely to own a firearm than the nonvictimized, and there is further evidence to suggest that *fear* of crime is also not a very important factor. One study that allows a differentiation between ownership of sport guns and protection guns (Lizotte and Bordua, 1980) reports that the violent crime rate is the only significant predictor of gun ownership for protection. The general thrust of findings in this area, however, is that crime or the fear of crime is at best a minor factor in the private ownership of most firearms.

Although there is much speculation, surprisingly little empirical research has been done on firearms as a cause of criminal violence. Most of the studies in this area depend on gross comparisons of crime and weapons ownership rates across large and heterogeneous geographical aggregates (nations, regions, states, or counties) that differ in far too many (typically uncontrolled) ways for much of substance to be concluded from the results. Truly decisive evidence—for example, evidence on the ensuing criminality of people who acquire firearms—does not exist.

As an example of the difficulties encountered in this area of the literature, much is often made of the fact that the rate of private firearms ownership and the rate of violent crime (especially homicide) are higher in the South than in other regions of the country. Newton and Zimring (1969) were among the first to point this out, and the result is widely cited in subsequent literature as evidence that guns cause crime. In fact, this regional correspondence in crime and weapons ownership says little or nothing about private firearms as a cause of crime, for the following reasons:

1. The distinctiveness of the South in weapons ownership is due almost entirely to the high rate at which shoulder weapons are owned there. The ownership of handguns, in contrast, is not very much more prevalent in the South than in other regions. Yet, the largest share of violent crimes committed with firearms is committed with handguns. Reference to the evidence on the South essentially links homicide (and other violent crime) with the disproportionate ownership of a class of firearms seldom used in homicide (or other violent crime), a tenuous link at best.

2. In the same vein, in the South as in all other regions, weapons ownership is highest in rural and small-town areas, whereas criminal violence of the sort at issue here is concentrated in the larger cities. It is likewise tenuous to attribute urban crime to the possession of weaponry in small-town and rural areas, but this attribution is also directly implied in the regional comparison being discussed.

3. There is persuasive evidence that the high rate of criminal violence in the South is due mainly to the lower prevailing socioeconomic conditions of the region. The higher rate of weapons ownership, in contrast, is probably linked to early socialization of Southern males and to greater opportunities for the sporting uses of guns. Thus, the regional correlation between guns and crime may well be simply fortuituous and cannot, in any case, be taken as evidence that private firearms are a cause of criminal violence.

Other evidence, derived from other kinds of research designs, has also been presented in the literature to show that guns are a cause of crime, but none is any more conclusive than the regional evidence just discussed. We conclude from the review that there is little or no conclusive, or even suggestive, evidence to show that gun ownership among the population as a whole is, per se, an important cause of criminal violence.

Whether private firearms are an important *deterrent* to crime is likewise uncertain. Again, logical and methodological difficulties prevent a firm or

conclusive estimate of the rate at which crime is deterred by firearms possession among real or potential victims. It is clear that much crime occurs in
circumstances in which the victim's ownership of a gun would be irrelevant:
for example, street crime (most of which occurs while the victim is away
from his or her firearms) or the burglary of unoccupied residences. But these
facts say nothing about the effectiveness of weaponry as a deterrent to crimes
occurring in situations where they are potentially deterrable.

There is some evidence that the risk to a home robber or to a burglar
striking an occupied residence of being shot and wounded or killed by the
intended victim is on the same order of magnitude as the risk to the same
criminal of being apprehended, convicted, and imprisoned for the crime (both
probabilities appear to be on the order of 1 to 2%) (Kleck, 1979b). It is
thus plausible that much crime is deterred because those who would otherwise
commit it fear the possibility of being shot in the process, just as it is plausible
that the fear of serving time for one's offense also prevents some crime.

Evidence on the uses of firearms by victims in crimes that are potentially
deterrable suggests that the probability of a "successful" victimization decreases, but the probability of injury or death to the victim increases if one
uses a gun in defense.

Chapter 7 concludes with a review of existing evidence on the actual uses
of firearms in self-defense. Roughly 25% of the total private armament appears
to be owned primarily for protection or self-defense, and approximately 40–
50% of all handguns are owned primarily for this purpose. Survey evidence
for 1978 shows that about 15% of the respondents or members of their
households have used a gun in self-defense at some point in their lives, and
about one-half of this use was in defense against animals. It also seems that
about 7% of the nation's adults carry handguns with them for protection
outside the home. The proportion of U.S. adults who have actually *fired* a
gun in self-defense appears to fall somewhere between 2 and 6%.

Chapter 8, "How Much Crime? How Much Violence?," shifts attention
away from the ownership of firearms among the general population and
toward the criminal uses and abuses of guns and other weapons. Although
the definitions of "violence" and "criminal violence" are themselves problematic, and the available data are generally unreliable and incomplete, the
FBI's annual *Uniform Crime Reports* (UCR) and the several criminal victimization surveys provide the broad outlines of the problem of crime and violence
in the society.

Data from UCR for the index crimes of homicide, robbery, and aggravated
assault all show the same general pattern over time: namely, fairly sharp
increases from the early 1960's through the early 1970's, a peak in the rates
occurring in about 1974 or 1975, small declines through 1978, and some
increase in the years since. For example, between 1960 and 1978, the homicide

rate increased from about 5 to about 9 homicides per 100,000 population. The percentage of homicides committed with firearms also increased, from 53 to 63%. Of the homicides committed with firearms, approximately three-quarters involved handguns.

Likewise, the total number of robberies of all types increased roughly four-fold over the two decades. Of the total robberies occurring, between three-fifths and two-thirds were armed robberies. Among the armed robberies specifically, about 60–65% involved a firearm, and the rest were committed with knives or other weapons. There appears to have been some increase in the percentage of all robberies committed with a firearm: in 1967 about 36%, and in 1974 about 45% of all robberies were done with a gun.

The trend in aggravated assault is similar. The number of such assaults increased approximately threefold from 1960 to 1978. Proportionally, only a few aggravated assaults are committed with firearms, although this percentage has also apparently risen. In 1964, for example, about 15% of all aggravated assaults involved a gun, and in 1978 the proportion was about 22%.

Comparisons of these UCR data with evidence from the criminal victimization surveys are hazardous for several reasons that are reviewed in Chapter 8. In general, the victimization data suggest that between 25 and 50% of all criminal incidents are unreported to the police, with the percentage unreported varying by the seriousness of the crime. The victimization surveys also suggest that about 10% of all criminal incidents qualify as "violent crimes," that is, are crimes against the person, whereas the remaining 90% are property crimes; these proportions accord reasonably well with the proportions estimated from UCR data.

The trend in the suicide rate is also up over the past two decades, although not so sharply as the trends in other violent crimes such as homicide. In 1960, there were about 20,000 suicides, and in 1977, about 30,000. The percentage of suicides committed with firearms also appears to have increased somewhat over the same time span. Trends in attempted suicide, or in the proportion attempted with a firearm, are intrinsically unknowable, although there seems to be some consensus that perhaps 8 to 10 attempted suicides occur for every successful one.

Chapter 8 also reviews evidence on death from firearms accidents. As a percentage of all accidental deaths, deaths from firearms accidents have been more or less stable, hovering around 2% for as long as data have been collected. Of the total accidental firearms deaths, about 40% are due to hunting accidents.

Data on accidental firearms injuries are extremely unreliable, because of the (presumably) large fraction that is unreported, and, as a result, published estimates of the annual number of such injuries vary widely (between tens and hundreds of thousands). Our best guess for 1975 (the reference year in this analysis), based on data from the National Health Surveys, is about

170 ± 75 thousand injuries due to firearms accidents, roughly one-thirtieth the number of injuries sustained from "cutting and piercing" instruments.

Considering all sources of firearms deaths for the reference year of 1975, the most recent year for which reasonably complete data are available, we estimate that something on the order of 30,000 deaths occur annually as a result of the criminal, accidental, and suicidal uses of firearms. We further estimate, for the same year, that there were approximately 900,000 additional "incidents" where firearms were *either* present, brandished, or fired in criminal incidents, *or* where firearms were involved in injury-producing accidents, *or* where firearms were used in attempted suicides, *or* where firearms were involved in citizen–police encounters. We thus estimate, as a reasonable first approximation to the correct order of magnitude, an annual total of roughly one million gun incidents—i.e., instances in which a firearm of some sort was involved in some kind of violent or criminal incident (whether intentional or accidental, whether fired or unfired, whether fatal or not).

The preceding estimates are useful indicators of the approximate magnitude of the overall "guns, crime, and violence" problem in the United States, but we emphasize that they are approximate indicators only. We have taken 1975 as the reference year in the analysis because it is the most recent year for which complete data covering all relevant topics are available. More recent data, however, suggest that the years 1974 and 1975 were high points for gun violence over the previous decade. Further, these estimates include large numbers of incidents that are in no sense chargeable gun crimes: they include an estimate of accidental injuries resulting from firearms (for which figures are very unreliable) and they include estimates of suicides attempted with firearms (for which figures are also very unreliable). As a precise number, our estimate—one million annual gun incidents—cannot be taken seriously. A more appropriate phrasing of the results would be that the total number of gun incidents of all sorts in any year falls somewhere in the range of 100,000 to 1,000,000, and, in all probability, somewhere toward the upper end of that range.

In Chapter 9 the focus turns to "The Firearms Used in Crime." Remarkably, *no* nationally representative data are available on the weapons used in violent crime, with the partial exception of homicide. Such evidence as exists is taken, almost without exception, from small-scale studies in a single community or state.

A key issue in Chapter 9 is whether "crime guns" are sufficiently distinct from legitimate firearms owned by law-abiding citizens to allow for special legislative focus on them. It is not possible to answer this question at present for two reasons: (1) except for the rough distribution between handguns and long guns, virtually nothing is known about the characteristics of legitimate guns in private hands (for example, the preferred calibers, barrel lengths, age, cost, and so on); and (2) even less is known about the weapons used in crime. Whether crime guns are, in general, different from legitimate guns obviously cannot be determined until more is known about both types of firearm.

Evidence from several sources makes it clear that the handgun is the preferred firearm in most crimes involving firearms. On the basis of evidence from the most generalizable study in the literature, we estimate that in 1971 (the only year covered in this study), approximately 260,000 firearms were confiscated by state and local police, and of these, about 70% were handguns. Other studies report handgun percentages in the same range. Thus, the criminal use of guns involves largely handguns (although it is also important to remember that about a third of all crime guns are shoulder weapons).

Several studies have tried to estimate the proportion of "Saturday Night Specials" (SNSs) in the crime gun category. Unfortunately, the very definition of Saturday Night Special is highly ambiguous, and so the question cannot be answered definitively. Results from several of these studies confirm that concealability is an important factor in crime guns, but concealability is only one among several variables implied in the concept of Saturday Night Special.

Most studies of crime guns suffer from the absence of a proper comparison standard, namely, empirically reliable information on noncrime guns. Brill (1977), for example, notes that expensive firearms were as common in his sample of crime guns as inexpensive firearms, and he uses this finding to argue against the popular idea that most crime guns are cheap Saturday Night Specials. But the distribution by quality, price, or value among crime guns themselves is relatively uninformative unless one also knows the corresponding distribution among noncrime guns. (For example, if one-half of his sample were cheap SNSs, but only one-tenth of all private handguns were of the same sort, then his finding would *support* the idea that cheap SNSs are overrepresented among the firearms used in crime.)

Evidence that concealability is a major factor distinguishing crime from noncrime guns comes from several sources. First, handguns predominate among crime guns, whereas shoulder weapons are by far the more common firearm owned by the larger population. Second, in all studies reporting pertinent evidence, about 70 to 75% of all crime handguns have barrel lengths of 3 inches or less, that is, are of a size that makes them readily concealable. Finally, in the one study reporting evidence on the issue, slightly more than one-third of the confiscated shoulder weapons had been modified to shorter barrel lengths. (In contrast, there is no evidence to suggest that criminals prefer smaller *caliber* guns than the gun-owning population at large, or is there evidence that criminals prefer cheaper weapons.)

Handguns confiscated and traced are often found to have crossed state lines before having been used in a criminal incident. This is especially true

of guns confiscated in jurisdictions with relatively more restrictive gun regulations. Obviously, the flow across jurisdictional lines of firearms into criminal
hands tends strongly to vitiate the effects of jurisdiction-specific gun control
measures.

Stolen handguns apparently contribute substantially to the potential supply
of crime firearms. On the basis of 1975 statistics and a few assumptions,
we estimate that approximately 275,000 handguns are stolen from private
residences each year. To this total, one would have also to add thefts from
dealers, manufacturers, importers, shippers, and so on. To be sure, not all
stolen handguns eventually end up in criminal hands. Many, we presume,
go the route of much other stolen property—that is, they are "fenced" and
then sold through various outlets to the general private firearms market. It
is an interesting (and, as far as we can tell, unresearched) question whether
the proportion of stolen firearms among crime guns is any higher than the
proportion among the legitimate private firearms stock.

Several studies also confirm that crime guns tend to be relatively "young"
guns. About one-half of all confiscated handguns prove to have been manufactured in the previous 3–5 years. How this compares with the age distribution
of legitimate handguns owned by the population at large is completely unknown.

Chapter 10, "On the Matter of Criminal Motivations," reviews existing
evidence on the widely held view that much homicide, and criminal violence
in general, does not result so much from initially lethal intent as it does
from escalations of otherwise relatively petty quarrels that become lethal or
injurious simply because firearms are available. The basic issues were discussed
briefly above: essentially, the question is whether there would be less criminal
violence if there were fewer guns.

Here, as in most other areas of the literature, the available research is
highly inconclusive. The evidence is firm that attacks with a gun lead to the
death of the victim approximately two to six times more often than attacks
with knives. This *might* imply that guns are intrinsically more lethal (in which
case their restriction might lower the homicide rate), but it might imply only
that people who are intent on bringing death to their victim preferentially
choose firearms as the means (in which case firearms restrictions would not
lower the homicide rate). Nothing in the literature allows one to choose definitively between these possibilities.

Much of the evidence commonly cited on behalf of the contention that
most homicide does not result from a prior intent to kill turns out, on closer
inspection, not to bear on the matter of intent one way or the other. For
example, most homicide involves people known to each other before the
incident, and it often involves family members. Many authors infer from this
fact that these homicides are largely unintentional—"crimes of passion" that

turn lethal in the mythical "moment of rage" or distress. It is, however, plain that homicides among family members could just as easily result from prior intent as from any other circumstance; the evidence on victim–offender relationships, although of great interest in itself, says little or nothing about the issue considered in Chapter 10. We conclude that much the same is true of most of the other evidence commonly cited on behalf of the "ambiguous intentions" hypothesis, for example, that homicides are frequently accompanied by altercations among the parties, or that one or both parties had been drinking. All of these facts are interesting, but none of them bears directly on the matter of intent.

Chapter 10 also reviews briefly some experimental evidence on the hypothesis that "even the casual sight of a gun may catalyze violence" (Curtis, 1974: 108). There are perhaps three or four studies in the literature that provide support for this hypothesis, but an equal number does not. The relevance of the behaviors of undergraduates in a laboratory setting for an understanding of criminal violence is, certainly, always open to question.

Analysis of the effects of weapons choice in robberies tends also to show that robberies committed with firearms are more likely to lead to the death of the victim than robberies committed by other means. Because it seems plausible that the underlying motive in all robberies is the same (economic gain to the offender), the evidence from robberies is the strongest in the literature for showing that a gun is intrinsically more lethal than other weapons, presumably after possible differences in underlying motive have been eliminated. But even here there are complicating factors. First, as Cook (1980a, 1981) has persuasively argued, many of the robbery-connected homicides do *not* appear to have resulted from an underlying motivation for economic gain so much as from the innate brutality of the offenders, with the robbery itself being committed more or less as an afterthought. This again suggests differential motivations as a possible explanation for the lethality differential even in the case of armed robbery. Second, although the probability of death to the victim is higher in gun robberies than other armed robberies, the probability of serious but nonfatal injury is substantially lower, owing, presumably, to the fact that fewer victims attempt to resist a gun robbery in the first place. Also, the average take in a nongun robbery is roughly one-third the average take in a robbery committed with a firearm, presumably because robbers armed with guns seek more lucrative victims. These considerations suggest the possibility that in a hypothetical "no guns" condition, the total number of robberies committed would sharply increase (to compensate for the lower profitability of each nongun robbery) and the rate of personal injury would also sharply increase (because in the nongun robbery victims are more likely to resist and thus be injured). It is also conceivable that there would be some "substitution" of victims, with robbers more apt to strike relatively more vulnerable targets (e.g., women, the handicapped, the very young, or the very old).

The concluding part of this volume deals with "Weapons and Their Control." In Chapter 11, we review the evidence from two recent national surveys on "Public Opinion and Gun Control," that is, we consider what the public wants and does not want by way of stricter firearms regulations. Both surveys were conducted in 1978: one was sponsored by the National Rifle Association, and the other by the Center for the Study and Prevention of Handgun Violence. Together, the surveys are virtually encyclopedic in their coverage of public thinking on gun control issues.

Although the reports in which the survey results are presented differ, at times sharply, in their emphasis and the conclusions advanced from the data, the empirical findings are notably consistent wherever direct comparison is possible. Large majorities of the public favor measures that would require the registration or licensing of firearms, both for new purchases and for firearms presently owned. The public would *not* favor such measures if their costs were inordinately high, and there is considerable sentiment that any such measure would be effective only were it uniform across all the states. Equally large majorities oppose an outright ban on private handgun ownership, although there is a majority sentiment favoring a ban on the manufacture and sale of cheap, low-quality handguns. Majorities approaching 90% believe that they have a right to own a gun; but large majorities also agree that a licensing requirement for handgun ownership would not violate their rights.

Despite the high levels of support for registration or licensing measures, no more than about half the population feel that these measures would cause crime to decrease; many measures other than firearms regulations are thought to be more effective toward this end. Further, most of those who believe that crime would decrease with stricter weapons legislation also believe that the decrease would only be small. It therefore follows that many people support such measures for reasons other than their presumed effects on the crime rate.

There is nearly unanimous sentiment that criminals will always be able to acquire guns, no matter what legislation is passed, and thus that stricter controls would mainly affect average law-abiding citizens. There is also widespread popular support for the idea of strict and mandatory sentences for people committing crimes with guns. There is little popular support for the idea that gun controls would be a violation of our basic freedoms.

In general, the opinion data suggest as a useful although not precise metaphor that most people feel that governments should be just as careful about who is allowed to own and use a gun as they are about who is allowed to own and use an automobile or other potentially dangerous items. Gun control measures that enjoy large majority support (namely, registration and licensing) are all similar to measures currently employed to regulate automobile owner- ship and use; measures substantially more strict than these generally do not curry much favor. The undertone to public thinking on gun control thus seems to be that firearms, as automobiles, are *intrinsically* hazardous, and that governments should keep track of them for that reason alone. Whether the act of keeping track would itself have any effect on crime or violence seems to be taken as a different issue altogether.

Chapter 12, "Regulating Firearms: An Overview of Federal, State, and Local Practices," briefly summarizes the existing measures for firearms control in the United States. As many have noted previously, existing measures encom- pass a vast congeries of Federal, state, and local regulations, many of them working at cross-purposes with others. Jurisdictions with extremely restrictive gun control policies often abut jurisdictions with barely any controls at all. This fact, plus the evidence suggesting a substantial interstate commerce in crime guns, makes it altogether plain that gun control measures in a single jurisdiction will have no direct or necessary implication for the availability of firearms for illicit criminal purposes in that same jurisdiction.

Chapter 13 considers "Weapons Control Legislation and Effects on Violent Crime." Here the issue is the extent to which various legislative initiatives have actually achieved their intended goals.

Studies relevant to this topic fall into three broad categories: (1) studies that compare crime rates across jurisdictions (typically, cities or states) with variable weapons control legislation in force; (2) "process" studies that examine the actual implementation of various gun control measures; and (3) time- series or before–after studies that follow trends in crime before and after the introduction of a new legislative measure.

Studies of the first type depend critically on the ability of the analyst to model the crime phenomena in question; this is simply because jurisdictions differ in many ways other than in gun control measures on the books, which might plausibly affect crime rates. Conclusions about the impact of firearms controls are thus valid only to the extent that these extraneous factors are modeled and held constant in the analysis. And since there is, as yet, no firm theory of crime and how it is produced, none of the studies of this type can be said to provide conclusive evidence on whether or how firearms controls influence crime rates.

"Process" studies have generally been more informative in that they often point out major gaps between the legislation-as-enacted and the legislation- as-implemented; indifferent or hostile implementation of even the most aggres- sive and well-considered measures will necessarily mitigate legislative effects. Zimring's (1975) analysis of the implementation of the Gun Control Act of

1968 and Beha's (1977) study of the implementation of the Massachusetts Bartley-Fox Amendment are both excellent examples of the advantages that accrue from studies of this type.

All else equal, before–after studies are useful designs for examining the impact of programs, and some research of this type has been done on various gun control measures. Crude comparisons of crime rates at two time points (one before and one after enactment) are, of course, of little or no value. As in the case of cross-sectional studies, the processes that govern the operation of the time series being analyzed must be understood and modeled if the impact analysis is to have meaning. That is, one must have some method of estimating what would have happened in the time series had the measure not been introduced in order for perturbations in the time series after enactment (either positive or negative) to be legitimately taken as evidence of program effects. So here, too, the need for an empirically based theory of crime and how it is produced is apparent.

The concluding chapter of the volume considers "Some Policy Implications" that flow from the current state of knowledge about weapons, crime, and violence in the United States. In general, the research literature is far more remarkable for what it does *not* allow one to conclude than for what it does. Our most important "policy" conclusion is therefore that we need more and better research before we can state with even modest assurance what the likely effects of one or another policy intervention are going to be. Many of the proposals that have been made to deal with the problem of gun violence are based on rather Herculean assumptions that have never been adequately researched.

It *is* clear that enormous numbers of Americans own guns and enjoy the recreational activities that firearms make possible. The sheer number of firearms owned and the centrality of "The Gun" in some quarters of American culture make it obvious that any sort of stricter gun control policy is going to be highly intrusive, is going to impinge on the prerogatives and rights (whether real or perceived) of perhaps half the households in the United States, and is therefore something not to be undertaken lightly. It is also clear that gun control measures enacted in the past have had modest or no effects in reducing violent crime, and it is likewise clear that some fraction of the violence we live with—perhaps the larger fraction—would continue to occur even in the complete absence of guns. We conclude that the probable benefits of stricter gun controls (itself a highly nebulous concept) in terms of crime reduction are at best uncertain, and at worst close to nil, and that most such measures would pose rather high social costs. For these and other reasons spelled out in the last chapter, our view is that the prospects for ameliorating the problem of criminal violence through stricter controls over the civilian ownership, purchase, or use of firearms are dim.

I

WEAPONS

TWO

HOW MANY GUNS IN PRIVATE HANDS?

Estimates of the total number of firearms now in private hands in the United States vary from a lower limit of about 50 million to an upper limit of 200 million or more (Newton and Zimring, 1969; Wright and Marston, 1975).[1]

[1] The range among *empirically credible* estimates of the total number of private weapons is, as we discuss later in the chapter, much narrower. Many of the estimates that appear in print are better described as rough guesses or wild surmise. Sherrill offers this comment: "Just how many guns are floating around the country is anybody's guess; 'experts' have appeared before Congressional committees in recent years to estimate everything up to 200 million guns. . . . The National Commission on the Causes and Prevention of Violence guessed 90 million in 1969. It's a guessing game that depends very much on the mood: shortly after John Kennedy's assassination, a writer for *The Reporter* magazine got carried away and estimated one *billion* guns in America" (1973: 13).

One of the problems in this area is that although everyone seems ready to provide an estimate, very few of these accounts present any description of the methods by which the estimate was obtained. A passage from Bruce-Biggs (1976: 38) is a case in point. "While estimates vary widely," the author notes, "it can be credibly argued that there are at least 140 million firearms in private hands in the United States today." However, no "credible argument" in favor of this figure accompanies the passage; also, there is no footnote to the number, no reference to a study, and no description of the basis for the 140-million estimate. From what appears in the text, this number might well have been pulled from a hat. Note, too, the unjustifiable certainty of the formulation, ". . . *at least* 140 million," suggesting (wrongly, as we shall discuss) that the true number is not less than 140 million weapons. In fact, the best current evidence suggests 140 million as the plausible *upper bound* of the true number, and the best guess is thus that the true number is somewhere below this estimate.

On the topic of unjustifiable certainty, some mention might also be made of the "problem of significant digits." For example, one source reports, in all apparent seriousness, that the total number of weapons now in private hands in the United States is 135,578,778 (Speigler and Sweeney, 1975: 3)—a representation in nine significant digits of a number that is, in truth, known only to within ± 20,000,000! But unlike the large majority of such estimates, Spiegler and Sweeney's number at least has the strong advantage that the methods by which it was calculated are also reported in full.

25

In the absence of a vigorous national program of weapons registration, covering both new purchases and weapons currently in private hands and applied uniformly across all 50 states, it is very unlikely that the exact number of privately owned firearms will ever be known, even to the nearest few million. All methods for estimating this quantity are necessarily inferential and thus subject to errors of unknown seriousness. On the other hand, the approximate order of magnitude is known with reasonable certainty; it appears that there are not fewer than 100 million firearms now in private hands in the country.

It must be emphasized in advance that every effort to estimate the domestic weapons stock is based on a wide assortment of implicit and explicit assumptions, most of which have never been adequately researched. The same is true of the estimates undertaken in this chapter. The estimates provided here are "better" only in the restricted sense that we have tried to be completely explicit about every assumption we have made, not in the sense that we have made "better" assumptions.

Approaches to estimating the amount of private weaponry can be categorized into "supply-side" and "demand-side" methods. The supply-side approach involves calculating the total number of firearms produced domestically each year and adding to that the number of imported firearms. Additional allowances must, of course, be made for the number of firearms taken out of use each year through loss, destruction, confiscation, obsolescence, exportation or other means.

There are a number of well-recognized problems with this approach. First, although domestic production of firearms can be estimated more or less accurately, at least for recent decades, imports of firearms cannot be. According to Newton and Zimring (1969), the two major import flows that cannot be accurately known are (1) firearms imported into the country by returning servicemen, and (2) firearms imported by private citizens. The relatively high incidence of weapons ownership among veterans (see Chapter 6) suggests that the first source may not be trivial. Newton and Zimring note that "firearms purchased by the military since 1940, less those in current use, total approximately 14,000,000," of which about 2 million have been sold or given to foreign countries (1969: 4). There is thus a "surplus" of 12 million weapons, some fraction of which is now in private hands. This estimate covers the period through 1968 and therefore does *not* include the bulk of the Vietnam era or the weapons brought back to the United States by veterans of that war. Concerning the second source of imports, as Newton and Zimring have also pointed out, customs law allows returning U.S. citizens to import up to three firearms without a formal customs declaration. Since the number of Americans traveling abroad in any typical year is in the tens of millions (travelers to Canada and Mexico included), it is apparent that the total flow of weaponry from this source might also be substantial.[2]

A second problem with the supply-side approach is that no good estimate is available of the number of weapons taken out of use in a typical year.[3]

---

[2] These surplus military weapons and private imports are two of the three great unknowns in the supply-side estimating equation; the third, discussed below, is the rate at which weapons are taken out of use. Thus, all supply-side estimates must make assumptions about these three quantities or rates. The figure of 12 million surplus military weapons is a convenient one for later purposes. Since this figure includes all military weapons produced in the period, less the number sold or given away to other countries, it represents the absolute upper limit of the total number of surplus military weapons available to the private domestic market as of 1968. Now, some very large share of these weapons will have been lost in combat, abandoned, scrapped, and so on. For purposes of some of the calculations undertaken later in this chapter, we make the convenient assumption that these losses from the surplus military supply balance out additions through private imports, such that the total flow of weapons into the country unaccounted for by production and import data is just 12 million weapons. As with all such assumptions, this one is very unlikely to be literally true, but it is probably close enough for our purposes. Another problem is that the 12-million figure for military guns counts only weapons made in the United States. Foreign military weapons imported by returning servicemen are therefore not included. The magnitude of this potential flow is completely unknown.

A major source of subtraction from the potential domestic supply is the exportation of U.S. weapons to other countries—an "obvious" factor that, nonetheless, has not been considered in previous supply-side calculations. Data discussed later in the text suggest that roughly one domestically manufactured firearm in 10 is exported to another country. There are, as far as we can tell, no available estimates of illegal exportation, although at least some exportation of this sort can be assumed to occur.

[3] According to Spiegler and Sweeney (1975: 2), the U.S. Bureau of Alcohol, Tobacco, and Firearms (ATF) "estimates that guns annually worn out, destroyed, exported, or seized as contraband total about 250,000." Although this estimate is often cited in the literature (e.g., Comptroller General, 1978: 18), we have not encountered a specific reference to an ATF source or publication in connection with it, so we are unable to determine how the estimate was constructed and, thus, whether it is reasonable or not. Spiegler and Sweeney maintain that "this figure appears to be too low." On the basis of data from three Ohio cities, these authors project that some 447,000 guns are confiscated by municipal police alone, nationwide, in an average year; police confiscations, in turn, are only one of several mechanisms through which weapons can be removed from serviceability.

Better data than those available to Speigler and Sweeney, reviewed in a later chapter, suggest about 260,000 police weapons confiscations per year. It is, however, also the case that such confiscations do not always remove the weapon in question from the potential private stock, since weapons confiscated by police sometimes turn up again in private hands, through either licit or illicit means.

Newton and Zimring (1969: 5) report that the useful life of a gun ranges between 10,000 and 100,000 rounds fired. They also note that roughly 4.4 billion rounds of ammunition were manufactured in 1967, which, on an assumption of roughly 100 million weapons, works out to an average of about 44 rounds fired per weapon per year. On the basis of these figures alone, the average weapon would be expected to last for several hundreds of years.

How long the average weapon actually lasts, of course, is a function of its initial quality,

With proper care, a firearm remains serviceable more or less indefinitely; however, no study of maintenance behaviors among firearms owners has ever been conducted. Police confiscations of weapons occasionally involve firearms manufactured in the 19th century; the handgun fired at President Gerald Ford by Squeaky Fromm was manufactured in 1911. Specialists in antique firearms often restore weapons several centuries old into quite serviceable condition. It is thus conceivable that a very large fraction of all weapons manufactured or imported in the 20th century are still serviceable or could at least be made serviceable with the proper attention.

Figures from Newton and Zimring (1969: Table 1-1) show a total domestic production of 91 million firearms between 1899 and 1968, and a total import flow from known sources of 11 million firearms since 1918, for a total base-figure of roughly 102 million firearms available as of 1968. It can be assumed that both of these component numbers are subject to high degrees of error, especially the portion of them that depends on records from the turn of the century. Nonetheless, they seem to be the best (most complete) figures available for the period up to 1968. To these figures must be added total inward flow of firearms from unknown sources; likewise, the total number of firearms taken out of use must be subtracted. Having no good information

----

the rate at which it is fired, and the care that it is given. With the possible partial exception of the first factor, essentially no information is available on any of these questions.

As we discuss later, Newton and Zimring make no attempt to correct their supply-side data for weaponry taken out of use; their estimate of total weaponry is just the simple sum of known production and importation from 1899 to 1968. It seems highly unlikely, however, that much turn-of-the-century armament is still serviceable or in use. The assumption that *all* of it remains in use seems odd. They justify this treatment with the note that "a firearm can be expected to last indefinitely if given proper care" (1969: 5), but this is hardly a persuasive argument. An automobile will also last indefinitely "if given proper care." This hypothetical possibility, however, says nothing about the care that autos or guns *actually* receive or about how long the average auto or gun lasts *in fact*.

It is, of course, also true that old and dilapidated automobiles can, with adequate attention, be restored to a functioning, indeed pristine, condition, and the same is true of old guns. Many firearms buffs who have read this material have called our attention to one or another centuries-old firearm that they or their acquaintances have restored to serviceable condition. However, these examples do not address the issue of the *average* lifetime of a private weapon. Whether the typical gun owner lavishes the same care on his or her firearms that gun buffs lavish on theirs is an open empirical question.

It is always risky to reason by metaphor, but the parallel with private automobiles seems potentially informative. The purchase price of a new firearm will seldom run to more than several hundreds of dollars, whereas the purchase price of a new car runs to several thousands. Yet, the average private automobile receives indifferent maintenance at best, and the average lifetime of a new car cannot be more than 10 or 15 years. Why, then, would one expect the average firearm to receive better care and maintenance than the average automobile? Or to have a substantially longer life span?

on either of these quantities, Newton and Zimring make the convenient (but not implausible) assumption that the necessary additions and subtractions simply cancel each other out. Thus, the 1968 supply-side estimate is 102 million weapons in private hands.

An update of these figures through the decade of the 1970's is shown in Table 2-1, which presents data from the U.S. *Statistical Abstract* on weapons production and imports from 1969 through 1976, the most recent year for which data are available. It cannot be assumed that the figures shown are entirely reliable. Every *Statistical Abstract* contains a table similar to Table 2-1, and there are some discrepancies in the reported numbers from one *Abstract* to the next. All such discrepancies, however, involve only the import figures; the figures on domestic production are consistent. Data in Table 2-1 are in all cases taken from the 1977 version of the figures, on the assumption that the discrepancies reflect errors in the earlier compilations that have been corrected for more recent ones.[4]

From 1969 through 1976, annual domestic production averaged about 5.4 million weapons, and imports averaged about 960,000 weapons, resulting in the addition of about 6.3 million new weapons to the domestic market each year since the Newton–Zimring data were originally compiled. Both these rates are substantially higher than the rates that prevailed earlier in the century; on the basis of Newton and Zimring's data, for example, annual domestic production averaged only about 1.3 million firearms from 1899 to 1968, and imports averaged about 200,000 firearms. The rate at which new weapons are presently being added, in short, is about four times the rate that prevailed during the first half of the 20th century. These data therefore suggest that the sharp upturn in weapons sales, especially in handgun sales, noted by Newton and Zimring (1969: Ch. 4) for the decade of the 1960's has persisted more or less unabated to the present.

The data from Table 2-1 allow us to extend the supply-side estimate to 1978. If 6.3 million new weapons have been added to the domestic market

---

[4] Estimates of the total amount of firearms based on the 1977 version of the figures are therefore somewhat lower than those based on earlier compilations of the "same" figures. Spiegler and Sweeney (1975: Appendix A), for example, using the earlier figures (the only ones available to them as of their writing), show an annual average of about 1.1 million imported firearms from 1969 through 1974, as compared with the annual average of about 958 thousand shown in Table 2-1. Because we have only assumed that the more recently published figures are the more accurate ones, prudence might suggest that one split the difference, in which case the reasonable guess is that imports have been averaging about 1 million new weapons per year. Since imports in either case are only about one-fifth or less of the annual domestic production, it is clear that these discrepancies in the import figures have only modest effects on estimates of the total number of weapons being added to the market yearly.

The definitive discussion of ambiguities in the supply-side data, especially the import data, is provided by Zimring (1975); see also the following chapter.

TABLE 2-1. *Firearms production and imports, 1969–1976 (in thousands)*

Firearms	1969	1970	1971	1972	1973	1974	1975	1976	X̄s
Domestic production									
Handguns	2840	NA[a]	NA	NA	1734	1715	2024	1833	2029
Rifles	⎫	NA	NA	NA	1830	2099	2123	2091	⎫
Shotguns	⎭ 2450	NA	NA	NA	1280	1825	1621	1301	⎭ 3324
Imports									
Handguns	349	227	301	486	299	259	462	270	329
Rifles	207	237	243	197	195	188	166	157	199
Shotguns	334	363	406	535	420	456	457	468	430
Totals	6180	NA	NA	NA	5758	6542	6852	6120	6290

[a] NA, not available.
Source: *Statistical Abstract of the United States,* 1977: Table 289.

each year since 1968, and if we assume that none of the 1968-era weapons have been taken out of use since, then the 1978 supply-side estimate is the original 1968 figure, 102 million, plus 6.3 million additional each year for the past 10 years, for a grand total of about 165 million weapons. This figure amounts to the total known production and importation of weapons in the United States in the 20th century. If we add an additional 12 million from surplus military stocks and other unknown import flows, we are left with an estimate of about 177 million as the absolute upper limit of the possible number of serviceable firearms now in private hands in the United States. Since at least *some* of these 177 million will have been taken out of use in the century, we may confidently conclude that the total number is not more than about 180 million weapons and that the true present number must be less than that—by an amount equal to the number of these weapons that are no longer serviceable or in use.

As we have already noted, the Newton–Zimring supply-side calculation is based on the simple assumption that additions to the supply from unknown sources balance out subtractions from the supply due to weapons taken out of use, and although this assumption is not implausible, it is nonetheless just a guess. Further, for weapons manufactured early in the century, it is likely to be in serious error, because we can reasonably assume that the probability of a weapon being serviceable today is a very strong function of the number of years that have elapsed since it was first manufactured. The fraction of weapons manufactured in 1900 that are still in use today, in other words, must be relatively small, certainly smaller than the fraction of those manufactured in, say, 1950 that are still in use today. These considerations suggest that it may be useful to think of these production and import numbers in terms of weapon *half-lives*. Following the well-known physical analog, we may conceive of a weapon's half-life as the number of years that must elapse before one-half of any year's production has been taken out of use; in this sense, then, the half-life is just the number of years that the "average" weapon survives. Obviously, no one knows for sure what the true half-lives of weapons are; and there are other complications: half-lives for imports may be much shorter than those for domestic production; half-lives for handguns may be shorter than for long guns; certainly, the lifetime of any particular weapon will depend quite strongly on patterns of maintenance and use. But, as with Newton and Zimring, we are free to make some assumptions, which can in turn be used to correct the production and import figures for half-life decay and thus to generate a "best guess" about the total numbers of weapons now in private hands.

To emphasize the "iffiness" of these calculations, and to show quite directly how the final figures depend heavily on the initial assumptions, all our estimates are generated for assumed half-lives of 30 and 50 years. It is a very rare consumer good that has an expected usable lifetime as long as 30 years, so we believe these assumptions to be quite generous. To give some idea of what these assumptions amount to, the 30-year half-life would mean that about 20% of all weapons manufactured in 1900 are still serviceable and in use in 1978; under the 50-year half-life assumption, the fraction of weapons manufactured in 1900 surviving to 1978 would be just over one-third.

Given an assumed half-life (HL), the relationship between original production and import numbers and the numbers of presently serviceable weapons surviving is determined by Eq. (1):

$$N_p = N_m (0.5)^{T/HL} \tag{1}$$

where N_p = the number of weapons surviving; N_m = the number of weapons manufactured; T = the elapsed time between manufacture date and the present; and HL = the assumed half-life (either 30 or 50 years).

Using the production and import data through 1968 from Newton and Zimring (1969: Table 4-1), the update of those figures through 1978 (from Table 2-1, above), and Eq. (1), one can project the number of weapons surviving to either 1968 or 1978, as in Table 2-2. The table shows, separately for each decade, the best guess as to the total number of weapons made or imported and the elapsed time between the origin year and either 1968 or 1978. The table further shows both fractions and numbers of weapons from each decade of origin that survive to either 1968 or 1978, assuming half-lives of 30 and 50 years, respectively.

According to these projections, the number of serviceable firearms remaining in private hands as of 1968 was somewhere between 61 and 74 million. If we add 12 million to these figures to allow for surplus military weapons and inward flows from other sources, and if we make no further corrections for decay among these additional 12 million, our projections give between 73 and 86 million privately owned weapons in 1968, compared with the estimate of 102 million originally provided by Newton and Zimring. The original figure is thus plausible only if either (1) the total from unknown sources is very much more than 12 million weapons, which seems unlikely because this is the *total* number of unaccounted-for surplus military weapons through 1968, or (2) the actual half-life of a weapon is very much more than 50 years, which also does not seem likely. We thus conclude that the figure of 102 million for 1968 is implausibly high and that the actual number of weapons in private hands as of 1968 was probably closer to 86 than to 102 million.

Projections to 1978 give a total figure between 106 and 124 million for privately owned weapons; adding the 12 million weapons otherwise unaccounted for increases the guess to between 118 and 136 million weapons in private hands as of 1978. We may thus decrease our guess about the

TABLE 2-2. Projected numbers of privately owned weapons, using import and manufacturing data and assumed weapons half-lives (HL) of 30 and 50 years

Year of origin	Nm[a]	T(1968)[b]	T(1978)[b]	HL = 30 years				HL = 50 years			
				f(1968)[c]	N(1968)[d]	f(1978)[c]	N(1978)[d]	f(1968)[c]	N(1968)[d]	f(1978)[c]	N(1978)[d]
1899–08	10.6	64	74	.228	2.4	.181	1.9	.412	4.4	.358	3.8
1909–18	10.6	54	64	.287	3.0	.228	2.4	.473	5.0	.412	4.4
1919–28	10.6	44	54	.362	3.8	.287	3.0	.543	5.8	.473	5.0
1929–38	10.6	34	44	.456	4.8	.362	3.8	.624	6.6	.543	5.8
1939–48	10.6	24	34	.574	6.1	.456	4.8	.717	7.6	.624	6.6
1949–58	20.0	14	24	.724	14.5	.574	11.5	.824	16.5	.717	14.3
1959–68	29.2	4	14	.912	26.6	.724	21.1	.946	27.6	.824	24.1
1969–78	63.0	—	4	—	—	.912	57.5	—	—	.946	59.6
Total	165.2				61.2		106.0		73.5		123.6

[a] Number of firearms manufactured or imported in the indicated period, in millions.
[b] Average elapsed time between date of manufacture and 1968 or 1978.
[c] Fraction of the original number surviving until 1968 or 1978, where HL = 30 or 50 years.
[d] Actual number of weapons surviving until 1968 or 1978, where HL = 30 or 50 years, in millions.
Sources: Production and import data through 1968 are from Newton and Zimring (1969: Table 4-1); figures for 1969–1978 are from Table 2-1, above.

upper limit of the number from about 180 million (total production and imports in the 20th century) to about 140 million (the number that would have survived under an assumed half-life of 50 years plus an additional 12 million not counted in the production and import data). We therefore conclude that there are not more than about 140 million serviceable firearms in private hands in the United States as of 1978. The actual number will be less than 140 million if either (1) the 12 million added on is too high, or (2) the average lifetime of a weapon is less than 50 years.

It is useful at this point to introduce another consideration that is not taken into account either in the Newton–Zimring original or in its subsequent updates, and that is the *exportation* of weapons made in the United States to other countries. Certainly, an exported weapon would normally no longer be available for purchase in the domestic weapons market, and so the estimate of the domestic firearms supply must be appropriately discounted by this additional factor. As far as we can determine, there are no readily available figures for U.S. weapons exportation before about 1970. The December 1980 issue of *American Firearms Industry Magazine,* however, gives production and exportation figures for the decade of the 1970s. According to this source, the total 1979 domestic firearms production amounted to just over 5.4 million firearms (consistent with the data in Table 2-1), of which about 540,000 were exported to other countries. Data on other years in the decade show about the same proportion of exports (that is, about 10%). Thus, the data on domestic production (given in Table 2-1 and used in calculating the figures in Table 2-2) should be further reduced by approximately 10%, which further lowers the empirically credible upper limit of the true number to at most 130 million domestically owned firearms.

The demand-side approach uses national survey data on weapons owner-ship. Harris, Gallup, the National Opinion Research Center, and other survey organizations have been asking respondents whether they own a gun (or keep one in the house) more or less regularly since 1959 (Erskine, 1972). The proportion of U.S. households responding yes has consistently hovered around 50% (Wright, 1981).[5] Some (although not many) of the national surveys follow up the ownership question with an item asking for the total

[5] Trend data from the surveys on weapons ownership are presented and discussed in Chapter 5. There are, as noted in the text, many possible sources of ambiguity in the survey-based estimates, not the least being the varying definitions that respondents might have in mind when asked about "guns." We should also note that some fraction of the private weapons ownership detected by the survey method would not, strictly speaking, be "private" but would rather consist of firearms owned for occupational purposes (e.g., by policemen and other security forces). For more on this issue, see Chapter 4. Although most credible national surveys show ownership proportions very close to 50%, some surveys have found proportions as low as 42% and others as high as 59%, making it virtually certain that the true proportion is between 40 and 60%.

number of weapons owned, typically by type of weapon. The data on numbers owned can thus be used to calculate an average number of weapons owned per household; this average can in turn be multiplied by the total number of households to generate an estimate of the total numbers of weapons in private hands.

Survey evidence available to Newton and Zimring (1969) allowed for two of these kinds of estimates. The first is derived from a 1968 Harris Poll sponsored by the National Commission on the Causes and Prevention of Violence. Results from the poll, as reported by Newton and Zimring, showed 49% of all households owning a firearm, and an average of 2.24 firearms owned by each weapons-owning household. Given just over 60 million households in the United States as of 1968, these findings project to a total of 66 million privately owned weapons—well below the initial supply-side estimate of 102 million weapons, but quite consistent with the "corrections" of that estimate shown in Table 2-2. A second estimate is derived from a 1966 Gallup finding that 59% of all U.S. families owned a gun. Using the 2.24 average from the Harris data and the same population base, one can project the Gallup finding to a total of about 80 million privately owned weapons, again well below the original supply-side calculation but clearly within the range suggested by our Table 2-2 corrections.

Because the 1966 Gallup percentage (of 59%) gives a final number much closer to the initial supply-side estimate that the 1968 Harris percentage (of 49%), Newton and Zimring ignore the Harris-based estimate in their subsequent calculations and conclude that the survey data show some 80 million guns in private hands. Even this figure is about 20 million short of the supply-side estimate of 102 million. Lacking any better way to resolve the apparent discrepancy, Newton and Zimring conclude with an estimate that is simply an average of the final supply- and demand-side estimates; their "bottom line," in short, is a total of 90 million privately owned guns.

Newton and Zimring are predictably concerned by the wide discrepancy between 66 (or even 80) and 102 million weapons. They assume that the survey approach is faulty for two reasons: (1) respondents may not always know about all the weapons owned by other members of the household and may therefore report incorrectly low numbers, and (2) far more important, many people may be reluctant to say that they own a weapon, even if they do. In the latter case, the argument is usually that various "demand characteristics" of the interview situation may prevent people from revealing these "darker" aspects of themselves (on this, see, for example, Bruce-Biggs, 1976; Kleck, 1979a). This argument, however, depends on the largely unresearched assumption that many weapons owners are somehow embarrassed because they own a gun and thus hesitate to "fess up" when asked. And yet, one-half of all respondents freely admit to possessing a weapon, which should give some reason for skepticism about the "demand characteristics" interpretation.[6]

The Newton–Zimring analysis of the discrepancy thus assumes that the survey estimates are too low. It may also be that the supply-side estimates, as in Table 2-2 and the ensuing discussion, are too high. The range suggested by our "corrections" of the Newton–Zimring data is between 61 and 86 million weapons as of 1968, a range within which both Harris and Gallup survey estimates fall. In other words, if the assumptions we have made to correct the initial figures are accurate, then both supply- and demand-side estimates give approximately the same results.

On the other hand, we may be reasonably certain that the survey approach underestimates weapons possessed illegally and those kept primarily or exclusively for illicit purposes, so all such demand-side estimates should definitely be taken as lower-bound estimates. The lowest such estimate is the Harris-based estimate, 66 million weapons; the highest plausible figure from Table 2-2 is 86 million weapons; the best guess is thus that there were probably not fewer than 66 million and probably not more than 86 million guns in private hands in the United States as of 1968.

The survey approach, of course, is not free of problems. Although we are not convinced that demand characteristics are one of them, the following doubtlessly are:

1. As Newton and Zimring point out, respondents may not know about weapons owned by the family or kept in the house. For obvious reasons, about one-half the respondents in any national survey are women, whereas most gun owners are presumably men. It may be that many women are unaware of weapons owned by their husbands or are incorrectly informed about the total number.

2. Most weapons ownership questions from the national surveys ask

---

[6] One must distinguish between matters that would be offensive or sensitive in well-educated liberal circles and matters that would be offensive or sensitive in the circles in which the vast majority of people travel. In discussing our research with other academics and social scientists, we have often been told, "I don't know a single person who owns a gun!" In these circles, gun ownership may very well be socially undesirable, and the few gun owners who travel in these circles may be embarrassed by (or at least sensitive or defensive about) their weaponry. Outside these rarefied circles, however, every second family appears to possess a weapon; and in places other than the very largest cities, it is the unusual family that does *not* possess at least one gun. Among the masses weapons ownership is quite evidently *not* socially undesirable, since, as we note in the text, half of all families freely admit to possessing a weapon when asked. In other words, our feeling is that the "social desirability" argument amounts in this case to an inappropriate projection of the standards and values of the people who write about weapons onto the people who own them.

whether there is a gun in the home. Interpreted literally, this would exclude guns kept in garages or glove compartments, those stored in gun clubs or shooting ranges, or those kept in any other place outside the home.

3. Likewise, many of the national survey questions ask specifically about the respondent, for example, "Do you have a gun in your home?" (the Gallup item) or "Do you own a firearm?" (the Harris item). Weapons owned by family members other than respondents may thus be underreported by this question.

4. The survey approach allows respondents to use their own subjective definitions of what constitutes a gun, and these definitions are obviously free to vary from one respondent to the next. For example, entirely serviceable weaponry whose main function in the household is decorative (e.g., rifles hung over fireplaces) may or may not be reported; weapons purchased long ago and stored in some out-of-the-way place (to be retrieved "just in case") may be forgotten; and gas-operated or pump-operated weaponry may or may not fall into the respondent's definition of a gun.

5. Finally and potentially most important, as we demonstrate below, survey data on numbers of weapons owned per household are invariably taken (or at least reported) in categories, especially at the upper end of the scale. For example, the Harris poll reported by Newton and Zimring used "four or more weapons" as the highest ownership category. "Four or more," in turn, is an exceedingly broad range, covering all households with anywhere from four to dozens and dozens of firearms. The calculation of an "average" number of weapons owned per weapons-owning household from categorical data such as these therefore requires an assumption about the true midpoint of the "four or more weapons" range.

To indicate the seriousness of this problem, Table 2-3 presents the Harris ownership data as reported in Newton and Zimring (1969: Table 2-1), the data from which their Harris-based estimate of 66 million firearms is derived. Note the category "four or more weapons." If one assumes that the true average number of weapons in households possessing "four or more weapons" is just five weapons, then the total number of weapons owned by households in that category is about 30 million and the projected total number of weapons in private hands is about 68.7 million, or just about the figure that Newton and Zimring report. If, on the other hand, one assumes that the true average number of weapons in households owning more than four is as high as 10 weapons, then these households possessed (in 1968) some 60 million weapons total, and the projected total number of weapons in private hands for that year becomes 98.7 million, very close to the 102 million figure generated by the initial supply-side approach. In short, whether there is any genuine discrepancy or not between supply- and demand-side approaches turns entirely

TABLE 2-3. *Newton–Zimring–Harris data on numbers of weapons owned (1968)*

Firearms owned	Millions of households	Total weaponry (millions)	
		Assumption A[a]	Assumption B[b]
None	30.8 (51%)	0	0
One	12.1 (20%)	12.1	12.1
Two	7.9 (13%)	15.8	15.8
Three	3.6 (6%)	10.8	10.8
Four or more	6.0 (10%)	30.0	60.0
Total	60.4 (100)	68.7	98.7

[a] Assumption A: The average number of weapons owned among families owning four or more weapons is five weapons.

[b] Assumption B: The average number of weapons owned among families owning four or more weapons is 10 weapons.

Source: Newton and Zimring, 1969: Table 2-1.

on the guess one is willing to make about the average number of weapons owned by families owning "four or more" of them.

There is a rather comforting symmetry to all this. The supply-side approach (as corrected in Table 2-2) gives a lower bound of 61 million firearms under the most restrictive assumptions, and an upper bound of 102 million firearms under the least restrictive assumptions (in this case, under the initial Newton–Zimring assumptions). Likewise, the demand-side approach gives a lower bound of about 66 million firearms under the more restrictive assumption (that the "four or more" average is five weapons) and an upper bound of about 99 million firearms under the less restrictive assumption (that the "four or more" average is 10 weapons). All this makes it virtually certain that the true value in 1968 fell somewhere in the range of 80 ± 20 million weapons in private hands.

It must also be emphasized that the discrepancy that is so prominent in the Newton–Zimring report may result entirely from assumptions made about the numbers produced by each method, not from the numbers themselves. It also appears that the discrepancy is greatly inflated because Newton and Zimring make very liberal assumptions about the supply-side data and very conservative assumptions about the demand-side data. Given the inherent uncertainties of both methods and taking into account the considerations enumerated here, one is necessarily *much* more impressed by the consistency of estimates across methods than by the discrepancies.[7]

[7] All this amply demonstrates what is known in computer science as the GIGO principle. GIGO is an acronym for "Garbage In, Garbage Out." One's estimate of the total number of privately owned weapons can be made to vary by some 40 million weapons simply by substituting

The most recent survey data on numbers of weapons owned are from a 1978 survey conducted by Decision-Making Information, Inc. (DMI), under commission to the National Rifle Association. (See Chapters 7 and 11 for a secondary analysis and discussion of the DMI survey.) Ownership data from the DMI survey are shown in Table 2-4.

A number of findings reported in the table warrant emphasis in present context:

1. The ownership proportion from the survey is 47%, very close to the 1968 Harris proportion of 49% and broadly consistent with virtually all other survey estimates, the 1966 Gallup estimate being the major prominent exception.

2. Altogether, a mere 1% of the sample refused to answer the gun ownership question. By way of contrast, this is roughly one-tenth the proportion who typically refuse to answer a question on total family income, which gives some indication of the relative sensitivity of guns versus income in the minds of the American population. That only 1% refuse to answer the gun ownership question again casts some doubt on the "demand characteristics" argument.

3. According to DMI, 1% of all households own between five and nine handguns, and an additional 1% own 10 or more handguns. This means that *one-half* the households possessing more than five such weapons actually

---

one set of plausible assumptions for another. Given the sensitivity of the final numbers to the assumptions that produce them, any concern over discrepancies between methods is premature until one has, to the extent possible, researched the assumptions in question. Because the indicated research has, for the most part, *not* been conducted, our presentation emphasizes the general agreement across methods, with the advance understanding that all estimates are subject to great fluctuation as better information becomes available.

Most discussions of the surface discrepancy between supply and demand data on weapons ownership do not consider any of these issues. Kleck (1979a: 895), for example, has noted the same discrepancy that we have been discussing in the text: "While the commission's Task Force on Firearms [the Newton–Zimring report] estimated, based on manufacturer's records and importation data, a stock of about 100 million guns in the United States in 1968, estimates derived from the Harris survey indicate only about 66 million guns owned." That, as we have seen, is an accurate depiction of the results reported by Newton and Zimring. But what do these results suggest? In Kleck's view, they suggest that "a substantial number of gun owners were lying or 'forgetting' about guns they owned. Other national surveys of course faced this same problem" (1979a: 895). Even a modest curiosity about how the Newton–Zimring numbers were produced would caution against such a conclusion; Kleck himself acknowledges that "the [supply-side] measurement method does not take account of losses of firearms due to destruction, misplacement, or deterioration. . . ." As our own review demonstrates, there is more than ample reason to conclude that the discrepancy results more from assumptions made about the evidence than from inherent deficiencies in either measurement technique. The appropriate conclusion to be drawn from the Newton–Zimring discrepancy is thus that all estimates (of any parameter) are highly sensitive to the assumptions from which they are derived.

TABLE 2-4. *DMI data on numbers of weapons owned (1978)*

Do you have guns of any kind in your home?	
Yes	47%
No	52%
Refused	1%
[IF YES] Are there any pistols, revolvers, or other handguns in your home? [IF YES]: How many?	
None	46%
One	30%
Two	8%
3–4	4%
5–9	1%
10 +	1%
Yes only	8%
Refused	4%
Are there any shotguns or rifles in your home? [IF YES]: How many?	
None	14%
One	29%
Two	21%
3–4	16%
5–9	5%
10 +	2%
Yes only	9%
Refused	4%

Source: Decision-Making Information, Inc., 1978: 70.

possess at least 10 of them. Likewise, 5% of all households own between five and nine long guns, and an additional 2% own 10 or more long guns, which means that roughly one-third of all households owning more than five actually own at least 10. These data thus strongly suggest that the true midpoint of the range "four or more weapons" may be *much* higher than five weapons, or, in other words, that the discrepant Harris-based estimate of 66 million total weapons results mostly from an implausibly low guess.[8]

[8] Phrasing the conclusion more precisely, the DMI data confirm that *as of 1978,* the average number of weapons owned by households owning four or more of them was substantially greater than five weapons. The equivalent average *as of 1968* is basically unknown, the calculation depending entirely on a guess about the midpoint of the "4+" range. There is strong inferential evidence, reviewed in Chapter 5, that this critical average—the average number owned by households owning at least one—may have itself increased substantially over the decade. Given this possibility, it would obviously be unwise to make inferences about the 1968 value on the basis of 1978 data.

4. Note, finally, that 12% of the handgun owners and 13% of the long gun owners did not provide information on the number of weapons they owned (shown as "Yes only" and "Refused" in Table 2-4), which introduces an additional complication in calculating a total number of weapons from these data.

Our estimate from these data of the total number of firearms in private hands as of 1978 is based on these assumptions: (1) There was a total of 75 million households in the United States in 1978. (2) The distribution of numbers of weapons owned among the "Yes Only" and "Refused" categories is identical to the distribution among people who answered the "how many weapons?" question. (3) The midpoint of the range "5–9 weapons" is 7 weapons. And (4) the midpoint of the range "10 or more weapons" is 12 weapons. Of these four assumptions, only the last is likely to be seriously problematic. If the "10 or more" category contains a sizeable number of weapons collectors, as it very probably does, and if the average collection contains, say, 25 or more firearms, then our assumption about the true midpoint of the "10 or more" range (12 weapons) will no doubt be much too low. Lacking any useful data on the matter, we simply note that these assumptions and the data in Table 2-4 then project out to an estimate of 112 million weapons in private hands in 1978, very close to the 106 million supply figure calculated in Table 2-2 on the 30-year half-life assumption and somewhat below the 124 million figure derived from the 50-year half-life assumption. Thus, just as we concluded earlier that the true 1968 figure almost certainly fell between 60 and 100 million, so may we conclude that the present (1978) figure probably falls between 100 and 125 million, or between 100 and 140 million if our figure of 12 million weapons from fugitive sources is added in. Here, too, one should be more impressed by the order-of-magnitude agreement across methods than by minor discrepancies that reflect nothing more than one's initial assumptions. *The substantive conclusion is therefore that there are probably not fewer than 100 million, and probably not more than 140 million privately owned firearms in the United States at the present time.*

The distribution of these private weapons by weapons type has been estimated by many observers; two of these estimates are shown in Table 2-5. The first is the estimate of Newton and Zimring (1969), and the second is based on the update of the Newton–Zimring efforts reported by Spiegler and Sweeney (1975). Although there is much disagreement in the literature over the total number of weapons, there is a fair consensus over the relative proportions: virtually all studies report percentage distributions very close to those shown in Table 2-5.

Rifles are the most popular type of private weaponry, by a thin margin;

TABLE 2-5. *Distribution of private firearms by type*

	1968[a]		1974[b]	
Firearms	N	%	N	%
Rifles	35,000,000	39	50,000,000	37
Shotguns	31,000,000	34	45,000,000	33
Handguns	24,000,000	27	50,000,000	30
Totals	90,000,000	100	135,000,000	100

[a] Source: Newton and Zimring, 1969: 6.
[b] Source: Spiegler and Sweeney, 1975: 3.

shotguns are a close second. Approximately two-thirds of the total firearms are thus long guns; the remaining one-third are handguns. The available estimates are that there are approximately 30–40 million handguns in the United States at present.

Subject to several qualifications discussed in later chapters, the assumption may be made that most of the private long guns are owned and used primarily for sporting purposes; the same would also be true for some fraction of the handguns (see Chapter 3). However, "self-defense" is the most commonly cited reason for owing handguns, and by far most firearms used for criminal or illicit purposes are handguns. For these reasons, most (but not all) of the debate over gun control has focused on the control of handguns.

Aside from the approximate total number, then, what else do we know about the existing handgun supply? Unfortunately, relatively little. Table 2-1 gave a rough picture of the distribution of domestics versus imports; approximately three-quarters of the handguns now owned privately were manufactured (or assembled) in the United States. Spiegler and Sweeney (1975: 4) have compiled data on calibers for the domestic production of handguns for the years 1973 and 1974; these data are shown in Table 2-6. Revolvers (essentially, handguns with rotating ammunition chambers) are by far the more popular, outnumbering pistols (any handgun other than a revolver) by about 2.5 to 1. Just over one-half of all the handguns (53%) can be classified as small-caliber, namely, .32 caliber or less; the rest are large-caliber weapons (.38 caliber or more). According to these data, the most popular handgun currently being manufactured in the United States is a .38 caliber revolver, followed closely by a .22 caliber revolver; .357 caliber revolvers and .25 caliber pistols are tied for third. As far as we have been able to determine, no study of the equivalent distributions among imported handguns has ever been done, although there is a recurring surmise that most imported handguns are of the small-caliber type.

To summarize briefly, the substantive conclusion to be drawn at this point

TABLE 2-6. *Domestic handgun production by caliber,
1973–1974*

Caliber	Revolvers	Pistols	Total	% of Total
.22	854,000	321,000	1,176,000	34
.25	—	436,000	436,000	13
.32	217,000	2,000	219,000	6
.38	879,000	50,000	928,000	27
9 mm	—	72,000	72,000	2
.357	436,000	—	436,000	13
.44	79,000	—	79,000	2
.45	21,000	83,000	104,000	3
Total	2,486,000	964,000	3,449,000	100
% of Total	72	28	100	

Source: Spiegler and Sweeney, 1975: 4.

is that there were a total of about 80 million weapons in the United States in 1968, and about 120 million of them in 1978—an increase whose possible causes are considered in the following three chapters. In passing, it can be noted that all the estimates reported here are substantially *lower* than the estimates commonly supplied by advocates and polemicists on either side of the Great Gun War. We have in the previous pages laid out in rather precise detail the assumptions and calculations on which our guesses are based, and we invite others who favor different estimates to do likewise. It should also be noted that it is generally in the best interests of *both* sides to overstate the private ownership of guns: the pro-gun-control forces, that is, are interested in the highest possible numbers because they illustrate in the most dramatic way the extent and urgency of the "gun problem," and the anti-gun-control forces are interested in the highest possible numbers because they illustrate most dramatically the number of citizens whose rights and prerogatives would be infringed by additional weapons regulations.

Although it would certainly be nice to know the exact figures, and especially nice to know the approximate accuracy even of our order-of-magnitude figures, these estimates of the total weaponry are no doubt more than "close enough" for all practical, that is to say for all policy, purposes. Whether the true number is "only" 100,000,000, or "fully" 140,000,000, the fact remains that "by whatever measure, the United States has an abundance of firearms" (Newton and Zimring, 1969: 7). It is, in short, the general abundance more than the exact figure that defines the relevant policy considerations of the weapons issue. The considerations in question are these:

1. Any effort to curtail the private ownership or use of firearms will necessarily affect the lives of about one-half the families in the nation. Such a

procedure would be highly intrusive and, in a democratic society, not one to be undertaken lightly. The sheer numbers involved make the issue of compliance highly salient in this context; the same numbers also raise an obvious concern about the potential political opposition that any such measure might face. There is, on the other hand, persuasive evidence that many, perhaps most, weapons owners would *not* object to stricter regulations concerning firearms ownership or use (Wright and Marston, 1975); among nonowners, the proportion who would not object is even higher. (Public opinion data relevant to weapons issues are reviewed in Chapter 11.) So it assuredly cannot be concluded from the evidence on total numbers that opposition to stricter laws would be intense, only that such a possibility exists and that any such law would impinge on a very large fraction of the total population.

2. Any new legislation establishing registration or permit mechanisms enacted retroactively so as to cover not only new purchases but also weapons currently in private hands will face a literal mountain of at least 100 million weapons to be registered or licensed. The administrative labors necessary to process this many firearms are potentially very great. Precise cost estimates, of course, are extremely speculative. Not all gun owners would comply with any such regulation, and although this would raise a question about the effectiveness of the regulation, it would at least reduce the costs. Then, too, many of the weapons now in private hands have already been registered or issued permits under existing state or local laws. Cook (1979b), for instance, estimates that roughly two-thirds of the U.S. population live in states where local police are already required to investigate a prospective handgun purchaser before the sale is made. Assuming that some procedure for eliminating duplication and overlap could be devised, such that any weapon already registered or licensed would be exempt from a new retroactive provision, the total costs would also be substantially lower. Our purpose here, however, is not to generate a best-guess estimate of the costs of new national gun legislation, but rather only to note that even under the most favorable assumptions, the costs will not be trivial.

3. Given the total number of guns now in private hands, the potential effective lifetime of each weapon, and the evident impossibility of confiscating or otherwise removing from use any more than a small fraction of them, it is apparent that the potential supply of weapons that *could* be used for illicit or criminal purposes is more than ample for the next several centuries, even if the worldwide production of new weaponry were completely halted today. Those 100 million or so weapons already in private hands mean that the hypothetically possible "ideal" state of "no guns, therefore no gun crimes" will be exceedingly difficult—quite probably impossible—to attain.

Three

RECENT TRENDS IN WEAPONS OWNERSHIP:
I. Sport and Recreational Demand

THE TREND IN WEAPONS SUPPLY

Because the total number of firearms now in private hands is known only very approximately (within about 20 million weapons), it follows that knowledge about trends in that number is even less reliable. There is a consensus among all observers that the total amount of private weaponry has increased in recent years, but estimates of the magnitude of the increase are, for obvious reasons, as variable as estimates of the total numbers. Our best guess about the 1968 number, based on calculations in the previous chapter, is approximately 80 ± 20 million firearms; our best guess about the current (1978) number is approximately 120 ± 20 million firearms. Taking these figures seriously, the total trend over the past decade amounts to something between zero and 80 million "new" weapons. The first problem one encounters in trying to analyze the trend toward an increase in weaponry, in short, is that there is very little trustworthy information on just how extensive it has been.

Trend data on production and imports for the period 1900–1968 are given by Newton and Zimring (1969: Table 4-1). Between 1900 and 1948, an average of about 10 million firearms per decade (or about 1 million firearms per year) was added to the domestic supply. In the next decade (1949–1958), the figure roughly doubled (to about 20 million), and then increased by yet another 10 million (to about 30 million) in the decade 1959–1968. By far the largest increases, especially during the 1960's, were in handgun production and imports. It is the handgun increase in particular that leads Newton and Zimring to speak of the "domestic arms buildup."

The upturn in *handgun* supply during the decade of the 1960's was apparently quite pronounced. According to Newton and Zimring (1969: Table

4-1), total production and imports of handguns averaged roughly 2.7 million sidearms per decade through 1949; jumped to 4.2 million for the decade 1949–1958; and jumped even more sharply, to 10.2 million, between 1959 and 1968. During the 1960's, then, the total domestic supply of handguns apparently increased by about 1 million *each year*.

The more recent production and import figures, covering the 10 years since the Newton–Zimring compilation, show an acceleration of these trends (Table 2-1). The projections of the previous chapter suggest that between 1969 and 1978, as many as 65 million new firearms may have been added to the domestic supply, roughly *twice* the number added during the previous decade. All evidence from the production and import figures therefore converges on the conclusion that *the total number of guns available to the private U.S. market is substantially higher at present than at any previous time in American history.*

This, it appears, is especially true of the total *handgun* supply. The update of handgun production and import figures (Table 2-1) shows roughly 2.4 million additional handguns available on the market *each year* (on average) since 1969, which gives a total increase of about 24 million handguns since the original Newton–Zimring report. Possibly more accurate data, shown in Table 3-1, give an average annual increase of about 1,994,000 handguns. Over the last decade, then, the *gross* increase in supply has been in the range of 20–25 million handguns. Interestingly, this is about the same as Newton and Zimring's estimate of the *total* number of handguns introduced into the U.S. market from 1899 to 1968. Thus, the number of handguns in the United States appears to have approximately doubled since the Gun Control Act of 1968.

The provisions of the 1968 legislation are discussed more fully in a later chapter. In the main, the Gun Control Act of 1968 was designed to deal with interstate firearms commerce and with firearms importation. Although the actual legislative intent is somewhat unclear (see Cook, 1979b), the implementation of the 1968 legislation in essence amounted to a ban on imports of cheap, low-quality handguns, the so-called Saturday Night Specials. This ban, however, did not extend to the importation of most of the parts from which such handguns are assembled or to the domestic manufacture or assembly of such weapons.

Efforts to evaluate the effects of the 1968 legislation on the total handgun supply are hampered mostly by the lack of adequate time-series supply data (Zimring, 1975), especially with regard to imported weapons, the major focus of the Act. Zimring notes that two Federal agencies now maintain data on handgun imports: the Bureau of the Census and the Bureau of Alcohol, Tobacco, and Firearms (ATF). Since 1969, both agencies have published estimates of handgun imports, and in the five reporting years between 1969 and 1973, the *average* discrepancy between estimates was 162,000 handguns (Zimring, 1975: Table 4). Estimates by the ATF, moreover, are always higher than the Census estimates, and the magnitude of the discrepancy is larger in more recent years. (In 1973, for example, the Census estimates a total of 309,000 imported handguns, whereas the ATF estimate for the same year is 901,000.) One certainly hopes, along with Zimring, that "the two federal agencies in charge of compiling these data might attempt to resolve such a glaring discrepancy" (1975: 168).

Table 3-1 shows "best guesses" for handgun production and importation from 1960 to 1976; the figures differ slightly from those shown earlier in Table 2-1, but not in any major or serious way. Given the wide discrepancies in the data bases, none of the values reported in the table can be taken entirely seriously, but they do adequately indicate the rough magnitudes and give at least some crude index of the effects of the 1968 legislation.

These data sustain several reasonably obvious conclusions. First, it is apparent that the 1968 legislation responded to a genuine problem. Between 1960 and 1968, the annual importation of handguns increased by about 900%— up from 128,000 imported handguns in 1960 to about 1.2 million imports in 1968. To speak of these handguns "flooding the domestic market" is therefore no exaggeration. Second, imports of handguns in the year immediately following the legislation, and in every year since, were drastically lower than the all-time high figure registered for 1968: from a 1968 base figure of 1.3 million, imports of handguns dropped to 354,000 in 1969 and to 254,000 in 1970; they have averaged only about 365,000 per year since 1968, about one-third of the 1968 figure. These data suggest that the Gun Control Act of 1968 did achieve, at least in part, its objective of stemming the flow of "cheap imported handguns" into the domestic market; as Zimring says, the effect on handgun imports was "immediate and substantial" (1975: 169).

There was, however, very little effect on the *total* annual increase in the handgun supply. Much of the losses from the import flow that occurred in 1969 and later have been compensated by increases in domestic handgun production (and assembly). The total of new handguns entering the market in the years 1969–1972 was indeed somewhat lower than the peak 1968 figure, but since 1973 the number of new handguns yearly has averaged approximately 2.2 million, more than 90% of the 1968 value. The overall effect of the 1968 legislation, then, was apparently not so much to reduce the total numbers of handguns available as to cause some substitution of domestic for imported arms. Much of this substitution may well have amounted to cheap handguns assembled by foreign workers from foreign parts being replaced by cheap handguns assembled by American workers from foreign parts (Comptroller General, 1978: 4). Looking at Table 3-1,

TABLE 3-1. Handgun production and imports, 1960–1976 (in thousands)

Handgun	1960	1965	1966	1967	1968	1969	1970	1971	1972	1973	1974	1975	1976
Domestic production	475[a]	666[a]	700[a]	926[a]	1,259[a]	1,367[b]	1,394[b]	1,421[b]	1,667[b]	1,609[b]	1,715[a]	2,024[a]	1,883[a]
Imports	128[a]	347[a]	513[a]	747[a]	1,155[a]	354[c]	254[c]	352[c]	366[c]	605[c]	259[a]	462[a]	270[a]
Total	603	1,013	1,213	1,673	2,414	1,721	1,648	1,773	2,033	2,214	1,974	2,486	2,103

[a] Source: Statistical Abstract of the United States, 1975 (p. 156) and 1977 (p. 175).
[b] Source: Zimring, 1975: Table 5.
[c] Source: Zimring, 1975: Table 4. Numbers in all cases are the numerical average of high (ATF) and low (Census) estimates.

one gets the unmistakable impression that the 1968 legislation was something of a boon to the domestic arms industry, but probably little else. Despite the 1968 legislation, the best available data suggest that handguns are still being added to the U.S. market at the approximate gross rate of 2 to 2.5 million per year. This, of course, is in addition to the annual growth in long gun supply, which has been averaging about 4 million weapons per year.[1]

Where have all these new weapons gone? What are the sources of the increased firearms demand? What do the trends and their sources reveal about the nature of private weaponry in the United States today? These and a range of closely related issues constitute the subject matter of this and the next two chapters.

The recent sharp upturn in weapons manufacturing and importation has occasioned much anxious hand-wringing in pro-gun-control circles. Even the phrases used to refer to the trend are typically alarmist: "the flood of guns," "the domestic arms build-up," "the domestic arms race," and so on. One author (Clotfelter, 1977) speaks of the "almost breathtaking increase in the stock of handguns." The persistent analogy drawn in these sources to the international arms race is presumably intentional: the imagery is often that the American population is arming itself for some sort of impending show-down. Just who the contending parties in this showdown will be is seldom made explicit, such matters being left to the reader's imagination, but the customary insinuation is that the parties in question are socially or ideologically defined: whites are arming themselves for a war against blacks, the "straights" are arming for combat against the counterculturals, or the victims (real or potential) are getting ready to shoot it out with the violent offenders.

The range of speculations implied in these accounts collectively represent what can be called, with due apologies to Hunter S. Thompson, the "fear and loathing" hypothesis—namely, the notion that the recent weapons trend is ultimately rooted in rising fears and anxieties about crime, unrest, rebellion, civil disorders, and the related pathologies of modern, especially urban, life. This hypothesis has been advanced by a number of authors and has been the object of at least some research. The relevant studies are reviewed later, in Chapter 5. In advance, however, we note that the surface plausibility of the hypothesis depends on an extraordinarily uncharitable depiction of the motives and psychology of a very substantial fraction of the American population. Taken to its extreme, the "fear and loathing" hypothesis suggests that tens of millions of Americans have, in the past 10 years, gone out and pur-

---

[1] For a very similar analysis of the 1968 legislation and its effects on firearms supply, see Jerry Landauer, "Gunmaking Booms in the US . . . ," in *The New York Times* 8 June 1971: 49 ff. As a minor historical aside, we note that Landauer's main informant for the article is one G. Gordon Liddy, at the time the Treasury Department's resident in-house firearms expert.

chased a firearm in the anticipation of possibly having to shoot somebody for some reason someday. Uncharitable or not, this may well have been the case, and certainly little purpose is served in prejudging the issue. However, one would normally insist on very powerful evidence before advancing such a condemnatory conclusion, and one would also normally insist that all possible alternative explanations be given their due. In the following chapters, then, we give as much credence as the evidence allows to alternative hypotheses about the weapons trend, just because the "fear and loathing" explanation has such awesome and troubling implications.

HOUSEHOLD INCREASE

Crudely, our focus in the ensuing trend analysis is on the decades of the 1960's and 1970's, the period of most rapid growth in firearms supply. Most of the analysis focuses specifically on the most recent decade, the period between the initial compilation of weapons data by Newton and Zimring (1969) and the present. It is thus worth emphasizing that the size of the American population and, in particular, the number of U.S. households, grew quite substantially during this period, and that raw compilations of production and import data (such as those in Tables 2-1 and 3-1) are typically *not* adjusted to take this increase into account.

The 1968 projections undertaken by Newton and Zimring are based on a total of just over 60 million U.S. households. Partly because of an increase in population size, and partly because of an increase in the rate of household formation, the number of U.S. households at present is just about 75 million. The difference (15 million new households) represents a 25% increase over the 1968 figure. The implication is that the firearm supply must also have increased by some similar proportion in order for the average density of armament among U.S. families to remain constant in this period.[2]

[2] The 25% increase in number of households is, of course, substantially larger than the growth of United States population during the period. For purposes of the present analysis, we are thus assuming that households are the relevant ownership unit for private firearms, not specific individuals. Given that the available survey data on weapons ownership deal almost exclusively with household ownership, we have very little alternative to this assumption.

The disproportionate increase in the number of U.S. households mostly reflects that the baby-boom postwar generations reached the stage of forming households during the period. (The vanguard of the baby boom was the 1947 generation, which turned 25 in 1972.) The baby boom has posed supply problems for virtually every institution it has touched: it was responsible for the very rapid growth in elementary and secondary education in the 1950's and the growth of higher education in the 1960's; it has posed formidable unemployment and underemployment problems, as well as serious housing shortages, in the 1970's; and it is only a matter of time before the baby boom creates a national shortage of burial space. Part (by

As noted above, the number of new weapons that need to be accounted for in a trend analysis lies somewhere between zero and 80 million. For convenience, let us take the midpoint of that range as the correct value, in which case we need to account for about 40 million new weapons. This is rather fewer than the 65 million suggested by the projections from Table 2-1 and the above discussion, but the 65-million figure represents only the *gross* increase in supply. To achieve a measure of the net increase, we have to subtract from the gross figure the number of weapons taken out of use during the period, including the fraction (roughly 10%) that is exported to other countries. Since 80 million is our "best guess" value for the total number of weapons in 1968, and 120 million our best guess for 1978, then the difference, 40 million new weapons, is our best guess as to the total weapons increase.

With these numbers in mind, a simple calculation gives the amount by which the total weapons supply would have to have increased just to keep pace with the increasing number of households. Because the rate of increase in the number of households was about 25% between 1969 and 1978, the initial 1968 supply of weapons (80 million) would also have had to increase by 25%, or by some 20 million weapons. Another way to look at these numbers is that the first 20 million "net" weapons (i.e., those over and beyond the "replacement" weapons) produced or imported between 1969 and 1978 would be absorbed just among new households, assuming, of course, that rates of weapons ownership (and average numbers of weapons owned) would be the same for both new and old households. The conclusion, then, is that perhaps as much as one-half of the trend in weaponry over the past decade is a reflection only of growth in the number of U.S. households. The true growth in supply, net of the replacement proportion and net of that portion

---

our analysis, half) of the recent net upsurge in weapons supply reflects nothing other than the coming of age of these generations—their collective achievement of a stage in the life cycle in which purchasing household weapons would begin to be considered.

For the record, the following tabulation provides data from the *Statistical Abstract* (1977: 42) on the numbers of U.S. households:

Year	Millions of households
1960	52.6
1965	57.3
1970	62.9
1975	71.1
1976	72.9
1977	74.4 (Projected)
1980	78.8 (Projected)

due just to household increase, would therefore amount to about 20 million, rather than 40 million, or 65 million, weapons.

On the other hand, even conservative projections show an increase in weapons supply substantially in excess of the 20 million or so new weapons necessary to supply new families; the total growth has been roughly twice the growth attributable just to household increase. Growth in the number of households to be supplied is thus an important part, but assuredly not the whole, of the weapons trend story.

These corrections in the trend for household growth can, of course, be applied to the type-specific trends as well as to the total (Table 3-2). The numerical values shown in Table 3-2 are taken directly from Table 2-5; the 1968 numbers are as reported by Newton and Zimring (1969), and the "actual present values" are taken from the update of the Newton–Zimring numbers reported by Spiegler and Sweeney (1975). The "predicted present values" are calculated simply by adding 25% in each case to the observed 1968 values; the "excess" values are simply the differences between "predicted" and "actual" present values.

These corrections for household growth leave an excess of 22.5 million new weapons to be accounted for by other factors. This figure reflects the net growth in weapons supply over and above that necessary to keep pace with household growth. It represents a *net* growth of 25% in weapons supply over the 1968 values. As Table 3.2 shows, this 25% net growth has two distinct components: a long gun component, whose growth was proportionally

TABLE 3-2. *The weapons trend by weapons type, discounted for growth in number of U.S. households (in millions of weapons)*

Type	1968 Value[a]	Predicted present value[b]	Actual present value[c]	Excess[d]	Excess as a % of 1968 value[e]
Rifles	35	43.75	50	6.25	18
Shotguns	31	38.75	45	6.25	20
Handguns	24	30.00	40	10.0	42
Total	90	112.5	135	22.5	25

[a] Source: Newton and Zimring, 1969: 6.

[b] The 1968 value + 25%.

[c] Source: Spiegler and Sweeney, 1975: 3.

[d] Difference between "predicted" and "actual" present values.

[e] This column expresses the excess weapons as a percentage of the initial 1968 value, and is thus a measure of net percentage growth in the weapons supply as discounted for the growth in numbers of families.

rather less than the total growth, and a handgun component, whose growth was proportionally sharply higher than the total growth. The excess present handguns amount to 42% of the 1968 value, compared with 18 and 20%, respectively, for the excesses in rifles and shotguns. We may thus agree with many observers that the growth in handgun supply over the last decade has been substantial and quite disproportionate to the total growth in households.

After household growth has been discounted, then, the evidence suggests that a trend analysis needs to account for some 12–13 million excess long guns, and some 10 million excess handguns over the last 10 years.

SPORT AND RECREATION DEMAND

Newton and Zimring, and most other commentators, acknowledge that at least some share of the trend reflects nothing more ominous than an increase in the popularity of sporting and recreational activities requiring firearms. As with the production of guns, for example, the production of clay pigeons approximately doubled during the 1960's; membership in trap and skeet shooting clubs also doubled during the same period (Newton and Zimring, 1969: 20). As these authors also point out, the percentage increase in expenditures for sporting weaponry and ammunition between 1960 and 1966 (72%) was almost exactly the same as the percentage increase in expenditures on fishing equipment and tackle in the same period. Some nontrivial fraction of the domestic arms build-up, in short, apparently reveals more about leisure-time preferences and pursuits than it reveals about the "fear and loathing" of the American population.

In general, the growth of interest in outdoor recreation over the past several years has been rather extraordinary. Some sense of the magnitude of this trend is imparted by Table 3-3, which reports time-series data from the *Statistical Abstract* on various outdoor sporting activities and expenditures from 1960 to 1976. In 1960, as an example, there were about 79 million visits to the National Park system; by 1970, the figure had more than doubled to 172 million visits; and in the six years following, the visitation figure rose to 268 million, about 3.5 times the number of visits registered in 1960. Visits to state parks show an equivalent trend in the period, having approximately doubled between 1960 and 1975. Between 1970 and 1975 alone, annual expenditures on recreation of all forms increased by some 25 *billion* dollars. The annual growth in hunting and fishing licenses issued is much less spectacular but nonetheless substantial: between 1970 and 1975, for example, the number of fishing licenses issued annually increased by about 3.6 million,

TABLE 3-3. *Trends in outdoor recreation*

Trend	1960	1965	1970	1972	1973	1974	1975	1976
Visits to the National Park System ($\times 10^5$)	79.2	121.3	172.0	211.6	215.6	217.4	238.8	267.7
Visits to state parks ($\times 10^6$)	259	391[a]	483	—	—	—	566	—
Total recreation expenditures ($\times \$10^9$)	17.9	25.9	41.0	49.1	55.2	60.8	66.0	—
Fishing licenses sold ($\times 10^6$)	23.3	25.0	31.1	33.0	33.5	34.3	34.7	—
Hunting licenses sold ($\times 10^6$)	18.4	19.4	22.2	22.2	23.3	25.1	25.9	—
Federal duck stamps ($\times 10^6$)	1.6	1.6	2.1	2.4	2.2	2.0	2.2	—
Sport fishermen and hunting ($\times 10^6$)	30.4	32.9	36.3	—	—	—	—	—
Recreational vehicles sold ($\times 10^3$)	62.6[b]	192.8	472.0	747.5	752.5	529.2	552.0	656.3

[a] Data for 1967.
[b] Data for 1961.

Source: *Statistical Abstract of the United States, 1977*: pp. 232, 234, 235, 237, 643.

and the number of hunting licenses, by about 3.7 million.[3] Note, finally, the trends in sales of so-called recreational vehicles—mostly campers and motor homes. Sales of these vehicles peaked just before the Arab oil embargo of 1973 and have been down noticeably ever since. Still, in 1976, approximately 656,000 of these vehicles were sold in the U.S. market, 10 times the number sold in 1961. All available indicators therefore suggest that the decade of the 1970's has witnessed a continuation, and in some cases an unmistakable acceleration, of the growth trends in outdoor recreation activities noted by Newton and Zimring for the decade of the 1960's.

All of the trends shown in Table 3-3 exceed the growth that would be expected just on the basis of population increase, even the relatively modest annual increases in hunting licenses issued. Trends in hunting, net of the general trend in population, are shown in Table 3-4. Note that because hunting licenses are issued to *individuals*, not to families, the appropriate norm in this discussion is the growth in total population, not the growth in total number of households, as in the earlier discussion.

For purposes of this table, we have created a measure of "total hunters" by summing, for each year, the number of hunting licenses issued and the number of Federal duck stamps sold. The total number of hunters, thus defined, increased by 3.8 million between 1970 and 1975, from 24.3 to 28.1 million. The last line of the table expresses these values as a rate per 1000 population; as shown, the number of hunters per 1000 population also increased between 1970 and 1975, from 119 per 1000 in 1970 to 132 per 1000 in 1975.

Table 3-4 permits us to calculate the amount by which the total number of hunters increased beyond that which would be expected on the basis of population growth alone. In 1970, for example, the observed hunter rate was 119 per thousand. Had this rate remained constant, the total number of hunters in 1975 would be $119/1000 \times 213$ million $= 25.4$ million, the predicted number of 1975 hunters. The observed value for 1975, in contrast, is 28.1 million hunters, an excess over the five years of 2.7 million hunters.

[3] Newton and Zimring (1969: Table 4-4) also report trend data on hunting licenses issued; their values are rather lower than the values shown in our Table 3-3. For example, their 1965 value is 14.3 million licenses, versus our 1965 value of 19.4 million—a discrepancy of some 5 million hunters. Independent evidence suggests that our numbers are the more accurate. In the same year (1965), Gallup asked a national sample, "Do you [or your spouse] go hunting?" Roughly 36% of the sample responded yes. Assuming one hunter per household and about 60 million households, this finding therefore gives 0.36×60 million $= 21.6$ million hunters in 1965. Newton and Zimring conclude from their data that "the number of licensed hunters . . . has remained relatively stable since 1958" (1969: 20). This has *not* been true in the years since 1968, however; the data in Table 3-3 show an average annual increase in licensed hunters for the period 1970–1975 of just under 1 million new hunters per year. The recent hunting trends are discussed in detail in the text.

TABLE 3-4. *Trends in number of hunters, 1960–1975*[a]

Trend	1960	1970	1975
Number of hunting licenses (in millions)	18.4	22.2	25.9
Number of duck stamps (in millions)	1.6	2.1	2.2
Total hunters (in millions)	20.0	24.3	28.1
Total population (in millions)	180	204	213
Hunters/1000 population	111	119	132

[a] Hunting data are the same as in Table 3-3, above.
Source: *Statistical Abstract of the United States,* 1977: Tables 10 and 389.

This value suggests that the number of new hunters (hunters in excess of the number predicted from population growth alone) has averaged about 540,000 per year. In other words, even discounting population growth, some half-million additional individuals per year have taken up hunting. For the whole decade of 1969 through 1978, then, approximately 5.4 million excess hunters have been added (540,000 each year over a total of 10 years). If we assume that each of these new hunters outfits himself or herself with one and only one long gun, these figures indicate that about 5.4 million of the total net growth of 12.5 million excess long guns, or about 43%, can be attributed just to the increase in hunters over the decade, leaving about 7 million new long guns to be explained by other factors.

These projections, moreover, are doubtlessly conservative for a number of reasons. First, the measure of total hunters is in truth a measure of total *legal* hunters (i.e., a measure of hunting licenses and duck stamps issued). The number of people who hunt without a license and the trend in the number are obviously unknown, but it is at least possible that the growth in unlicensed hunting has exceeded the growth in licensed hunting, and if so, the share of the total trend attributable to increased hunting would be even higher than the 42% figure calculated above.

Second, our projection of 5.4 million new long guns due to new hunters is based on the assumption that each hunter is equipped with one and only one long gun. Since each hunter must have *at least* one gun, this too is obviously a conservative estimate; at least some hunters will outfit themselves with two or more guns.[4] The most recent evidence on numbers of weapons owned (the 1978 DMI survey mentioned in Chapter 2) suggests that the average number owned by households owning at least one weapon is somewhat more than three weapons (precisely, 3.17). Among families who own

[4] We are, for present purposes, simply ignoring the (presumably small) numbers who hunt with weapons other than firearms, for example, bows and arrows.

weapons *and* hunt, the average may be higher.[5] If new hunters armed themselves at the average rate for all families owning at least one weapon, then the increase in demand for guns due to new hunters between 1969 and 1978 would be roughly 16.2 million weapons. This would amount to *all* of the net growth in long guns (12.5 million) and some 40–50% of the net growth in handguns (10 million) as well. Indeed, if the total excess firearms are in fact 22.5 million weapons (as calculated in Table 3-2), and each new hunter armed himself or herself at the average rate of three weapons, the growth in demand due just to these new hunters would amount to about 72% of the net growth in supply of weapons of all types.

The idea that each new hunter would arm up with more than one gun is by no means inconceivable. A rifle is an appropriate hunting weapon for some game (squirrels and deer, for example, are usually hunted with rifles), but shotguns are necessary for other game (for example, all bird hunting is done with shotguns, and fast-moving small game, such as rabbits, are also usually hunted with shotguns). A hunter wishing to shoot, say, squirrels and game birds would therefore require at least one rifle and at least one shotgun. As the kinds of game to be hunted increase, the amount of necessary weaponry also increases. A deer rifle, for example, is virtually useless for hunting squirrels; a small-caliber rifle that would be used to hunt squirrels, likewise, would be largely useless in hunting deer. In the same vein, larger shotguns (12-gauge or 16-gauge) are necessary for game-bird hunting, whereas smaller shotguns (20-gauge or .410-gauge) are more appropriate for game such as rabbit. A hunter who chose, for example, to hunt deer, squirrel, rabbit, and pheasant (four of the more commonly hunted animals) would find it convenient to own four different guns. The idea that each new hunter would arm up with at least one rifle and one shotgun is therefore not implausible, in which case the demand for new long guns posed by new hunters works out to about 10.8 million, 86% of the 12.5 million excess in long guns.

Also, although handguns are not often used to hunt game, they sometimes are. Even if they are seldom used by hunters to take game, they are nonetheless often carried by hunters and other outdoors sports people along with long guns, typically for use against the snakes that one sometimes encounters when traipsing through the woods. In some respects, a quality sidearm is part of the standard regalia for the *de rigueur* sportsman and thus falls in the same class of objects as a good hunting knife, a hunting jacket, an ammuni-

---

[5] We say, "may be higher" because it is not possible to confirm that numbers of weapons owned by hunting families are in fact greater than the numbers owned by nonhunting families. The DMI data would be useful in addressing this (and many other) issues but, so far, the National Rifle Association has refused to release the data for secondary analysis. Several other surveys contain both a gun ownership question and a hunting question, but none of them asks specifically about the number of weapons possessed.

tion belt, and the related accouterments that no serious huntsman would be without. Thus, the idea that new hunters also account for at least some share of the increase in handgun demand is also not inconceivable.[6]

[6] In the pro-control literature, one often hears it said that there is "no legitimate sporting use" for handguns, with the possible exception of plinking and target shooting. In fact, even a very cursory examination of the gun-sport magazines (for example, *Guns and Ammo, Gun World, Field and Stream,* or any of perhaps 25 others) will confirm that handguns are used for all kinds of sporting and recreational purposes. In the survey conducted by Decision-Making Information, Inc., handgun owners were asked why they owned a handgun. Although self-defense was the most common answer, given by 40%, approximately 9% mentioned hunting as the most important reason; another 17% mentioned target shooting; 14% mentioned gun collection; and 6% said they "just like to have one." The total number of sport or recreational responses (hunting, target shooting, and collecting) therefore approximately equals the number of self-defense responses. In other words, the number of handguns possessed primarily for "legitimate" sporting purposes probably rivals the number owned for "illegitimate" self-defensive purposes.

Virtually *every* issue of *every* gun-sport magazine will contain one or more reviews of various sporting handguns. Most of them also run occasional pieces on so-called trail guns, which are the small, readily concealable handguns that one would typically never associate with legitimate sporting uses. One of these discussions ("Pack a Trail Gun," by Claud Hamilton in the December 1979 issue of *Gun World*) enumerates the reasons why an outdoors person might want to carry such a weapon: for example, "encounters with dangerous wild creatures" (specifically snakes, angry wolverines, rabid foxes, and so on); "your ability to signal for help" in the case of a serious accident; "also, if you would ever be plunged suddenly into a survival situation without transport or food, a handgun can put food in the pot when it is desperately needed." Similar themes can be found in any of a very large number of articles on trail guns that are run, month in and month out, in all the major gun magazines. Anyone who takes the time to read these magazines will quickly agree with our conclusion, that sporting and recreational uses would definitely account for at least some share of the handgun trend.

Some of the most enthusiastically reviewed trail guns are the very small, relatively cheap, short-barreled, readily concealable, small-caliber, foreign-made handguns that are, in some circles, treated as virtually synonymous with "crime gun" or Saturday Night Special. Hamilton's (1979) article on trail guns is especially informative on this matter. In general, he notes, "a trail gun ought to be the lightest in weight, smallest in size, and, if possible, made of stainless steel." He adds, "the first choice of many would be the light frame .22 long rifle pistol or revolver. . . ." "An alternative," he suggests, ". . . is pocket pistols as trail guns. These mostly European-manufactured pistols are usually encountered in .32 or .38 ACP caliber. I have to admit that when it comes to small size and compactness they beat out even the little .22s." Hamilton continues, "these are invariably pistols of the finest craftsmanship and beautifully made. These little pistols are at best short-range point-and-shoot affairs not intended for work beyond about seven yards." Concerning the little .22 handguns, Hamilton notes that they "have a lot going for them. Most of the decent ones are accurate and can be fine small game getters." Our purpose here, of course, is not to dwell on the wonders of little pistols, but merely to point out that the oft-encountered assertion that these kinds of handguns have "no legitimate sporting or recreational purpose" is very insistently contradicted by the testimony of people who use exactly these kinds of guns for sport and recreation all the time.

On the same theme, it can be noted that hunting with handguns, although perhaps not commonplace, nonetheless does occur, perhaps at a growing rate. Most states at least allow hunting with handguns, and some of them have recently set aside special seasons specifically

The preceding depicts hunting mainly as a leisure or recreational activity, but not all hunting is appropriately characterized in this fashion. For some people, hunting is an activity that generates "income in kind," or, in other words, is an activity undertaken to augment the family's protein supply. There is, in fact, some evidence to suggest that "meat hunters" (people who hunt primarily for the food) are the *modal type* (Kellert, 1978).[7] In Kellert's study, conducted for the U.S. Fish and Wildlife Service, meat hunters represented approximately 44% of all the people in the sample who had hunted in the previous five years. "Sports hunters" were the second largest category, representing 39% of the total; these people hunt primarily because it gets them out of doors and affords them an opportunity to display their marksmanship and outdoors prowess. Finally, there are what Kellert calls the "nature hunters," representing 17%, who hunt primarily for inner-directed, virtually mystical, reasons. As one of them, quoted by Kellert, expresses it, "It's death that makes the spark of life glow most brightly, measure for measure." These findings suggest that perhaps no more than about half of all hunting is appropriately characterized as recreational. The remainder apparently has more utilitarian motivations.

In this vein, it should also be pointed out that, although it is possible to spend very large sums of money on high-quality hunting weapons, perfectly serviceable weaponry can be purchased for very modest amounts. Current winter catalogs for both Sears and Penney, for example, list several models of rifles and shotguns that retail for less than $100; both also show a single-shot .22 caliber rifle (of the sort that might be used, for instance, to hunt squirrels) that retails for less than $35. Ammunition is also relatively inexpensive; a box of .22 caliber "longs," useful for small game, retails for less than $5. Hunting licenses rarely cost more than $10. If one did not care about being a truly stylish hunter and went about it as cheaply as possible, it appears that one could start from scratch and purchase an entire season of, say, squirrel hunting—weapon, ammunition, and license—for less than $50. This is substantially less, for example, than what the average skier would expect to spend in one weekend on the slopes, much less than what a serious flyfisher would expect to pay for a decent graphite rod, very much less than the price of a snowmobile, and so on. If one were interested in being outdoors

---

for this purpose (just as many states have special bow-hunting seasons). The reason for hunting with a handgun would presumably be much the same as for hunting with a bow, namely, that it increases the sport of the hunt and allows one to demonstrate a higher degree of prowess with the weapon. It can also be mentioned that there is now a rather wide assortment of handguns manufactured and marketed specifically for hunting purposes, e.g., single-shot pistols in large calibers and with long barrels, all of which would be essentially useless for self-defense.

[7] We have been unable to procur a copy of the Kellert report; the following discussion is based on a summary of the report published by *Sports Illustrated* magazine, 2 January 1979.

and actually doing something once there, hunting seems to be potentially one of the cheaper ways to do it.[8]

The relatively small sums of money necessary to take up hunting and the evidence from Kellert that much of it is undertaken mainly to procure food suggest that at least part of the recent increase in hunting, and the corresponding increase in demand for weaponry, may be attributable to many of the same factors that have recently sparked interest in vegetable gardens and wood stoves, namely, the decay of the domestic economic situation. Growing vegetables, heating with wood, and hunting for meat are all "labor-intensive" activities, requiring relatively modest initial capital outlays, whose results make at least some difference in a family's overall financial circumstances in troubled economic times. All three activities also have direct "use value"; that is, they are intrinsically enjoyable leisure-time pursuits, whether or not they bring other benefits. It is thus possible that some (possibly a large) share of the domestic arms build-up is only a utilitarian response to a decaying domestic economy.

Hunting is the most common, but by no means the only sporting activity requiring firearms; others include target shooting, gun collecting, and skeet and trap shooting. The trend data on hunting are at best thin, but published trend data on other sporting uses of firearms are practically nonexistent, except for the few fragments compiled by Newton and Zimring (1969). Thus, any effort to discount the overall weapons trend for sporting uses of firearms other than hunting is a very inferential and perilous activity. However, there is at least enough information to piece together a rough guess about the approximate magnitudes.

In this case, the relevant information is taken from the 1978 survey conducted by Decision-Making Information, Inc. (DMI). One of the items in the survey, asked of gun owners only, read as follows: "I have a list of reasons why people own guns. Please listen while I read it and then tell me the most important reason *you* have a gun." Fifty-four percent of the gun owners who answered the question gave hunting as the most important reason; 10% said target shooting, 7% indicated gun collecting, and the rest answered with a variety of other nonsporting (mostly self-defense) reasons. The total sporting responses other than hunting therefore constituted 17%, which is just about one-third of the proportion who mentioned hunting specifically. From these data it can be inferred that the total number of people engaged in shooting

---

[8] Along these same lines, Bruce-Biggs (1976: 38) has pointed out that the price of firearms has dropped considerably, relative to average incomes, over the 20th century. The standard of comparison in this case is the classic Winchester 94 deer rifle, which has been in continuous production (in approximately the same form) since 1894. In 1900, the price of the Winchester 94 was 2.5 times the average worker's weekly take-home pay; in 1960, 91% of the average weekly pay; and in 1970, only 75% of the average weekly pay.

sports other than hunting is about one-third of the total number of hunters. If, in turn, our guess in Table 3-4 about the total number of hunters is correct (28.1 million in 1975), there would have been about 9.4 million additional firearms sportspeople (collectors included) in the same year.

Again, we can use these numbers to project an "excess" of sports shooters and collectors. In order to make such a projection, we assume that the disproportionate rate of increase (beyond that of population growth) observed for hunting was matched by an exactly equivalent net rate of increase in other gun sports. If this were the case and all the other necessary assumptions were also met, then we would guess that in 1970 there were 8.1 million nonhunting sports shooters or collectors (one-third of the 24.3 million hunters estimated for the same year). This amounts to about 39.7 per 1,000 population in 1970. At the same rate, the predicted number of sports shooters and collectors in 1975 would have been about 8.5 million (39.7/1000 × 213 million population), whereas the direct calculation of this number showed about 9.4 million (one-third the observed number of 1975 hunters). These calculations—although admittedly very conjectural—therefore suggest an excess of some 900,000 sports shooters over 5 years, or an excess of some 1.8 million over the whole 10-year period from 1969 to 1978. Again, assuming one and only one gun per each of these excess sports shooters or collectors, the net growth in this category would account for approximately 8% of the total net increase in weapons supply of all sorts (1.8 million divided by the total net excess of 22.5 million = 8%).

Although it can be assumed that most (but not all) of the new hunting demand would be concentrated in the long gun category, the same cannot be assumed about the new demand for weaponry for gun sports other than hunting. The DMI data discussed above are presented in two parts, one part showing the responses for all gun owners (which was noted above), and a second part showing responses for handgun owners only (as discussed in footnote 6). The proportion of handgun owners mentioning target shooting as the primary reason for ownership was 17%, close to twice the 10% figure registered for all gun owners irrespective of type. Likewise, the proportion mentioning gun collection among handgun owners was 14%, or twice the 7% figure registered for all gun owners. From this information, it can be safely inferred that some substantial share of the new gun demand posed by new nonhunting sportspeople would definitely be a handgun demand. In other words, some share of the excess handguns as reported in Table 3-2 has been absorbed by net growth in the nonhunting gun sports.

Consider, for example, the matter of handgun collections. Collecting handguns is evidently a popular activity. According to the DMI survey, 23% of the nation's families possess a handgun, and of these families, 14% mention collecting as the primary reason. Thus, some 3.2% of the nation's families

$(0.23 \times 0.14 = 0.032)$ would qualify as handgun collectors by these admittedly approximate standards. With a base of 75 million families, this figure gives 2.4 million handgun collectors as of 1978. For obvious reasons, the typical handgun collector would tend to own and acquire handguns at somewhat more than the average rate. If each of the 1978 handgun collectors added just two handguns to their collection in the previous 10 years, collecting alone would account for nearly one-half of the excess handgun supply projected in Table 3.2. Also, as noted above, target shooting is given as a reason for owning a handgun somewhat more commonly than mentioned as a reason for owning a long gun, so at least some of the growth in target shooting, as well as collecting, would also result in an increase in the handgun demand. The essential point here is that any new demand for weapons posed by increases in sporting or recreational uses of firearms would not necessarily be restricted to a demand for long guns; part of this new demand would be for handguns as well.

It might, of course, be objected that the typical short-barreled, small-caliber, cheaply made Saturday Night Special is not an appropriate weapon for either collecting or target shooting, and it is also not the kind of sidearm that hunters would usually be interested in carrying (but see footnote 6). As far as we know, however, nobody has ever studied the kinds of handguns that handgun collectors collect, and so the assumption that they do not collect Saturday Night Specials is gratuitous. These days, people collect empty beer cans, old comic books, Beatles memorabilia, and thousands upon thousands of other commodities of dubious cultural value, and, this being the case, it is perfectly reasonable that many people might collect Saturday Night Specials as well. A more serious problem is that nobody knows for certain (or even to a first approximation) just how many Saturday Night Specials are represented by the figures in Table 3-2. There is, first of all, no agreed-upon definition of just what a Saturday Night Special is (e.g., Cook, 1979a), and even if there were, the available supply data are not sufficiently detailed in terms of such characteristics as cost, caliber, quality of construction, and barrel length to estimate the proportion of new handguns that are indeed SNSs. We can thus agree that sport and recreation uses probably contribute relatively little to the demand for SNSs, but we cannot say just how many handguns fall into this category.

All the preceding projections are, of course, distressingly speculative, but the hard evidence needed to make them something other than speculative simply does not exist. It is therefore impossible to state precisely just how many of the net excess guns should be attributed to sport and recreational demand. Our projections suggest a total of about 7.2 million new shooters over the decade (hunters and nonhunters combined). If these new shooters all acquired weapons at the average rate shown in the DMI survey (3.17

guns each), then the total demand growth is for 22.8 million weapons, or for 100% of the net growth that remains after household increase, replacement stock, and exportation have been taken into account. At the outer bound of possibility, the suggestion is that household increase and disproportionate growth of interest in the shooting sports account for *all* of the net remaining weapons trend, in handguns and long guns alike. If, alternatively, all these new shooters armed up at the average rate of 2 guns each, the total ensuing demand would be for about 15 million weapons—or all of the remaining excess long guns and about a third to half of the remaining excess handguns. Therefore, when the demand increase due to sport and recreational growth is factored out, there remain no more than a few million long guns and probably not more than about 5–8 million handguns to be ascribed to other uses.

SUMMARY

Between 1969 and 1978, roughly 65 million new firearms were either manufactured domestically or imported into the United States. Some (about one-tenth) of the domestic production was exported to other countries, and some of the remaining increase in supply must be seen simply as a supply of replacements for weapons taken out of use permanently (through confiscation, obsolescence, or decay) over the decade. These factors apparently leave an initial gross increase in firearms supply amounting to about 40 million guns.

Over the same decade, the number of U.S. households increased by about 25%. In order to maintain a constant average density of weapons ownership across households, the 1968 supply (of 80 million guns) would also have had to increase by 25%, or by 20 million guns, about half of the remaining excess.

Over the same decade, the *proportion* of U.S. citizens using firearms for hunting and other sporting purposes also increased, and various pieces of evidence and some (plausible, although typically untested) assumptions suggest that the consequent growth in sporting demand for weapons amounted to essentially all the remaining net growth in shoulder weapons and a third to half of the remaining net growth in handguns.

Explaining the remaining excess weapons is the topic of the following two chapters.

FOUR

RECENT TRENDS IN WEAPONS OWNERSHIP:
II. The Police Demand for Armament

The production and import data that we have taken as the measure of trends in supply exclude military weapons but they do *not* exclude weapons manufactured for, shipped to, or purchased by Federal, state, local, and private police. This chapter therefore considers the question: What share of the remaining "excess" weapons has been absorbed by enhanced armament demands among the police?

A caveat is again in order. There is, on the whole, relatively little distinction between the police arms market and the more general private firearms market. Many policemen purchase their official arms as private citizens, not as police officers; even of the 50 largest police departments, more than 20% do not supply a regulation-issue sidearm for their officers. Thus, much of the police demand for small arms is contained within the more general private demand that has been considered in the previous two chapters. Specifically, police armament is reflected in the existing supply-side data and would also show up in the demand-side (that is, survey) data as well.

The possibility that police demand accounts for a nontrivial fraction of the total increase in demand has not been seriously considered by anyone. There is very little reliable information on police arsenal or armament policies and virtually no hard information on any recent policy trends. Our effort to discount from the total increase in demand the portion attributable to enhanced demand among the police is therefore even more speculative than the discounts undertaken in the previous chapter. Still, there is more than ample evidence that police demand for weaponry has increased quite substantially and represents a sizable fraction of the total growth in demand.

Increased demand for police weapons necessarily arises from two sources: first, from increases in the total numbers of armed police officers, and second, from increases in the average numbers of weapons with which officers are armed. The first source can be called the "personnel" trend, and the second

65

the "armaments policy" trend. Neither of them can be estimated in any precise quantitative way, but fragmentary data strongly suggest that both trends have been upward over the past 10 years.

THE PERSONNEL TREND

Table 4-1 shows indicators from various governmental sources on the personnel trend among U.S. public police during the 1970's. These data confirm that public police expenditures and employment have increased dramatically in the last decade. (There has been a parallel and possibly even sharper increase in the number of private police as well, which would also enhance the growth of legitimate weapons demand. The growth of private police, however, is not considered in this chapter. See Kakalik and Wildhorn, 1971, and the National Advisory Committee on Criminal Justice Standards and Goals, 1976, for exhaustive studies of U.S. private security forces.) Between 1970 and 1975, for example, total expenditures on criminal justice at all governmental levels *doubled*. During the same period, gross total employment in criminal justice increased from 852,000 to 1,129,000, roughly a 33% increase. Figures for total *police* employment show similar trends: between 1970 and 1975, the total number of police (at all levels) increased from 548,000 to 670,000—a 22% increase—and the same pattern emerges from all other indicators.

Unfortunately, although all trend series show the same general pattern, none of them gives a precise numerical estimate of the trend over the last decade in the total number of armed public servants of all sorts at all levels. Total police employment would obviously include some fraction of unarmed personnel (clerks, custodial, EDP staff, for example); likewise, some fraction of armed public servants would not be in police employment (e.g., prison guards, and Treasury agents). A further complication arises from the often wide discrepancies among the various trend indicators. For example, item 3 of Table 4-1 shows 508,000 and 599,000 state and local police employees in 1970 and 1975, respectively. Item 4 gives figures of 450,000 and 556,000, respectively, a discrepancy amounting to about 40–50 thousand police. In the same vein, the 1977 *Uniform Crime Report* estimate of sworn full-time police officers is 437,000, whereas a secondary analysis of the machine-readable data of the Law Enforcement Assistance Administration (LEAA) gives 551,000, a discrepancy of about 110,000 police. It would thus appear, remarkably, that the actual number of American police is itself known only to within about 50,000 officers.

In the face of these uncertainties, what estimates can be made of the total police personnel trend in the decade? We begin with some findings

TABLE 4-1. *Indicators of the "personnel trend" among U.S. public police*

Indicator	1965	1970	1972	1973	1974	1975	1976	1977
1. Total expenditures on criminal justice, all government levels (in billions of $)[a]	4.57	8.57	11.72	13.05	14.95	17.25		
2. Gross employment in criminal justice (in 1000's)[a]								
Federal		61				98		
State		175				274		
Local		617				757		
Total		852				1129		
3. Police employment only (in 1000's)[a]								
Federal		40				70		
State		57				100		
Local		451				499		
Total		548				670		
4. State and local police and corrections employment (in 1000's)[b]								
Police	349	450	486	511	539	556		
Corrections	111	142	178	187	203	214		
Total	460	592	664	698	742	770		
5. Full-time law enforcement officers (in 1000's)[c]						411	418	437

[a] Source: *Statistical Abstract of the United States,* 1977: Table 297.

[b] Source: *Ibid.,* Table 299.

[c] Source: *Uniform Crime Reports,* 1975 (p. 221), 1976 (p. 223), and 1977 (p. 222).

from a recent survey of police departments, known as the "Police Equipment Survey of 1972" (PES72). The survey is based on a known 1972 universe of 12,836 state and local departments. The sample design was stratified by LEAA region and by departmental size, and it generated a total N of 528 departments. Of this total, 444 departments returned the questionnaire, a respectable response rate of 84%.

Part of PES72 deals with "Handguns and Handgun Ammunition" (Bergman, Bunten, and Klaus, 1977). The survey contained several questions on handgun use among police officers, and these questions were used to estimate the number of "officers carrying . . . handguns in U.S. police departments on duty" in 1972 (1977: Table 1-3). The estimate, weighted to remove sampling disproportionalities, is 484,752, or, let us say, 485,000 handgun-armed state and local policemen.

As it happens, this estimate is within a thousand of the total state and local police employment data reported in item 4 of Table 4-1 for the same year. This correspondence suggests that we may take the trend data from item 4 as a close approximation to the actual increase in numbers of armed on-duty police officers over the decade. Thus, in 1970, our guess is that there were 450,000 armed, on-duty state and local police; in 1975, the corresponding guess is 556,000—an increase of 106,000 over 5 years and a projected increase of 212,000 over the decade. To estimate the total increase in armed public servants *at all levels,* we have only to add (1) increases among *Federal* police, and (2) increases for all categories of armed public servants *other than* armed on-duty police officers.

Item 2 of Table 4-1 shows total criminal justice employment at state and local levels to have been 1,031,000 in 1975; our guess is that this includes 556,000 armed police. At state and local levels, then, the proportion of armed officers to total criminal justice employment is about 0.54. If the same proportion holds at the Federal level, then there would have been about 53,000 armed Federal police in 1975 (54% of 98,000 Federal criminal justice employees) and about 33,000 in 1970, an increase of about 20,000 over 5 years, or about 40,000 over 10 years. Adding these estimates to the previous total gives an overall growth of some 252,000 police over the decade.

The proportion of corrections personnel (other than police) who are armed while on duty appears to be unknown. If the proportion is on the order of 10%, then state and local corrections personnel alone would add approximately 20,000 to the above totals, and there would also be some increase in the corresponding Federal category as well. These considerations therefore suggest, as a conservative estimate, a total increase between 1969 and 1978 of about 250,000 men—a quarter-million new police in the last decade.

Projecting the demand for new weaponry that this personnel trend poses requires only that we know the average rate at which new policemen are armed. However, there is very little evidence on this topic. The following account is pieced together primarily from three sources: (1) the PES72 survey, (2) a somewhat similar 1977 mailback survey of the 50 largest departments done by the Police Foundation (Heaphy, 1978), and (3) a review of articles, notes, and advertisements in roughly the last five years of *The Police Chief* (the official publication of the International Association of Chiefs of Police).

The standard service sidearm of American police is the .38 caliber revolver with a 4-inch barrel—the famous "Police Special." In PES72, about 80% of all officers were armed with .38 Special handguns. The second most popular service sidearm is the .357 Magnum revolver, carried by 17%, and only small fractions of officers were found to carry other weapons. As a "first cut" through the probable armament of 250,000 new police, then, we assume at least one service sidearm each.

The 1977 Police Foundation survey shows similar results. Again, the .38 caliber revolver is by far the most commonly prescribed on-duty weapon, used in 44 of the 50 largest departments. However, 14 of the 50 list some other handgun as well, either as the required sidearm or as an acceptable alternative. Also of interest, 11 of these 50 departments require officers to supply their own sidearms; among the smaller departments, one assumes that this proportion would be even higher.

Many officers, of course, carry additional weapons while on duty as "an added safety factor" (Eastman, 1969: 285). These weapons often consist of concealed handguns, carried to provide back-up firepower if the officer is disarmed of his service revolver or if it fails to operate for any reason. Unfortunately, there is no reliable information on the proportion who routinely carry back-up handguns, but some fragmentary evidence suggests that the proportion may be very high:

1. Both concealable handguns and the leather with which to carry them are featured prominently in the armaments advertisements of *The Police Chief.* The October 1977 "equipment issue" has four advertisements for leg holsters and one for a leather police boot with a built-in holster, all designed and marketed explicitly for concealment of back-up handguns.

2. There is much evident concern among arms manufacturers to design, build, and market the "ideal" concealable police handgun. One article in *The Police Chief,* entitled "Design Evolution of the Detonics .45 ACP," discusses Detonics' "quest for the so-called ideal police handgun" (Marlow, 1977: 30). Such a gun would be small enough to be concealed, yet have adequate "stopping power" and "intimidation value" (two of the manufacturers' favorite euphemisms). Photographs show that Detonics' .45 ACP pistol is no larger than a man's hand, yet offers "the brute force of a .45 automatic in a handgun the size of a snub-nosed .38 revolver" (Marlow, 1977: 32). One assumes that arms manufacturers try to develop these concealable police weapons because a sizable market for them exists.

3. Several articles in *The Police Chief* and other police publications over the past 5 years have discussed the problem of murdered police officers. In 10–15% of these cases, officers are slain with their own service sidearms, and carrying a back-up weapon is one useful hedge against this possibility. Indeed, at least one article on "Gun Retention" (O'Neill, 1979: 22), published in the *FBI Law Enforcement Bulletin,* recommends carrying back-up weapons as good police practice: "An auxiliary weapon, concealed and readily accessible, should be carried in the event the primary weapon is compromised."

The understandable desire of police to be prepared for all eventualities would therefore suggest that carrying a concealed back-up weapon would at least be strongly considered by most or all officers.

4. Many U.S. police are required by departmental policies to be armed at all times, even when off duty. In the 1977 Police Foundation survey, 24 of the 50 departments affirmed that "department policy *requires* officers to be armed off duty" (Heaphy, 1978), and all but three of the remaining departments said that this was "optional." PES72 also contained an item on off-duty handgun use; 78% of the responding departments provided data on the calibers of their officers' off-duty weapons (Bergman, Bunten, and Klaus, 1977: 19). The standard service revolver, because of its bulk and barrel length, is not well-suited for concealed off-duty use; thus the proportion of police who own and carry a second, concealable, back-up handgun must be very large indeed.

We therefore conclude, as a not unreasonable guess, that the standard in-service personal armament of U.S. police consists of at least two handguns— one a service sidearm, and the second a smaller weapon carried concealed (or at least kept in readiness for off-duty use). Actual police armament, however, must average even more than two handguns per officer. Owing to the nature of police work, it is reasonable to assume that departments or officers themselves maintain some reserve supply of handguns, such that replacements are always at hand. Informal queries of a few departments in Massachusetts confirms that this is the case. Police handguns presumably wear out much more quickly than handguns owned by private citizens. For obvious reasons, one may also assume that even modest deteriorations in the condition of police weapons would cause them to be taken out of use. Also, police sidearms are carried daily and are thus subject to normal wear and tear far beyond that of the more typical private citizen's handgun, which presumably spends much of its lifetime in storage.

PES72 contains some information on the issue of gun deterioration. A late, open-ended item asked about handgun problems encountered by police departments. About half the departments (45%) responded, and among them, problems with the revolver mechanism and cylinder were by far the most frequently mentioned. Examples include "cylinder had excess play," "weapon bought new and used approximately three months," and "after carrying this gun in a holster for several years, the rotating mechanism wears so much that the bullets do not line up with the barrel, causing a spray of lead to fly out of the side of the chamber" (Bergman, Bunten, and Klaus, 1977: 23). Problems with "hammer/firing pin," "misfires," "trigger," and "age, wear and tear" were also commonly mentioned. The impression one gains from these materials is that police handguns wear out rather quickly even if they are not often fired; the precision mechanisms and alignments apparently wear and foul just because of the normal jostling they receive when carried in the holster. Indeed, judging from the above comments, the lifetime of the average police handgun might well fall somewhere between several months and several years (in contrast to the 30- and 50-year half-lives assumed for privately owned weapons in Chapter 2).

Three apparently quite plausible assumptions—(1) that police strongly prefer *not* to be without a service handgun for any reason, (2) that police handguns deteriorate at a relatively rapid rate, and (3) that even minor "bugs" in the condition of a service handgun would cause it to be decommissioned—therefore suggest that most or all in service police handguns are backed up with spares. If we assume that each personal police handgun is backed up with one replacement weapon, and that every policeman carries or possesses two handguns for which replacements might be needed, then each officer would account, on the average, for a total of four handguns. The quarter-million new police projected above for the decade would, under these assumptions, represent a demand for about one million new handguns.

It is possible that this estimate of four handguns per officer is too high. Our guess that every officer carries or possesses at least two handguns is itself a liberal inference from the evidence, and our guess about arsenal back-ups is entirely a speculation. On the other hand, this estimate may also be much too low. For example, it appears that at least 75% (and conceivably much more than 75%) of all U.S. police are required to be armed at all times, both on-duty and off; some additional officers presumably choose to be armed at all times even if not required. One therefore readily imagines that many officers own large numbers of handguns, each well suited for some particular on-duty or off-duty use. In some respects, the need to be armed is a wardrobe problem that can be solved by owning a variety of weapons. Because more than 20% of the 50 largest departments require officers to supply their own sidearms, it is also evident that many policemen are plugged into the private handgun market. Further, the police are presumably quite knowledgeable about and expert in the use of sidearms, and the police magazines literally swarm with advertisements for the newest developments in handguns. The idea that many policemen would own large numbers of handguns for official or semi-official use is therefore not at all implausible, and this gives some indirect reason for confidence that the four-per-officer average is probably not far off the mark.

A quarter-million new police would cause some corresponding increase in the demand for police *long guns* as well. Less is known about police shoulder weapons than about police handguns. However, most police cruisers are outfitted with at least one shoulder weapon, and many are outfitted with very many more than one. The "Command Car" for Quincy, Illinois (a small city in central Illinois, 1970 population of about 45,000), for example, is outfitted with two "riot-grade shotguns" and a high-powered "anti-sniper rifle" with scope, plus several hundred rounds of ammunition for each weapon, and, of course, the officers' personal handguns (Cramer and Scott, 1978: 69). Long gun armaments in Philadelphia's "Stakeout Cars" are even more substantial: according to one source, these Philadelphia police cars each carry two M-70 Winchester .30/06 rifles with scopes and 200 rounds of ammunition, two M-12 Winchester 12-gauge police shotguns with 100 rounds of 00 buck-shot ammunition, one .45-caliber Thompson submachine gun with 500 rounds of ammunition, and one .30-caliber M-1 assault carbine with 200 rounds of ammunition (Pinto, 1971: 74). Moreover, *The Police Chief* bristles with rifle and shotgun advertisements, and training in shoulder weapons is routinely included in virtually all police firearms training courses. It is therefore obvious that a quarter-million new police would also account for at least some of the growth in shoulder weapons.

The discussion to this point has dealt just with conventional police weapons, most of them the same weapons that ordinary citizens might purchase. Police are also armed, however, with a variety of more exotic weapons for which little or no private demand exists, e.g., automatic weapons (such as the Thompson submachine guns mentioned above), devices for delivering tear gas canisters, tranquilizer guns, and an assortment of chemical weapons (tear gas, Mace, and so on). It is not clear (and apparently cannot be determined) whether the production and import figures include these armaments. There are, however, at least two reasons to assume that they might. First, many exotic weapons (especially the tear gas and tranquilizer dart guns) are very similar to conventional guns in design, manufacture, and general outward appearance. Second, they are manufactured by the same firms that manufacture conventional police weapons. It is therefore at least possible that the supply figures include some fraction of exotic weaponry, the demand for which is almost exclusively concentrated among the police.

THE ARMAMENTS POLICY TREND

New police represent only the first of two potentially large sources of increase in armaments demand; the second would be an increase over the decade in the average rate at which all police (new or old) are armed. In other words, the growth in demand may also be due to recent changes in standard police armament practices and policies.

Police armament practices have been the object of much outcry and some speculation but surprisingly little research. There is, however, some reason to suppose that demand increases resulting from changes in police weapons policies are probably at least as great as, and conceivably much greater than, the increase resulting from the personnel trend.

The general context for the ensuing discussion is well known and requires only a brief note here. The key event in recent police armament policies is Vietnam, in two related senses. First, Vietnam was a high-technology war, and since the middle 1960's, much of the small-arms technology developed for Vietnam has been transferred into domestic police arms. Second, domestic protest against the war, and a host of related disturbances, posed for police a set of combat or quasi-combat situations for which they were, in general, not prepared—in temperament, training, or equipment. The general trend in police arms policies since then seems rooted in a determination that this potentially dangerous state of unpreparedness shall never again be.

Police response to the post-Vietnam realities manifests itself in many ways. Articles on police training, for example, tend more and more to emphasize topics such as stress training, crowd control, human and community relations, psychology, and so on; the current thinking is that the cop on the beat should command the skills necessary to respond coolly and effectively to unconventional situations. But this has been accompanied by a parallel realization that, these days, the police also need to be prepared for virtually any combat situation they might, sooner or later, confront. The result appears to have been something very close to what has been called a "police arms race" (Steele, 1979: 33), that is, a sharp and recent increase in both the numbers and kinds of firearms routinely stocked by U.S. police departments.

The direct observational evidence necessary to confirm this conclusion—for example, yearly data on police arsenals—does not appear to exist, and so our case for a "more and better" weapons trend among the police is circumstantial. We can, however, demonstrate the following points: (1) There is a dazzling variety of new weaponry being developed and marketed for domestic police use. (2) Both the arms manufacturers and the professional police journals promote this new weaponry as essential or desirable. (3) During the post-Vietnam period, the funds needed to buy into the "more and better" weapons market were amply available. These first three points demonstrate, in the language of criminal proceedings, both opportunity and motive for departments to get into the "police arms race." We also present (4) "hearsay" evidence from presumably knowledgeable experts that something like a "police arms race" is indeed under way, (5) one piece of evidence suggesting that innovations in police weapons tend to diffuse quickly, and (6) some fragments of direct evidence on actual changes in police armament policies, practices, and standards over the decade.

1. That new weaponry is constantly being developed and marketed for police use is instantly obvious from the arms advertisements in journals such

as *The Police Chief.* Virtually all arms manufacturers advertise their wares in these journals. For example, the October 1977 equipment issue of *The Police Chief* contains rifle, shotgun, and handgun advertisements from Smith and Wesson, Winchester Arms, Ruger, Detonics Inc., Dan Wesson, Ithacagun, and many others—all touting this or that "new and improved" weapon. Remington Arms has a six-page "glossy" in the August 1977 issue introducing its new Model 870P police shotgun (headline: "More than Just a Shotgun . . . It's a 12-Gauge Law Enforcement System . . ."). These advertisements strongly suggest that manufacturers invest substantial sums in research and development of new police weapons—partly to equip police with the best weapons that modern firearms science can offer, and partly, of course, to capture a share of what is clearly a very sizable market.

In some respects, marketing police arms is much like marketing any other consumer good. This year's model is invariably a "new, improved" version. Thus, the advertisements typically emphasize the better sighting characteristics of a new handgun; or the sturdier, more reliable construction of a new shotgun; or the greater accuracy and firepower of a new rifle. But in the marketing of police arms, there are at least two other considerations. First, the manufacturers consistently exploit an understandable desire to be equipped with the very best firearms available. In a combat situation, one never knows in advance what weaponry the other side will command, but one hopes it is not superior to the weapons available to the police. Since, in general, the other side has access to the same weapons supply, the unmistakable conclusion is to arm the police with the newest, best, and most "improved" equipment—indeed, that it would be irresponsible to arm them with anything less. Second, one also cannot anticipate just what *kinds* of combat situations police might face, and this makes it possible to exploit a "what if . . ." mentality. For example, very few local police departments will ever encounter a sniper, but at least some will. What if your department is the one? Is it not best to arm up in advance with the appropriate weaponry? Again, would it not be irresponsible to do otherwise?

Another indicator of the rate at which new police arms are developed is that many gun magazines run either occasional articles or regular monthly columns reviewing the latest police weapons, and they do not seem ever to be short of material.

2. The implicit themes of the weapons advertisements are reinforced in the professional police literature, which is thick with articles of these sorts: (a) reviews of new weapons, (b) discussions of "unconventional" police situations (riots, hostage and sniper situations, and so on) in which specialized arms might be useful or necessary, (c) articles on police weapons training, (d) descriptions of actual experiences in which specialized weaponry was used to good effect.

For example, *The Police Chief* for October 1977 contains 36 articles, of which six deal specifically with weapons: there are two articles on police firearms training, one on the Monadnock Prosecutor PR-24 nightstick, a long article on police body armor, one article on a new police handgun, and a brief item on "Handgun Control." The *FBI Law Enforcement Bulletin* also regularly features articles dealing with police weapons and firearms policies, as do virtually all other police journals and magazines.

Professionalism is, of course, something of concern to virtually all departments, and one function of these journals is to keep local police informed about prevailing professional standards. In the area of weapons, the prevailing standard is very much that a truly professional department should be prepared for all possible combat situations, much the same theme as the manufacturers themselves promote.

3. From 1969 to the present, the Federal government funneled very large sums of money into state and local departments, mostly through the conduit of the Law Enforcement Assistance Administration. Between 1970 and 1976, LEAA allocations to departments averaged about $750 million per year (United States Department of Justice, *Sourcebook of Criminal Justice Statistics*, 1977: 97). LEAA apparently does not know just how much of this was spent on arms purchases, but this use of LEAA funds was sufficiently common to have generated much controversy in the early 1970s. (See, for example, *The New York Times* 27 June 1972: 36; or 19 February 1973: 26.) Much of the controversy, to be sure, was focused not on small arms, but on armored personnel carriers, police helicopters, even an occasional tank. The essential point, however, is that departments looking to upgrade their small arms arsenals, to buy some of the "new and better" weaponry, or simply to stockpile small arms supplies would have found ample Federal monies available.

In sum, for the period covered by our analysis, there were large numbers of new weapons being developed and marketed for police use, and most police departments would have had both reasons and funds to purchase them.

4. That many departments in fact made these purchases and continue to do so seems to be common knowledge among authoritative sources who write about police arms practices for national publications. Articles dealing with police arms regularly refer, often quite explicitly, to a recent "more and better" weapons trend among the police. The phrase, "police arms race," is itself taken directly from an article in *Guns* magazine for December 1979 (Steele, 1979), and similarly explicit acknowledgements can be found in many sources. A *New York Times* article on SWAT (see below), appearing on 14 July 1975, notes that "some policemen are arming themselves to the teeth in para-military imitation of the latest techniques introduced in the big cities." Another *Times* article (27 March 1977) on high-powered police arms makes

explicit reference to "a nationwide shift [among the police] toward more powerful and more deadly weapons." A discussion of dumdum bullets in *Newsweek* magazine of 9 September 1974 refers explicitly to "the increasing use of heavy weapons by the police." A report released in late 1974 by the Massachusetts Research Center and discussed in a *Times* editorial of 11 November 1974 remarks on a "definite trend towards more powerful bullets and weapons capable of shooting higher velocity bullets." Thus, police writers for publications as diverse as *Guns* magazine and *The New York Times* agree that there has been some recent trend toward "more and better" police weapons.

5. No one has yet systematically studied the diffusion of small-arms technology among the police. Evidence on chemical weapons, however, suggests that innovations tend to diffuse rapidly. A survey conducted by the International Association of Chiefs of Police in 1970 found that, even at that early date, *four departments in five* had already purchased at least some of the chemical spray weapons (e.g., Mace) then coming onto the market. (See *The New York Times*, 22 February 1970: 88.)

6. There is some direct evidence on changes in police arms policies over the decade, all tending to confirm the general drift of our argument:

Standardization. State-wide standardization of local police policies is one theme in the "professionalization" movement, and in some states (for example, Oregon and New Jersey) this has meant a movement toward standardized police armament (see, e.g., *The Police Chief*, March 1976; or *The New York Times*, 27 March 1977). No one knows just how widespread the trend toward standardized arms policies is. If it has been at all common, the implications for demand in police weapons are potentially substantial, since every officer carrying a nonconforming firearm would be in the market for new weapons.

Officer Disarmings. Moorman (1976) and Giuffrida, Moorman, and Roth (1978) have analyzed the problem of officer disarming and subsequent slaying in some detail. They make a plausible case that the Police Special service revolver is itself partly at fault. Virtually all Police Specials are double-action revolvers whose firing is a simple matter of "point gun, pull trigger." One solution is therefore to carry a sidearm that is not so simple to fire, for example, semiautomatic pistols, which must be cocked before they will fire, which require both hands to cock, which not everyone would know how to operate. (Moorman [1976: 275] reports on 13 cases known to him "in which suspects forcibly took a semiautomatic from the uniformed officer but didn't know how to operate the weapon.") Moorman has conducted several surveys of California departments to monitor trends toward semiautomatic pistols. He reports that "the number of municipal and county law enforcement agencies that have mandated the 9 mm [semiautomatic pistol] as the on duty service sidearm for sworn uniformed personnel increased from 17 in September 1974 to 31 in January 1976" (1976: 275). The number of officers involved in this shift is from 1677 to 3463. "There are indeed," Moorman concludes, "an increasing number of semiautomatics being carried . . ." (1976: 275). No one knows whether this California trend generalizes nationally. If it does, the possible implications for police weapons demand are obvious.

Special Weapons and Tactics (SWAT). One of the most controversial instances of the Vietnamization of U.S. police is the so-called Special Weapons and Tactics, or SWAT, team. Basically, a SWAT team is an elite police commando unit, modeled roughly on the Green Berets or Rangers and trained to deal with unconventional, especially combat, situations. Some SWAT squads predate the period under analysis, but SWAT is mainly a 1970's phenomenon. According to *The New York Times* (14 July 1975), there were about 500 SWAT teams "on line" in 1975; by 1977, there were about 3000, with the number continuing to grow by perhaps 200 squads each year. The *Times* also notes that as of 1977, the FBI SWAT training program had "a large backlog of applicants."

The diffusion of SWAT to 3000 departments is strong evidence for the "be prepared" mentality discussed above. Few departments will ever encounter a SWAT-type situation over any reasonable time span; the *Times* articles on SWAT emphasize that most units are idle most of the time. But ". . . what if . . . ?" As Nicholas Fratto, Chief of Police for Cambridge, Massachusetts, expresses it: "We think it [SWAT] is a good idea to have. We have a lot of very important people in Cambridge. In the event something happened, we would want to know what to do" (quoted in *The New York Times,* 2 May 1977).

One important characteristic of SWAT squads is that they are heavily armed. The standard team consists "of five officers armed with a high powered sniper rifle, automatic weapons, and shotguns" (*The New York Times,* 14 July 1975). Given the number of squads, their recency, and the large amounts of weaponry involved, the contribution of SWAT to overall growth in police weapons demand is potentially substantial.

Hot Loads, Dumdums, and the Ammunition Controversy. A parallel to the search for the "ideal police handgun" is the search for ideal ammunition. The ammunition quest poses a definite minimax optimizing problem: one wants a bullet of sufficient weight and velocity to provide ample "stopping power," but not one so powerful as to pose a danger to bystanders through "overpenetration" or whose firing causes too much recoil or flinching. For years, the optimum police bullet was thought to be the low-velocity 158-grain .38-caliber cartridge, standard ammunition issue in most departments as of 1972 (according to PES72). Two widely publicized studies done in 1974 and 1975, however, called this conventional wisdom into doubt.

The first, on "the wounding effects of commercially available handgun ammunition suitable for police use" (DiMaio et al., 1974), was reported in the *FBI Law Enforcement Bulletin*. The report notes, "the .38 Special [the cartridge described in the previous paragraph] is the cartridge most widely used by police in the United States. In the past few years, many law enforcement organizations have expressed dissatisfaction with the wounding effectiveness of this cartridge. Because of this dissatisfaction, many organizations have begun using the new high-velocity .38 Special loadings or have shifted to the use of other weapons, such as the .357 or .41 magnum" (1974: 6). (Note, again, the explicit trend acknowledgment.) Results confirm the noted dissatisfaction: "The traditional 158 gr round nose (RN) loadings for the .38 Special are relatively ineffective" and "the high velocity round is significantly superior" (1974: 6). The report, however, warns that "some of the high velocity loadings for the .38 *should not* be fired in small and/or alloy frame revolvers due to the extreme pressure developed" (1974: 8). From this warning it can be inferred that at least some departments that wanted to follow these recommendations would have had to buy not just hotter cartridges but also weapons designed to handle them safely.

The study is especially enthusiastic about the 9-mm Parabellum cartridge, found to be "superior to most .38 Special loadings and a number of the .357 Magnum soft point and hollow point loadings" as well (1974: 5), i.e., superior to the ammunition then in use in virtually all departments. Departments interested in this "superior" cartridge would, of course, also need to buy 9-mm sidearms.

The study concludes with a strong endorsement of the 9-mm pistol: "We found that the 9 mm loadings are pleasant to shoot. In view of the wide range and the excellent performances of the 9 mm loadings, as well as the equality in wounding effectiveness with the .45 Automatic, the 9 mm is probably *the best available caliber for police use,* if a semiautomatic pistol is to be used" [1974: 7, our emphasis]. According to PES72, fewer than 1% of U.S. police used 9-mm weapons in 1972, so any movement to arm them with "the best available caliber" would create a large new demand for 9-mm sidearms.

These findings were reinforced in a study conducted by LEAA and the National Bureau of Standards and released in 1975 (see *The New York Times,* 9 August 1975). According to the *Times,* the key recommendation is that "policemen should change their standard ammunition from the traditional low-velocity 158 grain .38-caliber bullet to one with more 'stopping power' ". The possible implications for police weapons demand are again clear: many departments wanting to conform to the recommendation would have to purchase service handguns capable of firing the recommended hotter ammunition.

There is episodic evidence that many departments took these recommendations to heart. In 1974, the American Civil Liberties Union charged that police in Massachusetts, Connecticut, California, Hawaii, Pennsylvania, Texas, Virginia, and Washington had begun to use higher velocity hollow-nosed or dumdum bullets (*The New York Times,* 11 November 1974: 28). Later charges add Wisconsin, Tennessee, Mississippi, and New Jersey to the list (*The New York Times,* 16 January 1975: 21; 27 March 1977). To emphasize, in many cases, these changes in ammunition policy would require the purchase of new weapons.

Very little of the evidence on the trend in police arms policy lends itself to precise quantification. It seems plausible that shoulder armaments for new police, weaponry for SWAT squads, and a little experimentation with "new and improved" police rifles and shotguns would easily account for the few million shoulder weapons not yet accounted for by other sources. But how many of the remaining 5–8 million excess handguns have gone to the police? Earlier, we suggested about 1 million handguns to arm new police. The evidence reviewed above makes it clear that there would have also been at least some demand for new handguns emanating from "old" police as well. The question, then, is just how many?

Fortunately, there is one useful piece of information on total police demand for handguns in a single (presumably typical) year. The 1977 Census of Manufacturers' "Preliminary Report on Small Arms" (issued in May 1979) shows product shipments from small-arms manufacturers for both 1972 and 1977. As of the preliminary report, the 1977 data are only partially compiled, but some of the 1972 data are reported with a breakdown showing "shipments to Government (Federal, state, local, etc.)" and "other shipments." Unfortunately, this breakdown is reported only for center-fire pistols and revolvers; no similar breakdown is given for rifles or shotguns, or for rim-fire pistols, and there is no similar breakdown for any of the 1977 data.

According to these data, 998,000 center-fire pistols and revolvers were shipped in 1972, of which 251,000 were shipped to Federal, state, or local governments. In at least one year, then, government demand (assumed to be predominantly or exclusively a police demand) for handguns represented approximately one-quarter of the total demand. Further, this figure understates the actual police demand, since "shipments to government" would obviously *not* include any weapons purchased independently by officers themselves. Government, in short, is a big handgun consumer. If the 1972 data are adequately representative, then total government consumption of handguns for the decade would be about 10 times 251,000 guns, or just over 2.5 million handguns, a sizable fraction of the remaining handgun excess. We conclude that the net excess weaponry that remains to be accounted for consists of no more than about 5 million handguns.

FIVE

RECENT TRENDS IN WEAPONS OWNERSHIP:
III. "Fear and Loathing" and the Mass Demand for Defensive Weapons

The unfortunate cycle continues: the rise in street crime causes nervous people to buy guns for protection, and those very guns eventually cause more accidents, more crime, and more national paranoia. This deadly cycle must be broken. (From *A Shooting Gallery Called America,* pamphlet issued by the Massachusetts Council on Crime and Corrections, Inc., 1974)

Firearms purchases in recent years have often been motivated by fear of crime, violence, and civil disorder, as well as the fear that stricter firearms laws may make guns harder to obtain in the future. . . . Growing interest in shooting sports may explain much of the increase in long gun sales, but it does not account for the dramatic increase in handgun sales. (Newton and Zimring, 1969: 21, 22)

The tremendous increase in the sale of handguns in the United States in the last decade is evidence of the defensive reaction of many Americans. For a certain segment of our population, the possession of a handgun is apparently a viable reaction to the perception of threat in the environment. . . . (Northwood, Westgard, and Barb, 1978: 69)

The domestic arms race is a relatively recent development, probably spurred by the fact and fear of rising street crime rates and the civil disorders in the mid-1960's, and possibly by the anticipation of stricter gun laws. (Spiegler and Sweeney, 1975: 3)

The belief that possession of a handgun in the home or on the person offers one security and the ability to protect oneself . . . has apparently contributed to the rapid increase in handgun sales during the last ten years. (Alviani and Drake, 1975: 6)

The revolt involves the use of guns. In East Flatbush, and Corona, and all those other places where the white working class lives, people are forming gun clubs and self-defense leagues and talking about what they will do if real race rioting breaks out. (Hamill, 1970: 21)

As the preceding quotations illustrate, the notion that "fear of crime, violence, and civil disorder" underlies the recent weapons trend has become commonplace in the literature, especially among authors favoring stricter weapons controls. Indeed, in the pro-control literature, the trend itself is often cited as a self-evident demonstration that stricter firearms controls are essential. That the number of weapons in private hands has increased is easy enough to demonstrate with a simple compilation of import and production data. That the weapons increase reflects rising national fear and paranoia seems plausible enough, in the absence of any information to the contrary. The substantive conclusion is thus that the population is arming itself as a hedge against a fearful and unknown future. And because the prospect of citizens preparing to shoot one another to death over cultural, racial, ideological, or social disputes is something that any civilized nation would try to avoid, the policy conclusion is also straightforward: "something" must be done to stem the flow of weapons into private hands, to "break the deadly cycle."

There is a parallel line of argumentation among those opposed to stricter weapons controls—one, interestingly, that shares a key premise with the pro-control argument. Many of those opposed to stricter controls would agree that "fear and loathing" are the predominant sources of the recent weapons trend. Among anti-control forces, however, the fear is seen to be legitimate, and the purchase of a weapon is seen as a realistic and efficacious defense. People, in short, have become fearful for good reason and have thus purchased weapons for equally good reason: it has become a dangerous world, and private weaponry enhances one's safety within it. From this point of view, then, the recent weapons trend testifies that stricter gun controls are *not* desirable. Advocates of this position argue that further controls on private weaponry would only deprive the citizenry of access to an important (and, they hasten to add, Constitutionally guaranteed) means of protecting self and family against rape, pillage, and plunder.

Despite what appears to be a nearly uniform consensus that rising national anxieties underlie the recent weapons trend, the analyses in the previous chapters suggest that the total contribution of "fear and loathing" to the trend may in fact be quite small. Summarizing briefly: The gross addition to the weapons supply over the last decade apparently was within the range of 60–65 million weapons. Of these weapons some 20–25 million either were exported or functioned as replacements for weapons lost over the 10 years; the initial net increase is thus on the order of 40 million guns. Of these 40 million excess weapons, about 20 million are accounted for simply by growth in the number of U.S. households. Of the 20 million that then remain, on the order of 15 million can apparently be accounted for by disproportionate increases in the popularity of hunting, collecting, and the other shooting sports. Corrections for these factors thus leave an excess of no more than about 5–8 million guns, of which perhaps one-half can be accounted for through enhanced arms demand among the U.S. police. The number of excess weapons remaining to be explained by other factors is thus on the order of 5 million guns.

Few of the existing studies of the trend pay much serious attention to *any* of these alternative possible explanations. Indeed, no compilation of data on the weapons trend that we have seen goes even so far as to correct the data for growth in the number of U.S. households, the minimum first step in any serious trend analysis. Rather, most of the available accounts simply assume that the weapons trend reflects an increasing "fear of crime, violence, and civil disorder," as though this were somehow a self-evident proposition.

The work by Spiegler and Sweeney, quoted at the beginning of this chapter, provides one among many possible examples. Their data consist of a bar chart showing estimates of "guns added to the U.S. civilian market" for selected years from 1962 to 1974 (1975: 3). As with all other versions of the supply data, this chart shows an unmistakable upward trend. No additional evidence bearing on the sources of the trend is presented anywhere in the report. Their conclusion, that the trend results from "the fact and fear of rising street crime rates and the civil disorders in the mid-1960's," is an assertion for which no direct evidence is presented.

In a summary section, Spiegler and Sweeney remark, "while the blessings of liberty should include shooting for hunt and sport, . . . it is doubtful whether the founding fathers could have foreseen the scope of the domestic arms race, especially in handguns, a device not well suited for either hunt or sport, but rather as a weapon, which has resulted in a gun in every other home" (1975: 1). There are two aspects of this passage that warrant comment. First, there is the *stipulation* (as opposed to demonstration) that handguns have no (or, at best, very limited) sport or recreational applications. This is, as we shall see later, a key premise in the "fear and loathing" argument: if there are no "legitimate" uses of handguns, then what except fear and loathing can possibly account for the handgun trend? And yet, no serious empirical study of sport and recreational uses of handguns has ever been undertaken; such evidence as does exist suggests a rather extensive sport and recreational use.

A second notable aspect of the passage is the suggestion that the "domestic arms race" has "resulted in a gun in every other home," as though "a gun in every other home" is somehow a new or recent development. In fact, there has been a gun in every other home for as long as anyone has bothered to ask the question in a national survey.

SURVEY DATA ON THE WEAPONS TREND

The only *direct* (as opposed to inferential) evidence on trends in the mass demand for weaponry is contained among the several national surveys conducted since 1959 that have included a gun ownership question. Gallup first asked the question in 1959 and has included it periodically in many surveys since; the National Opinion Research Center (NORC) has asked the question in several of the General Social Surveys. Trend data from these national polls and surveys for the period 1959–1977 are shown in Table 5-1.

These and all other available survey data on private ownership of guns show that approximately one-half the families in the United States possess at least one gun and that this proportion has been approximately constant for the last two decades. This conclusion, of course, seems immediately to contradict the data on weapons supply, which show very substantial increases in weaponry, especially in the last 10 years. In the literature, typically, this disparity is resolved by the simple assertion that the survey data are invalid: that many people in fact own weapons but deny it to survey interviewers. There are, however, other equally plausible explanations.

The total number of weapons in private hands is a function of three variable parameters: the total number of families, the proportion of those families who own at least one gun, and the average number of guns owned by families owning at least one of them. The survey data shown in Table 5-1, of course, pertain only to the second of these parameters. A constant proportion owning a weapon is thus *not* inconsistent with the large supply increases if there have been proportionate increases in either or both of the remaining two parameters.

The effects of growth in the number of U.S. households were calculated in Chapter 3; about half the net growth in supply can be attributed to this source alone. If one therefore grants, not unreasonably, that all existing evi-

TABLE 5-1. *Survey data on trends in mass weapons ownership, 1959–1977*

Percentage ownership[a]	1959	1965	1966	1972	1973	1974	1976	1977
No guns	50.8	52.0	52.6	55.5	51.4	52.9	52.0	48.9
Shotgun	32.2	32.8	32.1	26.0	27.5	27.8	27.9	31.0
Rifle	27.4	24.3	27.7	24.6	29.1	26.7	28.0	30.1
Handgun	12.6	14.5	15.1	15.4	19.8	19.7	21.4	20.5
N	1538	3492	3541	1541	1504	1484	1499	1530

[a] Columns do not sum to 100% because families may own more than one type of weapon.
Source: Gallup Polls Nos. 616, 704, 733, and 852 (1959–1972); NORC General Social Surveys (1973–1977).

dence is equally valid—that the supply data are real and the survey data equally real—then it follows deductively that the rest of the disparity between supply-side and demand-side trend estimates must be accounted for by an increase in the average number of weapons owned by families owning at least one of them.

Indeed, given the conclusions of the previous chapters, the necessary increase in this parameter can be readily calculated. In 1968, we estimate, there were approximately 80 million guns and some 60 million U.S. households, one-half of which owned a gun. The average number owned among the one-half that owned at least one gun must therefore have been approximately $80/30 = 2.67$ guns per gun-owning household. Calculations for 1978 suggest some 120 million guns dispersed over one-half of 75 million households, for an average of about $120/37.5 = 3.20$ weapons per gun-owning household. In other words, if over the decade the average number of guns owned by families owning at least one of them had increased by just one-half a gun, all the apparent disparity between the supply-side and demand-side trend estimates would be eliminated.

Unfortunately, the projected increase in this parameter cannot be independently tested. Although many surveys ask the simple ownership question, very few of them follow it up with a question on how many guns the respondent owns; and the best existing survey data on "how many guns" have already been used in calculating the total number of guns in private hands (see Chapter 2). The case that this average has increased is therefore mainly logical, not empirical.

The logical case, however, is reasonably strong. If this average has *not* increased, and if the supply increase is *in fact* genuine, then the only remaining possibility is that the true proportion of U.S. families owning a gun has increased. Since the existing surveys show no such increase, to argue for this possibility is equivalent to arguing that the survey data are invalid. But if they are invalid, then why or how do they give estimates of total weaponry that are generally quite consistent with the supply-side estimates?

The interpretation that we offer is bolstered by the data in Table 5-1 on gun ownership by weapons type. Although the proportion owning at least one firearm of any type has been roughly constant throughout the time series, the proportion saying that they own a *handgun* has nearly doubled, increasing from 13% in 1959 to 21% in 1977. In contrast, the proportions claiming to own rifles and shotguns have been roughly constant, as has the proportion owning no weapons at all. These data therefore confirm that the tendency to own more than one *type* of firearm, given that one possesses at least one of any type, has increased over the past 20 years, and this pattern can only result from purchases of additional weapons by families that already own at least one weapon.

The implication, of course, is that most of the remaining excess firearms in the supply trend may well be accounted for by additional purchases of guns' among families already owning one or more weapons. The data on weapons type suggest that this may be especially true of the remaining excess handguns. If this speculation is substantially correct, then the remaining weapons trend takes on an entirely different cast. That is, we would not be dealing with first-time purchases by "nervous" and "paranoid" citizens who were largely unfamiliar with small arms, but rather with second, third, or fourth purchases among families who have *always* owned guns and who are (one assumes) comfortable with them and familiar with their use. It seems reasonably obvious that from the standpoint of "public safety," the transition from no-guns to one-gun is considerably more "alarming" than the transition from several to several + 1 weapons.

But why, it may be asked, would a family that already owns one or more guns want to purchase additional ones? Surely, one or two guns is enough. This argument, however, assumes that weaponry is somehow a thing apart, qualitatively different from any other kind of consumer purchase. We suggest, in contrast, that the purchase of additional weaponry by families who routinely own guns is not very different from the purchase of additional stereo equipment by stereo buffs or of new ski equipment by ski buffs. In other words, people own guns mainly because they enjoy them and the activities they make possible. Weapons-owning families presumably purchase additional guns for much the same reason that TV-owning families often purchase additional TVs, namely, because these are simply the kinds of things they like to buy when their incomes rise.

The most "alarming" aspect of the data shown in Table 5-1 is the distinct upturn in handgun ownership over the two decades. A crude analysis of this handgun trend is shown in Table 5-2, which reports for the years 1959 and 1976 the percentages of various population subgroups saying they possess at least one handgun. This analysis shows nothing very sharp or distinctive. In particular, these data do *not* suggest that some population subgroups are arming themselves at a greatly disproportionate rate, in contrast to what one might expect from the "fear and loathing" hypothesis. The increasing proportion owning a handgun has been concentrated in (but certainly not restricted to) the South, a region where rates of weapons ownership have always been relatively high (see Chapter 6). All told, Southern handgun ownership increased by just over 13 percentage points during the period, compared with a 6.4-point increase outside the South. That the trend has been disporportionate in a region traditionally high in private weapons ownership adds additional support to the interpretation that much of the recent trend reflects additional purchases of weapons among families that already own weapons.

Also, the handgun trend has been slightly disproportionate in middle-sized cities, which show increases on the order of 15 percentage points during

TABLE 5-2. *Percent owning a handgun by social back-*
ground characteristics, 1959–1976

Characteristic	% Owning handgun		
	1959[a]	1976[b]	Change
Total U.S. population	12.6	21.4	8.8
(N)	(1538)	(1499)	
By political party			
Democrat	13.7	21.9	8.2
Independent	10.7	21.6	10.9
Republican	12.5	20.7	8.2
By religion			
Protestant	14.0	25.8	11.8
Catholic	10.9	13.3	2.4
Jew	1.9	14.8	12.9
By heads occupation			
White collar	13.6	21.9	8.3
Blue collar	12.8	24.7	11.9
Farm	12.3	19.5	7.2
By education			
Less than high school	10.1	21.3	11.2
High school graduate	16.1	20.0	3.9
Some college	19.9	25.8	5.9
College graduate	8.3	20.5	12.2
By age			
18–30	11.5	19.1	7.6
31–54	13.7	23.2	9.5
55+	11.6	21.3	9.7
By sex			
Men	14.6	25.6	11.0
Women	10.7	18.1	7.4
By race			
White	12.9	21.5	8.6
Non-white	10.2	20.3	10.1
By city size			
Open country, farm	16.3	25.8	9.5
City less than 10,000	13.5	23.8	10.3
10,000–50,000	15.1	30.0	14.9
50,000–250,000	8.1	23.0	14.9
250,000 and up	9.7	15.8	6.1
By region			
South	16.9	30.1	13.2
Non-South	10.9	17.3	6.4

[a] Source: AIPO (Gallup) No. 616.
[b] Source: 1976 NORC GSS.

the period. Interestingly, the increase in the larger urban areas (those with a population over 250,000) amounted to only about 6 percentage points, somewhat *below* the increase for the population as a whole, and this, too, is the opposite of what "fear and loathing" would lead one to expect.

There are two final items of interest in the table. First, the increase in handgun ownership has been concentrated at the extremes of the education distribution: ownership among both high-school dropouts and college graduates increased more sharply (by 11 to 12 percentage points) than in the population as a whole. Second, the ownership increase was also disproportionate among Protestants and Jews; Catholics show virtually no increase in handgun ownership at all during the period. The Jewish increase was particularly pronounced: in 1959, 2% or less of the Jewish population owned a handgun; in 1976, the figure was nearly 15%.

The rest of the variables in the table show little or nothing of interest. The handgun trend has been approximately the same among blacks and whites, among men and women, and across all age, occupation, and political party categories. Even the differences by region, city size, and religion are modest. The most prudent conclusion to be drawn from these data is therefore that the increase in handgun ownership has cut more or less equally throughout all sociodemographic sectors of contemporary American society.

A somewhat more complicated version of these data is shown in Table 5-3. This table is identical to Table 5-2 except that a control for city size has been introduced. In order to achieve respectable cell sizes throughout the table, city size has been collapsed to three categories: rural, which here means anything under 10,000 population; middle-sized, everything between 10,000 and 250,000; and urban, everything from a quarter-million up. The table then reports, within each of these three city sizes, the proportions of various population subgroups saying they own a handgun, for both 1959 and 1976. The rows denoted by δ report the simple increase (or decrease) in each proportion over the period. Thus, for example, one can see in the first line of the table that in 1959, 15.7% of all rural Protestants owned a handgun (column one); that in 1976, ownership among rural Protestants had increased to 26.1% (column 2); and that this increase amounted to 10.4 percentage points (column 3).

In the total sample, the increase in handgun ownership over the period amounted to just about 9 percentage points, so any increase exceeding 9 points is "disproportionate." Given the usual margin of survey error, however, and that many of the comparisons reported in the table are sustained by distressingly small cell sizes, it makes sense to insist on a certain distance from the 9-point average as the minimum difference worth discussing. For present purposes, a 15-point increase seems a reasonable, if necessarily arbitrary, criterion. Where, then, did handgun ownership increase by more than 15 percentage points in the 1959–1976 period?

TABLE 5-3. *Trends in handgun ownership by city size and selected background variables*

| | % Owning handgun | | | | | | | | |
| | <10,000 | | | 10–250,000 | | | 250,000+ | | |
	1959	1976	δ	1959	1976	δ	1959	1976	δ
Religion									
Protestant	15.7	26.1	10.4	12.7	30.3	17.6	11.7	19.6	7.9
Catholic	15.6	22.2	6.6	9.4	12.3	2.9	8.5	11.0	2.5
Jew	—	—	—	—	20.0	—	2.1	12.5	10.4
Head's occupation									
White collar	25.0	24.7	−0.3	11.9	28.6	16.7	6.6	13.4	6.8
Blue collar	16.5	26.1	9.6	12.7	25.8	13.1	9.4	21.9	12.5
Farm	12.4	24.1	11.7	—	—	—	—	—	—
Education									
Less than high school	12.6	25.5	12.9	6.9	24.2	17.3	8.3	12.7	4.4
High school graduate	23.1	22.3	−0.8	15.5	23.2	7.7	10.8	14.5	3.7
Some college	19.0	31.1	12.1	30.8	27.0	−3.8	15.4	22.2	6.8
College graduate	10.3	25.7	15.4	12.0	23.2	11.2	5.3	15.7	10.4
Age									
18–30	12.9	23.8	10.9	10.9	20.6	9.7	10.0	15.0	5.0
31–54	18.0	25.9	7.9	13.4	27.1	13.7	9.1	16.8	7.7
55+	13.3	25.0	11.7	8.5	23.0	14.5	11.5	15.2	3.7
Sex									
Male	18.8	31.4	12.6	13.0	25.6	12.6	10.4	20.9	10.5
Female	12.5	19.6	7.1	10.1	22.7	12.6	9.0	11.6	2.6
Race									
White	15.8	25.2	9.4	12.4	23.8	11.4	9.5	15.6	6.1
Non-white	13.5	17.6	4.1	0.0	26.3	26.3	11.5	17.6	6.1
Region									
South	19.2	28.4	9.2	17.4	34.5	17.1	12.9	24.5	11.6
Non-South	11.6	22.5	10.9	7.8	18.1	10.3	7.7	13.6	5.9

a Dash indicates *N* < 10.

With one exception, *all* the increases of 15 points or more are registered among respondents from middle-sized cities. The sole exception is that college-graduated respondents from rural areas showed a 15.4 point increase. In the middle-sized cities, subgroups showing trends in excess of the criterion include Protestants, white-collar workers, high-school dropouts, nonwhites, and Southerners. Geographically, then, the largest increase in handgun ownership has occurred in middle-sized Southern cities. In contrast, the handgun trend in large non-Southern cities (amounting overall to 5.9 percentage points) is among the more modest shown anywhere in the table.

Strictly, these data rule out very little of the speculation on motivations underlying the recent weaponry trends; the data tell us something about the "who" of the issue, but little or nothing of the "why." However, these data do pose some puzzles that any adequate theory about the causes of the trend, including "fear and loathing," must address: Why, for example, is the trend sharper in the South than outside of it? Why has it been concentrated in middle-sized cities? Or among Protestants and Jews but not Catholics? Why do non-whites in middle-sized cities show such a sharp increase in hand-gun ownership, when both rural and urban non-whites show no equivalent trend?

Because many of the variables shown in Table 5-3 are intercorrelated, it is difficult to determine just which of these effects are robust and independent of the others, and which are not. In order to separate the genuine from the spurious, we have also performed a regression analysis of handgun ownership (coded as a dummy variable, where 1 = owns a handgun and 0 = does not) on selected background variables.[1] The results of this analysis are shown

[1] Regression analysis is a statistical technique that allows one to analyze a large number of variables simultaneously. In the present case, the analysis treats handgun ownership as a simple, linear additive function of the various background variables shown in the table. In Table 5.4, the b coefficients, or unstandardized multiple regression coefficients, show the average increase or decrease in the probability of owning a handgun that results from a one-unit change in the corresponding independent (or background) variable, with all the other variables in the equation held constant.

"Dummy variable" is a conventional statistical term that refers to a variable taking on only two values (typically, zero and one). Sex is an example: in the regression analysis, women are given the value 0 for the variable sex, and men the value 1. Purely nominal or categorical variables (that is, variables with no inherent rank-ordering to their categories, such as region and religion) can also be treated as sequences of dummy variables in a regression analysis. Religion, for example, can be represented as a sequence of variables along the following lines (shown in the tabulation):

Respondent	Yes	No
Protestant	1	0
Catholic	1	0
Jewish	1	0
Other	1	0

For technical statistical reasons, when a variable such as religion is entered in the equation, one of the categories of the variable must be omitted; in the regression analysis reported in Table 5.4, Protestant is the omitted category for the religion variable.

An "interaction term" is used to assess the effect of unique combinations of categories of the independent variables on the dependent variable. (In this case, the dependent variable is handgun ownership, and the independent variables, also called the "regressor set," are the several background variables in the analysis.) To illustrate, the effect of sex is shown in the coefficient in Table 5-4. The data base for the regression is a merger of both the 1959 Gallup survey and the 1976 NORC survey. Accordingly, year varies across respondents and is therefore entered in the regressor set. The remaining independent variables are just those shown in previous tables, treated as dummy variables where appropriate (see footnote 1). Finally, to assess the effects of the background characteristics on the trends, each of the independent variables has also been entered as an interaction term with year.

Results of the regression analysis suggest the following conclusions. First, R^2 for the total regression is less than 6%. Although this is "significantly" more than zero variance explained, it is not much more. This means that handgun ownership is largely (but not exclusively) random with respect to the variables considered in this analysis, or, in other words, that handgun owners are not very much different from nonowners in terms of these social characteristics.

Second, the main effect for year is 0.112. This suggests that, net of all variables considered in the table, the increase in handgun ownership over the period would have been some 11.2 percentage points, rather than the 8.8-percentage-point increase that was actually observed. That the coefficient for year (0.112) is larger than the zero-order effect (0.088) and statistically significant (at the 0.10 level) implies that the handgun *trend* is also not adequately explained by the independent variables included in the regression. For example, if it were the case that the trend reflected only increases in the relative size of population subgroups that always owned handguns at a relatively high rate (if, that is, the trend were a simple artifact of demographic changes), then the coefficient for year would be zero and insignificant. That more of the trend is left after all these variables have been taken into account than there was to begin with is thus evidence that the trend has been largely independent of the variables in this analysis.

The main effects reported in the table are all much as one would expect given the zero-order results. Net of all other variables and of year, handgun

---

for the sex variable; the effect of race, in the coefficient for the race variable. To show the effect of being a *black female,* however, would require the inclusion of an interaction term over and beyond the variables for sex and race. (In the present case, the only interaction terms that have been entered are terms expressing the interaction of background characteristics with year. This is a convenient statistical device for determining whether the increase in handgun ownership over time was concentrated in particular sociodemographic subgroups of the population.)

R^2 is a measure of the ability of the independent variables to account for, or explain, the variability of the dependent variable, handgun ownership. If handgun ownership was perfectly accounted for by the variables in the regressor set, R^2 would be equal to 1.00; and if handgun ownership was completely unrelated to the variables in the regressor set, R^2 would be equal to zero.

TABLE 5-4. *Multiple regression of handgun ownership on year, selected background variables, and year-by-background interactions*

Variable	b^a	S.E.[b]	Significance[c]
Main effects			
Year (1976 = 1)	.112	.068	.098
Catholic (=1)[d]	−.012	.023	NS[f]
Jew (=1)	−.082	.056	NS
Other (=1)	−.064	.051	NS
West (=1)[e]	.068	.030	.024
East (=1)	−.010	.025	NS
South (=1)	.066	.027	.013
Age (in years)	.000	.000	NS
Sex (male = 1)	.040	.019	.032
Race (white = 1)	.029	.032	NS
Urban (=1)	−.053	.024	.025
Middle (=1)	−.038	.025	NS
Education	.017	.007	.014
Blue collar (=1)	.010	.010	NS
Interactions with Year			
Catholic	−.069	.033	.037
Jew	.047	.093	NS
Other	−.044	.063	NS
West	.010	.042	NS
East	−.031	.037	NS
South	.042	.037	NS
Sex	.037	.027	NS
Race	−.004	.047	NS
Urban	−.004	.035	NS
Middle	.049	.035	NS
Education	−.008	.009	NS
Blue collar	−.011	.014	NS

$$R^2 = .059$$
$$F = 7.172$$
$$p = .000$$
$$\alpha^g = .011$$

[a] Unstandardized multiple regression coefficient.
[b] Standard error (SE) of the estimate of the b coefficient.
[c] T-test against the null that the true coefficient equals zero.
[d] For the religion dummies, Protestant is the omitted category.
[e] For the region dummies, Midwest is the omitted category.
[f] NS: $p > 0.10$.
[g] The regression intercept.

ownership is significantly *higher* in the South (0.066) and West (0.068) than in the omitted region, the Midwest. Men are slightly *more* likely to report a family handgun than are women; handguns are *less* common in urban areas than elsewhere; the tendency to own a handgun *increases* with respondent's education.

Of the 12 interactions of these variables with year, only one is significant: the interaction between year and the Catholic dummy. Net of all other variables shown in the table, that is, Catholics showed a smaller increase in handgun ownership in the period than would otherwise have been expected (−0.067). That none of the other interactions achieves significance again indicates that the trends are not adequately explained by the variables contained in this model.

In general, it appears that little of substance can be concluded on the basis of these data; most of the legitimate conclusions are negative. That is, the trend revealed in these data turns out to be largely independent of the various sociodemographic factors available for analysis. It can at least be noted, however, that many patterns that would be consistent with "fear and loathing" as an explanation are *not* observed in these data: the trend, for example, is not distinctively sharper in larger urban areas than in smaller places, and is not clearly concentrated in any one particular social, racial, or ideological group. The major positive conclusion is thus that the increase in the proportion of the population owning a handgun has been more or less uniform across all major sectors of the society.

EMPIRICAL STUDIES OF "FEAR AND LOATHING"

After the obviously polemical and the essentially polemical "studies" are discounted, the amount of empirically credible research on "fear and loathing" that remains is unimpressive in quantity and inconclusive in substance. Indeed, there are no more than a handful of legitimate studies of the topic, and the few studies that have been conducted generally do *not* show very substantial fear and loathing effects.

Newton and Zimring (1969) remain by far the most widely cited source among authors arguing the fear and loathing theme. Their evidence on the supply trends was reviewed in an earlier chapter. Unlike most other accounts, theirs contains at least some effort to compile data on sport and recreational weapons uses, and there is an explicit acknowledgement that "to some extent these dramatic increases in gun sales merely reflect increased shooting sports activity" (1969: 20). "Yet," they continue, "increases in hunting and sport shooting only partly account for the spiraling sale of firearms and can have little to do with handguns. Firearms purchases in recent years have often been motivated by fear of crime, violence, and civil disorder, as well as the fear that stricter firearms laws may make guns harder to obtain in the future" (1969: 21).

Some of the sport and recreation data compiled by Newton and Zimring suggest, as does our analysis in Chapter 3, that the portion of the trend attributable to this source may be quite large. But ascribing any large portion of the total weapons increase to sport and recreational demand would sit poorly with the overall themes of the rest of the report. They thus conclude their discussion of the trend on the following note: "Growing interest in shooting sports may explain much of the increase in long gun sales, but it does not account for the dramatic increase in handgun sales. Fear of crime, violence, and civil disorder, and perhaps the anticipation of stricter firearms laws, appear also to have stimulated sales of handguns in recent years" (1969: 22).

This, it will be noted, is a pretty firm conclusion, and so one expects to find, somewhere in the report, persuasive evidence that "fear of crime . . ." has motivated a large fraction of recent weapons purchases. Evidence along these lines is not amply abundant in the report. The conclusion, rather, is sustained by two fragments of evidence, neither of which is persuasive, and by one critical stipulation that happens also to be incorrect. The evidence is presented below.

1. Newton and Zimring emphasize that "self-defense is the most frequently given reason for owning a handgun" (1969: 21). In support, they cite a finding from a 1966 NORC survey that asked: "Is there a gun, pistol, rifle, or shotgun in the house that is used for the protection of the household, even though it is also used for sport or something else?" Overall, 37% of the respondents (and therefore, about three-quarters of the weapons-owning respondents) said yes. Newton and Zimring also report that about 95% of the "shooters" in a 1964 poll mentioned hunting as a "good reason" for owning a shoulder weapon, but only 16% gave this as a good reason for owning a handgun; in contrast, self-defense was mentioned as a good reason for owning a handgun by 71%.

Because in our view, people should be seen as expert informants on the conditions of their own existence, these findings constitute strong evidence that must be taken seriously. The question is, evidence for what? The data do show, unmistakably, that perhaps two-thirds to three-fourths of the people who own guns own them at least in part for self-defense. Given the wording of the question, it is impossible to ascertain how many people own them *primarily* or *exclusively* for self-defense, and so this question fails to bear on any possible sporting uses of these same weapons. That guns are owned in part for self-defense clearly does not rule out other ownership reasons, since virtually all hunting or sporting weapons could also be used, should the situation arise, for self-defense.

In addition, the question does not ask about protection against *what*. The presumption is that most or all of these defensive weapons are to protect against other human beings, but, in at least some cases, the self-defense in question would be protection against "snakes, angry wolverines, and rabid foxes," to borrow a phrase quoted earlier. The fear of aggressive fauna would hardly constitute evidence in favor of Newton and Zimring's hypothesis.

Some indirect evidence on the ownership of weapons for defense against animals is contained in the 1978 poll conducted by Decision-Making Information, Inc. (DMI), noted in several previous contexts. One question in the poll asked whether people had "ever used a gun, even if it wasn't fired, for self-protection." Altogether, 12% of the sample responded yes. A follow-up asked: "Was this to protect against an animal or a person?" *One-half* the responses to this question referred to protection against animals (DMI, 1978: 116). How weapons get used is an imperfect indicator of why they are owned in the first place, and so this is only indirect evidence. But it suggests that perhaps one-half of all "defensive" weapons are for defense against animals as opposed to other human beings.

Other aspects of Newton and Zimring's treatment of these data warrant comment. Their conclusion is that "self-defense is the most frequently given reason for owning a *handgun.*" The NORC question, however, does not differentiate between handguns and long guns (in fact, it conscientiously collapses any such distinction) and so does not bear directly on this conclusion. Thus, the only evidence cited in the report that does pertain directly to the authors' conclusion is the finding from the 1964 poll of "shooters." That poll, however, did *not* ask people why they owned a gun; it asked "shooters" to give opinions on what good reasons for owning various kinds of guns would be—a separate matter entirely. The 1966 NORC result is also cited as evidence that "many Americans keep loaded firearms in homes, businesses, and on their persons for the purpose of protection" (1969: 61). This assertion is an unwarranted interpretation of the evidence: the finding itself indicates nothing about the proportion of families who keep *loaded* guns in their house, but only about the proportion who own guns (loaded or not), at least in part, for protective purposes.

The preceding aside, the most serious problem with the data on reasons for ownership in the context is that they do not, in and of themselves, relate directly to the question at issue, namely, the sources of the handgun *trend*. To explain the handgun trend on the basis of these kinds of data, one would have to show either that (a) the number of gun owners citing defense or protection as a reason for ownership had increased, or (b) the numbers of people feeling some need for protection or defense had increased over time. Either of these possibilities may, of course, be true; given the events of the 1960's, the second (if not the first) may be self-evident. But there is again no direct evidence cited or presented anywhere in the Newton–Zimring report that bears on either points (a) or (b).

The most current and probably best evidence on why people own guns is contained in the 1978 DMI poll (see Table 5-5). The DMI question is less ambiguous than the NORC question because it asks specifically for the "most important reason" for weapons ownership. Focusing for the moment on the "all guns" column in Table 5-5, "self-defense at home" is mentioned as the primary reason by just one in five weapons owners; the large majority (71%) mention some sport or recreational use (hunting, target shooting, or collecting). From this, it can be correctly inferred that "self-defense at home" is *not* the "most frequently given reason" for owning a weapon. But we could certainly not conclude from this that fear and loathing is *not* the explanation of the weapons trend. The Newton-Zimring inference from their 1966 survey data is therefore a non sequitur.

Other aspects of the DMI data also deserve some emphasis here. *First,* consistent with the conclusion from Newton and Zimring, "self-defense at home" *is* the modal reason for owning a *handgun.* At the same time, the proportion of handgun owners giving this answer was 40%, which means that the clear majority gave some other reason. This finding therefore supports the conclusion that most handguns are owned for reasons other than self-defense, contrary to Newton and Zimring's depiction.

Second, 5% of the handgun owners mention "protection at work" and 8% mention "law enforcement or security job" as the primary reasons for owning the handgun. "Protection at work" is somewhat ambiguous in context; presumably, this includes people such as truckers, taxi cab drivers, possibly foresters or farmers, or those in other nonsecurity occupations in which carry-

TABLE 5-5. *Reason for gun ownership*[a]

Reason	All guns (%)	Handguns only (%)
Self-defense at home	20	40
Protection at work	1	5
Law enforcement or security job	3	8
Part of a gun collection	7	14
Target shooting	10	17
Hunting	54	9
Just like to have one	3	6
Missing data (DK, NA, etc.)	2	1
	100%	100%

[a] The survey question reads: "I have a list of reasons why people own guns. Please listen while I read it and then tell me the most important reason *you* have a gun."

Source: DMI, 1979: 40; all results are from DMI's December 1978, poll.

ing a gun provides a useful hedge against the unknown. "Law enforcement or security job," however, is more clear-cut; this issue was discussed in Chapter 4. The weapons demand projected from that chapter was based on a total number of armed public servants somewhere in the range of 750,000 plus some additional (and hard to estimate) number of armed private servants (that is, private police and security forces). If the guess that recurs in the literature on private security, that there are as many private as public police, is correct, then we would project a total security employment somewhere in the range of 1.5 million people. According to the DMI data, 23% of the nation's households possess a handgun, and of these, 8% say that the main reason is a law enforcement or security job. On the basis of a total of 75 million households, the DMI data thus give (75 million) (0.23) (0.08) = 1,380,000 as the total armed security employment, encouragingly close to the corresponding estimates in Chapter 4.

Third, 14% of the handgun owners mention "gun collection," 17% mention target shooting, and 9% mention "hunting" as the primary reason for owning a handgun. The sport and recreation answers therefore amount to 40% of the total, the same proportion who gave "self-defense at home" as the primary reason. This finding suggests that sport and recreation have at least as much to do with owning handguns as self-defense has. Working again from a base of 75 million households, the proportions shown in Table 5-5 project out to totals of 2.9 million handgun target shooters in the nation as a whole, 2.4 million handgun collectors, and 1.6 million people who hunt with handguns (here assuming one and only one shooter per gun-owning household). The conclusion from Newton and Zimring, "that hunting and sport shooting . . . can have little to do with handguns," is, in our view, sharply undercut by these results.

Finally, 20% of all gun owners (handgun or otherwise) mention "self-defense at home" as the primary ownership reason, which implies that roughly four of five privately owned weapons are possessed for reasons other than fear and loathing. Since gun owners represent about one-half the total population of households, the proportion of all American households possessing a firearm of any sort *primarily* for self-defense is therefore on the order of 10%. (Contrast this, for example, with the imagery of "a gun in every other home," as advanced in Speigler and Sweeney, above.) If this proportion of 20% has been constant over the past two decades, then one could suggest, reasonably, that some 20% of the excess weapons supply (as estimated earlier) has been absorbed in fear and loathing demand. Given an initial weapons excess of 40 million guns, one can calculate a total demand for such defensive weapons of (0.2) (40 million) = 8 million firearms, which agrees quite respectably with the 5 million net excess guns projected at the close of the previous chapter.

2. Aside from the evidence on reasons for gun ownership, the only other fragment of evidence presented in the Newton–Zimring report bearing on "fear of crime . . ." and its effects on weapons demand is a chart showing trend data on permits to purchase firearms in Detroit for the years 1965–1968 (see Figure 5-1). These data are apparently presented to show that applications for permits to purchase weapons respond to racial incidents and civil disorders. Even if the data showed this clearly and unambiguously, there would be a question whether results from "Murder City" generalize to the nation as a whole. But the graph does not clearly show the presumed fear and loathing effect even for Detroit. The data do reveal an unmistakable upward trend in *applications* to purchase a weapon (*not* in their actual purchase), but it does not reveal any clear "spike" or "break" in the time series corresponding, even with appropriate lags, to the points designating "racial incident" and "civil disorder." (It should also be kept in mind that the total population of metropolitan Detroit during this period was about 4.4 million, whereas the quarterly permits to purchase number in the range of 1–6 thousand.)

The data in Figure 5-1 show that the number of people in Detroit wishing to purchase a legal firearm increased quite regularly from 1965 to 1968, but they say little or nothing about why. Fear and loathing is one possible explanation that is neither confirmed nor ruled out by these data. Nonetheless, Newton and Zimring's Detroit chart is commonly cited in the pro-control literature as nearly definitive proof on the fear and loathing point (e.g., Comptroller General, 1978: 21).

3. The most compelling argument for fear and loathing is thus the simple *stipulation* that sport or recreation "can have little to do with handguns" (Newton and Zimring, 1969: 21), as in the Speigler–Sweeney passage already discussed. A sport or recreational explanation of the handgun trend is therefore ruled out on a priori grounds. This purely logical argument, however, is directly contradicted by the DMI findings and by other information presented in Chapter 3. To be sure, these DMI and other data do *not* demonstrate that sport and recreation actually account for the handgun trend, only that they may. But this explanation cannot be ruled out solely on a priori grounds.

Thus, the source most commonly cited in the literature as demonstrating a fear and loathing effect turns out to contain virtually no evidence at all pointing to such a conclusion. At best, the evidence is ambiguous and the stated conclusions premature. Much the same is true for most other direct inquiries into fear and loathing as a factor in the trend. For example, Wright and Marston (1975) examined 1973 survey evidence on correlates of weapons ownership in cities and suburbs (of population 250,000 and up). The fear and loathing interpretation requires *at least* that direct measures of fear and loathing correlate with gun ownership, but these authors found very little to

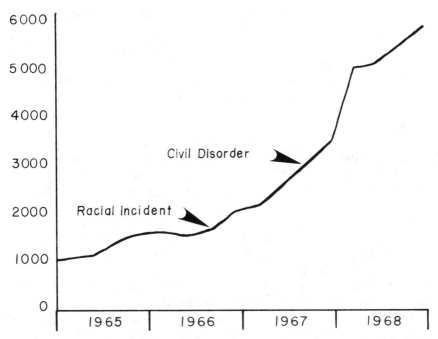

FIG. 5-1. New permits to purchase firearms in Detroit, Michigan (by quarter), 1965–1968. (Reproduced from Newton and Zimring, 1969: 22.)

suggest such a pattern. Indeed, people who expressed some fears about venturing out alone at night were somewhat *less* likely to own a gun than those who did not. Weapons ownership was also disproportionately *low* among people who had been burglarized or threatened with force in the previous year, and among those living in integrated neighborhoods. All these findings are directly opposite to what a fear and loathing interpretation would lead one to expect (Wright and Marston, 1975: 101–103).

Several other survey studies have reported similar patterns. For example, Williams and McGrath conclude from another analysis of the 1973 NORC data that "there is not a statistically significant degree of association between victim status and gun ownership" (1976: 27). Here, too, it is reported that there is a *"negative* relationship between fear in the neighborhood and gun ownership" (1976: 27–28). In contrast, Caetano (1979) used a broader measure of victimization (including victimization occurring over the previous 5 years rather than 1, and victimization of family and close acquaintances as well as of the respondent) but a substantially less compelling sample (467 night students at California State College, San Bernadino). He found a significant correlation (gamma = 0.24) between criminal victimization and gun ownership. This correlation, however, was somewhat less than half the correlation between parental and respondent gun ownership (gamma = 0.55). (There is considerable evidence from many sources that adult weapons ownership is a function of early socialization; see the following chapter.) Further, among several categories of respondents (women, the young, non-whites, and the lower classes), the relationship with gun ownership was either insignificant or reversed.

The most recent and most sophisticated analysis of the NORC weapons ownership data has been done by DeFronzo (1979), based on merged data from the 1973, 1974, 1976, and 1977 General Social Surveys. As in all previous NORC-based analyses, having been victimized by a crime had no statistically significant effect on handgun ownership (see also Garofalo, 1979). Likewise, the fear of crime had no statistically significant effect. "These findings provide no support for the popular belief that the fear of criminal victimization acts independently to increase the ownership of handguns in the population" (DeFronzo, 1979: 339).

Northwood, Westgard, and Barb (1978) have analyzed applications for permits to carry a concealed weapon in Seattle. Across the sample of applications analyzed, "only 18.5% . . . claim prior victimization as a reason for carrying a concealed weapon" (1978: 71), which suggests that "this factor alone is not sufficient to explain gun application behavior in general." In a further analysis, they looked at the relationship between per capita applications and the crime rate across Seattle census tracts. "The results suggest a low and statistically insignificant relationship to gun application rates. Thus, the notion that a 'crime threat' is a major determiner for people to arm themselves is not convincing" (1978: 71).

Bordua and Lizotte (1979) have analyzed the incidence of Firearms Owners Identification Cards (FOICs) across Illinois counties. (These cards are required for all legally possessed weapons in the state.) *No* measure of the county crime rate was significantly related to FOICs for either males or minors. Legal ownership among women was, however, significantly related to the cube of the county's violent crime rate and to the proportion of young blacks in the county. This analysis thus suggests that adult women, but not minors or adult men, tend to buy guns at least in part as a response to crime.

Individual-level survey data for Illinois have also been analyzed by Lizotte and Bordua (1980). Their data allow them to differentiate directly between weapons owned for sport and weapons owned for purposes of self-defense; the former outnumber the latter by about three to one. No measure of crime, victimization, perceived crime, proximity to blacks, fear, or racism correlates with ownership for sport, which is to say that the ownership of most weapons (the three-quarters majority) is independent of fear and loathing.

With regard to protection guns, "violent crime in the county is the only significant predictor" (Lizotte and Bordua, 1980: 239). Apparently, "people's defensive ownership of guns is totally a function of violent crime in the area. It is *not* an extension of a general home defense orientation or a product of any of the other variables in the model, such as violent attitudes or racism" (1980: 239). Defensive ownership was also uncorrelated with proximity to blacks, direct criminal victimization, fear of crime, and the perceived crime rate. Thus, even here, the bulk of the evidence is inconsistent with the fear and loathing theme.

One final effort to examine fear and loathing as a factor in the handgun trend is that of Clotfelter (1977). Six states with good time-series data on handgun sales were studied. Independent variables included violent crime rates (taken from *Uniform Crime Reports*) and indices of civil disorder events both for the states and for the nation as a whole. The findings provided only limited support for fear and loathing. Civil disorder incidents *for the country as a whole* "represent an important determinant of handgun demand," but "disorders *within a state* have no independent effect" (1977: 13, our emphasis). There was also *no significant effect* for violent crime rates: "The strong upward trend in [handgun] sales cannot be explained by . . . rising violent crime rates" (1977: 13). The time-series data (1977: Fig. 1) show an unmistakable spike centered on 1967–1968, with a general upward linear trend on either side of the spike. One interpretation is thus that there was a one-time surge in handgun demand corresponding approximately with the major civil disorders of the late 1960's, which is consistent with the fear and loathing hypothesis. But this finding obviously does not explain the persistence of the trend into the 1970's. As Clotfelter notes, "much of the demand for handguns remains unexplained, however, as illustrated by the strong upward trends in purchases over the last decade."

These are not the only studies that have looked at fear and loathing, but they adequately illustrate the general point, namely, that there is *no* credible study *anywhere* in the literature that shows, clearly and unmistakably, a fear and loathing effect in the weapons trend. This, of course, is not to say that there is no such effect, but only that no one has yet been able to find it.

Why not? The most parsimonious explanation, of course, is either that the effect does not exist or that it is so subtle as to escape detection by existing methods of research. In either case, it seems obvious that the overall contribution of fear and loathing to the recent "domestic arms build-up" is very much smaller than commonly suggested in the standard accounts. As Chapters 3 and 4 have argued, by far the largest share of the "excess' weaponry of the last decade must be ascribed to other sources, most of which are relatively benign from the societal viewpoint.

SIX

CHARACTERISTICS OF PRIVATE WEAPONS OWNERS

This chapter reviews the available research on characteristics of the people and households that possess weaponry, that is, how owners and nonowners differ in social background, locale, and personal outlooks. Our purpose is essentially to determine where in the society the private ownership of weapons is concentrated.

There are at least two important distinctions that need to be introduced. First is the distinction between *personal* and *household* ownership of weapons. It seems reasonable to assume that guns are owned by individuals, and it is the characteristics of these individuals that are at issue here. However, much of the available survey data on weapons ownership is based on a question that asks about guns kept *in the house,* whether they belong to the respondent or to some other family member. In turn, much of the descriptive literature on the correlates of ownership deals not with individual owners but with the characteristics of the households within which they reside—a separate matter.

Second, it is essential to distinguish among various *types* of private weaponry. Several distinctions might be considered in this context, for example, handguns versus shoulder weapons. Lizotte and Bordua (1980, and in press; Bordua and Lizotte, 1979), however, have made a persuasive case that the most critical distinction concerns the reasons that the weapon is owned: whether for sport and recreation, for protection and self-defense, or for illicit criminal purposes. Their research (reviewed in more detail below) strongly suggests that the characteristics of people who own weapons for sport and recreational purposes differ sharply from the characteristics of people who own protective or defensive weaponry. (It can also be assumed that the criminal ownership of weapons involves yet another qualitatively different type.) Unfortunately, most available research depends exclusively on the simple yes–no ownership question, such that all weapons owners, irrespective of their reasons for ownership, are treated equally.

The most recent nationally generalizable evidence on reasons for weapons

103

ownership was reviewed in the previous chapter (see Table 5-5). When the data for all types of guns are combined, slightly more than 70% of all owners give sport or recreation as their motive for possessing the weapon, and slightly less than 25% mention some sort of defensive or protective reason.[1] (The rest provide ambiguous responses or no response at all.) It follows, then, that most gun owners fall into the sport and recreational category, and, thus, that the available studies of weapons ownership (irrespective of type) are predominantly, but not exclusively, studies of sport and recreational owners. The presence within the gun ownership category of a substantial minority of people who own a weapon for other reasons, however, introduces more than a little ambiguity into many of the published results. For this reason, the following review places more emphasis on studies that maintain the distinction among ownership types and relatively less on studies that consider all gun owners equally, irrespective of their reasons for owning weapons.

LOCATIONAL VARIABLES: REGION AND CITY SIZE

All studies to have considered the matter report that weapons ownership is highest in rural areas and falls off as city size increases (e.g., Erskine, 1972; Hamilton, 1972: 546; Newton and Zimring, 1969; Wright and Marston, 1975). Evidence from the nationally representative survey by the National

---

[1] That most weapons are owned for recreational as opposed to defensive reasons is a common finding in the literature. In Bordua and Lizotte's Illinois survey, for example, recreational ownership exceeded defensive ownership by about 3 to 1. (This survey is reviewed in detail later in the chapter.) Deiner and Kerber (1979: 230) report that among their small sample of gun owners, "recreation . . . was the most frequently cited reason for owning a gun." Additional evidence on this point comes in the strong correlation between weapons ownership and hunting, the most common of the various gun sports. The following tabulation is based on the NORC General Social Survey for 1977, the only year in the series in which both a gun ownership and a hunting question were asked: *Do you (or your spouse) go hunting?*

Gun ownership	Yes	No	Total
Yes	85.4%	36.4%	50.7%
No	14.6%	63.5%	49.3%
N	444	1079	1518
%	29.2	70.8	

There are three findings of interest in this table. (1) Consistent with virtually all previous national household surveys, this too shows roughly half the households in the country possessing a weapon. (2) Roughly 30% of the national adult population hunts. This proportion is higher than would be expected on the basis of data on hunting licenses reviewed in Chapter 3 (an estimated hunting rate in 1975 of 132 hunters per 1,000 population). This implies either that many hunters are unlicensed or that many people who hunt do not hunt each and every year, or, of course, both. (3) Households with at least one hunter present are sharply more likely to own a weapon than households with no hunter present (85.4 vs. 36.4%), thus suggesting, again, a very strong link between recreational activities involving guns and weapons ownership.

Opinion Research Center (NORC) analyzed by Wright and Marston, revealed that the proportion owning any weapon falls off from 65.5% among rural residents to 30.5% of residents of cities with populations of 250,000 and above. The patterns for people owning only handguns are similar, but much less sharp: in the same data, the proportion owning a handgun ranges from 23.1% of the rural respondents to 15.3% of the urbanites. Thus, handgun ownership is rather more evenly distributed over city sizes than is the ownership of shoulder weapons, which tends to be sharply concentrated in smaller-sized areas.

The city-size pattern supports the contention that most private weaponry is owned for sport and recreational purposes, since most such purposes require access to open and unpopulated areas.[2]

[2] On the other hand, one must take care not to exaggerate. Skiing, for example, also requires access to "open and unpopulated areas," yet many city dwellers ski. Prime hunting land in upstate New York, to cite another example, is not more than a 2-hour drive from midtown Manhattan.

Direct evidence on hunting behavior by city size is contained in the NORC General Social Survey for 1977 (see footnote 1). The relevant tabulation from that survey based on the question "Do you (or your spouse) go hunting?" is as follows:

City size	Yes (%)	No (%)	N (= 100%)
Within SMSA[a]			
Over 250,000	12.7	87.3	267
50–250,000	21.3	78.7	160
Suburbs	20.4	79.6	358
Other incorporated	28.6	71.4	140
Other unincorporated	34.9	65.1	86
Not in SMSA			
10–49,999	37.4	62.6	99
2,500–9,999	44.4	55.6	99
< 2,500	40.3	59.7	72
Open country	50.8	49.2	246

[a] "SMSA" stands for Standard Metropolitan Statistical Area, which translates roughly into big cities and their surrounding counties.
Source: 1977 NORC GSS.

Again, several interesting points are revealed in this table. (1) Consistent with the point made in the text, hunting increases as city size decreases. The proportion who hunt is thus lowest among residents of large central cities (12.7%) and highest among people living in open country (50.8%). (2) The general pattern notwithstanding, there are nontrivial fractions who hunt in all categories of city size. Even in the largest central cities (size 250,000 and up), roughly one adult in eight hunts.

The tabulation below shows the relationship between city size and the proportion of people owning any weapon, as estimated from the combined NORC surveys for 1973, 1974, 1976, and 1977 (all surveys in the series containing the gun ownership question). As in all previous studies, ownership and city size are sharply and inversely related. In these combined data for

There is a similar consensus on the regional patterns in weapons ownership: private weaponry is more prevalent in the South (and West) than in other parts of the nation (e.g., Erskine, 1972; Newton and Zimring, 1969; Wright and Marston, 1975). The regional effect is also sizable: in Wright and Marston's data, the South–non-South difference amounted to 22 percentage points over all guns, and about 16 percentage points in handgun ownership.[3] Some re-

over 5000 respondents, the spread in ownership between most urban and most rural places amounts to 48 percentage points (27.2 to 75.3%).

The second column in this table shows the estimated ratio of hunters to gun owners over categories of city size; the cell entries show just the percentage of hunters (from the previous table) divided by the percentage of weapons owners (from this table). The general pattern revealed here is that this ratio increases as city size decreases, or, in other words, that the ownership of weapons for reasons other than hunting tends to be highest in the larger places. Still, even in the central cities, roughly half of all gun owners hunt.

City size	Percentage owning any weapon	Ratio of hunters to gun owners
Within SMSA		
Over 250,000	27.2	.47
50–250,000	44.5	.48
Suburbs	39.4	.52
Other incorporated	47.6	.60
Other unincorporated	56.6	.62
Not in SMSA		
10–49,999	54.8	.68
2,500–9,999	53.5	.83
< 2,500	66.9	.60
Open country	75.3	.67

[3] The following tabulation shows the proportion of weapons owners across regions, as estimated from the combined NORC data for all years in which the gun ownership question "Do you own a gun?" was asked:

Region	Own a gun?			
	Yes	No	NA	N (= 100%)
New England	23.8	75.8	0.4	277
Middle Atlantic	28.3	71.4	0.3	1029
E. North Central	50.2	49.1	0.7	1299
W. North Central	50.7	47.9	1.4	428
South Atlantic[a]	60.3	39.2	0.5	1156
E. South Central[a]	71.8	26.9	1.3	308
W. South Central[a]	55.1	44.3	0.6	474
Mountain	61.8	37.0	1.3	238
Pacific	39.4	59.4	1.2	779
Total	47.7	51.5	0.7	5988

[a] The South, by conventional definition.

search has attempted to link Southern weapons ownership with a presumed "regional subculture of violence." These studies are reviewed in detail later in this chapter.

Since the South is disproportionately rural, it may be wondered if the effects of region and city size are independent; the available evidence is that they are (e.g., O'Connor and Lizotte, 1978; Wright and Marston, 1975: Table 3). Indeed, both region and city size contribute significantly and independently to the probability of owning a weapon. Thus, weapons ownership is highest in rural Southern areas and lowest in the urbanized North.

Several investigators (e.g., Alviani and Drake, 1975: 1–2; Newton and Zimring, 1969) have noted the correspondence between regional rates of private weapons ownership and regional rates of violent crime. Specifically, the rate of violent crime (mainly homicide) is highest in regions where the private ownership of weapons is highest. On this basis, it is sometimes argued that private weapons ownership is a cause of violent crime. On the other hand, violent crime is much more prevalent in big cities than in rural areas, whereas for weapons ownership, just the opposite is true. As we discuss in some detail in the following chapter, the effect neither of region nor city size says *anything* about the possible causal relationships between private weaponry and criminal violence, a large number of assertions to the contrary notwithstanding.

SOCIAL STATUS: CLASS, RELIGION, RACE, AND SEX

In much of the popular literature on guns, there is a "commonly held viewpoint that [gun] ownership is more prevalent among . . . lower socio-economic classes" (Burr, 1977: 8). In contrast to this theme, there is substantial evidence that private weapons owners of all types are disproportionately affluent and middle class. In the Wright–Marston data, there was a 12-percentage-point difference in weapons ownership between the most and least prestigious groups. In the same data, there was nearly a 25-percentage-point difference between the most and least affluent, with ownership highest among the most affluent group (1975: Table 2). That weapons ownership tends to increase with income, or occupational prestige, or both, has subsequently been confirmed in several studies (e.g., Burr, 1977: 8; Lizotte and Bordua, 1980:

As in all other comparable data, the regional variation in weapons ownership is substantial. The lowest ownership rate comes among the New England states, and the highest, among the states in the East South Central region (Kentucky, Tennessee, Mississippi, and Alabama). The spread in ownership across these extreme cases amounts to 48 percentage points. Recoding the data into the conventional South and non-South categories, the ownership rates are 60.8 and 41.5%, respectively—broadly consistent with all other data.

237; O'Connor and Lizotte, 1978: Table 1). As far as we have been able to determine, no study has yet reported a contrary result.[4]

Effects of education on weapons ownership are less clear. Burr (1977) reports the regular pattern mentioned above, with ownership increasing as a function of years of education. In Wright and Marston's study, however, ownership was highest in the middle of the education distribution and generally lower at both extremes; and other investigators (e.g., Lizotte and Bordua, in press) report no significant educational effect.

Rather surprisingly, there is also a strong religious pattern in private weapons ownership, with white Protestants far more likely to possess a weapon than members of other religious groups (Wright and Marston, 1975; O'Connor and Lizotte, 1978: 424). Further, this effect is statistically independent of city size, region, and all measures of social status (Wright and Marston, 1975: Table 3) and is detectable both for all weapons and for handguns only. In magnitude, the religious effect rivals the effect of region; nonetheless, no further analysis of the religious effect, beyond that reported by Wright and Marston, has yet been published.[5]

The available evidence suggests no sharp or consistent differences in weapons ownership across racial groups. In the 1973 NORC data analyzed by Wright and Marston (1975), whites were slightly, but not substantially, more likely to own a weapon than non-whites. The data, however, revealed no difference in rates of handgun ownership. Burr (1977: 8) reports, on the basis of Florida data, that "a greater percentage of whites (47.3%) own handguns than do blacks (39.8%)." In contrast, an analysis of applications for permits to carry handguns in Seattle reports that "blacks are proportionally over-represented" among the applicant pool (Northwood, Westgard, and Barb, 1978: 70). Finally, there are some studies (e.g., Lizotte and Bordua, 1980: 237) that report insignificant race effects. Because some studies report ownership being higher among whites (by small margins), others report ownership higher among blacks (by small margins), and still others report no significant

---

[4] The income effect is readily detectable in the combined NORC data. Among the least affluent (total family incomes less than $3,000), 31.9% claim to possess a weapon; among the most affluent ($20,000 and above), the proportion is 55.2%—a spread of slightly more than 23 percentage points. Wright and Marston (1975) suggest several possible explanations of the income effect, perhaps the most plausible of which is that family weaponry is, in general, a discretionary purchase and thus tends to increase with family income.

[5] In the combined NORC data, the proportions owning any weapon are 54.7, 36.7, and 14.9% for Protestants, Catholics, and Jews, respectively. The Protestant–Catholic difference (18 percentage points) in these data is thus about as sharp as the South–non-South difference (19 percentage points). In contrast with the regional effect, however, virtually no literature is available on the religious effect. (For example, there is no literature at all arguing for a Protestant "subculture of violence.")

difference, the most prudent conclusion is very probably that weapons owner-ship is not linked in any important way to race.

As noted in the introduction, much of the available literature is based on surveys of household weapons ownership, and from these surveys the reported sex differences in weapons ownership are correspondingly small.[6] Studies that have included a question about *personal* weapons ownership, however, routinely report that ownership and use of weapons are sharply higher among males than among females (e.g., Kennett and Anderson, 1976; Lizotte and Bordua, 1980; Marks and Stokes, 1976; Northwood, Westgard, and Barb, 1978).

In general, the published literature strongly supports the conclusion that private weapons owners are predominantly rural and small-town middle-class Protestant males whose ownership of weapons is mostly for sport and recre-ational purposes. None of these relationships is perfect; in fact, most of them are fairly weak, and so there is substantial variation around this main theme. (There are, in other words, substantial numbers of weapons owners in all regions, all city sizes, and among all social, racial, and religious groups.) As to the conclusion itself, however, there is little serious empirical question.

THE SOUTHERN SUBCULTURE OF VIOLENCE

W. J. Cash, eminent observer of the American South, once remarked that "the South is another land, sharply differentiated from the rest of the American nation, and exhibiting within itself a remarkable homogeneity" (1940: vii). Around this belief has grown a large literature on Southern distinctiveness and culture (see Wright, Rossi, and Juravich, 1980, for a recent, though partial, review). One element of this distinctiveness is, as we have already noted, a substantially higher rate of personal weapons ownership in the South than elsewhere; another element, noted by many observers, is that the rates of interpersonal violence are also higher in the South than in other regions (e.g., Harries, 1974; Newton and Zimring, 1969). These facts have led several authors to argue that there is a distinctive "Southern subculture of violence"— that is, a package of cultural values transmitted within families and distinctive to the South that glorifies or condones violent behavior (e.g., Gastil, 1971; Hackney, 1969; Reed, 1971).

All the literature that has focused on this presumed subculture of violence

---

[6] In the combined NORC data, for example, which are based on a household ownership question, 53% of the males and 44% of the females report a weapon in the home. In contrast, studies based on individual ownership data routinely report that gun ownership is some four to five times more common among men than among women.

acknowledges that the simple zero-order effects noted above are not adequate, in and of themselves, for proving the subculture thesis. Region correlates with economic development, level of poverty, level of urbanization and industrialization, percentage non-white, and a large number of other factors that may account for the zero-order effects, independently of any subcultural explanation. (In less technical language, the distinctiveness of the South in rates of interpersonal violence may reflect only that the level of economic development is lower in the South than elsewhere and thus have nothing at all to do with violence-conducive subcultural values.) Thus, in advance of any further evidence, subcultural differences are but one among many plausible explanations of the regional effect.

Results of the initial empirical studies of the topic seemed to support the subcultural explanation (Gastil, 1971; Hackney, 1969). Both studies demonstrated a regional effect on the homicide rate that persisted even with certain relevant background variables held constant; that is, even net of various potential confounding effects (such as levels of socioeconomic status or percentage of non-whites), Southern states were found to have higher homicide rates than non-Southern states. But this is, as Loftin and Hill (1974) and Erlanger (1975) have pointed out, an extremely weak and indirect test of the subcultural explanation. In both analyses, the only measure of "Southern subculture" was region itself. Thus, both studies attribute to Southern subculture *all* of the regional effect *except* that portion due to the specific variables held constant in the regression analyses. This is a plausible attribution only if the control variables in the analyses exhaust all potential explanations of the effect other than subcultural differences—a very unlikely possibility. (There are also other, more technical, difficulties with both the Gastil and Hackney studies, reviewed thoroughly by Loftin and Hill, 1974.) Lacking any direct, independent measure of the values presumably contained within the subculture, neither study can be definitive about the contribution of these values to the regional differences in rates of interpersonal violence. It may thus be said that the Gastil and Hackney studies show results that are consistent with the "subculture of violence" hypothesis but inadequate to rule other plausible explanations out.

More recent and rather more sophisticated analyses show little or no support for the subcultural explanation, although none of the studies can be considered conclusive. Following procedures closely analogous to those of Gastil and of Hackney, but including more precisely defined situational variables among the regressor set, Loftin and Hill show no statistically significant residual effects for region in the state-by-state homicide rate, after relevant background variables have been controlled (1974: Tables 3 and 4). Indeed, most of the zero-order regional effect disappears with a control for the relative poverty levels across states. Contrasting with the Gastil–Hackney findings, these data therefore tend to support the conclusion that the Southern distinctiveness in interpersonal violence reflects mainly structural, situational, or socioeconomic factors, rather than subcultural ones.

However, even this may be a premature conclusion, as Loftin and Hill themselves point out: "The more appropriate conclusion is: our data and those analyzed by Gastil and Hackney are not adequate to delineate precise cultural and non-cultural effects" (1974: 722). The major shortfall in all such studies is the lack of a measure of regional culture that is independent of region itself.

The most recent inquiry into the subculture theory has been by O'Connor and Lizotte (1978). This analysis is based on survey data on individuals, rather than aggregate data on states (as were the studies by Gastil, Hackney, and Loftin and Hill). The approach of O'Connor and Lizotte has the advantage of avoiding certain aggregation effects that imperil the conclusions of the previous studies. Given the focus on data from individuals, the dependent variable in the analysis cannot be homicide *rate,* or, for that matter, any other measure of homicide, since murderers appear quite infrequently in any national sample, however large. Rather, the dependent variable is whether the respondent's household possesses a gun (more particularly, for the published part of the analysis, whether the household possesses a handgun). It is plausible, however, that a culture conducive to violence would support the ready availability of guns no less than their ready use as a means to settle interpersonal disputes; and, certainly, patterns of weapons ownership among individuals seem at least as plausible a test of the subcultural theory as homicide rates across states. Granting in advance, then, that the results from this study are not strictly comparable with the results reviewed above, we consider this test of the thesis as at least equally informative.

O'Connor and Lizotte reason, not unpersuasively, that if the regional distinctiveness in weapons ownership is a function of a violence-conducive subculture—a package of values transmitted within families as part of early socialization—then the effect for the region within which one was socialized would be greater than the effect for the region of current residence. Likewise, were the situational variables more important than those relating to the culture in which one was socialized, current residence should have the larger effect. The rationale here is obvious: the bulk of cultural learning takes place in early childhood, so if the tendency to own a weapon is a function of having been raised in a region-specific cultural setting, the region of birth should be a better predictor of weapons ownership than the region of current residence.

Data for the analysis were taken from the 1973 and 1974 NORC General Social Surveys; the dependent variable for the reported analysis is a dummy variable for pistol ownership. (The authors remark, however, that equivalent results were obtained when the ownership of any weapon was treated as the dependent variable.) Consistent with results reviewed earlier, the analysis showed a negative relationship with city size (both city size of present residence and city size of the respondent's residence at age 16), a sharp and positive relationship with income, and a strong positive effect on pistol ownership for being Protestant. The coefficient for region of *current* residence was also significant and in the expected direction (ownership significantly higher in the South); however, the coefficient for region of residence at age 16 was insignificant. These results thus appear to be more consistent with the "situational" than with the "cultural" explanation of the Southern distinctiveness in weapons ownership.

The effect for city size reported by O'Connor and Lizotte (1978) is consistent with the effect reported in all other studies: ownership is highest in rural places and falls off sharply as city size increases. The further interesting finding reported here is that, even net of the effects of city size of current residence (and other potentially confounding variables), there remains a strong, also negative, relationship with the size of the place where one was raised. That is, the more rural one's early environment, the more likely one will be to own a gun as an adult. This evidence is thus initially consistent with an argument, reviewed in more detail in the next section, that weapons ownership is a strong function of early socialization into what might be approximated by the term "gun culture"—a culture that glorifies not violence so much as rural values and activities and, specifically, the sporting uses of guns.

SOCIALIZATION

Much behavior of interest to the social sciences is demonstrably learned in the context of early childhood socialization. There is, for example, overpowering evidence that political party identification is mainly a result of early socialization; the evidence is simply that the party of one's parents is consistently the single best predictor of one's own party affiliation (e.g., Berelson, Lazarsfeld, and McPhee, 1954; Campbell *et al.,* 1956). The same is true of religious affiliation and, for that matter, many other things.

There is, in the same vein, substantial evidence that to an important extent private weapons ownership is also a function of early socialization into what may be called a gun culture. Some elements of this culture have been discussed in previous chapters.[7] A key value in this culture is the sporting use of weap-

---

[7] The following brief account of "the gun culture" is based mainly on impressionistic and episodic evidence. So far as we have been able to determine, no serious ethnographic study of this culture has ever been undertaken. Richard Hofstadter's well-known piece, "America As

ons—for hunting, target shooting, and other recreational purposes. The values of this culture are best typified as rural rather than urban: they emphasize independence, self-sufficiency, mastery over nature, closeness to the land, and so on. Within this culture, the ownership and use of firearms are both normal and normatively prescribed, and training in the operation and use of small arms is very much a part of what fathers are expected to provide to their sons—in short, this training is part and parcel of coming of age. The strong correlation between city size (both of current residence and of residence in one's youth) and weapons ownership is a good, if indirect, indicator of the predominantly rural nature of the culture in question (but see footnote 2).

As far as we have been able to determine, the first direct empirical evidence on the potential role of socialization in the private ownership of weapons is that of Marks and Stokes (1976). This research was not directly focused on correlates of weapons ownership, but rather on whether or not differential familiarity with firearms might be a plausible explanation for sex and regional differences in the suicide rate. Still, the findings are relevant to the concerns of this chapter. Data are based on questionnaires administered to students in two universities (one in Wisconsin, the other in Georgia), and so the sample is predominantly young.

One question asked whether the respondent had ever fired a gun; among a student sample, this is not an implausible indicator of "socialization" into firearms use. In the South, about 81% had (98% of the males, 59% of the females); in the North, 56% had (88 and 40% of the males and females, respectively). Notice that this pattern reproduces the known correlates of weapons ownership among adults (higher in the South and among males) and is thus consistent with an argument that ownership of weapons by adults is a function of early socialization.

Socialization into firearms use evidently begins at a relatively early age: among Southern males, for example, more than one-third of those who had ever fired a weapon (35.5%) reported first having fired one at age 9 or earlier, and 76% had fired a gun at least by age 12. Among Southern females, 43% had fired a gun before age 12. Outside the South, the equivalent percentages by the age of 12 are 55% for males and 42% for females. Large majorities of all groups (ranging from 66 to 94%) had first fired a gun at least before age 16. One obvious inference from these data is that large proportions of

---

A Gun Culture," is useful in this connection but is more in the nature of a diatribe than an empirical research study. Oddly enough, as the following review in the text makes plain, there is far more evidence on socialization into this culture than there is on the characteristics and values of the culture itself.

adult weapons-owners have experiences with the use of firearms stretching back well into childhood.

Virtually all (97%) of the respondents in the study who had ever fired a gun were introduced to small arms by men, mostly male relatives (typically, fathers). This, along with the tendency of men to own guns at a much higher rate, suggests that the gun culture is also heavily masculine as well as rural.

For most categories in the analysis, the tendency ever to have fired a weapon is strongly related to whether the respondent was reared in a home where guns were kept. Among Southern males reared in homes with a gun present, 99.4% (every respondent but one) had fired a gun; among Southern males reared in homes in which a gun was not owned, 91% had fired a gun. Thus, virtually all Southern males are exposed to weapons at an early age, whether their household possesses a gun or not. Among the remaining three groups (Southern females, non-Southern males and females), however, the effect of being reared in a gun-owning home is much stronger, with percentage differences in having fired a gun ranging from 23 to 35 points. Except for the Southern males, then, the evidence is strong that being reared in the gun culture (that is, in a household where guns are routinely present) is related to socialization into weapons use (that is, having at some time in early life fired a weapon). These results are also consistent with the argument that weapons ownership and use among adults are functions, at least in part, of socialization into the gun culture.

Several other studies have reported results consistent with the findings of Marks and Stokes, many showing even more directly the effects of early socialization on adult weapons ownership. For example, Deiner and Kerber (1979) have presented results from data on a small and nonrepresentative sample of Illinois men showing that "a major difference between gun-owners and nonowners was that the former group had been in a variety of situations which provided contact with guns" (1979: 230). In particular, gun owners in the study were much more likely to have grown up in rural areas and small towns than in the big cities (thus reproducing the common city-size result); further, and more relevantly, "eighty-six percent of the gun-owners' fathers owned guns, compared with only 30% for nonowners" (1979: 230). Also consistent with the findings of Marks and Stokes, 78% of the Deiner–Kerber gun owners had themselves owned a gun before age 18, again suggesting that socialization into gun use begins at an early age. Three additional findings of Deiner and Kerber are relevant to the socialization argument: (1) 43% of the owners had, as children, attended summer camps where shooting firearms was part of the program, compared with 22% of the nonowners. (2) 57% of the owners were military veterans, compared with 22% of the nonowners. (The effects of veteran's status on weapons ownership are considered in more detail later.) And (3) the gun owners were substantially more willing than the nonowners (92 vs. 52%) to purchase toy guns for their own children.

Caetano (1979) has reported additional results, unfortunately also based on a small atypical sample (in this case, 467 night students at Cal State, San Bernadino), that are consistent with the socialization argument. In this study, parental gun ownership and respondent gun ownership were correlated (gamma) at 0.55; parental ownership of weapons was thus, by far, the single best predictor of weapons ownership.

The most sophisticated, informative, and persuasive inquiry into socialization as an explanation of adult weapons ownership is the series of studies by Bordua and Lizotte (1979; Lizotte and Bordua, 1980, and in press). The first report in the series is based on county-level aggregate data for the state of Illinois. Illinois is one among several states that require some form of permit to possess any weapon legally; in Illinois, the requirement is for a "Firearm Owners Identification Card" (FOIC). In the Bordua and Lizotte analysis (1979), the number of such cards per county is treated as the dependent variable.

The analysis contains a large number of other county-level indicators, of which two groups are relevant to our topic. One is a set of indicators that index what the authors call "a firearms sporting culture"—that is, a cultural milieu that favors the sporting uses of weapons. In this case, the indicators are (1) the number of subscriptions to gun-sports magazines in the county; and (2) the number of hunting permits issued in the county in a single year (1973). A second set of indicators is constructed from county-specific murders, robberies, and aggravated assaults and thus indexes the county's violent crime rate. Both the crime and magazine variables are normed for county population.

Findings from the analysis are straightforward: "Our sporting culture variables are the only good predictors of male FOIC ownership. Hunting and sporting magazines both tend to drive up ownership. The crime rate of a county has no direct effect on male registered ownership" (Bordua and Lizotte, 1979: 162). Further, "for minors, the only predictor of FOIC ownership is adult male FOIC ownership, which has a strong positive effect" (p. 162). Among men and minors, then, FOIC ownership (in other words, legal ownership of weapons) responds as a variable far more strongly to the existence of a firearms sporting culture than to any indicator of violent crime. "We have found no empirical evidence at the aggregate level to support the assumption that men legally own firearms uniquely for protection as a response to violent crime" (1979: 162).

Findings for female FOIC ownership were rather different. Women's ownership, as men's, is related to hunting and the percentage of veterans in the county, and, like that of minors, is related to male ownership. For women, however, two additional factors are significant: the cube of the crime rate, and the percentage of young (18- to 34-year-old) blacks in the county. Thus, "other cultural and situational factors being equal, women seem to buy guns in response to crime" (1979: 163).

This aggregate analysis by Bordua and Lizotte therefore tends to support two conclusions: (1) that legal weapons ownership among men and minors is predominantly a function of exposure to and socialization into a gun-sports culture; and (2) that legal ownership among women responds in part to this culture *and* to crime or the fear of crime. The results for men and minors, of course, are broadly consistent with those of all other studies reviewed in this section.

A more detailed and fine-grained analysis, based on individual-level survey data, has also been published by these authors (Lizotte and Bordua, 1980). The study is based on 764 telephone interviews conducted in 1977 in Illinois. Respondents were first asked how many firearms they owned and, then, "For what purpose do you own the firearm(s)?" Respondents were probed for *all* reasons for firearms ownership, which means that both sporting and defensive ownership reasons could be given by any respondent. There are, thus, two dependent variables in the analysis: weapons ownership for sport and weapons ownership for self-defense. Any given respondent could be scored "yes" on either or both variables.

We note first that 18% of the respondents were scored as owning a gun for sport, and about 6% as owning a gun for defense.[8] The ratio of the two (roughly, 3 to 1) is thus consistent with all other data on the reasons for private weapons ownership (see e.g., Table 5-5, and footnote 1, this chapter). This comparison with previous findings cannot be exact, since in this study any respondent could possess a weapon for both reasons. Empirically, however, this outcome was exceedingly rare: "What is the probability of owning a gun for protection given the probability that a gun is owned for sport? The answer is zero. Owning a gun for protection is not a function of owning a gun for sport [and vice versa]" (Lizotte and Bordua, 1980: 240). As noted in the introduction to this chapter, these data strongly suggest that there are two distinct gun cultures—the first and substantially the larger being a culture of sport and recreation, and the second being a "culture" of defense.[9]

---

[8] We emphasize again that these figures refer to individual ownership of weapons. "While about 20% of respondents over age 18 own a gun, about 50% of families own at least one gun" (Lizotte and Bordua, 1980: fn. 2). These ownership data are thus broadly consistent with the available national survey data on the topic.

[9] "Culture" appears here in quotation marks because "there is no evidence of a subculture of defensive gun ownership. While we can locate a group of protective gun owners, there is no indication of contact among them. That is, having friends who own guns for protection

The authors' conclusion is that "those who own guns for sport are very different from those who own for protection" (1980: 240).

Analysis of these two categories of weapons ownership confirms this conclusion. "Income, sex, parents' gun ownership, and age at first gun are the only significant determinants of gun ownership for sport" (Lizotte and Bordua, 1980: 237). That is, ownership for sport increases with income (consistent with all previous research), is substantially higher among men than among women, is considerably higher among respondents reared in gun-owning households, and is also higher among people who themselves first acquired guns at relatively earlier ages. The conclusion is straightforward and thoroughly consistent with the socialization argument: "Gun ownership for sport is the result of financial status, sex, and the early socialization into gun use" (1980: 237).

Ownership for protection is entirely different and is predicted by none of the variables mentioned above: "Violent crime in the county is the *only* significant predictor of owning a gun for protection" (Lizotte and Bordua, 1980: 239; our emphasis). Of some additional interest is that gun ownership for defense "is not an extension of a general home defense orientation or a product of any of the other variables in the model, such as violent attitudes or racism" (1980: 239). Likewise, neither criminal victimization nor the perceived crime rate (i.e., fear of crime) predicted defensive ownership. The only distinguishing feature of the defensive gun owners in this study was that they resided in counties where the actual rate of violent crime was relatively high.

These findings allow us to qualify our conclusions about the effects of early socialization on adult weapons ownership in important ways that previous studies have not allowed. Primarily, there are two (legitimate) reasons for weapons ownership: sport and protection. Most gun owners—about three-quarters of the total—fall into the first of these categories, and their ownership of weapons is predominantly a function of early socialization into gun use. Thus, ownership for sport is essentially cultural in nature and reflects a package of values and favored activities passed from parents to children as part of coming of age. Ownership for protection, in contrast, is strongly determined situationally, responding mainly to the existence of violent crime, and largely (if not entirely) impervious to the effects of variables that account for sport ownership. As these data show clearly (at least for Illinois), sport owners and defensive owners are qualitatively different types.

does not predict the respondent's protective ownership" (Lizotte and Bordua, 1980: 239). However, some of these findings are recanted in a later "correction" (Lizotte, Bordua, and White, 1981).

A related theme in the socialization argument concerns military socialization into weapons ownership and use. That veterans are more likely than non-veterans to own a weapon has been reported in several studies (e.g., Erskine, 1972; Bordua and Lizotte, 1979; Newton and Zimring, 1969; Deiner and Kerber, 1979).[10] Several explanations for this effect have been offered: for example, that military experience socializes individuals directly into weapons use and that the socialization is then carried back to civilian life; or that veterans acquire guns while in the military and bring them back into civilian life; or that the military experience predisposes veterans to violent or authoritative outlooks, which in turn result in civilian weapons ownership.

Lizotte and Bordua (in press), in contrast, have considered the possibility that the relationship is spurious and that it reflects a process of self-selection into the military in the first place. The argument, in short, is that military service appeals preferentially to people from rural backgrounds. "Hence, veterans would be more likely to have been socialized into gun use at an early age, and more likely to continue this usage later in life" (in press: 2). The evidence from the Illinois phone survey is consistent with this interpretation. When the relevant socialization variables are held constant (parental gun ownership, age at first gun, etc.), the effect for veteran's status drops to insignificance. The most plausible interpretation is thus that early socialization into gun use predisposes individuals to enlist in the armed services *and* to own guns as adults, with no independent effect for veteran's status when early socialization is held constant.[11]

One additional strand of evidence worth reviewing here concerns how privately owned weapons are acquired and disposed of. Such evidence as there is on this topic (and, sadly, there is not very much) shows a very extensive "swap" market in private arms—which in turn suggests that private owners are known to one another and enter into interactions and exchanges on the basis of their gun ownership. Burr (1977) has presented evidence on the private acquisition of handguns in Florida: of the 433 handguns in his analysis, 43% were purchased from a retail dealer and 6% were bought from a pawn shop; thus, slightly less than half the handguns were acquired through normal retail channels. Roughly 16% were bought from a private party, 15% were received as gifts, and 7% were acquired through trades or exchanges. (The

---

[10] Two of the NORC General Social Surveys have both weapons ownership and a question on veteran's status. Among the veterans, 56% reported owning a household weapon; among the rest of the sample, the proportion was 47%. The difference is thus modest but consistent with other studies.

[11] The National Rifle Association has noted an interesting implication of the Lizotte–Bordua finding. The finding implies, rather directly, that early socialization into the gun culture predisposes individuals to enlist in the armed forces later in life, which suggests that the gun culture is positively functional for the success of the volunteer army.

rest were acquired in a variety of odd-lot fashions.) Thus, a sizable proportion of the "flow" in handguns takes place outside the usual retail channels, consistent with the argument of a gun culture.

Burr also inquired whether his respondents had ever sold or disposed of a handgun; 333 "disposed" handguns are represented in the sample. Of these, only 9% had been sold to a firearms dealer. The largest share (37%) had been sold to another private party, 11% had been traded, 2% had been pawned, and 16% had been given away as gifts. Rather surprisingly, about 10% had been "disposed of" by theft, and the remainder are scored as "other." So here, too, the evidence for a private "swap" market in firearms among gun owners is substantial.

The only recent national evidence on this topic is contained in the 1978 DMI survey discussed in previous chapters. The DMI format gives respondents "a list of places where guns can be obtained," then asks: "Please indicate the place where your family's last firearm was obtained." Results are very close to the Burr data for Florida handguns: 35% were obtained from a sporting goods or department store, 19% from a gun shop, and 2% from a pawnshop, for a total of 56% obtained through usual retail channels. Two percent were obtained at a gun show, 19% had been received as gifts, and 13% had been obtained through private sale or trade. (Again, the remainder are scored as "other" or as a refusal to answer the question.)[12]

The lessons from these "hard" data are reinforced by an enormous amount of impressionistic evidence on the private "swap" market in firearms. Virtually every gun-sports magazine runs a classified section where private owners advertise their willingness to trade. This private "swap" market is sufficiently extensive that there are entire publications devoted exclusively to servicing it. One such is a bimonthly magazine in newspaper format entitled *Shotgun News,* which advertises itself as "The Trading Post for Anything that Shoots." The typical issue consists mainly of small classified ads, most apparently placed by private owners, announcing firearms wanted or offered. The issue for 15 September 1980 runs to 224 pages and does not appear to be atypical in the least.

In summary, various fragments of evidence suggest the existence of a "gun culture," one that is predominantly male and rural in orientation and

---

[12] Newton and Zimring (1969: Ch. 3) present similar evidence from the 1968 Harris poll on "How Firearms Are Acquired." Their conclusion: "Almost half of all long guns, and more than half of all handguns, are acquired secondhand. New firearms and a large number of used firearms are purchased from sporting goods stores, hardware stores, and other firearms dealers. But about half of secondhand firearms are acquired from friends or other private parties" (1969: 15).

It has been pointed out by Burr and others that much firearms acquisition thus takes place outside "regulatable" channels, that is, as sales or trades between private individuals.

that glorifies the use of weaponry in sport. There is also substantial evidence (unfortunately, none based on nationally representative data) that early socialization into this culture is the predominant explanatory factor in private weapons ownership and use among adults, particularly among adult men who own weapons for sporting purposes. Ownership among adult women is apparently rather more complicated, responding in part to these socialization effects but also to crime or the fear of crime. Finally, there is no evidence that the ownership of weapons for self-defense results from early socialization.

PERSONALITY CHARACTERISTICS

Although there is a rather extensive speculative literature on the personality characteristics of private weapons owners (e.g., Daniels, Gilula, and Ochberg, 1970; Sherrill, 1973; Stickney, 1967), virtually nothing of empirical substance is known about this topic. The themes of the speculative literature are well known and, with few exceptions, condemnatory and derogatory. In one view (the psychoanalytic), weapons are phallic symbols representing male dominance and masculine power. A related theme concerns the presumed need for power and virility. Fear, psychological insecurity, authoritarianism, a tendency to violence, generalized pessimism, and so on, are also commonly advanced as personality abnormalities to explain weapons ownership.

Contrasting these themes, such evidence that exists suggests no sharp or distinctive personality differences between gun owners and nonowners.

The common hypothesis, that fear, in general, and fear of crime, in particular, would be correlated with weapons ownership, is contradicted by all available studies (e.g., DeFronzo, 1979; Lizotte and Bordua, 1980; Williams and McGrath, 1976; Wright and Marston, 1975); in fact, most of these studies report a slight tendency for weapons ownership to be *lower* among the more fearful.

Williams and McGrath (1976) have derived five personality or quasi-personality measures from the NORC General Social Survey data and examined their correlation with household weapons ownership. Fear, as already noted, was significantly correlated with weapons ownership, but in the opposite direction. Victimization by crime was *not* significantly correlated with weapons ownership (see also DeFronzo, 1979; Wright and Marston, 1975). There was a moderately strong negative correlation with a measure of sociopolitical liberalism (liberals being less likely to own guns). But this effect was reduced to statistical insignificance when city size was controlled, suggesting that the correlation with liberalism is spurious. A measure of violence-proneness was positively correlated with weapons ownership in the anticipated direction, but the correlation (gamma $= 0.2$) is modest at best. Finally, pessimism was found to be *negatively* correlated with ownership (gamma = −0.16): pessimists, that is, are slightly *less* likely to own guns. With the exception of violence-proneness, then, all the remaining effects are either insignificant or run in the direction opposite to that posited in the speculative literature.

Much the same results are reported in what is, to our knowledge, the only other empirical study of the topic, an analysis of 37 male gun owners and a matched sample of 23 nonowners published by Deiner and Kerber (1979). Some of these results were reviewed above. The study included a large number of personality measures, most of which were adapted from items from the California Psychological Inventory. Findings were straightforward: "This study demonstrates that gun ownership per se is *not* indicative of unusual motivations or of deviant personality characteristics" (1979: 237). There were some differences of potential interest: for example, "gun owners tended to be more open-minded and tended to have a higher need for power;" also, the gun owners were less sociable and affiliative (1979: 234). But these differences were modest, and the results for the gun owners were all well within the "normal" (vs. "abnormal") range. In sum, "there was no evidence in the present study that the average gun owner exhibits atypical personality characteristics" (1979: 236).

Although the Deiner–Kerber data are hardly definitive (indeed, they are scarcely better than nothing at all), these authors nonetheless have what we would consider to be the last word on the topic. Their article concludes with this observation: "Since about one-half of the households in the U.S. contain a gun, it seems somewhat unrealistic to attribute severe abnormal characteristics to the average gun owner (unless one is willing to see considerable pathology in most people)" (1979: 236).

CONCLUSIONS: THE "TYPICAL" GUN OWNER

We were once again proven a savage, uncontrollable, unpredictable, gun-ridden, and murderous people. . . .

> Robert Coles, commenting on
> Charles Whitman's slayings at
> the University of Texas.

Could any response be more American than that of the two New York youths who shot and killed a storekeeper because they asked for apple pie and he had offered them Danish pastry instead? Or the husband who shot and killed his wife for being thoughtless enough to run out of gas on the way home?

> Robert Sherrill, in *The
> Saturday Nite Special*, p. 5.

In the popular literature on guns (and even in much of the scholarly literature), the "typical" private weapons owner is often depicted as a virtual psychopath—unstable, violent, dangerous. The empirical research reviewed in this chapter leads to a sharply different portrait. The key findings are described below.

Most private weaponry is possessed for reasons of sport and recreation; sport guns apparently outnumber defensive guns by roughly three to one. The uses of weaponry for sport are correlated with city size, but not perfectly; large numbers of sport users can be found even in the largest central cities. Relative to nonowners, gun owners are disproportionally rural, Southern, male, Protestant, affluent, and middle class. Most adult weapons owners were socialized into the ownership and use of weapons during their early childhood and thus have experience in the use of weaponry spanning virtually the whole of their lives. There is no evidence suggesting them to be an especially unstable or violent or maladapted lot; their "personality profiles" are largely indistinct from those of the rest of the population.

SEVEN

ON CRIME AND PRIVATE WEAPONS

It is often remarked that the United States is among the most heavily armed private populations in the Western world, and, further, that the rates of criminal (and accidental) violence are higher here than virtually anyplace else. The relationship between these two facts is the topic of this chapter.

At least three distinct relationships between violent crime and the incidence of private weaponry have been hypothesized. First, it is possible that private weaponry is an important *cause* of criminal violence. This, for example, is the theme enunciated in a chapter title from the Newton–Zimring (1969) report: "More Firearms, More Firearms Violence." The underlying idea is that as more firearms are available, more crime comes to be committed with them. This view posits that much criminal violence is not intentional, but rather evolves in the "heat of the moment" and becomes criminal (e.g., assaultive or homicidal) only because the instruments of violence (firearms) are readily at hand. (On this subject, see Chapter 10.)

Second, it is possible that private weaponry is an important *effect* of criminal violence. This theme was reviewed in some detail in Chapter 5, and indirectly in Chapter 6. The general idea in this view is that people arm themselves as a way to defend against crime, violence, and the related pathologies of modern life.

Still a third possibility is that private weaponry is an important *deterrent* to criminal violence. As people arm themselves more heavily, their risk from criminal violence is correspondingly reduced.

It must be noted that these are not mutually exclusive possibilities. Certainly, at least some crimes occur only because the means with which to commit them are available. Likewise, at least some people purchase weapons in response to criminal violence. As intimated in the previous chapter, this may be especially true of the recent acquisitions of defense weapons among women. Finally, there is no doubt that at least some crimes at some times and some places are deterred because the potential victim is armed. The issue here, as elsewhere in this volume, concerns the relative proportionalities involved.

Further, all three hypothesized relationships could operate simultaneously. Crime, let us suppose, increases for whatever reason. As one response, the purchase of weapons for defensive reasons increases. The then-enhanced presence of private weaponry acts as a deterrent to some crimes (e.g., rape, burglary, and robbery) but functions to increase the prevalence of other crimes (assault, homicide, and firearms suicide). In this case, private weaponry would *respond* to some crimes, *deter* others, and *cause* still others, all at the same time.

Aside from the possibility that all three hypotheses could well be true, there are other serious barriers to choosing decisively among them. Some problems are strictly logical. For example, a deterred crime is a relatively undetected crime. This would be less true of crimes deterred "in process" (i.e., burglars frightened off by homeowners brandishing weapons) because, presumably, at least some such incidents would be reported to the police. But crimes that are never even attempted because of advance knowledge that the potential victim is armed (i.e., the burglary that does *not* occur because the homeowner is a well-known marksman) would never show up in any data source. Furthermore, even if it could be shown that certain types of crimes were just as common in areas with a high density of private weaponry as in areas where this density is low, the argument might still be made that the rate of crime would be even *higher* in the heavily armed areas if the citizenry were not quite so well armed. As is well known, the deterrence effect even of relatively direct criminal sanctions (e.g., sentencing) is notoriously difficult to estimate. Estimating the deterrent effects of private weaponry is certain to be more difficult still.

Other barriers are more methodological in character. First is the age-old problem of inferring cause from correlation. Even if it could be shown that violent crime was highest in areas where the private possession of weapons was highest, it would not be clear whether weaponry was causing crime, or crime was causing people to arm themselves in protection against it, or, of course, both.

It is also possible that such a relationship would be spurious. To cite one possible example, crime tends to increase as economic conditions deteriorate. Following a theme noted in an earlier chapter, it is also likely that hunting for meat increases as economic conditions deteriorate. Extrapolating from these possibilities, one might expect both high rates of crime and high rates of weapons purchases to occur in economically depressed areas—for example, the South. In this example, there would be a detectable *correlation* between crime and weaponry across region, but no *causal* relationship; rather, the correlation would be the spurious result of both variables being causally linked to underlying economic conditions.

One immediate implication of these points is that even demonstrable correlations between the density of private weapons and the crime rate over relatively large and heterogeneous geographical aggregates (e.g., nations, regions, states, and even counties) are, in themselves, relatively noninformative with respect to the issues of concern in this chapter. Even if the imputation of cause in such data were not a problem (and, of course, it always is), such large aggregates are far too gross and differ in too many (typically uncontrolled) ways for such comparisons to have much meaning.

Consider the extreme, but not uncommon, case of international comparisons. Much is often made, for example, of comparisons between the United States and the United Kingdom, or between the United States and other Western democracies. In general, the comparison consists of a simple note to the effect that there are more guns, and more gun violence, in the United States than somewhere else, and this is, in turn, taken as evidence that guns are a cause of crime and violence. There are at least two additional serious problems in taking these comparisons as evidence for a causal relationship between private weaponry and crime:

1. Cases for comparison are chosen purposively and selectively; different choices lead to different conclusions. As Bruce-Biggs (1976) has noted, for example, the density of private weaponry (i.e., proportional weapons possession by households) is at least as high in Norway and Switzerland as it is in the United States, but rates of criminal violence are very low in both nations.[1] In sharp contrast to the U.S.–England or U.S.–Canadian comparisons, the comparison with these nations suggests that there is nothing intrinsic to a high rate of private weapons possession that increases criminal violence. One may thus come to entirely opposite conclusions depending solely on which other nation is contrasted with the United States.

2. In general, any two nations (or, for that matter, any two regions, states, or counties) will differ in a large number of ways over and beyond differences in weapons ownership and in the local crime rate. Such differences may be historical, legal, cultural, or social and are generally manifold and multifaceted, both in nature and in effects. Strictly speaking, all such factors that might themselves affect the incidence of crime would have to be held constant before the direct effects of private weaponry on crime could be legitimately detected. Stated more directly, there are many differences between, say, the United States and England that *might* contribute to the difference in crime rate. In the absence of controls for these other potential causative factors,

---

[1] The high rate of weapons possession by households in these nations is, of course, a reflection of their policies regarding an armed reserve militia. See Bruce-Biggs (1976) for details and some interesting commentary on international gun comparisons in general.

the inference that the difference in crime results from differences in weapons ownership is gratuitous. To a greater or lesser extent, the same would be true of any two regions, states, counties, or other gross geographical aggregates.

The conclusion derived from these purely methodological considerations is that zero-order comparisons (holding none of the other potentially important variables constant) of weapons ownership and crime over large geographical aggregates tell us little or nothing about the possible causal relationship between these two factors. Unfortunately, this is the most common research design employed in this area of the literature.

In general, one's statistical ability to control many factors simultaneously increases with sample size; thus, legitimate causal inferences about private weaponry and crime are more readily made if the number of individual geographical aggregates being analyzed is relatively large. This would, for obvious reasons, tend to rule out regions of the country, and possibly even states, as useful units for such an analysis. In this vein, cities and counties are more likely and potentially more informative possibilities, and some city- and county-based studies have been undertaken, as reviewed below. Such studies have the further advantage that the units of analysis are smaller and more homogeneous; as a general rule, one's confidence in causal inference from ecological (that is, aggregative) correlation increases as the homogeneity of the underlying units increases.

However, using cities or counties as units in an analysis of the effects of private weaponry on crime, one encounters yet another formidable methodological problem, namely, getting reliable city-by-city or county-by-county estimates of the rate at which private weapons are possessed. Unlike crime data, which are routinely recorded for both city and county levels, there are no readily available data anywhere that show city- or county-level weapons ownership rates, least of all over large numbers of units. Further, the expense of generating such data for a large sample of cities or counties is insurmountably prohibitive. Comparative large-sample studies of cities or counties as units are, therefore, usually based on highly inferential and potentially quite unreliable estimates of across-unit differences in weapons ownership.

As previous comments suggest, most research that has looked at crime or violence as a function of private weapons ownership is based on aggregative data (data on geographical aggregates, not on individuals). One reason for this is that although in absolute terms, there is "a lot" of criminal violence in the United States, there is, proportionally, very little. We note in Chapter 8 that there are about a million "serious gun incidents" per year (this, calculated with the broadest possible definitions). In contrast, the total stock of private weaponry is on the order of 120 million guns. The proportion of gun offenders among private gun owners is therefore extremely low, and consequently few or no firearms offenders appear in population surveys of the average size. For this and other reasons (for example, the possible reluctance of respondents to report incidences of violent criminality among household members), the possibility of addressing the issue of private guns as a cause of criminal violence directly via population surveys appears to be quite limited. As a result, virtually all relevent studies are aggregative in nature and based on comparisons of rates (rates of crime on the one hand, rates of private weaponry on the other, both calculated over some geographical aggregate). This poses one final problem worth discussing in advance of the literature review itself, namely the problem of "connecting" private weaponry with crime when there is no direct evidence on the connection.

To illustrate with an example from the literature noted in Chapter 6, the South has a higher rate of private weapons ownership than any other U.S. region; the homicide rate is also higher in the South than elsewhere, as is the proportion of homicides committed with firearms (e.g., Newton and Zimring, 1969: 75). Thus, one might conclude (as Newton and Zimring do) that "more guns" equal "more gun crime." But how firm is this connection? First, the distinctiveness of the South in private weapons ownership is far sharper for shoulder weapons than for handguns; in Newton and Zimring's data, handgun ownership was actually higher in the West and Midwest than in the South. Yet most homicides involving firearms are committed with handguns, and this is just about as true in the South as in other regions. It seems rather tenuous to attribute homicide to the disproportionate ownership of a class of weaponry that is seldom involved in homicide. Further, in the South as elsewhere, weapons ownership (of all types) is sharply higher in rural than in large urban areas, whereas criminal violence (in the South as elsewhere) is concentrated in the large cities. Again, it seems rather tenuous to link urban murders with the ownership of guns in small-town and rural areas. But tenuous links of precisely these sorts are directly implied in the kinds of regional comparisons being discussed.

There is persuasive evidence in the literature that the Southern distinctiveness in homicidal violence results mainly from the higher level of impoverishment and generally lower socioeconomic conditions of the region (Loftin and Hill, 1974). This conclusion is plausible because crime everywhere (more particularly, violent crime of the sort at issue here) is far higher among the economically marginal than among the stable middle class. The Southern distinctiveness in private weapons ownership, in contrast, is almost certainly a function of differential early socialization into gun use for sport and the readier accessibility in the South of areas where the sporting use of weapons is possible. To the extent that these two points are valid, the correspondence of high levels of weapons ownership and high levels of criminal violence in the South relative to other regions is purely fortuitous and, in itself, says nothing about any possible causal relationship between private weaponry and crime.

IS CRIME A CAUSE OF PRIVATE WEAPONRY?

The role of crime and violence in spurring demand for private weaponry was considered in some detail in earlier chapters, and only a brief summary of relevant findings is necessary here. About three-quarters of private arms are owned for sport, recreational, or collecting reasons; the rest are owned for self-defense. At least some defensive weapons ownership, especially in rural, isolated areas, would be for defense against animals rather than other people. Proportionally, then, weapons owned primarily or exclusively for self-defense against other people probably amount to not more than 10–20% of the total private arms stock. It is, of course, possible (although not logically necessary) that many or most of these 10–20% are owned as a reaction either to crime or the fear of crime.

There is considerable evidence that the criminally victimized are *not* any more likely than the nonvictimized to possess a private weapon (DeFronzo, 1979; Lizotte and Bordua, 1980; Northwood, Westgard, and Barb, 1978; Williams and McGrath, 1976; Wright and Marston, 1975). Moreover, there is evidence that *fear* of crime is also not directly or strongly linked to weapons ownership (DeFronzo, 1979; Lizotte and Bordua, 1980; Wright and Marston, 1975). On the other hand, Bordua and Lizotte (1979) do find a significant correlation between county crime rates and legal weapons ownership among women across Illinois counties. In their individual-level survey data for the state, they find that violent crime in the county is a significant predictor of gun ownership for defense. Interestingly, in this survey, direct criminal victimization was not related to owning a defensive weapon, and neither was the respondent's stated fear of crime. Thus, one *cannot* attribute the correlation between gun ownership and county crime rate in these data to ownership among the criminally victimized. Rather, the correlation is apparently due to ownership among nonvictims living in the high-crime counties. Further, those most fearful of crime are not disproportionately represented among defensive weapons owners. In general, these findings are similar to those reported by Wright and Marston (1975) from national data on gun ownership in the large cities and their suburbs. One possible scenario to explain this pattern of results is that some people living in areas of higher-than-average criminality (but not those who have actually been victimized) get worried about their readiness to deal with a criminal attack, consequently arm themselves with a defensive weapon, and, then, because they are armed, fear crime less. The absence of an effect for fear of crime, that is, may reflect only that the initially most fearful arm themselves and then feel psychologically safer because of it.

Why are the criminally victimized themselves not more likely to possess a gun? One possibility, perhaps remote, is that their guns are among the items taken in the victimization. In this connection, it is useful to recall the finding from Burr's (1977) analysis of private handguns in Florida: about 10% of the handguns ever disposed of by his respondents were lost through theft. Another possibility is that criminal victimization is concentrated among categories of people (for example, women) who have never been socialized to use guns, or among other categories (for example, the old) who doubt their ability to use a weapon effectively, or among others (for example, the poor) who are unable to afford the price. Still another possibility is that the criminally victimized learn through first-hand experience the futility of private weaponry as a crime deterrent and thus do not bother to arm themselves, despite their victimization. Additional possible explanations could, of course, be suggested, but there is little or nothing in the published literature that would allow one to choose among them.

Thus, although there is at least some contrary evidence, the bulk of the available research suggests that crime, fear of crime, and related variables are in themselves not very important factors in most private weapons ownership. Most guns are owned for sport and recreation, and there is neither reason nor evidence to suggest crime as a factor in this type of ownership. At least some guns (and a substantial fraction of handguns, perhaps as many as 40–50%) are owned primarily for defense, and living in a high-crime area seems, at least in the one available study that differentiates between sport and defensive weapons, to be a significant factor in the ownership of weapons of this type. There is no evidence to show that the criminally victimized are more likely to own a gun, however, so the dynamics of the "crime and defensive weapons" equation are rather more complex than simply "get robbed, then buy a gun."

IS PRIVATE WEAPONRY A CAUSE OF CRIME?

> There was a domestic fight. A gun was there. And then somebody was dead. If you have described one, you have described them all.

This quotation from a televised interview with the Chief of the Homicide

Section of the Chicago Police Department was first cited in Newton and Zimring (1969: 43). It has since been widely cited throughout the literature as an epigrammatic, but nonetheless accurate, account of the etiology of much criminal violence. The essentials of the underlying theory of criminal violence are these: Much interpersonal violence in the society is *not* the result of premeditated intentionality on the part of the perpetrator, but rather arises in disputes, altercations, barroom fights, disagreements and fights between spouses, and other relatively trivial circumstances. Such disputes arise in one of two conditions: either a gun is present, or it is not. In the second condition, the parties dispute, then come to their senses, and except for the heightened interpersonal animosity, little harm is done. In the first condition, the parties dispute, blast away, and then come to their senses. By then, however, someone is injured or dead, and what would have been a minor dispute has been transformed, merely by the availability of a firearm, into an aggravated assault or homicide. In this view, then, the privately owned firearm is an important cause of criminal violence; it turns otherwise harmless disputes into violent criminal attacks.

Similar arguments are sometimes also made for robbery, rape, and a few other classes of crime. In these cases, it is thought that firearms, especially handguns, give potential offenders the courage (and means) to do what they would otherwise not be capable of doing. Lacking firearms, offenders would lack the psychic strength to engage in criminally violent acts.

A third argument in the same vein is that firearms themselves catalyze violent or aggressive tendencies. In other words, the presence of a gun pushes a potentially violent or aggressive person past the threshold between wanting to respond violently and actually responding in that fashion.

Thus, for these and a few other reasons, it is often argued that guns are themselves a cause of violent crime, that in the absence of guns much of what is now violent crime would be qualitatively different and, indeed, essentially benign. Therefore, if there were fewer guns in private hands, less criminal violence would be committed.

Initially, there would seem to be a certain logic to these points of view. Certainly, the presence of a firearm is a necessary (if not sufficient) condition for its use as an instrument of criminal violence. If there were no guns at all, then, certainly, no crimes could ever be committed with them. Given the numbers of guns already available, however, and the evident impossibility of removing more than a fraction of them from potential criminal abuse, the more serious research question is whether some reduction in the incidence of private weaponry would be followed by some similar reduction in the incidence of criminal violence. However, the possibilities for experimentally manipulating the rates of private weapons ownership are limited or nonexistent, and, further, few or no successful legislative efforts have achieved this end (see Chapter 13), least of all recently. Therefore, the only practical way to investigate this issue is to see whether there is less violent crime in areas with fewer privately owned weapons, and, of course, vice versa. But this design, in turn, is imperiled by the several inferential and methodological problems discussed at the beginning of this chapter. The implication, confirmed below, is that existing research is *not* definitive with respect to whether private weaponry is a cause of criminal violence.

As in many other areas of the literature, the first sustained empirical foray into these issues is that of Newton and Zimring (1969: Ch. 11). The chapter, "More Firearms, More Firearms Violence," uses three approaches to assess the causal impact of private firearms on criminal violence. "All approaches," they say, "provide evidence that the arms buildup, if it is partly a response to increased violence, also has contributed to it" (1969: 69).

The first approach is a case study of arms and violence in Detroit. The data show a sharp increase in the number of handgun permits issued in Detroit from 1965 to 1968; in 1965, about 5000 such permits were issued, and in 1968, nearly 18,000 (1969: 70). (On the implications of this increase, see also Chapter 5). The number of accidental firearms fatalities also increased during the same period, from 10 in 1965 to 32 in 1968. Thus, "firearms accident rates increased markedly during this period of surging urban armament" (1969: 70).

There are several problems with this conclusion. First, the data on "surging urban armament" are for handgun permits issued and are thus only an indirect indicator of the trend in handguns actually owned. (There is apparently no evidence on the number of people who do acquire a handgun once they have acquired a handgun permit. Presumably, the percentage is large, but it must be something less than 100%.) The data on fatal firearms accidents, however, are for all accidents reported, irrespective of type of weapon. Thus, there is apparently no way to discern whether the noted increase in fatal accidents is a rise in fatal *handgun* accidents, as their argument implies, or in accidents involving shoulder weapons.

A further problem is that the permit evidence is for the city of Detroit, whereas the data on accidental deaths are for the whole Wayne County area (which includes Detroit and 10 other relatively large communities). Whether the increase in accidental deaths *and* the handgun build-up were both concentrated in the same place therefore cannot be determined from these data.

A final point is that although the conclusion is given in terms of an increasing firearms accident *rate,* the data are the absolute numbers of accidents and are not converted to a rate. Presumably, the appropriate rate would in this case be the rate of fatal firearms accidents per handgun-owning household. Unfortunately, no one knows for sure how many Detroit households possessed a handgun in the early 1960's (Newton and Zimring do not report an estimate).

But we can estimate the number on the basis of a few assumptions. The 1960 population of the city of Detroit (*not* the surrounding metropolitan area) was about 1,670,000 people. In the same year, there were, on average, 3.33 people per household, which suggests roughly 502,000 Detroit households in 1960. Table 5-3 shows that among large non-Southern cities, the proportion of households owning a handgun was 0.077 in 1959. Simple multiplication thus gives an estimated 38,700 handgun-owning households in Detroit in 1960.

Suppose now that the number of handgun-owning households increased by 2000 per year in the years from 1961 to 1964, such that by 1964, it stood at 46,700. According to Newton and Zimring, an additional 5000 were added in 1965. (We are here assuming one permit per household.) The total in 1965 therefore stands at 51,700, and the 10 accidental firearms deaths reported for 1965 therefore represent a *rate* of 10/51,700, or approximately 2 accidental firearms deaths per 10,000 handgun-owning households. By 1968, again according to Newton and Zimring, handgun-owning households were growing by about 18,000 a year. Although it is difficult to infer the precise numbers from their graph, let us assume that the 1966, 1967, and 1968 additions were 6,000, 12,000, and 18,000, respectively, consistent with the notion of a "surge." This brings the 1968 total to 87,700 handgun-owning households (which would, as an aside, still represent only 17.5% of all Detroit households, within the realm of plausibility). Under these assumptions, the firearms accidental death rate in 1968 would be 32/87,700, or approximately 4 accidental firearms deaths per 10,000 handgun-owning households. This rate is very definitely an increase over that estimated for 1965; in fact, it is twice the 1965 rate, which is in some sense a "marked" increase. What these numbers show, which Newton and Zimring's numbers do not show, is that in both years, something in excess of 99.9% of all handgun-owning households did *not* experience a fatal firearms accident. These data are thus consistent with an argument that "new" handgun procurers in Detroit in the 1965–1968 era were somewhat less careful with their weapons than "old" handgun owners tended to be, but that well over 99.9% of all handgun-owners—new and old—were sufficiently careful not to have been involved in a fatal firearms accident.

"The increase in handgun sales is also reflected in trends in firearms suicides" (1969: 71). Again, there is reason for caution. Between 1965 and 1968, the total number of suicides in Wayne County actually declined, from 318 to 305 (see Newton and Zimring's Figure 11-3, p. 72), despite the "surging urban armament" available for self-destruction. On the other hand, the number of suicides committed with firearms (of all sorts) did increase from 84 to 113. When these numbers are converted to rates by using the figures estimated above, however, the 1965 rate is 84/51,700, or about 16 per 10,000 handgun households, and the 1968 rate is 113/87,700, or about 13 per 10,000 handgun households. In other words, there was a slight decline in the rate of firearms suicides. This suggests that the "new" handgun owners were actually somewhat *less* likely to kill themselves with their guns than "old" handgun owners had been.

"The most significant aftermath of the arms buildup in Detroit is its impact on crime" (1969: 72). To demonstrate this point directly, one would have to show that the people applying for permits and actually purchasing handguns during the period were more likely to commit subsequent crimes (of whatever sort) than the people who did not. The data, or course, contain no such direct demonstration: the subsequent criminality, if any, among the people applying for handgun permits between 1965 and 1968 is simply unknown. So the case that the arms build-up was somehow directly linked to an increase in crime is at best inferential.

Data from Newton and Zimring on homicide and aggravated assaults (1969: Figure 11-4, p. 73) show a modest increase in attacks not involving firearms between 1965 and 1968, and a very much sharper increase in attacks with guns. The number of attacks with a gun in 1968 is slightly more than twice the number in 1965. On the other hand, according to our earlier calculations, the number of handgun-owning households also increased in the period, by about 70%. Expressed as a rate, the increase is substantially less dramatic. The same is true of the evidence on armed robbery (1969: 74). Thus, of the various pieces of evidence presented on violent crimes in Detroit, the only one that shows a sharp and alarming increase in the rate per handgun-owning households is homicide with firearms (1969: Fig. 11-6, p. 74), which increased from 55 in 1965 to 279 in 1968. The corresponding rates are 11 and 32 per 10,000, respectively. The number of these homicides committed with "new" handguns is, of course, unknown.

For a variety of reasons, nothing of substance can be concluded from these data (or these kinds of data) about the causal role of private firearms ownership in criminal violence. There is no evidence anywhere that the "new" criminals and the "new" handgun owners were in fact the same people, or even that the former were drawn disproportionately from among the latter. As noted in the introduction to this chapter, it is at least possible that some or all of the "surge" in handgun permits was a response to the increase in crime, not a cause of it, a theme that Newton and Zimring themselves argue. And, certainly, other plausible explanations of the increase in crime may be adduced that have nothing to do directly with private handgun ownership—for example, the surge in black rage against their treatment by white society that accompanied the racial turmoil of 1967 and 1968. The conclusion, that the arms build-up in Detroit "contributed to increased violence," may well be correct, but it is not demonstrated by these data.

Newton and Zimring's second approach to the issue involves comparisons between the proportional ownership of firearms and the percentage of gun use in homicide and aggravated assault across four U.S. regions (1969: 75). The impossibility of drawing a sound causal inference from such data has already been discussed.

The third approach involves comparisons across eight U.S. cities. It consists of comparing proportions of crimes committed with guns over three categories of crime: homicide, robbery, and aggravated assault. The data show that cities with a high proportion of firearms involvement in any of the three types of crime also have high proportions of firearms involvement in the other two types, with rank-order correlations ranging from 0.6 to 0.9. Unfortunately, *there are no data in this comparison on city-by-city differences in private weapons ownership,* and so the correlation between rates of gun ownership and the proportional involvement of guns in these crimes across the eight cities cannot be computed. In general, cities with the highest proportional gun involvement in crime are in the South and West (Atlanta, Houston, and St. Louis are the "top three" in all three crime types). These are the regions where private weapons ownership is also disproportionally high. But, clearly, there is nothing in these data that suggests a direct causal link between weapons ownership city-by-city and rates of criminal violence city-by-city or rates at which firearms are used in violent crime city-by-city. It is possible that the city differences in proportional weapons involvement in crime reflect local judicial, prosecutorial, or sentencing practices, not the (possible, but undemonstrated) differences in private weapons ownership.

In sum, the evidence assembled in the Newton–Zimring report is inconclusive about whether private firearms are directly and causally linked to violent crime. To be sure, this hypothesis is consistent with their evidence, but it is neither confirmed nor denied by it. Truly definitive evidence, such as evidence on the subsequent criminality of new purchasers of handguns of the era, simply does not exist. These points notwithstanding, the Newton–Zimring chapter is often cited in the later literature as proof that guns cause crime.[2]

Newton and Zimring are not the only investigators to have researched this question, but they are among the relatively few. "Although there has been much popular discussion, surprisingly little serious empirical research

---

[2] See, e.g., Alviani and Drake (1975: 1): "the data on crime, accidents, and suicides involving handguns show close correlations between levels of ownership and the rate of each type of incident." As further evidence, these investigators also cite the regional comparisons discussed in the text. A very similar treatment of the Newton–Zimring results is found in a well-known publication of the Massachusetts Council on Crime and Correction, *A Shooting Gallery Called America,* especially pp. 1–2.

has studied directly the impact of levels of gun ownership on rates of violent crime" (Kleck, 1979a: 887).

The subsequent research, like that of Newton and Zimring, is also consistently inconclusive on the issue. Two of the more commonly cited studies (Fisher, 1976; and Seitz, 1972) actually do *not* contain a direct measure of firearms ownership, although both claim to offer evidence that firearms ownership per se increases criminal violence (specifically, homicide).

Murray (1975) has examined the relationship between five measures of "firearms violence" (firearms robberies, fatal firearms accidents, aggravated assault with a firearm, and suicide and homicide by firearm) and proportional handgun ownership across the 50 states and concludes that "it seems quite unlikely that the relative availability of handguns plays a significant part in explaining why some states have higher rates of acts of violence associated with firearms than others" (1975: 91). However, this study does not contain state-by-state estimates of handgun ownership. Rather, it is based on *regional* rates over four gross regions, with all states in the same region receiving the same "percent owning a handgun" score. This is, therefore, an extremely crude test of the hypothesis.

There are two time-series analyses in the literature claiming to show a positive association between homicide and gun ownership (Kleck, 1979a; Phillips and Votey, 1976), even with certain other relevant variables controlled. Kleck concludes, "gun ownership, whether measured as total guns or handguns [per capita], has a significant positive effect on the homicide rate" (1979a: 900); and, in a later passage, "coefficients estimating the effect of the homicide rate on either total gun ownership or handgun ownership are in the predicted direction." Thus, Kleck claims to have found a reciprocal causal relationship between gun ownership and homicide: "crime is a cause of gun ownership just as gun ownership is a cause of crime" (1979a: 908). But again there are some problems. For example, the effect on homicide for total guns (handguns and long guns combined) was somewhat stronger than the effect for handguns only. Since homicide is about four to five times more likely to be committed with a handgun than with a shoulder weapon, one would naturally expect the handgun variable to show the stronger effect. There are also some problems, acknowledged by Kleck, with the firearms measures (they are based on production and importation data; see Chapter 2). Finally, since all measures in this study are for the United States as a whole, there is no direct evidence to show that the gun increases and the homicide increases occured in the same area or areas of the country. The argument that "crime causes guns" would, of course, not require that the gun build-up and the homicide build-up be concentrated in the same area, since, to cite an example, people in Peoria might well purchase a weapon as a reaction to crime in Chicago.

But the weapons owned in Peoria could scarcely be the *cause* of criminal violence in Chicago, and so the reciprocal argument, that "guns cause crime," *does* require that the gun and crime build-ups be concentrated in the same places.[3]

Obviously, production and importation data for the nation as a whole cannot be used to estimate area-by-area variability in weapons possession. Thus, the only existing direct evidence on city-size and regional variations in the domestic arms build-up is that contained in the survey evidence analyzed in Chapter 5. That analysis, although necessarily rather crude given the nature of the data available, does not suggest a very close correspondence between the crime and handgun build-ups: the increasing proportional ownership of handguns was concentrated mainly in middle-sized cities with populations in the range of 10–250 thousand (i.e., in the Peorias), whereas the increase over the past decades in criminal violence has been concentrated mainly in the largest urban areas (i.e., the Chicagos).

In this context, it is relevant to cite once again Bordua and Lizotte's (1979) analysis of crime and weapons ownership across Illinois counties. Their evidence "implies that where the rate of legal firearms ownership is high, the crime rate is low," and thus, "it is implausible to assume that legal firearms ownership increases crime" (p. 159). The explanation is apparently simple: in Illinois, as elsewhere, gun ownership is predominantly rural, whereas violent crime is predominantly urban.

The most recent analysis of these topics is by Cook (1979), who has estimated the relationship between "gun density" and various indicators of the robbery rate over 50 large American cities. As with prior researchers, Cook has no direct measure of city-by-city variance in gun density, but constructs an apparently acceptable proxy measure by using the proportion of suicides and homicides committed with firearms. To demonstrate the validity of this indicator, data from the 50 cities are aggregated over geographical region, and the ensuing estimates of regional gun density are compared to the estimates generated from the National Opinion Research Center (NORC) General Social Surveys. The comparison, although not perfect, is reasonably close, and Cook rightly suggests that these indicators of gun density might therefore have wide applicability in other research situations.

Substantive findings are relatively straightforward: the indicator of gun density was unrelated to the overall robbery rate across 50 cities, but it was significantly related to the fraction of robberies committed with guns (1979: Tables 6 and 7) and, thus, to the gun-robbery rate. The indicator was also

---

[3] Since 1979, Kleck has reanalyzed these issues on a more current and broader data base (see Kleck, 1982). The more recent analysis suggests that "neither gun ownership in general, nor handgun ownership in particular, among the general law abiding population causes homicide" (Kates, 1982).

related to the rate of robbery homicides. The apparent interpretation is that guns do not cause robbery in the sense that they cause more robberies to be committed, but rather that they alter the mix of robbery types: where guns are readily available, robbers are more inclined to use them, and in areas where they are not, robbers are inclined to use other weapons instead, or no weapons. A general decline in gun availability, in short, would probably not lessen the number of robberies that occur, but it would increase the proportion committed with something other than a gun. Some possible effects of this "substitution" are discussed later, in Chapter 10. (As an aside, Cook's findings are inconsistent with the argument that many robbers would lack the psychic strength to commit their crimes in the absence of a gun, since over these 50 cities, the robbery rate is essentially unrelated to gun availability.)

In sum, there is some, but not much, evidence to suggest that at least some fraction of private weaponry is purchased as a reaction to crime; by far the largest share is purchased for entirely different reasons. There is little or no conclusive evidence to show that gun ownership among the larger population is, per se, an important cause of criminal violence. Most of the research designs employed in the literature would not allow for a decisive demonstration of such an effect, even if it did exist. Designs that would allow one to detect the effect usually require data that do not exist or would be prohibitively expensive to generate.

It is true by definition that gun crimes require guns, and it is true empirically that guns, mainly handguns, are involved in a very large share of criminally violent incidents. (In 1967, for example, firearms were involved in 63% of all U.S. homicides, 37% of all robberies, and 21% of all aggravated assaults [Newton and Zimring, 1969: 39], and more recent data show similar patterns [see Chapter 8].) But it does not follow from any of this that reducing the private ownership of weapons would be accompanied by similar reductions in the rates of violent crime, or (what amounts to the same thing) that private weapons ownership is itself a cause of violent crime.

It perhaps goes without saying that the "average" gun owner and the "average" criminal are worlds apart in background, social outlooks, and economic circumstances. The idea that common, ordinary citizens are somehow transformed into potential perpetrators of criminally violent acts once they have acquired a firearm seems far-fetched, most of all since there is substantial evidence that the typical gun owner is affluent, Protestant, and middle-class (see Chapter 6).

Again, it is true by definition that everyone who commits a crime with a firearm has a firearm in his or her possession when the crime is committed. In this sense, the gun is obviously a "cause" of the crime. But there is no good reason to suppose that people intent on arming themselves for criminal purposes would not be able to do so even if the general availability of firearms to the larger population were sharply restricted. Here it may be appropriate to recall the First Law of Economics, a law whose operation has been sharply in evidence in the case of Prohibition, marijuana and other drugs, prostitution, pornography, and a host of other banned activities and substances—namely, that demand creates its own supply. There is no evidence anywhere to show that reducing the availability of firearms *in general* likewise reduces their availability to persons with criminal intent, or that persons with criminal intent would not be able to arm themselves under any set of general restrictions on firearms.

On the other hand, it may be, and often is, argued that much criminal violence, especially homicide, does not result from criminal intent but rather evolves from empassioned disputes that become violent (or lethally violent) just because the gun is there. This line of argument is sufficiently common and important to the issues of this volume that it is exclusively focused upon in Chapter 10.

DOES PRIVATE WEAPONRY DETER CRIME?[4]

The presumed deterrence effect of private firearms is often touted in anti-gun-control sources as an important argument against stricter weapons controls. What evidence is there that private firearms are an effective deterrent to crime? Or that they are not?

The argument that firearms are *not* an effective crime deterrent is typically made on the basis of two kinds of evidence: (1) that much crime occurs in situations or locations where the ownership of a gun by the victim would not, even in principle, deter the crime, and (2) that the number of criminals actually shot by intended victims is very low.

Concerning the first of these points little need be said. The burglary of an unoccupied residence, the most common type of home burglary, is clearly not deterrable by any firearms kept in the home, since there is no one home to use them. Likewise, unless people walk the streets armed (and some do; see below), then private weaponry is not going to deter much or any street crime. But neither of these obvious facts bears on whether private weapons are useful deterrents to crimes that occur in a situation or area where they would be potentially deterrable, which is the more important empirical issue.

It is also true that in very few burglaries, robberies, or rapes does the victim shoot the offender (Newton and Zimring, 1969: 62–65; Yeager, Alviani, and Loving, 1976). Newton and Zimring note, for example, that over the period 1964–1968, roughly two burglaries in a thousand were foiled by the

---

[4] A revised and substantially expanded version of this section appears in Wright (1982).

intended victim shooting at the burglar; thus, some 99.8% were not.[5] The figure for armed robbery is somewhat higher, but still is low in absolute terms. Newton and Zimring's data suggest that about 2% of all robberies "result in the firearms injury or death of the robber" (1969: 63). Similar results in all cases are reported by Yeager and his associates.

Because about 90% of all home burglaries occur when no one is at home (Yeager, Alviani, and Loving, 1976: 1), the presented evidence for home burglary is somewhat misleading. If 2 in 1000 of all burglaries are foiled by the victim's use of a firearm, and 900 in 1000 occur with no one home, then the actual rate for burglaries committed with a person in the home is comparable to that reported for home robbery—roughly 2%. We may thus conclude that the risk to a home robber, or to a home burglar burglarizing an occupied residence, of being shot and wounded or killed by the intended victim is roughly 0.02.

This seems a relatively low risk in absolute terms, and one might therefore question whether a risk of this magnitude ever prevents potential burglars or robbers from getting into the business. Interestingly enough, however, this magnitude of risk apparently *exceeds* the risk to a burglar of being apprehended, charged, prosecuted, convicted, and sentenced for the crime (Kleck, 1979b: 11–12). In 1976, "the overall risk of a burglar being arrested and convicted was only about 1.8% for any given burglary. If half . . . received a prison sentence, then the risk of imprisonment was 0.9%." Since there is reason, and some evidence (e.g., Erlich, 1973; Tittle, 1969), to suppose that the possibility of imprisonment, however slight, deters at least some robbery and burglary (in the sense that it discourages people from ever robbing or burglarizing), and since the possibility of being shot and wounded or killed appears to be on the same order of magnitude, then it is plausible, as Kleck argues, that at least some potential robberies and burglaries never occur because the people who would otherwise commit them fear being shot by their intended victims. (Cook, 1979c, has made a similar point.)

[5] The figure, 2 per 1000, is a comparison between the number of burglars shot or wounded in the course of the crime and the total number of burglaries reported to the police. Burglars who were fired at but escaped and were never subsequently apprehended would presumably not show up in these data as deterred crimes, and so the calculated figure may be rather too low. Also, it is possible that many burglars are frightened off by the homeowner brandishing a weapon; these cases, presumably, should also count as deterred crimes but would not show up as such in these data. (All these points also apply to the calculated deterrence rate for robbery, as discussed below in the text.)

To avoid confusion, *burglary* is the unlawful entry into a structure to commit a felony or theft. *Robbery* is theft committed by force or the threat of force. A routine "breaking and entering" for the purpose of stealing is therefore a burglary, of which about 90% involve unoccupied residences. A "home robbery" would occur when the offender used force or the threat of force in order to steal.

Concerning burglary, it is also often noted that the probability is higher that a burglar will steal a weapon than be frightened off or actually shot by one (e.g., Yeager, Alviani, and Loving, 1976: 1). This may be relevant information for the homeowner who is considering the purchase of a defensive weapon, in that it compares the various risks and benefits that such a purchase might pose; but the result itself says nothing about whether the weapon, once purchased, effectively deters any crime or not.

Newton and Zimring (1969) as well as Yeager, Alviani, and Loving (1976) note that a private firearm is also more likely to be involved in a firearms accident than to be used for deterring a crime. (Other data on this point are reviewed later in this chapter.) But this, too, is relevant only to the risks and benefits that might ensue if a gun is purchased and is not relevant to the issue of deterrence effects per se.

Another interesting theme in the pamphlet by Yeager and his associates is that "the probability of being robbed, raped, or assaulted is low enough to seriously call into question the need for Americans to keep loaded guns on their persons or in their homes" (1976: 1). (How many private firearms are *kept loaded* is, of course, unknown.) Actually, the odds of being criminally victimized in any year are between 5 and 10 times higher than the odds of being victimized by a natural hazard of any sort (e.g., flood or earthquake) (Wright *et al.,* 1979), but one would certainly not want to argue that since the risk from natural hazards is so small, no protective measures against them need to be taken.

There is some evidence, reported by Yeager and colleagues and noted elsewhere as well, that the use of a weapon against a robber is an effective deterrent in some cases. Robberies, that is, are less likely to be successful if the intended victim takes self-defensive measures (55% success) than if not (85% success) (Yeager, Alviani, and Loving, 1976; see also Cook, 1980a). Thus, "use of a weapon for self-protection may be the most effective means of resisting a robbery" (Yeager, Alviani, and Loving, 1976: 1). On the other hand, the opportunity to use a weapon to defend against a robbery is rare, since most robbery occurs on the street with the victim unarmed, and it is also true that the death or injury of the victim is more likely if he or she resists than if not (Cook, 1980a; see also Chapter 10).

As far as can be determined, no evidence is available on the deterrence of crimes against business that results from weapons kept on the premises. One study, cited by Newton and Zimring (1969: 66), did show that roughly one small business in four has a gun for defense against crime on the premises.

The evidence from several studies on the relationship between gun ownership and victimization by crime was reviewed earlier in this chapter. In general, no demonstrable relationship exists. If weapons ownership were an effective crime deterrent, then, all else equal, one would expect less crime against armed than unarmed households, which the data do not show. But in this sense, weapons ownership would function only as a deterrent if the criminal knew in advance that the intended victim was armed, not a very likely possibility.

On the other hand, Kleck (1979b) has pointed out that although criminals may not know whether any specific household is armed, they might know that some areas of a state or city are more heavily armed than others and avoid them accordingly. In this case, we would expect less crime against households located in neighborhoods where the rate of weapons ownership was known to be high. This, however, must remain a speculation because no relevant data are known to exist.

With regard to deterrence of aggravated assaults, the scanty evidence available suggests that assaults are *less* likely to be completed if the victim uses a weapon than if no protective measures are taken (Kleck, 1979b: 13; Yeager, Alviani, and Loving, 1976).

In general, such evidence as exists on crime deterrence by private weaponry does *not* support the argument that guns are useless in deterring crime. The evidence does make it quite plain that most crime occurs in circumstances where the victim would have little or no chance to use a gun, even if one were possessed. On the other hand, in the relatively few cases in which there is opportunity to defend oneself with a gun, the evidence suggests that one is somewhat less likely to be successfully victimized if one is armed than if not.

At the same time, for the types of crimes in question (mainly, home burglary against occupied residences, home robberies, and aggravated assaults), the evidence also suggests that one is more likely to be injured or killed if one resists the offender in any way (whether with a weapon or with some other protective action) than if one merely capitulates. For crimes potentially deterrable by a private gun, then, the trade-off in defending oneself with a gun is between a somewhat lower "completion" rate and a somewhat higher probability of suffering bodily harm.

It is also possible, of course, that the single most important deterrent effect of private weaponry could never be detected even in the largest and most sophisticated research effort—namely, the *generalized* deterrence of crime that results from the high overall possession rate of firearms among U.S. households. In other words, there may be vast numbers of *potential* rapists, burglars, robbers, and assaulters in the general population who never commit a crime precisely because they know that many citizens are armed and they fear the possibility of getting shot. As Newton and Zimring have remarked, "it is certainly possible that the crime rate would be still higher were it not for firearms" (1969: 65). Obviously, there is no evidence that would allow one to examine this possibility.

If the real or potential deterrent effects of privately possessed weaponry are necessarily difficult to determine, the actual *use* of private weapons in self-defense is not. Indeed, two recent national surveys have explored this issue in some detail, and it is appropriate to conclude this chapter with a review of the more relevant findings.

The two surveys are, first, the 1978 survey carried out by Decision-Making Information, Inc. (DMI), which was commissioned by the National Rifle Association and noted in several previous chapters, and, second, a survey conducted in the same year by Cambridge Reports, Inc. (Patrick Caddell's polling outfit), under commission to the Center for the Study and Prevention of Handgun Violence. Both surveys are focused rather more directly on public opinion about gun control than on the uses of weapons in self-defense; a comparison of the public opinion results is contained in Chapter 11.[6] But both also have at least some information on the uses to which private weapons are put. Most of Caddell's questions along these lines focus on handgun accidents and on respondents' experiences with handgun threats or attacks. DMI's questions, in contrast, focus heavily on the uses of weapons by respondents for their own self-defense.

Table 7-1 shows the relevant question sequence and marginal results from the Caddell survey. Consistent with other studies (see Chapter 2), 24% of Caddell's respondents say that they possess a handgun, 17% (of the total, or 71% of those owning handguns only) say that they own a handgun "for protection or self-defense," and 7% (of the total, or 29% of the handgun owners only) say that they carry their handgun with them for protection outside the home.[7] Likewise, 3% of the total sample (or 13% of the handgun owners only) have "had to use" their weapon in self-defense: two-thirds of those who have had to use their weapon in this manner actually fired it. It thus appears that 2% of the total adult population of the country has at some time in their lives actually fired a handgun in self-defense.[8]

---

[6] Actually, DMI conducted two surveys for the NRA in 1978: one in person and one over the telephone. Both are surveys of registered voters only; in contrast, the Caddell survey is of all U.S. adults, whether registered to vote or not. Technical details on both surveys, and comparisons of their sample demographics, are presented in Chapter 11.

[7] Note that Caddell's figure—71% of *handgun* owners owning the gun for protection or self-defense—is much higher than the roughly 40% suggested in other sources (see Chapter 5). This discrepancy exists because the estimate of 40% is based on a question asking for the *most important reason* one owns a handgun, whereas Caddell's question would also pick up self-defense as a secondary or tertiary ownership reason.

[8] It is impossible to determine from Caddell's report just how much of this 2% consists, say, of veterans who have used sidearms in combat situations or of policemen or other security personnel using handguns in the context of their jobs. Presumably, these kinds of experiences would contribute a sizable fraction to the total. Recall that according to the data shown in Chapter 5, somewhere between 8 and 13% of all privately owned handguns are owned primarily for employment-related reasons.

TABLE 7-1. *Data on weapons experience and use from the Caddell survey*

[IF "YES" TO THE HANDGUN OWNERSHIP QUESTION]
Do you ever carry that handgun or pistol outside of the house with you for protection or not?

Yes	7%
Not sure	4%
No	15%
Don't own handgun	77%

Do you own a handgun for protection or self-defense purposes? [IF YES] Have you ever had to use it?

Yes, to threaten	1%
Yes, and I fired	2%
Yes, but never used it	14%
No to first question	83%

[IF "YES" TO ABOVE]
Where did you use it?

At home	1%
At business	—
On the street	—
Public facilities	1%
Other places	1%
Inapplicable	97%

Have you ever been involved in a handgun accident? [IF YES] Were you injured or not?

Yes, not injured	2%
Yes, injured	2%
No, never	96%

Has anyone in your family ever been involved in a handgun accident? [IF YES] Were they injured or not?

Yes, not injured	2%
Yes, injured	3%
Yes, killed	5%
No, never	89%

Has a close friend ever been involved in a handgun accident? [IF YES] Were they injured or not?

Yes, not injured	2%
Yes, injured	6%
Yes, killed	7%
No, never	85%

Have you ever been attacked or threatened with a handgun? [IF YES] Were you injured or not?

Yes, not injured	9%
Yes, injured	2%
No, never	89%

Has anyone in your family, beside yourself, ever been attacked or threatened with a handgun? [IF YES] Were they injured or not?

Yes, not injured	7%
Yes, injured	2%
Yes, killed	3%
No, never	88%

(*Continued*)

TABLE 7-1 (*Continued*)

Has a close personal friend ever been attacked or threatened with a handgun? [IF YES] Were they injured or not?

Yes, not injured	9%
Yes, injured	6%
Yes, killed	4%
No, never	82%

The text of Caddell's report tends to play down these self-defensive uses of weapons. "Almost half the time, the handgun was purchased in order to provide protection, although only 3% of the population has actually used a handgun for self-defense." And later, "since defense is a primary reason behind the ownership of many guns, it is interesting to see whether owners have actually used their handguns for protection. As the table shows, most have not." The theme here seems to be that, although many people buy their guns for self-protection, they are seldom used for that purpose, a point that might be used to undercut self-defense as a compelling reason to own a gun.

Caddell's data on accidents, threats, and attacks are featured more prominently. According to them, about 4% of the respondents have been involved in a handgun accident, half of the incidents resulting in personal injury. Likewise, 10% report that a family member has been involved in such an accident, and 15% report a similar experience for a "close personal friend." Caddell's data suggest that 5% of the adults in the United States have had a family member *killed* in a handgun accident, and 7% have had a close friend *killed* in the same manner.[9] The evidence on handgun threats and attacks is similar: 11% of the respondents say they have personally experienced such an attack, 13% report such an attack for a member of the family other than themselves,

[9] Caddell's figures for death from handgun accident and attack seem on the surface to be inordinately high. They are probably inflated to some extent by what is known in the survey literature as the "good respondent" syndrome—i.e., by the tendency of a few respondents to provide the answer that they think the investigator wishes to hear. It must also be kept in mind, however, that the frame of reference provided by the question is very broad, i.e., "Has *anyone* in your family *ever* been involved. . . ." In this case, "ever" could conceivably stretch back two or three generations (to, for example, grandparents and great-grandparents), and "anyone in your family" could include not just people in the immediate family, but also aunts, uncles, cousins, and various other extended family members. With these frames of reference in mind, the numbers from the Caddell survey are more plausible. Rephrasing slightly, imagine a single individual killed in a handgun accident or attack. That person would have two parents, four grandparents, unknown numbers of aunts, uncles, and cousins, and possibly some children who could then accurately report that a family member had, indeed, been killed in a handgun mishap. Note further that if the person were married, all the equivalent in-laws could, again accurately, make the same report.

and 19% report such an attack on a close personal friend.[10] Roughly half of all these attacks are said to have resulted in personal injury or death. Additional analysis reveals that both handgun accidents *and* handgun threats and attacks are more common among households possessing a handgun than among households who do not. "What these numbers say is this: handgun violence touches a lot of people in this country." Certainly, these data show that a handgun is at least as likely to be involved in an accident as it is to be fired in self-defense, consistent with the point made by Yeager and associates.

Table 7-2 presents the DMI data on weapons experience and uses. None of the DMI questions is precisely comparable to Caddell's, so direct comparisons between results should be made cautiously. Also, all of Caddell's questions ask about *handguns,* whereas the DMI items deal with all guns irrespective of type. A further important difference is that Caddell's questions on uses of self-defensive weapons ask for information only about the *respondent,* whereas the corresponding DMI questions ask about both the respondent and the respondent's family members. These differences in question format are of some interest in themselves: Restricting the questions to handguns only and to respondents only will necessarily show less use of defensive weapons than expanding the questions to include all guns and all family members.

According to the DMI data, 15% of all registered voters (or their family members) have used a gun for self-defense or other protective reasons at some point in their lives; in the DMI telephone poll, the corresponding percentage for an identical question was 12%. The telephone survey shows that roughly one-half of these uses of defensive weapons were to protect against a person. Of the 15% reporting a defensive weapons use in the face-to-face survey, 31% said that the incident was important enough to report to the police. The weapon was actually fired, it appears, in 40% of the incidents; 9% of the incidents apparently resulted in injury or death (presumably, to the other guy). A parallel series of questions about personal friends produced similar, but uniformly higher, numbers on all items.

The DMI face-to-face survey thus suggests that 6% of all registered voters *or their families* ($0.40 \times 0.15 = 0.06$) have, at some point in their lives, fired a weapon *of some sort* in self-defense. This finding is thus not inconsistent with Caddell's finding that 2% of all U.S. adults have *themselves* fired a *handgun* in self-defense. There is, in short, no serious disparity between the two findings.

[10] The NORC General Social Surveys have periodically asked, "Have you ever been threatened with a gun, or shot at?" The percentage responding "yes" varies between 16 and 20%, or somewhat higher than Caddell's 11% (for respondents only). Caddell's question, however, stipulates a *handgun* threat or attack, whereas the NORC item says nothing about the kind of gun, which would account for the difference in observed results.

TABLE 7-2. *Data on weapons experience and use from the DMI surveys*

Face-to-Face Survey
Have you yourself or a member of your household ever used a gun, even if it wasn't fired, for self-protection or for protection of property at home, at work, or elsewhere (except in military service or police work)?

Yes	15%
No	85%

[IF YES TO THE ABOVE QUESTION]
Was the incident important enough to report to the police?

Yes	31%
No	66%
Don't know	3%

Was the gun fired in the incident?

Yes	40%
No	56%
Don't know	5%

Was anyone killed or injured?

Yes	9%
No	86%
Don't know	6%

[ALL RESPONDENTS]
Has anyone else you know personally ever used a gun, even if it wasn't fired, for self-protection . . . [AS ABOVE]

Yes	27%
No	73%

[IF YES TO THE ABOVE]
Was the incident important enough to be reported to the police?

Yes	52%
No	47%
Don't know	2%

Was the gun fired in the incident?

Yes	47%
No	52%
Don't know	1%

Was anyone killed or injured?

Yes	24%
No	74%
Don't know	1%

Telephone Survey
Have you yourself or a member of your household ever used a gun, even if it wasn't fired, for self-protection . . . [AS ABOVE]? [IF YES] Was this to protect against an animal or a person?

Yes, an animal	5%
Yes, a person	5%
Yes, both	2%
No	88%

TABLE 7-2 (*Continued*)

And, have you, yourself, ever been in a situation where you needed a gun to protect yourself or your family or property but there was no gun available? [IF YES] Was this to protect against an animal or a person?

Yes, an animal	1%
Yes, a person	8%
Yes, both	1%
No	90%

DMI's telephone poll reveals another finding that figures prominently in its report. Ten percent of the DMI respondents said that they could recall a situation in which they "needed a gun but no gun was available." (Caddell has no comparable item with which this result might be compared.) Most of these incidents, it appears, involved a person rather than an animal.

In contrast to Caddell, DMI's report strongly emphasizes the frequency with which guns are used in self-defense. First, from the Executive Summary: "13 million [registered voters] live in households in which a family member has had to use a gun in defense of self, family, or property from another person. Further, 9.5 million registered voters can recall a situation in which they needed a gun for protection when none was available. . . . With this many voters having direct experience with guns as instruments of self-defense, it is no surprise that 83% feel 'most people who have guns in their homes feel safer because of it.' " All these themes are emphasized again in the body of the report. "Seven out of every one hundred respondents (or 6.6 million Americans) indicated that they or a member of their family had used a gun at some time to protect self or property against another person. Additionally, nine out of every hundred (8.5 million) indicated that they themselves had been in a situation where they needed a gun . . . but none was available to them." The next paragraph of the report emphasizes that "these data may *understate*" the true use of guns in self-defense "because people may fail to recall episodes in the 'distant past' where they used, or desperately needed but did not have, a gun." Then, bringing the argument to its most pointed conclusion (and incidentally, its most pointed contrast with the Caddell report): "It is sometimes asserted that firearms in general, and handguns in particular, have limited use for defensive purposes. . . . The surveys found that almost 14% of the American electorate, or about 13 million Americans, could recall a time when they or another member of their household had used a gun for protection. . . . Of those who remember such an experience, 40% indicated that the gun was fired . . . , 31% said that the incident was important enough to report to the police, and 9% responded that someone was killed or injured in the incident. It is clear that guns are frequently used for protection. In a substantial minority of those remembered instances of gun use, it was necessary to fire the weapon, although few such incidents resulted in injury or death."

As is evident from the passages quoted above, DMI's report and conclusions depend heavily on rhetorical formulations of key results. Note first the persistent translation of percentages into raw numbers. Via this device, a smallish percentage is transformed into, literally, millions and millions of people. A second prominent device is the occasional insertion of a word or a phrase to the actual wording of a question when the result is being discussed. Respondents were asked, for example, whether they could recall a situation "where you needed a gun . . . but there was no gun available." In the text, this becomes (at one point) *"desperately* needed but did not have a gun." Or consider the sentence, "in a substantial minority of those instances . . . , it was necessary to fire the weapon, although few such incidents resulted in injury or death." DMI's question, of course, asks only whether the weapon *was* fired and says nothing about whether it was *necessary* to fire it; these are, quite obviously, different things.

Despite the differences in emphasis and conclusions, both surveys touch enough common ground to sustain at least a few conclusions. First, as shown in all other studies, some 20–25% of all U.S. households possess a handgun, and about twice that percentage possess a weapon of some sort. Second, many (although certainly not all) handguns are owned for purposes of protection or self-defense; approximately 40% of the handgun owners in both surveys cite self-defense or protection as the primary reason they possess the weapon, and some additional percentage cite this as a secondary reason (see also Chapters 3 and 5). Third, at least some of the weapons that are owned for self-defense are actually used for this purpose at some point. Perhaps as many as 15% of all registered voters or their families have "used" a gun for self-defense; a rather lower percentage (7% in the Caddell survey) carry their weapons with them for defense outside the home; a lower percentage still say that they, personally, have "had to use" their handguns for self-defense (clearly a more restrictive phrasing than simply "used"); and the proportion of U.S. adults who have actually fired a weapon in self-defense is somewhere in the range of 2–6%. Fourth, the incidence of firearms accidents and handgun threats and attacks is at least as prevalent as, but not much more prevalent than, the incidence of uses of weapons for self-defense.

In sum, it is often said that "ownership of handguns by private citizens for self-protection against crime appears to provide more of a psychological belief in safety than actual deterrence to criminal behavior" (Yeager, Alviani, and Loving, 1976: 35). This conclusion is misleading in several related ways:

1. The vast bulk of private weaponry is not owned for self-protection, but for other reasons.

2. Of the weaponry possessed specifically and primarily for defense (perhaps 25% or so of the total armament), some share is not for self-protection against crime but for protection against animals; evidence from DMI intimates that this factor might account for as much as half the total defensive ownership.

3. In this day and age, a "psychological belief in safety" probably ought not be dismissed as a trivial benefit. If people feel safer because they own a gun, and in turn lead happier lives because they feel safer and more secure, then their guns make a direct and nontrivial contribution to their overall quality of life.

4. That private weapons are ineffective as crime deterrents has *not* been established directly in any source. Rather, in the case of crimes occurring in circumstances in which they are potentially deterrable by a private gun, the evidence suggests at least some modest deterrent effects. (To be sure, most crimes do occur in what might be referred to as nondeterrable situations.)

5. In owning a gun for protection (or any other reason), a homeowner runs some risk that the gun will be stolen or involved in an accident. This speaks to the potential costs of such a purchase, but not to the potential benefits, either psychological or objective.

6. At least some of the people who owns guns for self-defense actually use them for that purpose; the precise percentage is, of course, very difficult to determine, as are the ensuing effects on crime and violence in the society as a whole. It is certainly possible that the high rates of crime and violence that predominate in the United States are due primarily to the widespread ownership of guns. But it is also possible that the widespread ownership of guns keeps the rates of crime and violence well below what they might otherwise be. At present, there is no good evidence anywhere that would allow one to choose decisively between these possibilities.

II

CRIME AND VIOLENCE

EIGHT

HOW MUCH CRIME? HOW MUCH VIOLENCE?

In this chapter we examine the extent to which violence and violent crime feature in American life, drawing on a variety of sources.

The definitions of violence and violent crime have obvious implications for measuring the amount of such activity. In its broadest conception, violence might be defined to consist of all circumstances in which human life is threatened, injured, or extinguished by psychological or physical means. This definition would cover a very wide range of incidents such as abuse and neglect within the family, industrial and work-place hazards, and the psychological consequences from fear of crime. Although some commentators employ this broad definition, more commonly violence is defined as in typical American criminal codes by crime categories of murder, rape, aggravated assault, and robbery. In this chapter (as elsewhere in this volume), we use this narrower definition of violence mainly because it is employed in American statistical series. Other forms of violence, including child abuse and within-family violence, as well as those not involving physical force or its threat, are simply not measured in existing statistical series and cannot be included.

The most common definition of violent crime used by law enforcement agencies is derived from the FBI's annual *Uniform Crime Reports* (UCR), which present amounts of violent crime in four Index crime categories as reported by cooperating police departments: murder and nonnegligent manslaughter, forcible rape, robbery, and aggravated assault. A slightly broader interpretation of violent crime is used in the Law Enforcement Assistance Administration's (LEAA) victimization surveys, in which "crimes against persons" include simple and aggravated assault, and statutory and forcible rape, as well as robbery.

Index crime rates from UCR represent only a fraction of the actual levels of violent crime: those that are reported to or detected by the police and that the police record and report to the FBI. In contrast, the LEAA victim surveys reveal that the amount of violent crime that is unreported by victims varies from 25% to 50% depending on the type of crime. Black's (1970) analysis of police departmental practices in recording citizen complaints shows that a similar proportion of incidents do not become recorded officially by the police.

In the analysis that follows, the extent of violent crime in the United States is estimated, with the understanding that such crimes are bound to the definitions of violent crime used by law enforcement agencies.

The annual incidence of death and injury by violent means is just as difficult to define and estimate, because of the ambiguity about what constitutes "violence." For our purposes, we examine (1) those accidents that involve the use of weapons, (2) self-inflicted death and injury, i.e., suicide or attempted suicide, (3) police homicides (deaths caused by police officers), and (4) death and injury incurred by police officers.

Although our working definitions of "violent crime" and death and injury by "violent means" may not cover all conceivable forms of violence experienced by Americans, they do cover what is commonly considered violence, and violence on which data are available for trend descriptions.

LONGITUDINAL TRENDS IN VIOLENT CRIME: UCR STATISTICS

The FBI's *Uniform Crime Report* is an annual compilation of crimes reported to the police (the seven Index crimes) and arrest rates (for Index and non-Index offenses). Begun in 1930, these crime statistics are a major source of data for determining the incidence of crime. The limitations of the UCR are well known and are summarized below.

Citizen Reporting

Citizen discretion in reporting crimes contributes to the production of a UCR crime rate that is far below the actual level of crime. Wesley Skogan's (1974, 1976a) analysis of citizen reporting practices showed that the important factors in citizen reporting of crimes were the amount of financial loss, whether force was used, whether a weapon was used, the extent of injury sustained, and whether the assailant was a stranger.

Police Recording

Police underreporting of incidents stems from two major sources: the patrolmen who observe incidents and respond to complaints, and the policies of police departments in filtering such reports into official counts of incidents reported to the UCR. Donald Black's (1970) study of policing in three cities showed that patrolmen were more apt to make official reports if (1) the incident was serious (i.e., a felony), (2) the complainant preferred that an official report be made, (3) the alleged assailant was a stranger, and (4) the complainant was deferential to the officer. Official department counts of crimes can be influenced by the political milieu surrounding the department. Police departments may be under pressure to "keep the crime rate low" or to provide support for increased police department appropriations by producing a temporary "rise" in the crime rates. Flurries in crime recording and subsequent declines were documented by the President's Commission on Law Enforcement (1967: 22–25). Departments that are more honest or conscientious in their reporting practices may suffer the consequences of being judged lower in "police effectiveness" by citizens (Skogan, 1976b).

Crime Classification

Much discretion is exercised by police departments in reporting to the FBI once an incident has been detected. Offenses reported to the police may be downgraded to less serious offenses or simply ignored. Whether an incident is an aggravated assault or a simple assault often depends on an officer's subjective assessment of the amount of injury sustained by the victim. But in addition to *how* an incident is classified by the police, the UCR offense classification scheme can also be misleading and difficult to interpret. Specifically, UCR classification of crimes (1) utilizes broad legal labels that mask a variety of specific offenses within categories, (2) often includes attempted and completed incidents, (3) does not distinguish multiple-offense events from single ones, (4) does not indicate the seriousness of the offense (e.g., amounts of property loss and types of violence and personal harm involved), and (5) allows for numerous types of classification errors (Hindelang, Gottfredson, and Garofalo, 1978: 25).

Using the UCR for understanding longitudinal trends in the level and character of violent crime is problematic for the following reasons: (1) UCR crime rates probably reflect higher-than-actual proportions of serious crimes or crimes involving weapons, particularly firearms, since these crimes tend to be reported more consistently; (2) reporting practices of police departments vary to such an extent that inter-city differences or differences in rates among different demographic groups may be misleading; (3) the consequences of violent crimes for victims (e.g., level of injury sustained) cannot be ascertained from the crime classification; (4) longitudinal trends in violent crime rates may also reflect changes in political administrations, resources of departments, and changes in practices of record-keeping and reporting incidents to the FBI; and (5) the broad crime categories may mask wide differences in violent crime activities.

These problems with the UCR data are particularly relevant to analyses of trends over time, of the correlates of crime, and of intercity or regional comparisons of crime rates. The UCR crime statistics can be used with some confidence, however, in judging broad national trends in crime rates if one bears in mind that the "crime rate" is a mixture of actual levels of crime, police ability to detect and respond to crime, and departmental accuracy in reporting incidents. The following review of the UCR longitudinal trends (1960–1978) in violent crime presents a general picture of the rates of such crimes and patterns of weapon use.[1]

Criminal Homicide

From 1960 to 1978, the homicide rate has almost doubled, rising from 5 to 9 per 100,000 individuals (Table 8-1). The homicide rate actually peaked in 1974 at 9.8 per 100,000, then declined and stabilized to 9 per 100,000 from 1975 to 1978. The use of weapons in homicide has changed over the two decades: the use of firearms increased steadily from 53% in 1960, peaked in 1974 at 68%, and declined slightly to 63% in 1978. Handguns were the preferred weapon, accounting for about one-half of the homicides, and more than 75% of homicides were committed with firearms. Over time, handguns were used more often in homicides, increasing from 44% in 1966 to a peak of 54% from 1972 to 1974, and then declining to 49% in 1978. The use of rifles and shotguns in homicides has remained about the same since 1966. The overall increase in firearms use corresponds to decreases in other types of weapons used.

Often depicted as a "crime of passion" and thereby distinguished from other more economically motivated crimes, homicide may be more accurately portrayed as on a continuum with other types of violent crimes, distinguished from aggravated assault primarily by having death as an outcome. Richard Block's (1977b) longitudinal analysis of homicide, robbery, and aggravated assault shows that violent crimes that end in death (and thus labeled "criminal homicide") are very similar to other forms of criminal violence in which injury occurs (e.g., a robbery with injury or an aggravated assault). Whether an

---

[1] The tables presenting the trends in violent crime rates from the UCR show the data in 5-year intervals from 1960 to 1978 (additional years are included in certain tables to better show the weapons use trends). This selected presentation does not distort the trends, which are fairly smooth during the omitted years. Readers are referred to the original *Uniform Crime Reports* for the full year-by-year changes in crime rate.

TABLE 8-1. *Murder and non-negligent manslaughter trends from the UCR*

Year	Number	Rate/ 100,000	Firearms (%)			Total firearms	Cutting/ stabbing (%)	Other weapons (%)	Personal weapons (%)
			Handgun	Rifle	Shotgun				
1960	8,740	4.8	—[a]	—	—	53	24	12	11
1965	9,960	5.1	—	—	—	57	23	10	10
1966	11,040	5.6	44	7	9	60	23	8	9
1970	16,000	7.9	52	5	8	65	19	8	8
1975	20,510	9.6	51	6	9	66	18	8	9
1978	19,555	9.0	49	6	8	63	19	12	6

[a] No data or breakdown available.

Source: Data for frequency and rates/100,000 for 1960–1975 are from UCR, 1975, p. 49; 1978 data are from UCR, 1978, p. 7. Note that there are discrepancies between the yearly UCR figures and those shown in the UCR 1975 longitudinal trends for 1960–1975. Weapon use figures are from the individual yearly UCR reports.

incident is a fatal or a nonfatal violent crime may depend on what weapon is used. Under this interpretation, increases in the usage of more lethal weapons (i.e., firearms) in all violent crimes (see Tables 8-3 and 8-4) leads to increases in the homicide rates. In addition to Block's analysis, these trends have been observed in longitudinal studies of violent crime in Atlanta (Munford et al., 1976) and Cleveland (Hirsch *et al.,* 1973).

Rape

Rates of reported forcible rape and attempted rape have increased threefold from 1960 to 1978 (Table 8-2). Forcible rape is far more subject to nonreporting by the victim and to police discretion in recording incidents and making arrests. From a 1966 special survey on patterns of forcible rape, the FBI concluded that nearly 20% of the incidents of reported forcible rape were determined to be unfounded, i.e., judged not to be rape by the police or the courts (UCR, 1966). Clearly, the extent to which reported rape may be "unfounded" speaks to the problems of victims pressing charges against the rape offender (more often an acquaintance than a stranger). Of particular note for longitudinal trends is the shift in proportions of reported attempted versus completed rapes, with the completed forcible rape rate increasing from two-thirds to about three-fourths of all reported rapes.

TABLE 8-2. *Forcible rape trends from the UCR*

Year	Number	Rate/100,000	Rape (%)	
			Completed	Attempted
1960	17,190	9.6	—[a]	—[a]
1965	23,410	12.1	66	34
1970	37,990	18.7	71	29
1975	56,090	26.3	74	26
1978	67,130	30.8	75	24

[a] No data available.

Source: Data for frequency and rates/100,000 for 1960–1975 are from UCR, 1975, p. 49; 1978 data are from UCR, 1978, pp. 14 and 15. Note that there are discrepancies between the yearly UCR figures and those shown in the UCR 1975 longitudinal trends for 1960–1975. Rates/100,000 should be doubled, given that women are the targets of rapists.

Robbery

Rates of reported personal and commercial robbery increased about fourfold from 1960 to 1978 (Table 8-3). UCR did not begin reporting routinely on weapon use until 1974. Beginning in 1963 and until 1974, robberies were divided into two groups: armed and strong-armed. From 1963 to 1973, there was an increase in reported armed robberies from 59 to 66%. A special UCR survey of cities conducted in 1967 revealed that of all robberies, 36%

TABLE 8-3. *Robbery trends from the UCR*

Year	Number	Rate/100,000	Strong-armed (%)	Armed (%)	Type of weapon		
					Gun	Knife	Other blunt
1960	107,840	60.1	—[a]	—	—	—	—
1963	116,470	61.8	41	59	—	—	—
1965	138,690	71.7	42	58	—	—	—
1967	202,910	102.8	42	58	36	14	8
1970	349,860	172.1	37	63	—	—	—
1975	464,970	218.2	35	65	45	12	8
1978	417,040	191.3	37	63	41	13	9

[a] No data available.

Source: Data for frequency and rates/100,000 for 1960–1975 are from UCR 1975, p. 49; 1978 data are from UCR, 1978, p. 16. Note that there are discrepancies between the year UCR figures and those shown in the UCR 1975 longitudinal trends for 1960–1975. Weapon use figures are from the individual yearly UCR reports.

were committed with firearms, 14% with a knife or cutting instrument, and 8% with blunt objects.

The gradual increase from 1968 to 1974 in armed robberies corresponds to an increase in the use of firearms in robberies. In 1967, firearms were used in 36% of reported robberies, whereas in 1975, 45% of reported robberies involved firearms. From 1975 to 1978, the use of firearms declined somewhat to 41%, with an increase in the use of strong-armed tactics. The use of knives or other sharp instruments and blunt weapons remained constant from 1967 to 1978.

Aggravated Assault

Aggravated assault, by definition, involves the use of weapons or threat of use of weapons with the intention of inflicting injury. Rates of reported aggravated assault have shown a threefold increase since 1960 (Table 8-4). From 1960, the presence or use of a firearm in aggravated assault increased from 13 to 25% in 1975 and 22% in 1978, whereas the presence or use of a knife decreased from 44 to 23%. During this period, one also sees a gradual increase in the use of blunt objects (24–28%) and the use of personal weapons, such as fists (12–27%).

The general patterns emerging from this trend analysis are that UCR violent crime rates have increased by a factor of 2 to 4, with the rates accelerating during the late 1960's and early 1970's (Table 8-5). Homicide and robbery rates peaked in the mid-1970's and then stabilized or declined from 1975 to 1978, whereas rates of aggravated assault and rape continue to increase.

TABLE 8-4. *Aggravated assault trends from the UCR*

Year	Number	Rate/ 100,000	Firearm (%)	Knife (%)	Blunt weapon (%)	Personal weapon (%)	Other weapon (%)
1960	154,320	86.1	13	44	24	12	7
1965	215,330	111.3	17	36	22	25	—[a]
1970	334,970	164.8	24	28	24	23	—
1975	484,710	227.4	25	24	25	27	—
1978	588,102	255.9	22	23	28	27	—

[a] No data available. No data were collected on "other weapon" from 1964 to 1978.

Source: Data for frequency and rates/100,000 for 1960–1975 are from UCR, 1975, p. 49; 1978 data are from UCR, 1978, p. 20. Note that there are discrepancies between the yearly UCR figures and those shown in the UCR 1975 longitudinal trends for 1960–1975. Weapon use figures are from the UCRs for each year. Weapon use for 1960 is from a special survey conducted in that year.

TABLE 8-5. *Trends in proportion property and violent crime: UCR Index*
I offenses

Trend	1960	1965	1970	1975	1978
Rate/100,000 violent crime	160.9	200.2	363.5	481.5	486.9
Rate/100,000 violent and property	1887.2	2449.0	3984.5	5281.7	5109.3
Violent crime (%)	8.5	8.2	9.1	9.1	9.5

Among the three violent crimes for which there is information on weapons, one finds a uniform increase in the use of firearms from the early 1960's to the mid-1970's, at which point the use of firearms declined about 5%. The use of knives in homicides and aggravated assaults dropped, while knife use in robberies has remained constant over the two decades. The use of blunt objects has remained the same over this period for homicide and robbery. However, for aggravated assault, there has been a gradual increase in the use of blunt objects and personal weapons, corresponding to the decrease in knife use.

TRENDS IN VIOLENT CRIME FROM VICTIMIZATION SURVEYS

Victimization sample surveys were developed in the mid-1960's to provide more accurate estimates of the actual frequency of particular crimes, as well as to assess more comprehensively the nature of criminal incidents. Surveys first conducted for the President's Commission on Law Enforcement and Criminal Justice (Biderman *et al.,* 1967; Ennis, 1967; Reiss, 1967) worked out the basic approach and demonstrated the utility of victimization surveys. Late in 1969, work began on the development of a National Crime Survey (NCS), with collaboration between the LEAA of the Department of Justice and the Bureau of the Census. The NCS was first fielded in mid-1972, and 1973 marked the first complete year of the survey's operation. The victimization approach is a simple idea: Crimes are detected by asking samples of households whether or not household members have been victims of crimes during a given period immediately preceding the interview. This approach simply bypasses completely the steps in the UCR that involve reporting to police departments and police departments reporting to a central compiling agency, the FBI. Hence, victimization surveys provide more complete counts of crime incidents.

The crimes reported by the NCS generally correspond to the UCR Index offenses (excluding criminal homicide); however, the presentation of victimization data differs from that of the UCR. The personal crimes measured by the NCS include rape, personal robbery, simple assault, aggravated assault, and personal larceny; the household victimizations include burglary, household larceny, and motor vehicle theft; and the commerical victimizations include burglary and robbery of business establishments or other institutions.

It is important to note the differences between victim surveys and the UCR in measuring crime that pose problems in making comparisons between the two. First, victimization estimates and characteristics of victimizations are obtained from a national sample of households and commercial establishments or institutions and are therefore subject to sampling error. Victimization estimates may also be subject to error associated with respondent recall and response effects. Reiss' (1967) study of methodological problems of early victim surveys showed that 20% of people known to have reported incidents to the police failed to volunteer this information in victimization interviews. He also found that minor variations in the wording and timing of questions had substantial effects on response patterns (1967: 148–150). Although UCR data are not subject to sampling error, they are subject to population estimate errors in the computation of rates.

Second, with the exception of robbery and motor vehicle theft, it can be difficult and misleading to make comparisons between UCR and victim survey measures of crime. The UCR crime counts are those that are legally recognized criminal incidents, whereas the victimization estimates reflect respondent-defined criminal incidents. In one study, a lawyer reviewed the victim interview schedules and concluded that 20% of the incidents reported were not legally actionable offenses (Reiss, 1967: 151–152).

Third, "weapon use" is defined differently for the two measures. The definition of "weapon use" in the victim survey is threat of or actual use of a weapon, such as a firearm, knife, club, or bottle; it does not include "personal weapons," such as teeth or fists, as the UCR does.

Fourth, the UCR and surveys gather data from somewhat different population groups. UCR data cover crimes that occur (that is, have been reported) within a particular jurisdiction, whereas victimization surveys collect data from residents or establishments located in a jurisdiction, no matter where the crime occurred. There are also differences in coverage by age; victimization incidents are counted for individuals 12 years or older, whereas the UCR includes all age groups.

Victim Survey Estimates

Victimization data for personal incidents are organized in two ways: by the number of victimization incidents and the number of victimizations. Since any personal incident can involve more than one person, the number of victimizations exceeds the number of incidents. Table 8-6 presents the victimization rates for personal, household, and commercial crimes for 1973 through 1976. During this period, there were no substantial changes in the victimization rates for personal and commercial crimes of violence. The slight increase and then decrease in the rates of household and commercial theft are within the sampling error associated with these victimization estimates.

Table 8-7 presents the estimated total number of victimizations, violent and nonviolent, within the personal and commercial sectors (commercial violent crimes are robberies). About 25% of all personal victimizations were violent crimes, whereas only about 15% of the commercial victimizations were violent. If we exclude the category of simple assault without a weapon from these calculations (to make the information more comparable to the UCR's definition of violent crime), about 17% of all personal victimizations were violent from 1973 to 1976. The last line of Table 8-7 shows that about 9–10% of *all* victimizations are violent crimes—using a definition of violent crime that is comparable to that of the UCR. These percentages are similar to those found for the UCR Index offenses (see Table 8-5).

TABLE 8-6. *Trends in victimization rates from LEAA victim surveys*

	Rates per 1000[a]			
	1973	1974	1975	1976
Personal sector				
Crimes of violence	33.9	32.8	32.7	32.6
Rape	1.0	1.0	0.9	0.8
Robbery with injury	2.4	2.3	2.1	2.1
Robbery without injury	4.5	4.8	4.6	4.4
Aggravated assault with injury	3.4	3.3	3.3	3.4
Aggravated assault attempt, with weapon	7.0	7.0	6.3	6.4
Simple assault with injury	3.9	3.5	4.1	4.0
Simple assault attempt without weapon	11.8	10.9	11.4	11.4
Crimes of theft	93.4	94.9	95.8	96.1
Personal larceny with contact	3.2	3.1	3.1	2.9
Personal larceny without contact	90.3	91.7	92.9	93.2
Household sector				
Burglary, larceny, vehicle theft	221.2	234.7	236.1	229.4
Commerical sector				
Burglary	203.7	226.1	228.6	217.3
Robbery	38.8	38.8	39.4	38.5

[a] Rates per 1,000 persons, households, or commercial establishments.
Source: *Criminal Victimization in the United States,* 1973, 1974, 1975, and 1976.

TABLE 8-7. *Number of victimizations from LEAA victim surveys*

	Number of victimizations (in 1000's)			
	1973	1974	1975	1976
Crimes of personal violence	5,493.6	5,399.0	5,448.0	5,599.0
Crimes of personal violence (excluding simple assault attempts without weapon)	3,586.5	3,613.0	3,549.0	3,642.0
Total personal crimes	20,653.0	21,009.0	21,418.0	22,118.0
Crimes of commercial violence (robbery)	264.1	267.0	264.0	279.0
Total commercial crime	1,649.1	1,822.0	1,798.0	1,853.0
Total crime victimizations	37,656.9	39,694.0	40,483.0	41,170.0
Crimes of personal violence to total personal crime (%)	26.6	25.7	25.4	25.3
Crimes of commercial violence to total commercial crime (%)	16.0	14.6	14.7	15.0
Crimes of violence (excluding simple assault) to total crime (%)	10.2	9.8	9.4	9.5

Source: *Criminal Victimization in the United States,* 1973, 1974, 1975, and 1976.

The trends in weapon use in violent crime victimizations are shown in Table 8-8. In most categories, there has been a slight decline in the percentage of victimizations in which a weapon was used, from 40% in 1975 to 36% in 1976, a decline particularly apparent in the reports of personal robbery with injury and commercial robbery. The upper portion of the table shows that weapons are used in about 25% of rapes, 50% of personal robberies, 40% of attempted commercial robberies, 70% of completed commercial robberies, and 95% of aggravated assaults.

The lower portion of Table 8-8 shows the breakdown by the type of weapon used in these violent crime categories. The use of a gun has declined slightly in the crimes of robbery and attempted commercial robbery over this period. The estimates for the use of a gun in rape, although somewhat unstable because of the low incidence and the sample size, also showed a decline. The use of a gun appears to have been stable in aggravated assaults, with guns used in about a third of all assault victimizations. For personal robbery in which the victim sustained injury, firearms were used in about 10% of the incidents, whereas knives and other weapons were used in about 16% and 18–20% of the incidents, respectively. In contrast, for personal robbery in which the victim did not sustain any injury, firearms were used far more frequently (in about 20% of all such robberies). Knives were used about 20%

TABLE 8-8. *Trends in weapon use in crimes—LEAA victim surveys*

	Incidents with weapons (%)			
	1973	1974	1975	1976
Rape and attempted rape	24	30	24	27
Personal robbery with injury	47	45	52	38
Personal robbery without injury	49	49	49	48
Attempted commercial robbery	39	39	46	41
Completed commercial robbery	68	73	78	74
Aggravated assault	95	94	94	94
All incidents	38	39	40	36

	Types of weapons used (%)			
	1973	1974	1975	1976
Rape and attempted rape				
Gun	10	15	8	7
Knife	6	12	9	16
Other	7	1	7	6
Not ascertained	1	1	1	1
Personal robbery with injury				
Gun	8	9	11	6
Knife	16	17	16	11
Other	18	14	23	20
Not ascertained	5	5	6	4
Personal robbery without injury				
Gun	22	18	22	19
Knife	18	21	19	21
Other	8	8	9	8
Not ascertained	1	2	1	1
Attempted commercial robbery[a]				
Gun	21	17	31	23
Knife	11	12	9	8
Other	7	9	5	10
Completed commercial robbery[a]				
Gun	59	63	64	63
Knife	6	7	11	7
Other	3	3	3	4
Aggravated assault				
Gun	29	31	30	29
Knife	26	25	26	23
Other	35	24	37	39
Not ascertained	5	4	4	6

[a] For attempted and completed commercial robbery, information was collected on the type of weapon only if the weapon could be identified by those present; thus the category "not ascertained" is not used for these incidents.

Source: *Criminal Victimization in the United States,* 1973, 1974, 1975 and 1976; *Sourcebook of Criminal Statistics,* 1977 and 1978.

of the time, and other weapons were used less frequently. The presence of a firearm during a robbery may reduce the possibility of injury by intimidating the victim into compliance. A more detailed analysis of the reasons for the differences in use of firearms by crime categories is provided in Chapter 10.

In attempted commercial robberies, firearms were used in far lower proportions (about 20%) than in completed robberies (about 63%). Knives and other weapons were used to about the same degree for attempted or completed commercial robberies. The implication here is that the use of a firearm in a commercial robbery may greatly enhance the success of the perpetrator. Finally, for aggravated assaults, firearms, knives, and other weapons were used in roughly equal proportions of about 30–33% each during this period.

Table 8-9 turns these percentages and rates into numbers of incidents in which weapons were used, using 1975 as the base year. During 1975 there were an estimated 4.8 million incidents of personal and commercial violence, involving 5.7 million victimizations. Assuming that two weapons were used in incidents involving more than one weapon, about 4% of the incidents involved multiple use of weapons. For all incidents of personal and commercial violence, a total of 1.9 million weapons were used. Assuming that different weapons were used in each incident, these incidents involved over 700,000 firearms, 537,000 knives, 609,000 other weapons, and 81,000 weapons not specified. Weapons were employed in 40% of all incidents of violence; firearms were used in 15% of the incidents; knives in 11%; and other weapons in 13%.

Overall, our analysis of the victimization data shows *stability* over the 4-

TABLE 8-9. *Number of weapons used in incidents (1975)*

	Total incidents	Guns	Knives	Other	Unknown	Incidents with weapons
Rape and attempted rape	144,075	11,000	13,000	9,876	1,230	34,285
Personal robbery	958,410	177,299	171,350	128,087	26,332	478,880
Commercial robbery	264,400	147,750	28,165	9,613	1,517	181,528
Aggravated assault	1,232,980	364,488	324,278	461,173	52,244	1,160,168
Simple assault	2,211,607	—[a]	—	—	—	—
Total	4,811,472	700,637	537,170	608,749	81,328	1,855,373
Weapon use (%)		(15)	(11)	(13)	(1)	(40)

Total number of incidents with a weapon	1,855,373
Number of incidents with 1 weapon	72,506
Total number of incidents with 1+ weapons	1,927,879

[a] Weapons not used in simple assault.
Source: *Sourcebook of Criminal Justice Statistics,* 1977, Table 3.20.

year period, both in the rates of victimization and in the types of weapons used. These national trends, however, do mask differences among cities in the rate at which various weapon types are employed. From the victimization survey data of 13 cities collected in 1975, one finds large variation in weapon use in incidents, and, more specifically, in the use of firearms (*Sourcebook of Criminal Justice Statistics: 1977:* Tables 3.53 and 3.54). For example, weapon use in rape varies from 13% (for Dallas) to 58% (for New York); and for personal robbery, from a low of 37% (for Portland, Oregon) to a high of 64% (for Atlanta). Cities in which weapons are used in higher-than-average proportions include Atlanta, Chicago, Detroit, and New York. In contrast, weapon use is low in Dallas, Denver, and Portland. With one exception, cities having a high use of weapons in violent crimes are also those in which firearms are used more frequently. New York City is an anomalous case in which overall weapons use in crime is high, but knives or other weapons are used more frequently than firearms.

TRENDS IN ACCIDENTAL AND SELF-INFLICTED DEATH AND INJURY

In this section, we examine the longitudinal trends of death and injury from intentional, self-inflicted injury (suicides and attempted suicides) and accidents. It is well known that the assignment of labels of "suicide," "homicide" or "accident death" by law enforcement personnel, medical personnel, and friends or relatives (Douglas, 1967) is problematic. Nevertheless, such assignments constitute the only available data.

Sources for estimating deaths and injuries by violent, noncriminal means are from the National Center for Health Statistics (NCHS): its *Vital Statistics of the U.S.* and its annual National Health Survey (NHS).

Vital Statistics of the U.S. (more specifically, death statistics) are compiled through a Current Mortality Sample (CMS) collected each month by the NCHS from the 50 states, the District of Columbia, Chicago, and New York City. The CMS is a 10% systematic random sample of all death certificates (excluding fetal deaths) that have been filed in the jurisdiction.

The estimates of injuries in the NHS are derived from a multi-stage probability sample of households. During one week each month, a set of sample households is interviewed by the Bureau of the Census, and respondents are asked to provide information related to injuries they sustained within 2 weeks prior to the interview. Quarterly estimates are made by computing an average 2-week estimate produced by the 13 weekly samples and multiplying by 6.5. The annual injury total is the sum of the four quarters.

Because these two sources are based on either actual events (death certifi-

cates) or non-self-selected samples (household sample), they are likely to produce estimates of injuries and deaths that are higher than those generally
found from studies of emergency rooms, for example, where only a selected
subgroup of all injuries is counted. In addition, the death and injury estimates
derived here are subject to sampling error; in the case of the death data
this error is small, whereas that for the injury estimates is much larger.

Suicides

Table 8-10 presents trends in the estimated number of suicidal deaths
from 1960 to 1977. There has been a gradual increase in the rate per 100,000
persons, from 10.6 to 13.3; and the number of suicides has increased from
about 20,000 to 30,000 over the two decades. An important trend over time
has been the increase in suicides with the use of a firearm: from about 47%
of all suicides in 1960 to 56% in 1977. Suicide is a predominantly white
male activity: about two-thirds of the suicides are committed by men. Large
sex differences in means of suicide are also apparent, with men using firearms
much more often than women. In contrast, women are far more likely to

TABLE 8-10. *Trends in rates of suicide and means of death, 1960–1977*

Year	Number	Rate/ 100,000	Firearm (%)	Poison (%)	Hanging and strangulation (%)	Other (%)
1960	19,041	10.6	47	23	18	12
1965	21,507	11.1	46	28	15	11
1970	23,480	11.5	50	28	14	8
1975	27,063	12.7	55	24	13	8
1977	28,681	13.3	56	23	13	8

Means of suicide by sex

Year	Firearms (%)		Poison (%)		Hanging and strangulation (%)		Other (%)	
	Male	Female	Male	Female	Male	Female	Male	Female
1964	56	25	20	46	15	13	9	16
1970	58	30	20	48	15	12	7	10
1975	62	36	17	42	14	11	7	11
1977	63	36	16	42	14	11	7	11

Source: *Vital Statistics,* as reprinted in Table 301 of *Statistical Abstracts of the U.S. 1978.*
Means of death by sex for 1964 from NCHS Series 26, No. 5 (1967), p. 4.

use poisonous substances as the means of death. These sex differences in means of suicide have important implications for the incidence of attempted suicide that does not end in death (see below). However, the trend among women is toward increased use of firearms for suicide, from 25% in 1964 to 36% in 1977.

The incidence of attempted suicide is difficult to know with certainty; most authors believe that the ratio of attempted to completed suicide is on the order of 8:1 to 10:1. One study that examined patterns of attempted and completed suicide is that of Farberow and Schneidman (1961), conducted in Los Angeles during the late 1950's. Their estimates of the means of attempted suicide are plagued by technical deficiencies (e.g., low response rates in obtaining this information from physicians); in addition, it is uncertain whether their results for Los Angeles are generalizable to the nation and whether they are applicable today. We shall only highlight some of their findings to get a picture of this little-known phenomena.

In contrast to completed suicides, attempted (but unsuccessful) suicides are far more prevalent among females, a fact attributed to their preference for barbiturates or other pills taken in large doses. The use of firearms in attempted suicides is very low, and on the basis of Farberow and Schneidman's research is probably in the range of 3–6%. Tentatively, we can conclude that in the past 5 years, there have annually been approximately 200,000 to 300,000 attempted suicides, a small proportion of which were committed with firearms.

Accidental Deaths

Data on accidental deaths over the past 25 years show that there has been a slight decrease in rates, from 58.1 per 100,000 in 1966 to 47.9 per 100,000 in 1978 (National Safety Council, *Accident Facts,* 1975). This decrease has been largely due to a reduction in deaths from falls. Examining the seven major categories of accident deaths reveals that motor vehicle accidents account for 40–50% of all deaths annually over the last two decades. Except for increases in motor vehicle accidents and decreases in fatal accidents caused by falls, there is a remarkable similarity from decade to decade in the proportion of deaths attributed to various causes. Specifically, we find that firearms have accounted for only about 2% of all annual accidental deaths from 1953 to 1978.

In Table 8-11, the circumstances surrounding firearms-related accidental deaths are shown in more detail. From 1960 to 1978, there was a decrease in recreation-related deaths involving firearms (hunting accidents) from 6 to 3% of all deaths occurring from sporting or recreational activities. The propor-

TABLE 8-11. *Trends in circumstances surrounding fatal firearms accidents*

Year	Recreational deaths[a]		Home deaths[a]		Location of accident (%)		
	Total	w/Firearms	Total	w/Firearms	Hunting	Home	Other
1960	17,000	1,100 (6%)	28,000	1,200 (4%)	48	52	—
1966	20,000	1,000 (5%)	29,500	1,400 (5%)	40	55	5
1970	23,500	900 (4%)	27,000	1,400 (5%)	37	58	5
1975	23,000	900 (4%)	25,000	1,300 (5%)	38	55	7
1978	21,500	700 (3%)	23,000	900 (4%)	39	50	11

[a] Note that percentages for recreational and home deaths are approximate because the numbers were rounded off.

Source: National Safety Council *Accident Facts,* 1978, p. 74.

tion of deaths in which firearms were accidentally used in the home has remained stable at about 4 to 5% of all home accidents. Examining firearm-related accidental deaths from 1966 to the present, one finds that hunting accidents almost invariably constitute about 40% of this category and that the remaining deaths involve playing with firearms in the home or in other areas. Fatal firearms accidents occur predominantly among young males: in 1977 this group made up 85% of all deaths, with the largest age group at risk being 15- to 24-year-olds.

Injuries

Longitudinal trends over the last 25 years in the rates of accidental injuries resulting in restricted activity or in medical attention reveal that falls and bumping into people or objects, or being struck by objects, accounted for one-half of all accidental injuries sustained by the U.S. population in 1960, and 40% in the early 1970's. For our purposes, the categories of interest are those that are weapons-related. They include "discharge of a firearm" and "cutting or piercing instrument." In 1959–1961, injury estimates for "uncontrolled firearm or explosion" and "discharge of a firearm" were combined into a single category, whereas they were separately estimated for 1971–1972. However, the NHS (1976) cautions that estimates of firearms injuries are subject to large sampling error (in this case, a standard error that is over 45% of the size of the estimate). Our estimates, therefore, of the annual incidence of firearms-related injuries can only be approximate.

There are widely varying estimates of the incidence of firearms-related injuries cited in the literature. Askrant and Joliet (1968) estimated, on the basis of NHS 1959–1961 data, that over 100,000 injuries were annually sustained from firearms. On the other hand, Newton and Zimring (1969) estimated that the annual number of such injuries was 20,000, using a National Rifle Association study. For the 1970–1971 period, the NHS estimate is 155,000 injuries, with the 67% confidence interval covering the band from 82,500 to 217,500 injuries.

The NHS has not compiled more recent information on firearms-related injuries. Its publications from 1972 through 1977 show broad categories of types of injuries, the closest firearms-related category being injuries sustained by "contusions and lacerations." Thus, we need to estimate a firearms-related injury figure for 1975 based on prior estimates. Data from the NCHS show that firearms injuries constituted about 0.2 to 0.25% of all annual injuries in both 1959–61 and 1971–72. Applying this percentage to the total injuries for 1975 (76,192,000), we get about 183,000 firearms-related injuries.

In contrast, injuries sustained from "cutting and piercing instruments" (esti-mated for 1975 from 1959–61 and 1971–72 estimates) occur roughly 30 times more frequently. Although it is difficult to know all the types of "piercing instruments" involved in these injuries, and therefore whether all would be appropriately classified as weapons, it is clear that firearms are a far less prevalent source of injury than other potentially injurious objects (such as knives). Firearms, however, are far more lethal weapons, as evidenced by the injury-to-death ratios of these weapons—a ratio of 75:1.

POLICE HOMICIDE AND DEATHS AND ASSAULTS OF POLICE OFFICERS

The annual incidence of police homicide (also termed "intervention by police") is documented by the NCHS *Vital Statistics,* and the trends are shown in Table 8-12 for 1970 to 1977. From this table, one sees that there have been roughly 250 to 400 such deaths caused annually by the police and that, after 1974, police homicides appear to show a decreasing trend.

Deaths and assaults of police officers have been routinely collected by the FBI's UCR, and beginning in 1969 weapons used in assaults were tabu-lated. The counts of assaults and deaths of police officers shown in Table 8-12 are separate from those estimated by the victim surveys and contained in the UCR criminal homicide statistics. Until 1974, the UCR shows deaths of police officers incurred by weapons and accidents (largely motor vehicle

TABLE 8-12. *Trends in police homicides and deaths and injuries of police officers*[a]

Year	Police homicides	Police deaths	By weapons	By accidents	Police assaults	Type of assault weapon used (%)			
						Gun	Knife	Other	Personal
1960	245	48	28	20	9,621 (6/100)	—	—	—	—
1965	271	83	53	30	20,523 (11/100)	—	—	—	—
1970	333	146	100	46	43,171 (19/100)	5	3	13	79
1975	336	—	129	—	44,867 (15/100)	7	3	10	80
1978	—	—	93	—	56,130 (16/100)	5	3	10	82

[a] In 1971, the base number of police officers changed to include incidents in and officers from Puerto Rico, as well as Federal police officers. After 1973, no UCR data are shown for police deaths incurred by accidents. The UCR shows that 95–96% of police deaths by weapons are by firearms.

Sources: Police homicide data from the *Vital Statistics,* as reprinted in the *Statistical Abstract of the U.S., 1978,* Table 301. Police deaths and assaults from the UCR for the individual years.

accidents), but beginning in 1974 it shows only deaths from weapons. One sees that, as with the other statistics on criminal violence, deaths of police officers increased from 1960 to the mid-1970's and later declined. Roughly 100 officers annually are killed while performing their duties, and 95% of these deaths are incurred by firearms. The circumstances that have led to the killing of police officers over the past two decades are primarily the following: intervention in robberies in progress or pursuing robbery suspects, attempting arrests other than for robberies and burglaries, responding to domestic disturbance calls, and traffic pursuits and stops.

The number of assaults of police officers has increased from about 10,000 in 1960 to 56,000 in 1978. However, the rate of assault per 100 officers has remained steady since 1968, with about 15 to 17% of police officers annually assaulted. About 30 to 40% of these assaults result in injury to police officers. Weapons, such as guns, knives, and other types, are used in about 20% of all assaults, whereas personal weapons are used for the rest. Since 1969, when data were first collected, the use of various types of weapons has remained the same: about 5% of assaults involve firearms; 3%, knives; and 10%, other types of weapons. The circumstances surrounding assaults

of police officers are primarily the following: responding to domestic disturbance calls, attempting other arrests, handling or transporting prisoners, and
traffic pursuits and stops.

SUMMARY AND ESTIMATES OF VIOLENCE

In this chapter, we have considered the various circumstances by which
individuals die or are injured by violent criminal and noncriminal means.
Tables 8-13 and 8-14 present estimates of the annual death and injury, using

TABLE 8-13. *Estimates of violent crime and death and injury by violent means, 1975*

Crime/death/injury	Estimate (±)	67% C.I. range	% with Firearms
Deaths			
Murder and nonnegligent man-slaughter[b]	20,510 (NA)	20,510	63
Police officers[b]	129 (NA)	129	96
Police homicide[c]	336 (NA)	336	100
Suicide[c]	27,063 (550)	26,510–27,610	55
Firearms accidents[d]	2,380 (155)	1,125–2,535	100
	50,418	48,610–51,120	
Incidents of criminal violence, injury, and threat[a]			
Rape and attempted rape[e] (59%)	151,000 (18,000)	133,000–169,000	8
Aggravated assault[e] (36%)	1,590,000 (49,000)	1,541,000–1,639,000	30
Assault[e] (27%)	2,586,000 (65,000)	2,521,000–2,651,000	0
Personal robbery[e] (33%)	1,121,000 (41,000)	1,080,000–1,162,000	18
Commercial robbery[e]	264,000 (30,100)	234,300–294,500	56
Assaults of police[e] (42%)	44,900 (NA)	44,900	7
Firearms accidents[d]	183,000 (76,900)	106,100–259,900	100
Attempted suicide[f]	270,000 (NA)	270,000	3–6
	6,210,300	5,903,300–6,490,000	

[a] Percentages in parentheses show proportions of victims injured during the incident. NA, not available.
[b] *Uniform Crime Reports, 1975.*
[c] From National Center for Health Statistics, *Vital Statistics, 1975.*
[d] From NCHS and National Safety Council (based on 1971–1972 estimate).
[e] From *Criminal Victimization in the United States, 1975.*
[f] From based on a ratio of 10:1 attempted to completed suicides.

TABLE 8-14. *Proportion of annual deaths and injuries by violent means to total annual deaths and injuries, 1975*

		Percent of all deaths	Percent of all death, excluding health
Deaths			
Total deaths from criminal homicide, police homicide, suicide, and fire-arms accidents	50,418	3	33
Total deaths, other causes			
Accidents (except firearms)	100,650	5	67
Health-related	1,759,060	92	—
	1,910,128	100%	100%
Violence and injury			
Total incidents of violence, threat of violence and firearms accidents	6,210,000	The ratio of criminal and accidental violence to accidental injury is 1:12	
Total injuries by accidents (except fire-arms)	76,009,000		

Annual deaths and injuries attributed to firearms or the use of firearms for threat, 1975

Death by firearms	30,644
Criminal homicide	12,920
Police officers	123
Police homicide	336
Suicide	14,885
Firearms accidents	2,380
Injuries by firearms	896,778
Firearm use in victimizations	700,637
Assaults of police	3,141
Firearms accidents	183,000
Attempted suicide	10,000
Total injuries and deaths by firearms, 1975	927,422

1975 as the referent year.[2] For that year, there were 1.9 million deaths, of which more than 50,000 (or 3%) were caused by criminal homicide, suicides, firearms accidents, and police–citizen encounters. There were approximately

[2] We remind the readers of the trends in violence found earlier in this chapter: they peaked in 1974–1975 and have since shown a slight decline to 1978. Thus, the use of 1975 as the referent year for calculating the estimates of total violence by weapons may overestimate the more recent amount of violence. However, 1975 is the most recent year in which a full set of data from all necessary sources is available.

6.2 million incidents of criminal violence and injury by accidental or suicidal means; the ratio of these types of incidents to total accidental injuries experienced by Americans was 1:12.

Examining firearms as the weapon involved in annual death and injury (Table 8-14), we estimate that, in 1975, over 30,000 deaths resulted from the criminal, accidental, and suicidal use of firearms; and that almost 900,000 firearms were present, brandished, or fired in victimization incidents, accidents, attempted suicides, or police-citizen encounters. Thus, nearly 1 million deaths, injuries, accidents, victimizations, intimidations or other unfortunate incidents occurred in 1975 with the use of firearms.

Excluding health-related deaths, we find that deaths from criminal homicide, suicide, police–citizen encounters, and firearms accidents accounted for one-third of all annual deaths in 1975. With regard to the proportions of firearms-related deaths and injuries, 20% are incurred from the accidental use of firearms; 3% from suicide and attempted suicide; 1.5% from criminal homicide, and 0.5% from police–citizen encounters.

NINE

THE FIREARMS USED IN CRIME

What types of firearms are used in criminal violence? To what extent can "crime guns" be identified and separated from those that are bought and used for legitimate purposes? Is there enough of a difference between crime guns and legitimate guns to allow special legislative focus on the former? These and related issues are the topics of this chapter.

Little is known about the firearms used in crimes. Usually the depiction of crime guns is based on the characteristics of confiscated weapons. However, confiscated firearms often include *all* firearms recovered by the police, not just those directly related to a crime. This source of data makes it difficult to identify clearly the typical crime gun. In addition, the data on confiscated firearms are quite limited. There are no national statistics on the number and types of guns police confiscate or the reasons for confiscation, or is there a breakdown by the types of firearms associated with particular violent crimes (with the exception of homicide). Moreover, no national data exist on the features of guns annually manufactured and imported against which to compare the crime gun. Finally, there are no national data on the types and features of stolen guns and very few data on whether stolen weapons provide a major source of crime guns.

Within these limitations, a number of studies have attempted to describe crime guns on the basis of samples of firearms confiscated by the police. These studies are *Project Identification* (1976), *Project 300* (1976), *Project CUE* (undated), and Brill's (1977) *Firearm Abuse*. More detailed features of crime guns have been analyzed by Zimring (1976). The magnitude of the crime gun problem can be estimated by using the National Bureau of Standards' survey of police departments' annual number of firearms confiscated and features of these firearms (U.S. Department of Commerce, 1977). More tentative and indirect evidence of the types of firearms confiscated can be inferred by using the 1975 figures of the Bureau of Alcohol, Tobacco, and Firearms (ATF) on the types of guns for which trace requests were initiated

(Search Group, Inc., 1976). Last, Burr's (1977) study of patterns of handgun ownership for a sample of citizens and convicted felons in Florida is reviewed.

MAGNITUDE OF CRIME GUNS CONFISCATED: THE NBS SURVEY

A portion of the National Bureau of Standards' (NBS) 1972 survey of a sample of 440 state, county, and municipal police departments dealt with the numbers and types of firearms confiscated by departments in 1970 and 1971. Using the mean number of weapons confiscated per department and the total number of departments, we can derive an estimate of the total weapons confiscated in the United States in 1971. As Table 9-1 shows, we estimate in 1971 that over 260,000 firearms were confiscated by the nation's police departments. To be sure, not all of these are necessarily crime guns.

TABLE 9-1. *Estimated number of confiscated firearms, 1971*

Police department type	(1) Mean number confiscated per department [a]	(2) Number of departments [b]	Estimated confiscated handguns: column 1 × column 2
Handguns			
50 Largest cities	1,449	50	72,450
State	446	50	23,300
City (50 or more officers)	54	554	29,916
City (10–49 officers)	8	1,985	15,880
County	7.5	3,137	23,528
City (1–9 officers)	3	5,486	16,458
Township	1.5	1,574	2,361
		12,836	183,893
Shoulder guns			
50 Largest cities	451	50	22,550
State	62	50	3,100
City (50 or more officers)	25	554	13,850
City (10–49 officers)	5	1,985	9,925
County	7	3,137	21,959
City (1–9 officers)	1	5,486	5,486
Township	1	1,574	1,574
		12,836	78,444

[a] Mean is of those departments supplying information.

[b] This is the number of law enforcement agencies identified by LEAA in 1971; distribution of number of departments by type is taken from NBS (1977) Table 1.2-1, p. 3.

Source: U.S. Department of Commerce, NBS (1977), adapted from Tables 1.2-1 and 11A/ 1A-3, pp. 3 and 23.

TABLE 9-2. *Features of confiscated firearms by department type*

Police Department type	Estimated number of firearms confiscated in 1971			Handguns % of total	Total as a % of all estimated firearms confiscated ($N = 262{,}337$)
	Handguns	Shoulder weapons	Total		
50 Largest cities	72,450	22,550	95,000	76	36
State	23,300	3,100	26,400	88	10
City (50+)	29,916	13,850	43,766	68	17
City (10–49)	15,880	9,925	25,805	62	10
County	23,528	21,959	45,487	52	17
City (1–9)	16,458	5,486	21,944	75	8
Township	2,361	1,574	3,935	60	2
	183,893	78,444	262,337	70 (avg.)	100

The distribution of weapons confiscated by type and size of police department can also be estimated from the NBS survey (Table 9-2). Not unexpectedly, county and township departments (presumably located in more rural areas) confiscated proportionately fewer handguns (about 60%) than did police departments in the 50 largest cities (where 76% were handguns). Also, not surprisingly, over half of the confiscated firearms were concentrated in the largest departments (5% of the departments in the nation).

ATF PROJECT IDENTIFICATION

The first national study of the types of handguns confiscated by police was carried out by ATF (U.S. Bureau of Alcohol, Tobacco, and Firearms, 1976a) during 1973–1975. The initial phase of *Project Identification* was concerned with identifying the sources of handguns used in street crimes in order "to develop intelligence for ATF and police departments regarding illegal firearms dealers, firearms theft rings, and other suppliers of handguns to criminals" (ATF, 1976a: 3). For this initial phase and three subsequent phases of the project, a sample of 16 large metropolitan police departments collected data on all handguns received, recovered, or seized by them for specified periods of time (3–6 months).

The departments reported a total of 10,620 handguns, of which the ATF trace service successfully traced 7,815 (or 74%). Information about the circumstances surrounding the seizure, recovery, or receivership of handguns by the departments is not presented in the report, so again it is difficult to tell how many of these are actually crime guns. Brill's (1977) analysis of 10 cities shows that perhaps 20–25% of the handguns confiscated by the police are not associated with *any* criminal violation.

The ATF project does provide some description of the confiscated handguns. Over one-half were judged to be worth less than $50, 70% had barrel lengths of 3 inches or less, 60% were .32 caliber or less, 76% were revolvers, and 66% were purchased after 1968.

The ATF estimates that 45% of the confiscated handguns were Saturday Night Specials, their definition being a handgun that costs less than $50, of caliber .32 or smaller, and having a barrel length of 3 inches or less. Further, 624 of the 10,620 firearms confiscated (or 6%) had been stolen. (As we report below, this probably *under*estimates the actual proportion of confiscated firearms that are stolen.) Moreover, of all handguns that could be successfully traced, 23% came from pawn or loan shops. A special study of cities used in Phase IV of the project shows that of the handguns purchased from pawn or loan shops, about 60% were Saturday Night Specials, suggesting that such businesses may supply a disproportionate share of this type of handgun.

The ATF reported that except in those states with stringent regulations and licensing requirements for the purchase and sale of handguns, the majority of confiscated handguns were purchased in the state where the confiscation occurred. There are large variations among cities in the proportions purchased from other states, ranging from 13% for Dallas and 14% for Dade County (Miami) to 92% for Detroit and 96% for New York City. Overall, for all handguns confiscated and successfully traced, 57% came from out of state, a proportion that is strongly affected by the large number of confiscated handguns in New York City (2443). If New York City is excluded, 38% of confiscated firearms were purchased out-of-state. The following states were the major gun sources for the study cities: Florida, Georgia, Ohio, South Carolina, Texas, and Virginia.

Also included in the ATF report is the estimated "street age" of handguns confiscated. One-half of the handguns confiscated in Dallas, Denver, and Oakland had a street age of less than 3 years, whereas one-half of confiscated handguns from Kansas City had a street age of 6–7 years. However, Brill (1977: 94–95) has noted that the ATF's measures of street age are unsound: at times, the date at which the handgun was delivered to the first retailer was used as the beginning date; at other times, the date when it was sold to the first purchaser was used. ATF also apparently did not keep accurate figures of the date when the handgun was confiscated.[1]

[1] Brill asked ATF officials if they could provide more accurate information on the "end date" for confiscated handguns, but they could not. Indeed, one problem with the ATF report is that information on the study cities is inaccurate at times. For example, the report shows

Brill has noted several other problems with the *Project Identification* data. Because of the ways in which police departments keep records or inventories of gun confiscations, one cannot assume that a confiscated gun was involved in a crime. Brill estimates that 20–25% of firearms confiscated were *not* crime weapons. Instead, they were either (1) simply found by the police while on patrol, (2) voluntarily turned in by citizens, or (3) firearms owned by police officers who submitted them to the department's property room for safekeeping, testing, or as evidence for pending cases.

Another issue is the proportion of confiscated guns that were associated with illegal possession versus those that were actually used in violent crimes. Although the ATF study notes that "concealed weapons charges and street crimes" were the reasons that the police acquired the handguns, it does not show the proportions of handguns falling under each of these categories. Brill found that 50–60% of the crime guns were confiscated on illegal possession charges.

Brill notes that the ATF report often refers to confiscated handguns as "street crime" guns, and he attempts to examine this by analyzing confiscation data that he collected from eight of the 10 cities. He finds that 30–40% of handgun confiscations came from residences, 20–30% from the streets, 15–25% from automobiles, 10–15% from businesses, and 2% from other locations. Only a minority of these weapons were confiscated off the streets.

Other problems worth mentioning include the request by ATF that police departments *not* submit guns that were "too old to trace." Therefore, some unspecified amount of prescreening occurred that excluded an unknown number of "old guns" from the ATF study. In addition to prescreening by departments, ATF also screened out some guns. For example, Brill found that the New York City police Department submitted 3320 handgun descriptions for tracing, whereas ATF said that it received 2931 records.

Also some of the handguns that ATF was unable to trace were found in reanalysis to have been stolen. These missing data on thefts are especially prevalent among handguns stolen from manufacturers' factories, for which "records missing" is the reason given for an unsuccessful trace by ATF. In the same vein, Brill found that ATF had duplicated a large number of its traces and counted them twice, at least in New York.

Although Brill is critical of the ATF report, his analysis corroborates most of ATF's findings. Both studies found roughly similar proportions by caliber

---

that New York City handguns were confiscated from July to December 1973; however, Brill found that the handguns were actually confiscated during January to July of 1973. ATF apparently recorded the time during which the gun was *traced* as the time at which it was confiscated, a mistake that ATF officials admitted may have been made in other cities as well (Brill, 1977: 95).

of handguns confiscated: for ATF, 39% of handguns were .32 caliber or greater; for Brill, 45% were .32 Caliber or greater. Both studies conclude that the street age of confiscated handguns is relatively young.

Brill's analysis of confiscated firearms found that 82% were handguns, 11% were shotguns, and 7% were rifles. Comparable proportions were found in the NBS survey in 1971 (77% handguns, 23% shoulder weapons) (U.S. Department of Commerce, 1977: B-17), and in ATF's analysis of types of firearms traced in 1975 (79% handguns, 21% shoulder weapons) (Search Group, Inc., 1976: 10).

Brill comes to different conclusions about the quality of confiscated guns. His key theme is that most of these guns are not Saturday Night Specials. Our comparison of Brill's and ATF's findings, however, reveals small differences, especially given the great imprecision in estimating value. Brill finds that of the 5547 guns confiscated from the 10 cities in his study, 45% were manufactured by 10 companies. Thirty-five percent of the guns from these 10 sources were manufactured by companies that are predominantly engaged in making inexpensive handguns. The remaining 55% were manufactured by 60 other companies; and Brill notes, of this group of 60 companies, that "inexpensive guns appear not to have been any larger a part of this . . . category" (Brill, 1977: 48).

The ATF proportion of inexpensive handguns (less than $50) confiscated was 56%, and the percentage of Staturday Night Specials was 45%. We find little basis for concluding (as Brill does) that his results contradict the "widespread notion" (presumably based on the ATF report) "that so-called 'Saturday Night Specials' are the favorite crime weapon." He states that expensive firearms are found in these samples as often as inexpensive ones—the same result as was found in the ATF study. The difference in results has been somewhat overstated.

Brill does not report the proportion of confiscated firearms that are easily concealable. Since concealability has been reported to be a major feature of crime guns, this aspect of Brill's analysis is incomplete. Brill does present the caliber of confiscated handguns by five major types of crimes, and his results show that smaller-caliber handguns (.32 or smaller) were associated more with robberies and assault, whereas larger-caliber handguns were predominantly associated with murder. This result is consistent with Zimring's (1972) analysis of homicide guns and with ATF's *Project CUE* results.

As a further check on the cost of handguns, Brill analyzed 144 firearms confiscated in New York City. Using firearms catalogs to determine retail prices, this analysis showed that 31% of the firearms retailed for $60 or less. Obviously, these retail prices might not reflect what a person actually paid for a firearm (for example, it could have been stolen, purchased on the black market, or bought used).

In contrast to ATF's estimate of 6%, Brill believes that 20–25% of confiscated firearms were stolen at some point in their history. This higher proportion is based on a study of New York City firearms confiscated in a 1-month period in 1975. The same result is also found in a more intensive study of 300 handguns confiscated as part of *Project Identification* (termed *Project 300*). In two very small sample studies of 28 stolen firearms, Brill found that 41% had been stolen less than 6 months before being confiscated, and that half of the stolen firearms were taken from manufacturers, distributors, retailers, or in transit (Brill, 1977: 106).

Some corroborative data on the source of thefts that were *reported* to police are provided by the 365 stolen firearms that were part of New York City's *Project Identification* sample of confiscated firearms. Approximately 48% were reported stolen from manufacturers, dealers, or in transit; 35% were stolen in the course of burglaries and robberies; and the remaining 17% were stolen from unknown locations (Brill, 1977: 108).

A national estimate of the annual number of stolen firearms cannot be made with much precision. However, using data from a study of burglaries in Houston during the first quarter of 1976, Brill arrives at an estimate of 275,000 firearms stolen in reported incidents of burglary alone.[2]

Brill has also analyzed the types of handguns that move in interstate commerce. Of the 1364 New York City *Project Identification* firearms that were successfully traced, 773 (or 57%) were traced to retail purchases in Florida, Georgia, South Carolina, and Virginia. Of those traced to these states, 92% were attributed to 10 manufacturers. The differences between this sample (the "black-market" sample) and all types of firearms in the 10-city sample is large: far higher proportions of these black-market firearms were categorized as inexpensive, i.e., manufactured by companies that produce cheap firearms.

Zimring (1976) has analyzed in detail the street age of handguns confiscated in the ATF *Project Identification.* He concludes that the interpretation that crime guns are "new guns" should be qualified because a large share of untraceable guns were manufactured before 1969. Yet even the most conservative conclusion shows that fewer than half of all confiscated handguns could have originated before 1969 in seven of the eight cities.

ATF PROJECT 300

A sample of handguns confiscated during ATF's *Project Identification* was examined more closely to determine how handguns enter criminal channels,

---

[2] Brill acknowledges that Houston may be atypical insofar as it probably has a higher rate of firearms ownership than other urban areas. On the other hand, its reported burglary rate is relatively low. Houston's data may provide an accurate indicator of the number of firearms stolen because the city has no restrictions against having firearms in the home; thus, stolen firearms may more likely by reported to the police (Brill, 1977: 105).

as well as the life history of handguns from the time they are manufactured until they are involved in a crime. This study sought to trace 300 handguns from the first retail sale to the last known owner. Of the sample of 300, 256 (or 85%) were traced to the first retail purchaser.

The results of this study, called *Project 300* (U.S. Bureau of Alcohol, Tobacco, and Firearms, 1976b), show that of the initial 300 handguns, 22% had been stolen at some time in their history, 29% were identified as Saturday Night Specials, and 66% were confiscated as a result of a "street crime." (We assume that this figure includes both illegal possession and actual use in violent crimes.) The ATF report found that *all* the 256 handguns were either traced to or recovered in a state different from that of the first purchase (ATF, 1976b: 13)

Of special importance in this study are the significant proportions of first purchasers who had felony convictions (6%) or a record of criminal arrest (19%) at the time of purchase. An examination of the 40 first purchasers who used invalid identification at the time of purchase shows that 40% lived outside the state of purchase and 18% were convicted felons. ATF now does not allow retail dealers to accept Social Security cards as the only means of identification for firearms purchasers, since their study revealed that about one-third of the first purchasers using Social Security cards as their sole means of identification used fictitious names.

ATF PROJECT CUE

The ATF's *Concentrated Urban Enforcement* (CUE) project involved a concerted effort of increased ATF manpower and other investigative resources in the cities of Washington, D.C., Chicago, and Boston beginning in February 1976 (for Washington, D.C.) and July 1976 (for Boston and Chicago). The results of CUE through June 1977 are reported here; however, ATF's report on the project (undated) states that investigations are "ongoing."

There are four objectives of CUE: to step up prosecution efforts of federal firearms violations, to investigate and reduce major illegal sources of firearms, to educate dealers and audit their operations in compliance with federal law, and to trace all firearms confiscated in the three cities to determine the types and sources of these firearms and the flow of firearms from first retail purchaser.

Of the 22,072 handguns confiscated, about three-fourths were revolvers, over one-half had a caliber of .32 or less, three-fourths had a barrel length of 3 inches or less, and 27% were defined as Saturday Night Specials. Of the 6290 shoulder weapons confiscated, just over half were shotguns, and about one-third were classified as NFA (National Firearms Act) weapons (i.e., sawed-off shotguns and rifles). The features of confiscated handguns are similar to those found in *Project Identification.*

Of note were some differences in types of handguns and shoulder weapons confiscated in the three cities. The estimated value of handguns confiscated in Boston was higher (48% valued over $100) than in Washington and Chicago (36% and 33%, respectively, valued over $100). Since value is one of the criteria for determining a Saturday Night Special, Boston also had proportionately fewer of these types of handguns.

One of the important aspects of the CUE analysis is that it reports the types of firearms associated with particular types of violent crime. One-fifth of the confiscated firearms were associated with violent crime incidents: murder (4% of the firearms), robbery (4%), assault (13%), and rape (1%). The other 80% of the firearms were associated with "other" incidents; ATF does not provide a more detailed breakdown. Similar proportions of confiscated handguns and shoulder weapons were associated with each of the four types of violent crimes.

For the four crime types, there were no large differences in (1) the type of handgun employed (revolvers are the preferred type, constituting about 75–80% of the violent crime guns), (2) the caliber size (about half are .32 caliber or less), and (3) the barrel length of the handguns (70–75% are 3 inches or less). However, there were differences by crime type in the value of the weapon. Handguns used for murder and rape were more expensive than those used for assault and robbery.

The CUE analysis also shows that handguns are significantly more likely than long guns to have been purchased outside the state in which they were confiscated. Approximately 40% of handguns confiscated in Chicago and 48% of those confiscated in Boston were purchased outside the state. Moreover, an analysis of confiscated firearms by whether they were purchased inside or outside city jurisdictions shows even more dramatic differences. The proportions of confiscated firearms purchased outside city jurisdictions are 92% for Chicago, 81% for Washington, D.C., and 67% for Boston.

BURR'S STUDY OF FLORIDA CITIZENS AND CONVICTED FELONS

As we have seen, there is little direct evidence to compare handguns owned by legitimate owners and crime guns. One exception is a study conducted by D. E. S. Burr, who interviewed a sample of 808 Florida households and a sample of 277 convicted felons in five corrections institutions in Florida during 1977 in an attempt to discern differences in the types of handguns owned, how individuals in both groups came to possess them, and their reasons for owning handguns.

About 45% of Burr's Florida households acknowledged that they owned one or more handguns at the time of the interview, somewhat higher than the average handgun ownership for the South in 1976 (see Chapter 5). Of the 363 households admitting ownership, 304 gave the number of handguns owned: over 60% said that they owned one handgun; 18%, two handguns; 8%, three handguns, and 11%, four or more. The features of the Florida resident and felon handguns, sources of these handguns, reasons for purchase, and manner of disposal are shown in Table 9-3.

Some striking differences are found by comparing the features of handguns owned by each group. Although there are not large differences between the groups in the ownership of handguns of caliber .32 or smaller, higher proportions of Florida residents owned .22 caliber handguns than did the felons. Barrel length, however, shows a bigger difference: two-thirds of the inmates compared to just under one-third of Florida residents said that their handguns had barrel lengths of 3 inches or less. In addition, Florida residents paid more money for their handguns: Burr estimates that the average cost of a used handgun to the residents was $90, compared to an average of $35 paid by inmates for a private purchase. Burr learned in interviews with the inmates that a used handgun could be purchased on the street in any area of Florida for about $20 (Burr, 1977: 22).

These differences in cost can be understood, in part, by the differing sources from which Florida residents and inmates get their handguns. About 49% of the residents purchased their handguns from a retail dealer or a pawn shop, compared to 26% of the inmates. Most inmates got their handguns either by private-party sales (34%) or by theft (23%).

A tenth of the Florida residents indicated that they had had a handgun stolen from them. Burr found in his interviews with inmates who had been convicted of breaking and entering that handguns were often the most desirable merchandise to steal other than cash, since a handgun is easier to carry unnoticed from the premises, easier to dispose of for cash, and harder to trace than most other merchandise (Burr, 1977: 22).

Most respondents in both groups said that the primary reason for owning or carrying a handgun was protection, although Florida residents indicated more often that hunting and target practice were their reasons for owning handguns. Significantly, about 33% of Florida residents said that they carried handguns away from home on a daily basis, although only 14% said that they needed their handguns as part of their jobs.

The Glisson Amendment, a law stipulating a mandatory sentence of 3 years to life for the commission of specific felony offenses in which a handgun is used, was enacted in Florida to deter the use of firearms in violent crime. Burr found that although most of the Florida inmates knew of the Amendment,

TABLE 9-3. *Features of handguns owned by Florida residents and convicted felons*[a]

Feature	Residents (%)	Felons (%)
Caliber		
.22	29	18
.25	5	7
.32	9	20
.38	28	31
.45	13	2
Other	16	16
No answer	—	6
	100	100
	(511 handguns)	(176 handguns)
Barrel length		
2" or less	19	21
2.1–3"	11	46
3.1–4"	30	10
4" or more	40	23
	100	100
	(437 handguns)	(132 handguns)
Source of handgun		
Retail dealer	43	24
Pawn shop	6	2
Private party	16	34
Gift	15	5
Exchange or trade	7	1
Borrowed/found	3	4
Stolen	1	23
Other	10	7 (NA)
	100	100
	(433 handguns)	(176 handguns)
Manner of disposal		
Sold dealer or fence	9	6
Sold private	37	—
Sold nonstranger	—[d]	64
Sold stranger	—	15
Traded	11	—
Pawned	2	6
Stolen	10	—
Gave as gift	16	—
Other	15	9
	100	100
	(333 handguns)	

TABLE 9-3 (*continued*)

Reason for purchase
  Resident sample[b]

	N	% (of 363)
Protection	198	54
Hunting	63	17
Job requirement	28	8
Gun collector	31	8
Target practice	94	26
Other	46	13
	460	

  Felon sample[b,c]

		%
Protection		60
Hunting		3
Job requirement		6
Gun collector		2
Target practice		6
For use in felony		9
Other		11
No response		5
		102

Glisson Amendment (mandatory sentence of 3 years to life for the commission of specific felony offenses)[e]

	N	% of 277
Inmates aware of the Amendment	229	83
Inmates indicated that they would not be deterred by the Amendment (i.e., would continue to carry a handgun)	203	73

[a] Base N's for gun costs were not provided by Burr. The costs of handgun by both residents and felons are tabulated below:

	Residents		Felons	
	Mean	N		
Purchased new	$130	(246)	Public purchase	$70
Purchased used	$ 90	(204)	Private purchase	$35

[b] Percentages add to more than 100 because more than one reason was given.

[c] Burr does not show the real base N for these responses; although he computes the percentages with 102 as the base, it is likely that more than one reason was given by the inmates.

[d] —, Category not used.

[e] 69% of first offenders and 76% of multiple felony offenders stated that they would continue to carry a handgun.

about 75% would *not* be deterred by it; that is, they would continue to carry handguns on their person after release from prison.

SUMMARY

Our review of the available information on confiscated firearms provides some rough indication of the weapons used in crime. The characterization is not precise because many confiscated guns are not involved in criminal activity and most of the rest are confiscated on illegal possession charges. In addition, the data are very limited on the characteristics of legitimately owned firearms against which to compare the characteristics of crime guns. Thus, it is difficult to conclude that there is a particular "crime gun" type that is more likely to be preferred by those involved in violent crime, except for the obvious conclusion that handguns are preferred to shoulder weapons.

In most studies, 71–74% of the handguns confiscated had barrel lengths of 3 inches or less. The Cue study also showed that 34% of the confiscated shoulder weapons had been modified to shorter barrel lengths. Caliber does not appear to distinguish between legitimate and crime guns.

"Value" as a criterion proves very difficult to analyze, since the price paid for a gun eventually used for criminal purposes can be low or high, depending on the degree to which the supply and demand for black-market guns fluctuates in any jurisdiction. From the available studies, it appears that 40–50% of confiscated handguns have a value of $50 or less. We do not know, however, the proportion of all handguns manufactured that may also fall into this inexpensive category.

Overall, a large proportion of all confiscated handguns have crossed state lines, but the proportions of interstate sales may be dependent on the degree to which local or state laws are restrictive on the sale and possession of handguns. However, without comparable data on the interstate flow of *all* firearms, it is difficult to judge the source of guns for criminals in comparison to the source of guns for all owners.

Stolen handguns are a potentially important source of confiscated handguns. On the basis of 1975 statistics, perhaps as many as 275,000 handguns are stolen each year from legitimate handgun owners. Thefts from manufacturers, importers, dealers, etc., also constitute a significant proportion of stolen handguns; in New York City, such thefts accounted for half of all reported firearms thefts in 1973. However, it is not known whether all stolen guns become crime guns or whether they should be thought of much like all other stolen property (that is, the guns are fenced or sold to the general private firearms market). It is an unanswered question whether the proportion of stolen firearms among criminals is any higher than the proportion among the legitimate private firearms owners.

Our analysis of the CUE data reveals that of all firearms confiscated during 1976 and 1977 in Washington, Chicago, and Boston, only about 20% were associated with incidents of violent crime. The features of guns used in these violent crimes were different from those confiscated in other incidents; specifically, violent crime guns tended to cost more and to be of shorter barrel length. With respect to caliber, guns used in violent crimes (except rape) tended to be of larger caliber than handguns associated with other incidents. Using caliber, barrel length, and value of handguns, we find from these confiscation studies that Saturday Night Specials appear in confiscated handgun samples on the order of 25–33%.

Although it seems that the age of confiscated handguns is young (about one-half of handguns confiscated have a street life of 5 years or less), there are no comparable data on all private handguns to determine if a similar proportion are also young. However, given the large increases in firearms production over the past decade, we might assume that the age of handguns in legitimate hands is also relatively young.

TEN

ON THE MATTER OF CRIMINAL MOTIVATIONS

One of the most persistent debates in the "weapons and crime" literature concerns an issue involving criminal motivations, and that is whether restrictions in the availability of firearms would cause the number of violent crimes to decrease. As we have already noted, it is self-evident that if there were no guns, then no crimes could be committed with them. But a wide range of alternative weaponry would remain. Would the people who presently kill, rob, and assault with firearms not, in a "no-guns" condition, simply substitute some other weapon instead? And if so, then what would be the effect? Would death, injury, and destruction resulting from violent crimes or the number of crimes themselves increase, decrease, or remain the same?[1]

---

[1] It should be emphasized at the outset that the bulk of this chapter, and of the literature it reviews, is hypothetical in the sense that it speculates on what *might* happen were society somehow able to attain a "no guns" (or, in some cases, a "no handguns") condition. Given the numbers of guns already present on the scene, it is transparently obvious that such conditions would be exceedingly difficult, or impossible, to attain.

This point is sometimes granted, but with an important caveat. We know from contemporary existence the circumstances that obtain in a "many-guns" condition. We can theorize on the circumstances that might obtain in a hypothetical and admittedly unrealizable "no-guns" condition. Still, if we cannot achieve a "no-guns" condition, we can presumably at least reduce the total number. The inference is that the "fewer-guns" condition would produce a state of affairs somewhere between the "many-guns" and "no-guns" condition.

The critical inference, however, would follow only if the general reduction in firearms availability were accompanied by a proportional reduction in the availability of firearms to criminals for criminal use. It may be taken as self-evident that something in excess of 99% of all privately owned firearms are never involved in any sort of criminal act, and it is certainly possible (some would say extremely likely) that the criminally abused 1% would be the last guns touched by any sort of restrictive weapons policy. The implication is that society might have to come asymptotically close to the "no-guns" condition before any improvement over the "many-guns" condition is realized. There is, in short, no necessary linear proportionality between reductions in the general availability of firearms to the private market and reductions in the specific availability of firearms to people wishing to arm themselves for criminal or illicit purposes.

For a variety of reasons, the answers to these questions turn, mainly if not entirely, on the motivations that underlie violent criminal attacks. It should be understood that the discussion in this chapter refers to motivation in a psychological, rather than a legal, sense. The law recognizes rather fine gradations of motive: premeditated homicide, unpremeditated homicide, negligent manslaughter, non-negligent manslaughter, and so on. From a legal point of view, the strong intention to kill could be formed only seconds before the attack and would still be considered a premeditated homicide. The distinction we draw in this chapter is altogether insensitive to various legal niceties. It is the distinction between whether the perpetrator *wanted* to kill the victim (however long that desire had been in existence), to which we refer as an a priori intent to kill, or whether the death of the victim was an unwanted and unforseen outcome of the perpetrator's behaviors, a function of the "heat of the moment" and the availability of a suitable weapon. We are thus speaking of the psychological matter of *differential intentions,* and not addressing the more technical matter of legal culpability.

In this connection, Wolfgang (1958) has developed what is called the "weapons substitution" hypothesis. The hypothesis posits that the initial intent of the offender determines the choice of weapon. When the a priori intention is indeed to kill, firearms are chosen; when the a priori intention is not to kill, some other weapon will be chosen instead.

An implication is that the disproportionate lethality of firearms attacks (relative to attacks with any other weapon) is a spurious artifact of the initial intentions of the offender.[2] It is true, in other words, that gun attacks are more likely than any other kind of attack to end in the death of the victim. (Evidence on this point is reviewed later in the chapter.) But this is true, Wolfgang argues, only because the willful murderer prefers firearms over other weapons. If a firearm were not available, then some other weapon would be substituted with equally lethal results. Thus, "it is the contention of this observer that few homicides due to shooting could be avoided merely if a firearm were not immediately present, and that the offender would select some other weapon to achieve the same destructive goal" (Wolfgang, 1958: 83). The ready availability of firearms, in short, is a convenience to the intentional murderer, but certainly no necessity. Death by homicide would be just as common, in this view, whether firearms were readily available or not.

There is, without question, at least some class of homicides for which the weapons substitution argument is valid. People with a single-minded, thoroughly premeditated intention to kill will always find the means to do

---

[2] As Wolfgang himself says, "More than the availability of a shooting weapon is involved in homicide. . . . The type of weapon used appears to be, in part, the culmination of assault intentions or events and is only superficially related to causality" (1958: 82–83).

so, and if an efficient weapon such as a firearm is not around, the victim can always be poisoned, burned, stabbed, or, if all else fails, beaten to death with a stick. It is obvious that homicides of this sort will *not* be prevented or even modestly deterred by any kind of firearms legislation, or, for that matter, any other kind of legislation. There are simply too many objects in the world that can serve the purpose of destroying another human being.

The serious question, then, is not whether such a class of homicides exists, but whether this constitutes a large or small proportion of the total class of homicides committed. If the proportion of homicides resulting from a single-minded intent to kill is very large, there is probably very little that could be done to prevent them. If, on the other hand, the proportional contribution of willful killings to the total is very small, different implications follow. What, then, is the distribution of intentions among homicide offenders?

For a variety of reasons, this has proved to be an exceptionally difficult question to answer. Data generated through the criminal justice system are, in themselves, of little help, since the prosecution of a homicide as first-, second-, or third-degree, or as a manslaughter, depends more on plea-bargaining, the strength of the evidence, and other extraneous considerations than it does on determining what the offender had in mind when the incident began. There is also the problem of *intersubjectivity,* since the issue here turns entirely on determining the mental states of offenders at some time prior to their offense. Even in the best of circumstances, mental states are notoriously difficult to assess, and assessing the motives and intentions of murderers is assuredly not the best of circumstances. Even if the homicide did result from an unambiguous and single-minded prior intention to kill, it would be very much in the interests of the offender (and his attorney) to suppress this information.

Most efforts to assess the intentionality of homicides therefore attempt to infer intentions from the objective circumstances surrounding the incident. Probably the most widely cited and emulated effort along these lines is that of Zimring, who poses the critical issue as follows:

> If all homicides resulted from such a single-minded intention to kill as gangland killings, laws prohibiting firearms would not have a substantial effect on homicide. . . . But not all homicides are so unambiguously motivated. The question is: Do a significant proportion of homicides result from a less deliberate and deter-mined intention? If this question may be answered in the affirmative, and if the probable substitute for firearms in these situations is less likely to lead to death, then the elimination of guns would reduce the number of homicides (1968a: 721–722).

It must be granted that common sense and much episodic evidence seem strongly to favor Zimring's position. The daily newspapers and the pro-control literature are rife with accounts of homicides resulting from the most unimagin-ably trivial incidents—shoot-outs between two motorists over a dispute about positions in the gasoline line, a man shooting his wife to death because his supper was not quite up to expectation, a homicide that results from a dispute over a borrowed cigarette, or a teenager who blasts his mother with a shotgun because he was denied the use of the family car for the evening. In the face of these kinds of incidents, it is very hard to doubt that some large fraction of all homicide results from very little thought or advance planning, and that such incidents ultimately turn lethal not so much because anyone intended them to be, but simply because the weaponry at hand, a gun, is intrinsically lethal. That these kinds of incidents would be much less likely to result in death if the participants did not have access to firearms seems, on the surface at least, as firm a conclusion as anything could possibly be.

On the other hand, that such incidents occur tells us nothing about their relative frequency. People shooting one another to death over trivialities surely makes for good newspaper copy, and so these incidents tend to receive much publicity, perhaps more than their relative numbers would justify. Here, as in all other areas of public policy, episodic evidence and common sense are poor substitutes for serious scientific research. So, although we may grant that this episodic evidence seems strongly to favor Zimring's position, we must also ask whether the same applies to the more credible scientific evidence that he and other researchers have assembled.

Several items of evidence from Chicago for the middle 1960's convince Zimring that "a significant proportion (of homicides) do not result from an attack committed with a single-minded intention to kill" (1968a: 724). First, Zimring presents data on the relationship between victims and offenders in 554 homicide cases. In just over two-thirds of the cases, victims and offenders were friends, acquaintances, spouses, lovers, or otherwise related by family or conjugal ties. In an additional 6% of the cases, the victims were neighbors or business associates of the offenders. Victims and offenders were found to have no relationship to one another in only 22% of the homicides in the sample; in the remaining cases, the victim-offender relationship was undeter-mined. Thus, the large majority of all homicides involved persons known to one another prior to the attack.

That most homicides (and aggravated assaults) involve persons known to each other has been widely reported in all studies. For example, data from 17 American cities reported by Curtis (1974) showed that only 16% of all homicides, and 21% of all aggravated assaults, involve outright strangers. These figures increase somewhat if incidents involving police officers are added (to 17 and 31%, respectively). In either case, the evidence is broadly consistent with Zimring's Chicago results. Zimring's results have also been replicated in a large number of single-city U.S. studies, and they seem also to hold in most other nations for which data are available (Curtis, 1974).

We may thus take it as established that most violent assaults committed in the world, whether ultimately lethal or not, involve people who share some interpersonal knowledge or relationship prior to the assault.

But what can be inferred about motivations or intentions from this fact? The inference Zimring draws is that lethal attacks on family, friends, and acquaintances are not likely to involve single-minded, a priori intentions to kill, or, to rephrase, that most of these homicides result from escalations of otherwise petty and trivial quarrels that turn lethal just because firearms are available. But there is nothing in the data on victim–offender relationships per se to suggest such a conclusion. Strictly, the data tell us who gets murdered, but not why; the imputation of motive is just that—an imputation that is not directly demonstrated by these data.[3]

[3] The difficulties of inferring homicidal motives from data on victim–offender relationships are illustrated in a finding, reported by Block (1977), that between 1965 and 1974 the proportion of Chicago homicides involving people known to each other before the incident dropped from 76 to 57%. "While it is still true," Block concludes, "that most victims and offenders know each other before a killing, it is not nearly so true as in the past." Zimring himself has noted a similar pattern for the nation at large: "National data and studies of individual cities show that while the majority of all killings are still committed by friends or acquaintances of the victim, a substantial and increasing proportion of the 'new American homicide' is the outcome of robbery—an event where victim and offender are usually strangers" (1977: 317; see also Curtis, 1974: Table 3-2). Yet neither Block nor Zimring advances the obvious conclusion from this that Zimring's (1968a) treatment of the relationship data would suggest, namely, that the number of homicides involving "ambiguous intentions" has likewise sharply decreased.

The idea that domestic shootings involving family members are spontaneous "crimes of passion"—isolated outbursts occurring in the heat of circumstances and involving normally placid, nonviolent people—is a recurring image in the literature. It is, however, very difficult to square with a study of domestic killings in Kansas City, conducted by the Police Foundation (1977). That study showed that no fewer than 85% of all homicides involving family members had been preceded at some point in the past by some other violent incident sufficiently serious that the police were called in. Kleck has concluded from this finding that "domestic killings are rarely isolated outbursts of previously nonviolent people, but rather are usually part of a pattern of [domestic] violence engaged in by people who are known to the police and to others as violence prone" (1979b: 18).

The lesson from the Kansas City study is a very important one that deserves some emphasis. Reference to domestic homicides as a reason to reduce the private ownership of weapons has become commonplace in the pro-control literature, as it is the most obvious case of the "heat of the moment" dispute that turns lethal just because there is a firearm in the home. The imagery is, not infrequently, that of a bereaved spouse, head in hand, weeping uncontrollably over lethal behaviors committed in a fleeting and now much regretted moment of rage—the classic case of "ambiguous intention."

The Kansas City study makes it plain, in contrast to this imagery, that much domestic homicide is not an isolated occurrence or outbreak, but rather is the culminating event in a pattern of interpersonal abuse, hatred, and violence that stretches back well into the history of the parties involved. It is not hard to imagine that many of these homicides are preceded at some point by a comment like "If you do that to me again, I am going to shoot you." One does, and then the other does. The point, of course, is that the a priori intentionality in many cases of domestic homicide is not going to be nearly as ambiguous as it is depicted in the typical account.

That most homicides involve members of interpersonal relationships is, *in itself*, not inconsistent with a high level of prior intent. On the contrary, it seems likely that it would be much easier to work up an unambiguous hatred and subsequently lethal intention about someone known intimately than about an utter stranger. The fact that two people are known to each other assuredly does not mean that they are on mutually friendly terms. Typically, the only people one might have any *reason* to kill would be family, friends, and acquaintances. So the evidence on victim–offender relationships, although obviously of great interest in its own right, actually says very little about the motivations underlying homicide.

There is a second problem with these data, one that involves the matter of a comparison standard. Crudely, the available data suggest that about three-quarters of all homicides involve people known to each other before the attack. With what should this three-quarters figure be compared? Although we know of no evidence, it is a reasonable bet that some equally high proportion of *all* interactions that take place between human beings involve people known to each other before the interaction, in which case the 75% figure would be neither higher nor lower than what one would expect just on chance alone.

Zimring presents a second tabulation of evidence from police reports concerning the general circumstances surrounding homicide. These data are reproduced below as Table 10-1. Zimring's comments about the table and its implications are as follows: "82% of the homicides in Chicago in 1967 occurred as the result of altercations—domestic, money, liquor—precisely the situation

TABLE 10-1. *Circumstances surrounding 551 Chicago homicides in 1967*

Circumstance	Percentage	
Altercations		
General domestic	17	
Money	9	
Liquor	7	
Sex	2	
Triangle	6	82%
Racial	1	
Children	2	
Other	38	
Teen gang disputes	3	
Robbery	12	18%
Other motive	3	

Source: Zimring, 1968a: Table 2.

where the intention is more apt to be ambiguous rather than single-minded" (1968a: 729).[4]

This conclusion also seems unwarranted. The evidence does indeed show, first, that 82% of these homicides were accompanied by an altercation, however the police define this term. All this means is that most homicides occur in an atmosphere of interpersonal hostility or animosity between the parties, hardly a startling finding. The 82% figure is itself somewhat misleading. The examples mentioned in Zimring's text, "domestic, money, liquor," collectively account for only one-third of the homicides. By far the largest category shown is "other," which accounts for 38% of all homicides and nearly one-half of those involving altercations. The implications of the table for the point at issue would therefore seem to depend almost entirely on what those other altercations involve, and on this point the data are mute.

Most important, there is nothing in these data to show that homicides accompanied by altercations over domestic affairs, money, or liquor (or any other "passion") are not also frequently accompanied by determined intentions to kill. These altercations, that is, may represent only the presenting opportunity or context in which to actualize homicidal intentions. That such homicides reflect ambiguous rather than willful intentions is itself an untested assumption.

A third line of evidence said to favor the "ambiguous intentions" hypothesis involves comparisons between homicide victims and victims of aggravated assault. Zimring's hypothesis implies that most homicides begin as aggravated assaults and end as homicides only because the means chosen or available for assault tend to be lethal. The further implication is thus that homicides and aggravated assaults should differ only in outcome and in no other way. In this context, Zimring reports that "victims of homicides and victims of serious assaults are distributed quite similarly by race and sex among the population and differ substantially in these characteristics from the Chicago population as a whole" (1968a: 723). "The consistent similarity between homicide and assault across all variables reported in this volume" is also cited by Curtis (1974: 108) as evidence favoring the ambiguous intentions hypothesis; see also Block (1977) and Vinson (1974).

Both Zimring and Curtis demonstrate that black males are much more likely to be victims of (and offenders in) homicides and aggravated assaults than are black females or nonblacks of either sex. But, here again, nothing of direct relevance to the ambiguous intentions hypothesis follows. Zimring, Curtis, and others have shown that homicides and serious assaults are similar

[4] Virtually all available studies report very similar findings; altercations of the sort shown in Table 10-1 are routinely found to accompany between approximately 70 and 90% of all homicides (and aggravated assaults). (See Curtis, 1974; Table 3-1, for the most extensive available compilation of national data on this topic.) The empirical finding is therefore not in doubt; our question concerns only its interpretation.

in at least one important respect (namely, the race and sex of the victims), but not that they are similar in any respect relevant to hypotheses about underlying motivations.

Two final pieces of evidence are presented by Zimring on behalf of the ambiguous intentions hypothesis, neither compelling. The first is that "only 30% of the victims of fatal gunshot attacks in 1967 were wounded by more than one shot" (1968a: 723). Apparently, the point is that most murderers fire once, come to their senses, and fire no more; but this is, at best, a remote inference from the evidence. In any case, it is very difficult to see what the finding implies about the motivations of the people doing the shooting. One thing it might imply is that most murderers stop shooting once it is clear that the victim is dead. If one were to assume, not unreasonably, that pumping a dead body full of additional holes is the sort of behavior that results from enraged passions, then the finding that "only 30%" were wounded more than once might be interpreted as evidence that most (fully 70%) of these homicides do *not* involve enraged passions, just the opposite of what Zimring concludes. Unfortunately, the data do not contain any information on the number of rounds fired per homicide, but only on the number that hit the mark. But the data do at least suggest that a large fraction of murders involve one and only one shot—a level of marksmanship that one would probably not expect under conditions of outrage or duress.[5]

[5] Perhaps a parallel can be drawn here to the case of hunting and shooting deer. One of us (Wright) is a butcher by avocation and thus occasionally prepares deer carcasses for home freezers. Over the years in which he has pursued this hobby, his total sample size for deer carcasses is in the range of 15 to 20. The analogy between shooting deer and shooting people in a homicidal situation is obviously not very tight. On average, deer present a somewhat smaller target (the average deer might weigh in the range of 90 to 120 pounds); also, they tend to be on the move when shot at, and the conditions for shooting are usually not ideal, as there are brush, trees, and other obstacles in the way. On the other hand, the weaponry used to hunt deer is, one may assume, an order of magnitude better suited to the task than the weaponry used in the typical firearm homicide; the standard Saturday Night Special has an effective accurate range of tens of yards at most, whereas the typical deer rifle, outfitted with proper scope and sights, is accurate over several hundreds or even thousands of yards. We may also take it as self-evident that the average deer hunter is a better marksman than the average murderer, and also that the "underlying motivations" of the deer hunter when he pulls the trigger are utterly unambiguous: the intention is to kill the deer. The significance of Wright's experience in present context is that he is yet to encounter, over a sample of some 15–20 taken deer, even a single deer that was taken with one and only one shot. Indeed, the aura that surrounds the rare hunter who is capable of such a feat borders, in hunting circles, on the religious (as was intimated, for example, in *The Deer Hunter,* an Academy Award movie).

All this, of course, is nothing but a personal reminiscence. But it does suggest that capable marksmen, armed with highly accurate and efficient weaponry, aiming unambiguously to kill roughly man-sized targets, are seldom able to kill their prey with a single shot. That a much higher proportion of murderers, armed with much less impressive weaponry, kill with a single shot might therefore cause us to wonder just how ambiguous the underlying motives are.

"Finally, in 54% of the situations which led to homicide in 1967, the police noted that the offender or the victim or both had been drinking [alcohol] prior to the homicidal attack" (Zimring 1968a: 723). The suggestion here is that perhaps one-half of all homicides involve drunkenness on the part of one or both parties. But again, this is not a very revealing finding. First, there is again no comparison standard. With what should the 54% be compared? Even if it could be shown that this percentage is high, no implication about motive would necessarily follow. Drinking to work up the courage to do that which one has already decided to do is not exactly unheard of.

The point to be made here is *not* that most homicides involve willful and determined a priori intentions to kill, but rather that the evidence assembled by Zimring is not adequate to rule this possibility out. The conclusion drawn from these data, that "most homicide is not the result of a single-minded intention to kill at any cost" (Zimring, 1972: 97), may be correct, but it is not warranted by these data alone.

What of the second explicit premise in the argument, that the "probable substitute for firearms in these [homicidal] situations is less likely to lead to death?"[6] Zimring makes a reasonable case that the probable substitute weapon of choice would be knives, and we see no good reason to quarrel with this assumption.[7] In the Chicago data, knife attacks (irrespective of lethality) are

---

[6] We say "second explicit premise" because there is a third premise in Zimring's argument—namely, that some sort of policy could be devised and implemented whose effect would be actually to reduce the availability of firearms for illicit criminal purposes. Even if all the rest of Zimring's argument could be confirmed, the "less death" conclusion would follow only if this third premise were true, and although the validity of this premise is very much a complex and open question, the sheer numbers of weapons already in private hands in the United States (see Chapter 2) give one at least some reason to be skeptical. (See also footnote 1, above).

[7] To be sure, others *have* quarreled with this assumption. Kates (1978: 17ff), for example, considers that faced with a ban on *handguns,* killers and assaulters might opt for long guns as the substitute weapon. That shoulder weapons are already some two or three times more prevalent than handguns lends more than a little credence to this assumption. (Kates' argument does not directly address Zimring's analysis, since the comparisons drawn by Zimring are between all gun attacks, both with handguns and long guns, and all knife attacks. Zimring's speculations therefore relate to a hypothetical "no guns at all" situation, rather than the more limited "no handguns" situation. Kates' argument, however, is valid to the extent that a ban on handguns is a more probable "gun control" measure than a ban on all private weapons.)

Kates further argues that long guns are substantially *more* lethal than handguns—approximately four times more lethal, according to his sources, mainly because of the higher muzzle velocities attained by long guns and the more massive bullets that they fire. (Close-range attacks with shotguns, it appears, are even more lethal than short-range rifle attacks. One medical study, entitled "Gunshot Wounds of the Abdomen" (Taylor, 1973), remarks: "Shotgun injuries have not been compared with other bullet wounds of the abdomen as they are a thing apart. . . . [A]t close range, they are as deadly as a cannon" [quoted in Kates, 1978: 33].) What, then, would be the effect on homicide rates if, in a no-*handguns* condition, long guns were chosen as the substitute weapon? Kates calculates that the homicide rate would double if "half of the

about three times more common than firearms attacks anyway, and assaults with other forms of weaponry, hands and feet included, are comparatively rare. Results for 17 U.S. cities reported by Curtis (1974: Table 6-1) show somewhat, but not sharply, different results. In the Curtis sample of aggravated assaults, knives outnumber firearms by about two to one (versus about three to one in Zimring's Chicago data), and Curtis' data also show a substantially higher proportion of assaults with the hands and feet. These modest differences between the results of Zimring and of Curtis, however, are probably not very significant, least of all in respect to their possible implications for the choice of a substitute weapon. So let us assume, following Zimring, that in the absence of firearms, the assaults now committed with firearms would instead be committed with knives. To what conclusion does this assumption lead?

The data on the comparative lethality of gun and knife attacks are relatively unambiguous: attacks with guns result in death more commonly than attacks with knives. In Zimring's Chicago data, there were, all told, some 16,518 knife assaults (homicides and aggravated assaults combined) between 1965 and 1967, of which 391 were fatal. The fatality rate among knife attacks is therefore roughly $391/16,518 = 2.4\%$. In the same period, there were 6,360 gun assaults, of which 777 were fatal, for a fatality rate among gun attacks of 12.2%. The fatality rate for firearms attacks is thus approximately five times the rate for knife attacks. This estimate of 5:1 for differential lethality is rather higher than other estimates. For example, recalculations from Curtis' data (1974: Table 6-1) suggest that gun attacks are no more than about twice as lethal as knife attacks; data from Australia reported by Vinson (1974) suggest a differential of about three to one.[8] No study, however, reports that knife attacks are *more* lethal than gun attacks, so we may take it as

---

prospective killers substituted long guns while the other half went to knives, . . . even if," he adds, "we assume that *none* of those using knives succeeded in killing their victims" (1978: 20).

[8] Vinson's (1974) paper is virtually a point-by-point paraphrase of Zimring (1968a), based on data for Australia. With a few exceptions noted in the text, the Australian findings are identical on all points to Zimring's findings for Chicago.

Kleck (1979b) has pointed out that Zimring's initial (1968a) estimates of the comparative lethality of gun versus knife attacks are confounded seriously by sex differences in choice of weapon. Kleck recomputes Zimring's Table 5 to show that 87% of the gun assaulters were male, whereas only 65% of the knife assaulters were male; thus, women are disproportionate among the category of knife assaulters. Part of the lesser lethality of knife attacks may therefore stem only from the fact that women are less likely to command the physical strength necessary to kill with a knife. "These data," Kleck concludes, "serve to caution us that it is by no means obvious to just what degree guns are technologically deadlier than knives."

established that attacks with guns lead to the death of the victim more often than attacks with knives.[9]

What can be concluded from this fact? Zimring's conclusion is straightforward. "These figures," he says, "support the inference that if knives were substituted for guns, the homicide rate would drop significantly" (1968a: 728). But the data do not show this at all. What the data do show is that the people who presently attack with guns bring death to their victims more frequently than the people who presently attack with knives. That the people who now attack with guns would bring about less death if only knives were available would therefore follow only if the people who now attack with guns were no more likely to attack with an a priori intent to kill than are the people who now attack with knives: in other words, only if the ambiguous intentions hypothesis were confirmed. In the absence of better data, it remains a plausible hypothesis that persons who attack with a gun are more intent on killing—and therefore kill at a greater rate. That is, it is plausible that the difference inheres in characteristics of offenders, not in characteristics of their weapons.

Thus, whether rates of death from assault would decrease if knives were substituted for guns again turns on the question of whether knife attackers are motivated differently from gun attackers: whether, in Zimring's words, "the people who make homicidal attacks with firearms are radically different from those who make homicidal attacks with other weapons" (1968a: 726). To show that they are *not* radically different, Zimring reports two additional bits of information: (1) that, in general, knife killings are accompanied by the same kinds of altercations as gun killings; and (2) that firearms and knives

---

[9] There is, to be sure, a very serious "apples and oranges" problem with comparisons of this sort. Zimring's comparison, for example, is between the relative lethality of *all* gun attacks versus that of *all* knife attacks—"knife" here referring to *any* sharp-bladed or sharp-pointed instrument. The gun attack data therefore combine both handgun attacks and attacks with long guns. The inclusion of long gun attacks, especially shotgun attacks, tends, for obvious reasons, to raise the average lethality of gun attacks. Likewise, the knife attacks in the data include not only attacks with butcher knives, hunting knives, and other relatively heavy long-bladed weapons, but also attacks with pocket knives, pen knives, ice picks, possibly even forks and beer can openers (anything, in short, that the police classify as a "sharp instrument"). These inclusions, also for obvious reasons, tend to lower the average lethality of knife attacks.

A more informative comparison might therefore involve handgun attacks versus attacks with heavy, long-bladed knives. The available data do *not* suggest that the former are distinctively more lethal than the latter. One study of people hospitalized with penetrating abdominal wounds found that about 83% of those shot with handguns survived the attack; for those stabbed with butcher knives, the survival rate was 87%, a trivially small differential. (These findings are reported in Kates, 1978: 18.) Another medical study of abdominal trauma (Kyzoff, Shaftan, and Herbsman, 1966, quoted in Kates, 1978) concludes, "there is no reason to expect that a sharp knife inflicts less damage than a dull, low velocity bullet."

are used by whites and nonwhites in about the same proportions. But the hypothesis states only that gun and knife attackers must differ "radically" in motivation, so neither (1) nor (2) bears directly on the issue.

Zimring acknowledges that "it can be argued that because a knife is viewed as a less serious weapon than a gun, a lower proportion of knife attacks represent attacks in earnest" (1968a: 729). To show that the rate of earnest attacks is the same for both knife and gun attacks, Zimring presents evidence on wound locations (1968a: Table 7). On the basis of these data, about 70% of all knife wounds (lethal or otherwise) are to the chest, abdomen, head, face, back, and neck: "areas that are associated with serious attacks." In contrast, only 56% of gunshot wounds are to these same areas. Zimring draws three inferences from this comparison:

1. "Not all gun attacks can be *per se* considered attacks in earnest" (1968a: 731). The apparent reasoning here is that because about 40% of all gunshot wounds are not to "serious" locations, many of them must be inflicted by people who are not seriously intent on killing the victim. Since we certainly cannot assume that every murderer is a perfect marksman, or that every murder weapon is perfectly accurate, the possibility of a sound inference about motive from evidence on wound locations is obviously quite remote.

2. "A substantial proportion of the knife attacks reported to police appear to be attacks in earnest" (1968a: 732). Here, Zimring appears to be on somewhat firmer ground. Between 70 and 80% of all knife wounds in his study were inflicted in "serious" locations (as defined above). Some fraction of these may have been accidentally serious, to be sure. Still, Zimring's 70% figure does at least suggest that a substantial portion of knife attacks are indeed "in earnest," and this constitutes the strongest evidence yet encountered that the motives of gun and knife attackers may be similar. (If this line of reasoning is valid, however, then the similarity between knife and gun attacks is that a *high* proportion of both are in earnest. This would bolster the "differential lethality" argument but tend to undercut the "ambiguous motivations" argument.)

3. "There is no evidence that attacks in earnest are much more common with guns than with knives" (1968a: 732). This is one conclusion with which we can agree, so long as we also agree that there is no evidence that they are not. The issue is simply not resolved by these data.

Following Zimring, Curtis (1974) has also considered the issue of homicidal motivations. The basic observation is again that firearms are much more prevalent in homicides than in aggravated assaults, a zero-order result confirmed in all studies. There are, Curtis notes, at least two possible explanations for this: (1) "The crimes can be viewed as very similar in circumstance, with the differential in their seriousness largely explained by the fact that homicide offenders happen to have more deadly weapons at hand" (the Zimring argument), or (2) "the homicide offender is more determined to kill and therefore chooses the weapon most capable of achieving this end" (the Wolfgang hypothesis) (1974: 108).

Curtis favors the first hypothesis, what he calls the "accessibility argument," but his evidence is no more persuasive than Zimring's. One piece of this evidence has already been discussed, namely, "the consistent similarity between homicide and assault." "The low level of premeditation in homicide" is cited as a second piece of evidence. The data analyzed by Curtis in themselves do not bear on the premeditation issue: "We were unable to make an accurate count of premeditated homicides from the information available" (1974: 67). "But," Curtis continues, "legal and behavioral experts concur that careful planning over a considerable period of time have minimal import for the bulk of American homicides" (1974: 67). The sole reference cited in this connection is an estimate by Wolfgang and Ferracuti (1967: 141) that fewer than 5% of all U.S. homicides are premeditated. When we turn to the Wolfgang and Ferracuti materials to find the empirical basis of this estimate, however, we find that there is none, or at least none presented or referenced in the text itself. To be sure, the "expert testimony" is there: "Probably fewer than five percent of all known homicides are premediated, planned, intentional killings, and the individuals who commit them are most likely to be episodic offenders who have never had prior contact with the criminal law" (1967: 141). But no reference for this estimate is cited, no tabulation of data is presented, no footnote directing the skeptical reader to the source of this information is given. It may well be that fewer than 5% of all homicides fit this description, but there is no *evidence,* either from Curtis or from Wolfgang and Ferracuti, that shows or even implies this to be the case.

There is, in fact, some evidence suggesting that the proportion of premeditated homicides is several times higher than the Wolfgang–Ferracuti 5% estimate. One study traced a sample of homicides through the courts and found that about 16% of them were prosecuted as first-degree murder cases (i.e., murders with premeditation). Since the effect of plea-bargaining and related "extra-legal" pre-trial negotiations is always to reduce (and never to increase) the charge, it is clear that the proportion of actual premeditated homicides among this sample would be higher (by an unknown amount) than the 16% figure. Even when one ignores this potentially large downward bias, the empirically generated estimate from this study is some three times the rate suggested in the Wolfgang–Ferracuti passage. The study showing the 16% figure is Wolfgang's own study of Philadelphia homicides (1958: 303).

A third source of evidence said by Curtis to favor the "accessibility" argument is another that we have already discussed, namely, the high proportion of homicides that are accompanied by altercations (1974: 108), about which nothing more need be said.

Fourth, "Pittman and Handy's [1964] careful comparison of homicide and assault is consistent with" the accessibility argument (Curtis, 1974: 108). This source consists of an analysis of 241 aggravated assaults investigated by police in St. Louis for calendar year 1961. No criminal homicide cases are contained in the Pittman–Handy study; the "careful comparison" thus comes at the end of the article, where the St. Louis assault findings are compared briefly with Wolfgang's Philadelphia homicide findings (Pittman and Handy, 1964: 469–470). This comparison suggests that homicides and assaults are similar in the time and locations of occurrence, in "situational context" (that is, both crimes are typically accompanied by altercations), in victim–offender relationships prior to the incident, and in a few other ways; and that these crimes are different in type of weapon used, in alcohol involvement, and in a few other ways. As in the Zimring materials already discussed, nothing is presented in the Pittman–Handy analysis that bears directly on similarities or differences in underlying motivations.

Fifth, there is a reference to "supportive clinical findings." In addition to citing the episodic evidence that "every psychiatrist has treated patients who were thankful that guns were not around at one time or another in their lives" (1974: 108), Curtis refers to an experiment conducted by Berkowitz (1967) that suggests that "even the casual sight of a gun may catalyze violence" (1974: 108). Since the willful, intentional murderer is not very likely to seek out psychiatric counseling for his or her aggressive acts, the evidence from "every psychiatrist" must be heavily discounted. Berkowitz' experimental evidence is rather more compelling at first blush, all the more so because the findings are very much along the lines implied in Curtis' characterization. But even here, at least two important caveats must be inserted:

1. It is hazardous to assume that the behavior of undergraduate psychology students in a laboratory setting can be generalized to the behavior of criminals engaged in aggressive and violent acts bringing injury or death to the victim.

2. Kleck (1979b) has reviewed this experimental literature in some detail and reports the following conclusions: The initial experiment by Berkowitz and LePage (1967), and the follow-up work by Berkowitz (1968), have been replicated in some subsequent experiments (for example, Fordi, 1973; Leynes and Parke, 1975; Page and O'Neal, 1977), but not in others. Fischer, Kelm, and Rose (1969), for example, using a knife as the stimulus, found the predicted enhanced aggression among male but not female subjects. Turner and Simons (1974) found the predicted effects only in less apprehensive and less sophisticated subjects. And several studies, among them reports by Page and Scheidt (1971), Buss, Booker, and Buss (1972), and Ellis, Weiner, and Miller (1971), found no "weapons effect" at all. According to Kleck, the experimental literature thus contains at least three or four studies to suggest,

as Curtis puts it, that "even the casual sight of a gun may catalyze violence," but at least three more studies suggesting the opposite conclusion, and at least two additional studies suggesting that the nature of the effect varies according to characteristics of the subjects.

Finally, "perhaps the most objective validation yet [of the accessibility argument] comes from Zimring's data on fatal vs. nonfatal assaults in Chicago" (Curtis, 1974: 108). The Zimring study in question is the 1968 study discussed in great detail above, which neither supports nor rules out the hypothesis that most homicides result from ambiguous prior intentions to kill.

In later work, Zimring (1972) has also compared the relative lethality of attacks with handguns of various calibers, using data on 156 handgun fatalities (from a total of more than 1100 total handgun attacks) in Chicago in a 4-month period in 1970. The general pattern revealed by these data is straightforward: the lethality of the attack (that is, the proportion of attacks resulting in the death of the victim) regularly increased with the caliber of the weapon. Initially, this would suggest that the inherent lethality of a handgun increases with caliber, which tends to support the "technological efficiency" argument and thus, indirectly, tends to undercut the "differential motivations" argument.

Again, however, there are reasons for caution. It is certainly plausible, as Wolfgang argues, that the truly determined killers choose guns, and it is a straightforward extension that the more determined they are, the larger the caliber they choose. A second, and perhaps more likely, possibility is that the truly determined killer prefers a firearm and attacks with whatever firearm is available. In this case, what varies over the caliber of the weapon is not the underlying intent but the success of the killer in realizing his intent. Still a third possibility is that the larger handguns are intrinsically more accurate, and thus that what varies by caliber is again not intent but the efficacy of the weapon in realizing one's intent. One apparently certain implication of Zimring's result is that the substitution of higher-caliber for lower-caliber handguns would almost certainly cause the rate of handgun deaths to increase—as, for example, might occur in the face of a ban on small-caliber handguns (the Saturday Night Specials) that left all the heavier-duty equipment (the large-caliber handguns) on the market (see also Kleck, 1979b).

There are, in addition to the studies of Zimring and Curtis, a number of others that report similar findings and that are therefore often cited as support for the hypothesis of ambiguous intentions. But the general form of the evidence is very similar to that already discussed; typically, they provide information on victim–offender relationships; on the presence of altercations as surface rationales for the homicides; on the preferential use of firearms, especially handguns, in homicides as compared to aggravated assaults; and so on. All such studies necessarily suffer from the same general problem, namely, that in the absence of direct information on underlying motivations, these motivations must be inferred from the objective circumstances surrounding each case, an indirect and perilous inference.

Seitz (1972), however, has taken an entirely different approach to the issue, and because his study is among the more commonly cited, it bears examining in some detail.

As all other researchers in this area, Seitz also has no direct evidence on the motivations underlying homicidal attacks, and so his refutation of the Wolfgang argument in favor of Zimring's position is not based on the kind of direct comparison of motivations that one would very much like to see. The strategy, rather, is to draw out from Wolfgang's hypothesis an implication that can be directly tested, and to reach some conclusions about the hypothesis on the basis of that test.

According to Seitz, "basic to Wolfgang's 'murder by substitution' hypothesis are two questionable assumptions: all or most deadly attacks are motivated by a single-minded intention to kill and all or most weapons which might be substituted for a firearm are as lethal as firearms" (1972: 595–596). This formulation misrepresents Wolfgang's position in at least one important respect: Wolfgang does *not* argue that all substitute weapons are ipso facto as lethal as firearms, only that the substitute weapon would be just as lethal as a firearm *if the assailant were motivated by an unambiguous and willful intention to kill.* This assumption is substantially less "questionable" than Seitz' rendition of it. But questionable or not, neither of these assumptions is directly tested in Seitz' paper.

The main finding reported by Seitz, and said to be inconsistent with Wolfgang's hypothesis, is that "there is an astonishing .98 correlation between the firearm homicide rate and the total homicide rate based on aggregate data for the fifty states" (1972: 596). Since it is not at all obvious that Wolfgang's hypothesis implies a contrary result, we need to ask about the line of reasoning that leads from what Wolfgang has actually proposed to an implication about this correlation. The relevant passage is as follows:

> Given the substitution hypothesis [that is, Wolfgang's hypothesis], we have little reason to expect any correlation between the firearm homicide rate and the total homicide rate. In fact, if such a correlation does exist, the substitution hypothesis is apparently inadequate to explain the observed systematic relation, since the availability of firearms does vary from area to area. On the other hand, the substitution hypothesis leads us to believe that such a correlation does not exist. For in areas where firearms access is relatively restricted, we should expect some proportional decrease in the firearm homicide rate but observe no change whatsoever in the total homicide rate. In aggregate comparison, therefore, there should be little or no correlation between firearms homicide rates and total homicide rates. (Seitz, 1972: 596)

We quote this passage in full mainly because of a strong suspicion that it is a non sequitur. That is, we find nothing here to show that a low correlation between the firearm and total homicide rates is implied, even indirectly, in the Wolfgang hypothesis. Wolfgang's hypothesis does imply that in areas where there are no guns, people would murder with other weapons, more or less at the same rate. This might in turn imply that in areas with relatively fewer guns, there would be relatively fewer gun murders and relatively more murders by other means. A test of this implication on state-level aggregate data would therefore require that the availability of firearms for illicit or criminal or homicidal purposes itself vary substantially across states, and although it is clear that the density of private gun ownership does vary in this manner (see Chapter 6), this does not necessarily mean that the availability of firearms *for use in willful homicide* varies likewise (despite Seitz' assertion to the contrary). In fact, Seitz' position would seem to imply that there are at least some states where a truly determined and willful killer would find it very difficult to lay hands on the appropriate firearm, and this is a dubious proposition at best.[10] In short, it is not at all clear that the availability of firearms for criminal purposes varies *enough* across states to make state-level aggregate data useful for examining these issues.

In any case, it *is* clear that Wolfgang's hypothesis cannot be made to stand or fall on the basis of a methodological artifact, which Seitz' "astonishing" 0.98 correlation is, at least in substantial part. The artifice is simply that in every state, homicides with firearms constitute a large portion of the total homicides; in fact, as is well known, approximately half or more of all homicides are committed with firearms. Since firearms homicides represent a large fraction of all homicides, then, by construction, the rate of firearms homicide *must* be strongly correlated with the total homicide rate, with the magnitude of the necessary correlation determined strictly by the proportional contribution of firearms homicides to the total. What the 0.98 correlation implies, in short, is only that Seitz has the same variable (or nearly the same variable) on both sides of the equation.

In sum, none of the studies of homicide considered here confirms or rules out the hypothesis that most homicides result from willful and unambiguous

---

[10] Consider, for example, the case of New York City. In general, there are fewer private weapons in the Northeast than in other sections of the country; moreover, there are fewer in urban locations than in rural locations (see Chapter 6 for evidence on both points). Also, New York has as restrictive a set of firearms laws as any city in the country. But would we want to argue from these facts that the "availability" of firearms for criminal purposes is somehow less in New York City than in, say, Boise, Idaho, where the rates of private gun ownership are very much higher? Hardly. A recent guess, published in *The New York Times* for 2 March 1975, is that there are some 2 million *illegal handguns* within the city limits; and according to Cook (1978: 283), "18 percent of all U.S. robberies are committed in New York City alone."

intentions to kill. This, to emphasize a recurring but important theme, is not to argue that Wolfgang's alternative hypothesis is true, but only that the studies most often cited as showing it to be false do not show this at all. The essential point here is not that one hypothesis is consistent with the available evidence and the other not, but rather that most of the "evidence" assembled on either side of the issue has little or no relevance to it.

Ironically, some of the strongest evidence favoring the "ambiguous intentions" hypothesis about homicides comes not from studies of homicides, but from studies of robbery, particularly armed robbery. Armed robbery is an especially interesting crime in the present context because there is usually no uncertainty about the underlying motives. In most cases, the motive of robbery is economic gain to the offender.[11] And since the motive underlying most robbery tends to be the same, then the differences in outcomes of robberies presumably do not reflect differences in underlying motivations and would therefore reflect "something else." One possibility, for example, might be that differences in outcome reflect differences in the intrinsic lethality of weapons used to commit robberies, independent of the underlying motives of offenders. What, then, do the data on robberies show?

Cook (1976, 1978, 1980a) has proposed what he calls a "strategic choice" analysis of robbery. The essence of this analysis is "that observed robbery patterns are the aggregative result of choices made by individual robbers, and that these choices can be understood in terms of the robber's need to intimidate his victim and his desire to acquire as much money as possible with a minimum of effort" (1976: 173).[12] The two key choices that robbers must make are, first, who to rob, and second, with what weapon.

For a variety of subtle reasons, these two choices are intimately connected to each other. All else equal the first choice is a simple one: rob the most lucrative targets. But, as Cook points out, the most lucrative targets tend not to be the easiest targets, and vice versa. The very young and the very old, for example, are easy robbery targets, but not very lucrative; banks are very lucrative but not very easy to rob. Even restricting attention to noncommercial robberies, it is not hard to imagine that ease and profitability are negatively

[11] The exception would be an intentional homicide where the victim was robbed as an afterthought, which would be more murder than robbery, but which would probably be treated by the police as a "robbery homicide" (see Cook, 1978: 304). Cook's (1978) article presents some evidence that this exception is *not* typical of robbery homicides; in most such cases, the motive is robbery and the homicide is an "afterthought," not the reverse. Later work (Cook, 1979c, 1980a), however, suggests that slaying the victim may be the primary motive more frequently than initially assumed. The implication of this is discussed later in the text.

[12] Cook's phrasing here is not sexist so much as descriptive; according to his (1976: 175) data, "robbery is a male occupation, 96 percent of incidents involved male offenders (including 3 percent in which males and females worked together)."

related; the probability that potential victims are themselves armed and in a position to deter a robbery would certainly be expected to increase with the amount of cash or other valuables being carried. Thus, any choice to rob only the most lucrative targets would tend to be accompanied by a parallel choice to employ the most intimidating possible means of robbery, namely, a firearm. Alternatively, if a robber were content to rob only easy (and relatively unlucrative) targets, then a less intimidating weapon would suffice.

The essential point that flows from Cook's analysis, at least for our purposes, is that robbers arm themselves with firearms not because they have relatively more lethal intentions with respect to their eventual victims, but because they expect to be robbing relatively more lucrative targets and need a high level of intimidation in order to be successful. The death of the victim, when it occurs, is not the intention of the robber in most cases.

Death or injury to the victim is not an uncommon accompaniment to robbery. In 1974, for example, some 17% of all murders that occurred in the United States occurred during the course of a robbery (Cook, 1976: 181). Or, figuring from the other direction, roughly five of every thousand robberies result in the murder of the victim, and roughly six in every hundred result in personal injury (Cook, 1978: Tables 1 and 2). (Here, "personal injury" means injuries sufficiently serious that a medical expense is incurred by the victim as a result.) Thus, a very large majority of all robberies apparently involve "successful" threats by the perpetrator, capitulation by the victims, and no direct physical harm; in about 90 to 95% of the cases the threat of harm is apparently adequate. But in a nontrivial fraction of the cases (the remaining 5–10%), threat alone is not enough and some physical harm actually comes to the victim. It is the outcomes of these cases that bear on the themes of this chapter.

Data presented by Cook (1976: Table 10–4) suggest that approximately 38% of all robberies are unarmed; in 41% of the cases, robbers are armed with some weapon other than a firearm; and in the remaining 21% of the cases, the robber is armed with a gun—almost invariably a handgun. These data thus suggest that about a third of all *armed* robberies are committed with guns. A later estimate by the same author is rather higher, at 45% (Cook, 1978: 282), and 1974 data for Detroit reported by Zimring (1977: Table 1) show a figure as high as 70%. (Zimring's data also show some very evident long-term trends. First, the percentage of all robbery that is armed increases quite substantially in his data, from 49% in 1962 to 61% in 1974. Second, the fraction of armed robberies committed with a firearm also increases, from 41% in 1962 to 70% registered in the 1974 data.) Depending on year, city, and various intangibles, then, we may conclude that firearms are involved in something between one-third and two-thirds of all the armed robberies that get committed.

How do death and injury rates in robbery vary as a function of weapon? On the grounds that guns are more effective intimidators than any other weapon, it is sometimes argued that gun robberies should be *less* likely than other forms of robbery to result in harm to the victim. This argument asserts, in essence, that victims are less likely to resist, and thus less likely to be harmed, if the robber is armed with a gun. Indeed, most available studies of *personal injuries* in robbery tend to sustain this speculation. In Cook's (1976) data, for example, 6.2% of all robbery victims, irrespective of weapon, were injured to the extent that they incurred some medical expenses as a result. Among victims robbed with a gun, however, the proportion was only 2.8%; among those robbed with a knife, 6.6%; and among those robbed with any other weapon, 12.0%. Interestingly, 5.2% of the victims of *unarmed* robberies incurred some medical expense, approximately double the percentage of injured victims among those robbed with a gun. Similar results have also been reported by Cook and Nagin (1979), Conklin (1972), Block (1977a), and in most other studies that have examined robbery injuries as a function of weapon type. Cook's conclusions from these and similar data bear quoting. "Gun robberies," he writes, "are *least* likely to result in an injury requiring medical care, and a relatively low percentage (0.3 percent) result in serious injuries ($1,000 or more in medical expenses). A gun ordinarily eliminates the need for a robber to physically attack the victim in order to gain his compliance" (1976: 185).

All this, of course, speaks only to the issue of personal injuries and says nothing about deaths. No homicide victims *ever* appear in criminal victimization surveys, so Cook's 1976 data are not adequate to address this issue. Other data, however, show quite unmistakably that the death patterns are just the opposite of the injury patterns. In particular, whereas firearms robberies are substantially *less* likely than other forms of robbery to result in the injury of the victim, they are substantially *more* likely to result in the victim's death. Unpublished UCR data reported by Cook (1978), for example, show 7.66 robbery-connected murders per 1000 gun robberies, compared to 2.71 robbery-connected murders per 1000 nongun robberies, for a lethality differential of about 3 to 1 (Cook, 1978: Table 2). Zimring's Detroit data show the same pattern: "Death rates from gun robbery are consistently higher than those reported for other methods of attack" in all years in which data are available (1977: 321). As far as we can determine, there is no study in the published literature to contradict this conclusion. Robbery by gun is less likely to lead to injury, but more likely to lead to death, than robbery by any other means.

Why, then, are robbery-connected gun assaults substantially more lethal than robbery-connected assaults with other weaponry? If, as we have assumed, the underlying motive in all robberies is about the same, this difference cannot reflect differences in underlying motives. We tentatively suggest that the difference results mainly from the differential inherent lethality of guns relative to other weapons. Thus, the differential death rates in robberies committed with guns versus other weapons appear to be the only strong evidence available that gun assaults are more likely to lead to death than are assaults with other weapons, *independently of any possible confounding correlation with differences in underlying motivations*. If we further assume that the lethality in question is a property of the weapon, and not a property of the crime, then the enhanced lethality of guns would generalize across crimes, which in turn lends credence to the "differential lethality" interpretation of the homicide and aggravated assault data considered in great detail above.

But even here, there is reason for caution. Throughout this discussion, we have assumed that the underlying motive in all robbery is similar, namely, economic gain to the robber, and thus, that differences in outcomes do not reflect differences in underlying motive. More recent research by Cook (1979c, 1980a), however, has questioned whether economic gain is in fact the underlying motive in at least one important class of armed robberies: those in which the victim is slain (the critical type of robbery in this discussion). According to Cook's recent evidence, examples, and analysis, many robbery murders do not arise "accidentally" or "unintentionally," as the result of unforseen circumstances (e.g., victim resistance), but rather result from what is most appropriately described as the innate brutality (or violence proneness) of those doing the robbery. Explicitly, Cook's analysis shows that many of these robbery homicides occur for no other reason than the sheer thrill of watching someone die. This seems especially to be the case in robberies committed by more than one offender (e.g., gang robberies). If, as seems reasonable, the innately brutal preferentially arm themselves with firearms, then it is again possible that the lethality differential in the robbery case *also* reflects differences in a priori motive or intent, rather than inherent differences in the lethality of the weapon chosen. Thus it must be concluded that even the robbery data analyzed here are at least somewhat unclear with respect to their implications for the "ambiguous intentions" or "differential intentions" arguments.

The above point notwithstanding, the robbery data provide at least some reason to believe, along with Zimring, Curtis, and many others, that reduced availability of guns would lead to reduced death from violent crime. But the robbery data reported by Cook also suggest that this would not be a pure and unalloyed "plus" all across the board; the decrease in violent death, it appears, might be balanced off against some very undesirable increases, along the following lines:

1. If there were no guns with which to commit robberies, it is at least possible that the overall robbery rate would sharply increase. Presumably owing to the level of intimidation and the lucrativeness of targets chosen,

gun robberies are sharply more profitable than robberies committed by other means. In Cook's victimization data, for example, the average "take" in robberies committed with guns was $164, and only 22% of these robberies resulted in a zero take. In contrast, the average take in knife robberies was only $60, and 34% of them resulted in zero take. These figures suggest that a robber would have to substitute approximately three knife robberies to generate the same average profit generated in one gun robbery. The possible implications of this for the overall robbery rate are distressingly obvious.

2. The reduction in deaths that might occur in the "no-guns" condition would probably by accompanied by an increase in personal injuries. Knife robberies are at least twice as likely to involve an assault of the victim as are gun robberies, and robberies with other forms of weaponry are more likely still. Any wholesale replacement of gun robberies with other armed (but nongun) robberies would therefore presumably cause the overall rates of personal injury in robbery to increase, simply because fewer victims would be readily intimidated and there would be fewer cases in which the mere threat of violence was ample.

3. Since, in light of Cook's strategic choice analysis, guns permit access to more lucrative targets, the absence of guns would presumably cause robbers to focus on less lucrative and less resistant targets. Thus, a "no-guns" condition might lead to fewer robberies committed against healthy middle-aged males, but proportionally (or even absolutely) more robberies committed against women, the very young, and the elderly.

These potential "negative feedback loops" in the guns and robbery equation at least suggest the possibility that society would be not much better off under the "no-guns" conditions than it is under present conditions, at least insofar as death and injury resulting from robbery are concerned. Suppose, for example, that it were somehow possible to reduce the number of guns available for robbery to zero. Suppose, further, that in this condition all the robberies now committed with guns would be committed with some other armament, presumably knives. Assume that each present gun robbery would be replaced by three armed nongun robberies, in order to equalize the total profits under both arrangements. And suppose, finally, that the weapons-specific death and injury rates reported by Cook (1976, 1978) continued to hold. With these assumptions in hand, it is possible to construct Table 10-2, which projects total deaths and injuries resulting from robberies under the present and a hypothetical "no-guns" condition.

The projections for the present condition are based on a hypothetical 1000 robberies; Cook's death and injury rates suggest that under present conditions, these 1000 robberies would lead to roughly 3.75 victim deaths and some 58 victim injuries. These figures are approximately equivalent to the present death and injury rates from robberies of all sorts.

Projections to the "no-guns" condition are positively dreary. Note first

TABLE 10-2. *Projected deaths and injuries resulting from robberies under present and hypothetical "no-guns" conditions*[a]

Type	N	Death rate	Deaths	Injury rate	Injuries
Present condition (N = 1000 robberies)					
Gun	210	7.66/1,000	1.61	3/100	6
Other weapon	410			8/100	33
Unarmed	380	2.71/1,000	2.14	5/100	19
Totals	1000		3.75		58
"No-guns" condition (N = 1420 robberies)					
Gun	—	—	—	—	—
Other weapon	1040			8/100	83
Unarmed	380	2.71/1,000	3.85	5/100	19
Totals	1420		3.85		102

[a] See text for details.

that the "substitution" of three armed nongun robberies for each present gun robbery raises the total number of robberies from 1000 to 1420. Note further that in light of this increase, the total projected victim death does not decline; it is, rather, approximately the same as the number projected for the present condition (3.85 versus 3.75 deaths). Total victim injuries, however, approximately double, from 58 to 102. In short, considering only the death and injury that result from robbery, these figures intimate that a "no-gun" condition might effectively double the number of injuries incurred and leave the total number of deaths more or less unaffected.[13]

These projections, of course, are extremely conjectural and cannot under any circumstance be taken as "most probable case" scenarios. The point of Table 10-2 is only to illustrate some of the possible implications of the analyses of robbery by Cook and others. Additional complexities that are not reflected in the table would have to be incorporated for these projections to be taken seriously. For example, as Cook (1976) argues, the reduced profitability of robbery in the "no guns" condition might cause many potential robbers to forego robbery in favor of some more conventional business, and this deterrent might offset the anticipated robbery increases on which Table 10-2 is based.

[13] Indeed, the "no-guns" situation might even be worse than this depiction. The projections of Table 10-2 do not take into account any possible "substitution" of less resistant for more resistant targets of robbery, and yet Cook's strategic choice analysis implies that this would follow in a "no-guns" condition. In turn, injuries that were serious to an able-bodied healthy man might well prove fatal to an 80-year-old woman. If the "no-guns" condition caused substantially more robberies to be committed, say, against the very old, then some fraction of the projected injuries might, in fact, turn out to be projected deaths. In such a case, the advantages of the "no-guns" condition would be even dimmer.

Also, if the differential lethality of guns relative to other weaponry applied across crime types, then there would also be some drop in homicidal deaths (if not in robbery deaths), and these effects would have to be taken into account in any persuasive "probable case" scenario. Table 10-2 therefore does *not* amount to a "best guess" about what society might be like in the "no-guns" condition. Rather, it serves the much more modest, but nonetheless very useful function of demonstrating just how complex this whole matter of guns, crime, and violence is.

III

WEAPONS AND THEIR CONTROL

ELEVEN

PUBLIC OPINION AND GUN CONTROL

> Majorities of American voters believe that we do *not* need more laws governing the possession and use of firearms and that more firearms laws would *not* result in a decrease in the crime rate.

> It is clear that the vast majority of the public (both those who live with handguns and those who do not) want handgun licensing and registration. . . . [T]he American public wants some form of handgun control legislation.

As the above and apparently contradictory assertions demonstrate, the state of public thinking on the issues discussed in this volume is a matter of considerable debate, with both the proponents and opponents of stricter gun controls claiming the weight of majority opinion for their position. In itself, this is hardly remarkable: polemicists and advocates make frequent and routine use of phrases such as "public opinion," "most Americans," or the "vast majority" as symbolic and rhetorical devices. But in the present case, both sides also lay claim to a body of supporting evidence which is said to demonstrate that "public opinion" is favorable to their point of view. A detailed review of some of this evidence is thus the topic of the present chapter.[1]

Our attention focuses specifically on two rather large-scale national opinion polls conducted in 1978. The passages quoted above are from the Executive Summaries of the two reports in which the poll findings are presented. The first passage is from a report entitled "Attitudes of the American Electorate Toward Gun Control 1978." The report was prepared by Decision Making Information, Inc. (DMI), of Santa Ana, California, a private for-profit research and polling firm. The report is based on a national survey conducted during

---

[1] The material in this chapter is an expanded version of James Wright, 1981, "Public Opinion and Gun Control: A Comparison of Results from Two Recent National Surveys," *The Annals of the American Academy of Political and Social Science* 455 (May): 24–39.

1978 (actually, DMI conducted two surveys for the report; see below) and it was commissioned by the National Rifle Association.

The second passage is from a report entitled "An Analysis of Public Attitudes Toward Handgun Control," prepared by Cambridge Reports, Inc., Patrick Caddell's political polling firm. The Caddell report also derives from a large national survey conducted in 1978 and was commissioned by the Philadelphia-based Center for the Study and Prevention of Handgun Violence.[2]

Findings from the DMI polls have been cited and discussed in several of the previous chapters. Also, in Chapter 7, findings from both polls on the uses of private weaponry were compared. Here we focus more specifically on the evidence from the two surveys that pertains to public opinion about various aspects of guns and gun control.

This chapter is *not* a review of the published literature on public opinion and gun control per se, although some findings from this literature are noted where appropriate. Capable literature reviews in the area already exist (see the sources cited later in this chapter in footnote 9). Our focus here is specifically on comparing the results of the DMI and Caddell polls. A detailed comparison of the results of these two opinion surveys is instructive for several reasons. Of these, the most important involves the substance of the issue, namely, whether "most Americans" do or do not favor stricter weapons controls. Together, the two reports are nearly encyclopedic in their coverage of contemporary public opinion on weapons-related issues. As we show below, the comparison of results across surveys demonstrates that the majority opinion depends critically on the specific kinds of "stricter controls" envisioned, the likely costs, and the purposes that additional controls are meant to serve.

A subsidiary aim of the comparison is to evaluate what we shall call the "anti-survey hypothesis," which, at the most general level, states that surveys in essence *create* the reality they purport to measure. The general idea behind this hypothesis is that there is really no such thing as "public opinion" except as it is called into being by public opinion polls; respondents, it is said, simply "manufacture" the answers that they think the investigators want to hear. The kinds of answers one gets are thus (or perhaps, can be) predetermined by the hypotheses or political purposes of the investigators: one needs only to design the study in such a way as to generate whatever response one or one's client wishes to hear. The alternative possibility, of course, is that there is an underlying reality to public opinion, a reality that will tend to surface

---

[2] Strictly speaking, the Center for the Study and Prevention of Handgun Violence is not a lobbying organization, but rather a research and educational enterprise founded by Milton Eisenhower. The principal executive officers of the Center, however, are all active in pro-control lobbying organizations; for example, the Center's director, Mr. Nelson Shields, is also President of Handgun Control, Inc. (We thank Mr. Shields for his helpful and gracious commentary on earlier drafts of the material in this chapter.)

despite the a priori expectations, aims, or purposes or the researchers or their sponsors. A comparison between these two surveys thus provides a unique opportunity to consider whether and how poll findings are biased by the outlooks and ideologies of the organizations that conduct research or by the clients who pay for it.[3]

TECHNICAL COMPARISONS

Neither report was prepared for an academic audience; consequently, the amount of technical information provided about the two surveys is meager. As far as can be determined, however, both surveys were competently done and both appear to have been conducted well within the current standards and practices of survey research.

The Caddell survey is based on a national probability sample of adults aged 18 and over. The data consist of 1500 personal interviews conducted between April 20 and May 15, 1978, by Caddell's professional interviewing staff. No information about the response rate or field procedures is given. In addition to the textual narrative, the Caddell report includes a verbatim copy of the questionnaire with all marginal results displayed, including the coded marginal responses to various open-ended questions. (The "marginal results" are simply the percentages giving each of the various answers to the survey questions.) The report also provides a package of cross-tabulations of main dependent variables with sex, race, age, education, income, union membership, religion, region, and a few other background variables. No analysis more complex than two-variable cross-tabulations is discussed or presented in the report.

The DMI report is based on two surveys, both involving nationally representative samples of *registered voters* (rather than of all adults). The first consists of 1500 personal interviews conducted between May 19 and June 9, 1978, by DMI's professional interviewing staff.[4] (Note, then, that DMI's surveying began just 4 days after Caddell's ended.) The sample of registered voters

---

[3] Indeed, the situation here is most fortunate. DMI and Cambridge Reports, Inc., are both reasonably well-known and respected private research and polling firms. DMI works primarily for conservative candidates and causes, while Caddell works primarily for liberals. Both organizations were in the field with their studies at about the same time; both studies are concerned with essentially the same subject matter. With the exceptions of their own organizational proclivities and those of the study sponsors, then, all else is equal, or at least equal enough for the purposes at hand.

[4] Thus, both DMI's and Caddell's face-to-face surveys are said to be based on a final N of 1500 respondents. Whether these are exact or only approximate Ns cannot be determined from the reports themselves, so we treat them as if they were exact in this analysis.

was achieved by an initial filter question: people not currently registered to vote (or with no intention of registering before the November 1978 elections) were terminated from the interview. The second survey, also of registered voters, consisted of 1010 telephone interviews conducted during December 9–12; again, an initial filter question was used to determine eligibility for

TABLE 11-1. *Sample demographics for the DMI and Caddell surveys*[a]

Variable	DMI[b] (%)	Caddell (%)	March 1978 CPS (%)
Age[c]			
18–24	12	19	18
25–34	25	22	22
35–44	15	17	15
45–54	14	14	15
55–64	17	14	14
65 and over	17	14	15
Sex			
Male	50	51	49
Female	50	49	51
Education			
Less than high school	22	28	33
High school graduate	35	41[d]	36
Some college	25	19	17
College graduate	18	13	14
Race			
White	89	84	83
Non-white	11	16	17
Average Family Income ($)[e]	16,250	15,446	16,010

[a] Because of differences between the two surveys in terms of demographic questions asked and the response categories in which responses are coded, the variables shown in the table exhaust the direct demographic comparisons that are possible between the surveys.

[b] DMI data shown here are for the *face-to-face survey only*. (The telephone survey introduces additional biases related to the tendency to own a telephone that would obscure the direct comparisons being made here.)

[c] These are the DMI age categories; the Caddell categories are "off" by one year (thus, the figure shown in the first line under "Caddell" is the proportion 18–25, not 18–24; and in the second line, 26–35 rather than 25–34, etc.).

[d] Includes "high school graduates" (37%) and "technical/vocational" (4%).

[e] Neither report gives an average family income figure; the numbers shown here are means calculated from percentaged income distributions. The percentaged income data from each survey are as follows:

Income category	Assumed midpoint	Percentage
DMI		
Less than 5,000	2,500	15
5,000–9,999	7,500	17
10,000–14,999	12,500	18
15,000–19,999	17,500	18
20,000–29,999	25,000	20
30,000 and up	35,000	12
		100%
		($N = 1500$)
Caddell		
Less than 4,000	2,000	6
4,000–6,999	5,500	9
7,000–9,999	8,500	9
10,000–12,999	11,500	11
13,000–14,999	14,000	10
15,000–19,999	17,500	15
20,000–24,999	22,500	10
25,000 and up	30,000	13
		83%
		($N = 1500$)

Note, then, that the Caddell survey apparently generates 17% missing data on income, whereas in the DMI survey, the missing data on income are apparently omitted from the frequency distribution. The mean income for the Caddell survey reported in the table is thus based on an effective N of 1245 ($= .83 \times 1500$).

Source of CPS data: Current Population Reports. Population Characteristics, 1978 (No. 336), April 1979.

the sample.[5] No information on response rate is given for either DMI survey; some information on sample design and field operations is presented, however, and this information suggests that sound research procedures were employed. Unlike the Caddell report, the DMI report presents confidence limits for the results. The DMI report also contains a glossary defining technical terms used in the report and verbatim copies of both questionnaires showing all marginal results (including coded responses to various open-ended questions), but it contains no tabulations beyond those presented and discussed in the

[5] Unless otherwise noted in the text, we treat the two DMI surveys as a single survey throughout this chapter.

textual narrative. As in the Caddell report, no analysis more complex than two-variable cross-tabulations is presented.

There is an important difference in the substantive foci of the two reports: the Caddell report focuses almost exclusively on *handguns*, whereas the DMI report deals with handguns *and* long guns, which are then kept separate in the analysis.

Table 11-1 compares the sample demographics obtained in the two surveys; the table also shows comparable figures from the March 1978 Current Population Survey (CPS). Because of the additional complexities introduced by telephone samples, the DMI data shown in the table are from its face-to-face survey only. It is apparent that both surveys achieve demographic distributions that are respectably close to the "true" values (as indicated by the CPS data). The major differences between the surveys are all in the direction one would expect given the initial difference in sampling frames; that is, DMI's sample of registered voters is somewhat older, whiter, and more middle class than Caddell's sample of U.S. adults, and all of these variables are known to be related to whether one is registered to vote.[6]

Social status is also correlated with the tendency to own a weapon (see Chapter 6) and with attitudes toward gun control; in general, both weapons ownership and opposition to stricter weapons controls *increase* with social status.[7] For this reason alone, we would expect the DMI sample to be somewhat less supportive of gun control measures than the Caddell sample. However, the magnitude of the differences introduced by this factor should not be large, first because the socioeconomic differences between the surveys are themselves modest and second because the correlation of gun control attitudes with socioeconomic status is relatively weak (in the range of 0.1 to 0.2).[8]

---

[6] Note that both surveys report sex ratios very close to 50–50, the correct population value. It is well known that the correct sex ratio is very difficult to obtain with standard probability samples of households, because of the differential tendency of women to be present in the home at any particular moment. The reported sex ratios for the two surveys thus suggest either (1) that both organizations took extraordinary steps to execute a probability sample down to the individual level—a time-consuming and expensive undertaking; or (2) that both samples are probability samples down to the level of blocks or other enumeration areas and are quota samples (with sex defining the quotas) below the level of blocks. All things considered, the second possibility is the more likely.

[7] This finding is reported in the Caddell survey and is also reported in the academic literature reviewed in Chapter 6. That opposition to the Gallup "police permit" item (see text, below) *increases* with income is reported in Wright and Marston (1975).

[8] It must, of course, be emphasized that neither of these sampling frames is "better" than the other. "All adults" is an appropriate sampling frame for the study of public opinion; so is "all registered voters."

COMPARISONS OF SUBSTANTIVE FINDINGS

Pollsters have been measuring opinions about gun control in the United States since at least 1938. In the Gallup poll of that year, 79% of the public said they favored "gun control," and most surveys and polls conducted since then have reported more or less similar results. Erskine has reviewed the poll data on the topic from 1938 through 1972 and reports that "the vast majority of Americans have favored some kind of action for the control of civilian firearms at least as long as modern polling has been in existence" (1972: 455). The best-known question on gun control was instituted by Gallup in 1959. It reads: "Would you favor or oppose a law which would require a person to obtain a police permit before he or she could buy a gun?" The proportion favoring such a law stood at 75% in 1959 and has varied from 68% to 78% in all Gallup polls since. The National Opinion Research Center (NORC) has included the identical item in its annual General Social Survey; from 1972 through 1977, the proportion in favor of such a law varied between 70 and 75%.[9]

The other poll materials reviewed by Erskine, however, do not all uniformly suggest the same high pro-control percentages that are routinely revealed in the "police permit" question. One item from an Opinion Research Center poll for 1968, for example, asked: "Do you think that people like yourself have to be prepared to defend their homes against crime and violence, or can the police take care of that?" Somewhat more than one half the sample (52%) felt that people should "be prepared," and only 40% thought that such matters could be left to the police. In 1971, Harris asked a similar question: "Do you tend to agree or disagree that the way things are today, people should own guns for their own protection?" Forty-nine percent of the sample agreed with this viewpoint, 43% disagreed, and the remainder had no opinion. And in March 1968, Harris also found that 51% of the U.S. population would "use your gun to shoot other people in case of a riot." In the same Harris poll, 93% of the population agreed that "individual shootings can happen any time because it only takes one madman to shoot another man" and there was a 50–50 split on the statement that "control of guns might not cut down on violence at all."

The lesson to be learned here, rather an obvious one, is that public opinion is not of a piece on the gun control issue; as in all other areas of public

---

[9] There are several useful reviews of the existing poll data on gun control opinions. Erskine (1972) provides a compendium of virtually all relevant national results up through the early 1970's. See also Stinchcombe et al. (1980) and Schuman and Presser (1977–78) for more recent findings.

opinion measurement, different questions, posed in different ways, and dealing with different aspects of the issue, generate somewhat different results. A second lesson, also obvious, is that with some selective picking and choosing among topics, questions, and phrasings, one can elicit a very wide range of results. This wide range, of course, does not imply that public opinion is ephemeral or ill-formed, but rather that the issue itself is complex and multi-faceted.

Tables 11-2 and 11-3 display the question wordings and marginal results for all items from the two surveys that bear on opinions about gun control; the Caddell data are shown in Table 11-2, and the DMI data in Table 11-3.[10] Items are shown in the order in which they were presented to respondents, although originally other items (not shown) often intervened between those shown contiguously here; thus, the item numbers in the tables are given for ease of reference only. In Table 11-3, items 1 through 23 are from the DMI face-to-face survey, and 24 through 31 are from the telephone survey. Where it seems to matter, we show the question "lead-ins" as well as the questions themselves. Finally, all numbers in the tables are reported exactly as they appear in the respective reports, whether they add up to 100%, or include the missing data, or not.

The first notable aspect of the two tables is that, although both surveys are ostensibly about the same topic, *very few items are common to both surveys*. (The few exceptions are discussed below.) This again confirms that public opinion on gun control is sufficiently multifaceted that two entire surveys can be done on the topic and still touch relatively little common ground. The relative absence of items common to both surveys also intimates some selectivity on the part of both organizations as to the facets of opinion about gun control that they wish to explore, an intimation confirmed below.

Opinions on Specific Control Measures

Caddell has the more extensive question sequence on opinions about specific handgun control measures (CADDELL 1–17); DMI's questionnaires, surprisingly, contain rather little along these lines. The Caddell sequence is prefaced with a lead-in stipulating that the measures in question are for the purpose of "controlling handgun violence" and does not mention the control

---

[10] The listings in Tables 11-2 and 11-3 are nearly, but not entirely, complete. Both Caddell and DMI have rather extensive amounts of open-ended materials that are presented and discussed in the reports but not included in the tables shown here. DMI also has a long series on the effectiveness of various measures, including gun control measures, in fighting crime; these items and results are discussed later in this chapter but they are not included in the DMI table.

TABLE 11-2. *Public opinion on gun control: Results from the Caddell survey*

Here are some specific proposals that have been made for controlling handgun violence. Would you tell me whether you strongly favor, somewhat favor, somewhat oppose, or strongly oppose each proposal with respect to civilians only. Law enforcement personnel would not be affected.

	Strongly favor (%)	Somewhat favor (%)	Somewhat oppose (%)	Strongly oppose (%)	Do not know (%)
1. A crackdown on illegal sales.	72	13	5	6	5
2. Strengthening the rules for becoming a commercial handgun dealer.	63	18	7	5	7
3. Institute a waiting period before a handgun can be purchased to allow for a criminal records check.	74	14	4	3	5
4. Require prospective handgun purchasers to get a permit or license to purchase.	65	17	7	7	5
5. Require the registration of all handguns at the time of purchase or transfer.	67	17	5	7	5
6. Require the registration of all handguns now owned.	57	17	9	11	6
7. Require a license to own a handgun at all.	58	16	10	11	6
8. Make the rules for a license to own a handgun stricter.	55	17	10	11	8
9. Require a license to carry a handgun outside of one's house or business.	61	18	8	8	6
10. Make the rules for getting a license to carry a handgun . . . strict.	57	19	9	10	5
11. Require mandatory prison sentences for all persons using a gun in a crime.	68	15	6	6	6
12. Require mandatory prison sentences for all persons carrying a handgun . . . without a license.	38	17	17	21	8

TABLE 11-2 (continued)

13. Ban the future manufacture and sale of non-sporting type handguns.	33	15	20	21	11
14. Ban the future manufacture and sale of cheap, low-quality handguns.	54	16	10	13	7
15. Ban the future manufacture and sale of all handguns.	23	9	22	36	10
16. Use public funds to buy back and destroy existing handguns on a voluntary basis.	22	11	19	37	11
17. Use public funds to buy back and destroy existing handguns on a mandatory basis.	19	7	17	45	12

18. On [this card] are the phrases "favor banning all private ownership of handguns" and "oppose banning all private ownership of handguns," separated by seven blank spaces. I would like you to place yourself on the blank which best represents your position between the two opinions.

Favor banning	1	17%
	2	6
	3	8
Neutral	4	18
	5	8
	6	10
Oppose banning	7	33

19. Do you think it is possible to have effective controls on handguns without having controls on long guns, such as rifles and shotguns, or not?

Yes	37%
Not sure	23
No	40

The following are a number of arguments which are raised both for and against handgun control. Can you tell me if you strongly agree, agree, disagree, or strongly disagree with each one.

	Strongly agree (%)	Agree (%)	Disagree (%)	Strongly disagree (%)	Do Not know (%)
20. Requiring all handgun owners to be licensed would prevent law-abiding citizens from protecting themselves.	21	19	37	15	9
21. Requiring all handgun owners to be licensed would reduce crime.	21	28	28	14	10
22. Requiring all handgun owners to be licensed would violate people's constitutional rights.	17	19	37	16	11
23. Requiring all handgun owners to be licensed is just another step by government to interfere in people's lives and limit their freedom.	18	19	36	17	11
24. Requiring all handgun owners to be licensed would cut down on the number of violent crimes.	22	28	26	14	10
25. Requiring all handgun owners to be licensed is just the first step in confiscating all guns, including shotguns.	19	20	35	12	15
26. Requiring all handgun owners to be licensed is a good idea because it will defuse the pressure for total gun control.	17	30	24	9	21

27. Would you be much more inclined, somewhat more inclined, somewhat less inclined, or much less inclined to vote for a candidate who favored handgun controls?

Much more	22%
Somewhat more	27
Somewhat less	15
Much less	13
Do not know	23

225

TABLE 11-2 (*continued*)

28. Would you agree or disagree with the following statements: I would never vote for a political candidate who favored banning the sale of all handguns to private citizens.

Agree	37%
Do not know	24
Disagree	40

29. Gun control laws affect only law-abiding citizens, criminals will always be able to find guns.

Agree	78%
Do not know	10
Disagree	13

30. The only way to control handguns is by Federal law; state laws which allow them to be purchased in some states and not others are ineffective.

Agree	70%
Do not know	17
Disagree	14

TABLE 11-3. *Public opinion on gun control: Results from the DMI surveys*

Here is a list of various crimes. Look it over, please, and then tell me which three of these kinds of crimes you yourself are most afraid of for yourself and your family.

	First choice (%)	Second choice (%)	Third choice (%)
1. Murder by a friend or relative	6	3	4
2. Murder in the course of robbery, burglary, or another crime	34	16	13
3. Rape	16	20	13
4. Robbery, mugging	17	26	23
5. Burglary, theft	19	21	19
6. Vandalism	8	11	20
7. Fraud, embezzlement, or forgery	2	3	8

In recent years, there has been some attention paid to the laws about who can or cannot own a gun, and what kinds of guns people can buy.

8. In general, would you say there are: Already too many laws governing the possession and use of firearms, the present laws are about right, or that we need more laws?

Already too many	13%
About right	41
Need more	44
Do not know	2

9. And, if there were to be more firearms laws, would you expect the crime rate to decrease or increase? And would you expect that [*increase/decrease*] to be large or small?

Large increase	6%
Small increase	10
Stay the same	41
Small decrease	33
Large decrease	10

TABLE 11-3 (continued)

Sometimes the government asks us to report or give up something, with varying degrees of success.

	All (%)	Most (%)	Half (%)	Some (%)	None (%)
10. Suppose a law was passed that [outlawed smoking in] public places. How many smokers do you think would comply?	8	26	24	35	7
11. . . . prohibiting the sale or manufacture of hard liquor in your state. How many drinkers . . . do you think would stop drinking?	—	4	10	47	39
12. . . . requiring people to register their guns with the Federal government. How many gun owners do you think would comply?	4	25	28	39	4
13. . . . requiring people who wanted to sell or trade a gun or give one as a gift or bequest to do so through a licensed dealer and with a delay of three weeks, how many gun owners do you think would comply?	3	21	26	43	7
14. If a law was passed requiring people to turn in all their handguns to the Federal government, how many . . . would comply?	—	4	15	62	18

I would like to read you some statements that others have made. For each one, would you please tell me to what extent you agree or disagree with it . . .

	Strongly agree (%)	Agree (%)	Disagree (%)	Strongly disagree (%)
15. Occasional domestic shootings are tragic, but do not justify taking away the right of everyone to own a handgun.	20	52	22	6

228

16. A national gun registration program might well eventually lead to the confiscation of registered firearms by the government.	12	39	41	8
17. No private individual should be allowed to own a handgun.	5	11	46	38
18. Registration of handguns will not prevent criminals from acquiring or using them for illegal purposes.	48	43	8	2
19. Anyone having a gun while committing a violent crime should receive a severe and mandatory prison sentence.	53	40	6	1
20. Most people who have guns in their home feel safer because of it.	22	61	16	1
21. Prohibiting private possession of handguns will *not* lead to prohibiting all types of guns.	9	53	31	6

22. Do you believe that you, as a citizen, have a right to own a gun, or not?

Yes	89%
No	11

23. Do you believe that the Constitution of the United States gives you the right to keep and bear arms, or not?

Yes	87%
No	11
Do not know	2

24. Would you favor or oppose a law giving police the power to decide who may or may not own a firearm?

Favor	29%
Oppose	69
Do not know	3

TABLE 11-3 (continued)

25. As you know, about $20 billion is currently spent annually by Federal, state, and local governments on crime control or for such things as police, courts, and prisons. It has been estimated that a national gun registration program would cost about $4 billion per year, or about 20% of all dollars now spent on crime control.

Would you favor or oppose the Federal government's spending $4 billion to enact a gun registration program?

Favor	37%
Oppose	61
Do not know	2

26. Mr. Smith says he wouldn't mind government files being kept about his credit ratings, income, gun ownership, or medical reports. Mr. Jones is concerned about his loss of privacy if his personal information is kept in Federal or other government computers. [Which one do you agree with?]

Exactly like Smith	12%
Lean towards Smith	16
Lean towards Jones	34
Exactly like Jones	37
Do not know	1

I would like to read you some statements that others have made. For each one, would you please tell me to what extent you agree or disagree with it . . . .

	Strongly agree (%)	Agree (%)	Disagree (%)	Strongly disagree (%)	Do not know (%)
27. No private individual should be allowed to own a handgun.	5	12	52	31	1
28. Registration of handguns will not prevent criminals [see #18].	42	43	11	3	1

230

29. Assassination attempts on public officials could be avoided by banning private ownership of handguns.	4	14	52	29	2
30. Anyone using a gun while committing a violent crime should receive a severe and mandatory prison sentence.	59	34	5	1	2

31. Do you believe that you, as a citizen, have a right to own a gun or not?

Yes	87%
No	12
Do not know	1

231

of crime. As in most prior polls on the topic, Caddell finds large majorities favoring most, but not all, of the control measures asked about.

Some of the larger of Caddell's majorities are registered for relatively innocuous, easy-to-agree-with items. We should not be surprised to learn, for example, that some 85% would favor a "crackdown on illegal sales," since cracking down on anything illegal is bound to enjoy sizable majority support. Strengthening existing regulations or making them stricter is also something that most people would presumably find easy to support—for instance, "the rules for becoming a commercial handgun dealer" (81% favor making them stronger) or the rules for owning or carrying a handgun (72 and 76%, respectively, favor making them more strict). Toughening-up existing regulations and laws is what one might call a "Why Not?" item: the surprising finding from such items is not that so many people say they favor them, but rather that anybody says they do not.

Another useful point to keep in mind in this context is that many people may not be knowledgeable about just what the existing laws entail. An earlier (1975) survey by DMI revealed, in fact, a substantial degree of misinformation on the matter, and our own work in the area (see Chapter 12) confirms that it is sometimes very difficult to figure out just what the law is. If the public is in general ill-informed about the existing laws, rules, and regulations governing the ownership and use of weapons, then its opinion that the existing measures should be made tougher is rather difficult to interpret meaningfully.

All of the measures offered in the Caddell sequence that deal with permits to own handguns or registration of handguns also receive sizable majority support. About 82%, for example, favor requiring a permit or license in order to buy a handgun, and 84% favor the registration of such handguns at the time of purchase. As for the handguns now in private hands, 74% would favor requiring them to be licensed, and the same percentage would also favor their registration. Seventy-nine percent favor requiring a permit to carry a handgun outside the home, and 88% also like the idea of some "waiting period" as a part of the permit–registration process, "to allow for a criminal records check." These findings are all very similar to the findings from the Gallup "police permit" item.

One should be wary, however, of reading more into these results than is warranted. First, many states and local communities already have laws on the books that are similar to the measures discussed above. Cook and Blose (1981), for example, report that about two-thirds of the U.S. population already reside in jurisdictions that require handgun buyers to be screened by the police. In other words many of the large majorities obtained from the Caddell sequence may reflect more an endorsement of status quo conditions than a demand for new and more restrictive gun laws. Further, the specific measures being supported are all similar to measures taken to control other potentially lethal items whose use by irresponsible or incompetent people might lead to injury or harm. Perhaps a metaphorical parallel can be drawn here to the private automobile: all legally owned automobiles are registered with state governments, and all states require a license or a permit before one is allowed to drive. Likewise, or so the substantial majority seems to be saying, all privately owned handguns should also be registered, and one ought to be required to get a permit or a license to own or use them. What these data suggest, in short, is that most people feel that the ownership and use of handguns ought to be taken at least as seriously by governments as the ownership and use of automobiles.

Measures more extreme than those currently used to regulate automobile ownership and use, in general, do *not* enjoy much public support. Substantial majorities, for example, oppose a "buy back" law, such as was tried once in Baltimore and a few other places, either on a voluntary or mandatory basis. The idea of an outright ban on the manufacture, sale, or ownership of handguns is likewise rejected by large majorities, with the exception of a ban on the manufacture and sale of "cheap, low quality handguns," which is favored by 70%. (In this context, it would be useful to know how many people would favor a ban on the future manufacture and sale of cheap, low-quality automobiles, or, for that matter, on anything else that is cheap and of low-quality.)

There is very little in either DMI survey to compare with these results from Caddell. One item (DMI 8) shows that 13% feel that there are already too many laws governing the possession and use of firearms; these respondents, or so one presumes, are among the same people represented by the 10–20% opposing each of the Caddell registration and permit items already discussed. Approximately 41% say that "the present laws are about right" and 44% think that we need even more laws along these lines. Since the DMI question does not say anything about just *what* additional laws might be needed, one hardly knows what to make of the result; many of the Caddell items suggest measures similar to ones already in force (or a strengthening of those already in force), so the finding of 41% who feel that the present laws are about right is by no means inconsistent with the large majorities who favor many of the measures from the Caddell sequence. (The finding from "Do we need more laws?" figures very prominently in the DMI report and is, indeed, the finding being summarized in the opening DMI quotation in this chapter: "majorities . . . believe that we do *not* need more laws. . . .")[11]

---

[11] DMI's conclusion, although technically correct, is, of course, rather misleadingly stated. The actual result from its survey is that 41% say the present laws are about right, 44% say we need more gun laws, and 13% say there are already too many gun laws. Thus, none of the

The DMI survey also shows 69% opposing "a law giving police the power to decide who may or may not own a firearm" (DMI 24). This is DMI's version of the standard Gallup item, which asks about a law that would require "a person to obtain a police permit before he or she could buy a gun." But, again, there is no fundamental inconsistency between the DMI result and the result typically obtained with the Gallup item: requiring a police permit in order to purchase a weapon (which a sizable majority favors) is obviously not the same thing as giving police the power to decide who may or may not own a gun (which a sizable majority opposes). As is the case for most other permit mechanisms (for example, permits to use explosives or to have a parade), legislatures or other democratically elected bodies set the criteria by which the decision is made, and the functions of the police are to determine whether the criteria are satisfied and to issue the permit if they are.

The only other DMI item that relates directly to any of the Caddell items so far discussed is item 25, showing that 61% of the electorate would oppose "the Federal government's spending $4 billion to enact a gun registration program." However, wanting some sort of registration or permit system is not incompatible with not wanting it to cost $4 billion. The DMI item serves the useful purpose of convincing us that the public does not want a registration system *at any price*, but that it (or, rather, some three-quarters of it, according to the relevant Caddell items) wants it at some price less than $4 billion.

Banning the Manufacture, Sale, or Ownership of Weapons

Of the many available options for stricter gun controls, the only one explored directly in both surveys deals with an outright ban on the private ownership of handguns. Again, Caddell has the more extensive question series. Three Caddell items deal with bans on the manufacture and sale of handguns and one deals with a ban on private ownership; DMI asked a question about banning handgun ownership in both the face-to-face and telephone surveys.

As noted previously, about 70% of the adult population would apparently favor a ban on the manufacture and sale of Saturday Night Specials. A much lower percentage but, interestingly, still a plurality would "ban the future

---

three response options generates a *majority* response; the *modal* or *plurality* response is that more laws are needed. DMI's conclusion is a rather transparent attempt to create precisely the opposite impression.

Given the split revealed in the question, it is useful to point out that all three of the following "conclusions" are technically correct: (1) Majorities do *not* believe that the present laws are about right. (2) Majorities do *not* believe that there are already too many gun laws. (3) Majorities do *not* believe that more gun laws are needed.

manufacture and sale of non-sporting type handguns" (48% favor this ban, 41% oppose it, and the remainder have no opinion). As for banning "the future manufacture and sale of *all* handguns," however, the majority is opposed: 32% favor such a ban, 58% oppose it, and the remainder have no opinion.

Only a minority would favor an outright ban on the private ownership of *all* handguns. In the Caddell survey (CADDELL 18), 31% of the population say they would favor such a ban, 18% are neutral, and 51% are opposed. Recalculating the results with the neutrals omitted, we get a 62–38% split *against* an outright ban on private ownership of handguns. The comparable DMI item is rather different: it offers no neutral category and is framed as an "agree–disagree" item, in contrast with the seven-point self-rating item of Caddell. DMI found that 83 and 84% (in the telephone and personal interview surveys, respectively) *disagree* with the statement that "no private individual should be allowed to own a handgun." It is thus plain that a large majority of the U.S. population disapproves of the notion of an outright ban on the ownership of handguns; the size of the majority on this issue, however, does vary, apparently depending on the specific wording of the question and the context in which it is asked.

Weapons, Weapon Controls, and the Crime Rate

Both surveys have quite a few items probing people's opinions about what effects, if any, stricter weapons controls would have on the incidence of crime, particularly violent crime, in the country. Given the number of questions devoted to this topic, one must assume that both organizations believe that something of importance turns on this issue, so one point must be established in advance: whether the public *feels* that stricter gun controls would reduce the crime rate and whether stricter gun controls actually *would* reduce the crime rate are entirely separate questions, and only the former is at issue here. (The latter is considered in Chapter 13.)

Both surveys find immense majority support for the concept of mandatory and severe prison sentences for persons who use a gun to commit a crime. The Caddell majority on the relevant item is 83% (CADDELL 11); the DMI majority is 93% in both administrations of a comparable item (DMI 19 and 30). Caddell also finds a 55% majority favoring mandatory sentences for persons carrying handguns without a license, such as the Massachusetts Bartley-Fox law; DMI has no comparable item.

DMI asks: "If there were to be more firearms laws, would you expect the crime rate to decrease or increase?" One can only wish that the question had said something about *what kinds* of laws, or about the toughness of the enforcement. Still, the plurality, in this case 43%, expects that this would cause the crime rate to decrease, most only by a "small" amount. Another large minority (41%) feels that this measure would leave the crime rate unaffected, and the remaining 16% think that the crime rate would actually increase. Caddell's version of the item is in an agree–disagree format with no neutral or middle category; he finds 49% agreeing that "requiring all handgun owners to be licensed would reduce crime," 42% disagreeing, and 10% with no opinion (CADDELL 21). A later item asking specifically about *violent* crime produces nearly identical results (CADDELL 24). Obviously, people disagreeing with the Caddell item could believe either that this licensing provision would have no effect on crime or that it would actually cause crime to increase. One may also assume that most of the people who say they "don't know" to Caddell's item would, if pressed, respond "stay the same" to the DMI item. With these allowances for differences in question format and the response options provided, it is clear that the two surveys get very similar results; roughly 40–50% of the public think that crime would go down with stricter weapons controls, and the rest think that the crime rate would either not be affected or might even increase.[12]

It should also be noted that the proportion saying that they think the crime rate would go down under stricter gun controls is everywhere *lower* than the proportion who say they favor any measure involving licensing or registration of handguns. It must therefore follow that many people support such measures for reasons other than their assumed effects on the crime rate.[13]

Both surveys also find very large majorities who believe that criminals will always be able to get their hands on weapons, no matter what laws are passed. Caddell finds 78% agreeing that "gun control laws affect only law abiding citizens, criminals will always be able to find guns" (CADDELL 29). Likewise, 91% of the face-to-face respondents and 85% of the phone respondents in the DMI surveys agreed that "registration of handguns will not prevent criminals from acquiring or using them for illegal purposes" (DMI 18 and 28). Furthermore, 81% of DMI's phone respondents *disagree* that "assassination attempts on public officials could be avoided by banning private ownership of handguns" (DMI 29). (Caddell has no question on assassinations.)

---

[12] It is uncertain what people have in mind when they say that they think the crime rate would increase with stricter weapons controls. One possibility is that they believe private weaponry is a crime deterrent, and that the rate would thus increase as the deterrent was removed or restricted. Another possibility is that these people anticipate substantial noncompliance with stricter weapons controls, which would, by definition, increase the amount of "crime" being committed.

[13] It is anybody's guess what these other reasons might be. One possibility is that people feel that rates of accidental shootings would go down if tougher gun laws were enacted.

Weapons control as a way to control crime is the object of a long series of DMI questions which, for the sake of brevity, are not shown in Table 11-3. In this sequence, respondents were given a list of 17 measures that "have been proposed [to] fight crime" and asked to rate how effective they thought each measure would be. The measures ranged from "increasing punishment for using a gun or other deadly weapon while committing a crime," which was seen as the most effective of the 17 options (86% thought this would be effective), through "outlawing private possession of all handguns," which was rated as least effective (27% thought it would be effective). The general theme that surfaces in this question sequence is that most "get tough" measures (mandatory sentences for gun crimes, "making criminals pay damages to their victims," "increasing punishment for serious crimes," and so on) are perceived as being more effective crime-fighting devices than are most measures involving stricter controls on gun ownership or use among the general population. This, of course, is consistent with the previous findings that less than one half of the population feels that stricter controls would have any effect on lowering the crime rate at all, and that most who do anticipate such an effect expect that it would only be small. The one item from the DMI series that comes closest to an analogous Caddell item (CAD-DELL 21) asks about "requiring detailed record-keeping of guns purchases and sales by federally licensed gun dealers." Just over one-half (54%) felt that this would be "very effective" (rated 6 or 7 on a seven-point scale); in the Caddell item, the comparable proportion is 49%.

In the same vein, DMI also has a series of questions related to how many people respondents think would comply with various weapons control measures, if passed (DMI 10–14). Of course, how many people the public *thinks* would comply, and how many people actually *would* comply, are different questions. Still, the public anticipates a substantial degree of noncompliance, not only with new gun laws but also with laws outlawing smoking in public places or the sale and manufacture of hard liquor. On the item involving Federal registration of guns, for example, only 4% think that all gun owners would comply, 25% respond "most," and 28% say one-half; the remaining 43% think that less than one-half of all gun owners would comply with this measure. Anticipated compliance with measures more strict than Federal registration (DMI 13 and 14) is even lower. Clearly, a question to gun owners about whether *they*, personally, would comply with each of these measures might have been more informative, but neither DMI nor Caddell has such an item.[14]

---

[14] The Illinois survey conducted by Lizotte and Bordua (1980) apparently did ask respondents whether they personally would comply with stricter weapons regulations. Generally nonowners said they would comply and owners said they would not (Alan Lizotte, personal communication).

Personal Protection and Safety

According to DMI, 83% of the electorate believe that "people who have guns in their home feel safer because of it" (DMI 20). At the same time, a majority (52% of the total, 57% of those with an opinion) *rejects* the argument that "requiring all handgun owners to be licensed would prevent law-abiding citizens from protecting themselves" (CADDELL 20). Most people, in short, do *not* think that licensing handgun ownership would deprive people of the security they derive from owning weapons, so there is again no basic inconsistency in these results.

DMI has a seven-item sequence (DMI 1–7) asking people what kinds of crime they fear most. Murder in the course of another crime is apparently most feared, following by burglary, robbery, and rape; murder by a friend or relative and various white collar crimes are apparently feared least. "How do these findings relate to the issue of gun control?" the DMI report asks. "First, note that the anti-gun argument of reducing 'murder by a friend or relative' is not a crime which many fear. Note [too] that robbery/mugging, rape, and, to some extent, 'murder in the course of another crime' are crimes which possession of guns by intended victims tends to discourage or prevent— and these are crimes about which the public is *very* concerned. . . . Finally, note that precisely those crimes most likely to be reduced by gun ownership are those *less* feared by gun owners" (DMI, 1978: 17).

This is a creative but possibly misleading reading of the DMI results. Obviously, not many people would sit around in a high state of anxiety over the prospect of being murdered by a relative or close friend. That people do not fear this crime does not in any sense deny the well-known reality that most murders are committed by relatives and friends, and, of course, neither the lack of fear nor the reality of this crime says anything about whether its incidence would be reduced by stricter gun controls. Also, that DMI's gun owners are less fearful of certain kinds of crimes than the nonowners cannot be interpreted in the absence of additional controls for region and city size, since weapons ownership is disproportionately a rural, small-town phenomenon, whereas the kinds of crimes being asked about in the sequence are disproportionately urban (see Chapter 7). On the average, that is, gun owners may very well be less fearful of a mugging or a rape, as DMI reports, but that may reflect only that the average gun owner lives in a place where mugging and rapes are relatively rare.

The Right to Keep and Bear Arms

Eighty-nine percent of the respondents in DMI's personal survey, and 87% in the phone survey, believe that they "as a citizen have a right to own a gun." In the personal survey, 78% also said that the Constitution gives them that right. (See DMI 22, 23, and 31.) But at the same time, a substantial majority of Caddell's respondents (53% of the total, 60% of those with an opinion) *disagree* with the statement that "requiring all handgun owners to be licensed would violate people's constitutional rights" (CADDELL 22). Thus, most Americans believe that they have a right to own a gun, and most also believe that requiring a license for handgun ownership would not be a violation of that right. Again, there is no inconsistency: most people, it appears, understand that *all* rights and freedoms in a democratic society are subject to at least some constraints, the right to keep and bear arms apparently included.

"One Thing Leads to Another"

The more dramatic anti-control polemicists have in the past argued that registration or permit mechanisms for handgun ownership or use are "just the first step" toward regulation of all guns, then confiscation of all guns, and then, once the population has been disarmed and lacks the means to resist, the decimation of all our freedoms. To emphasize a recurring theme, whether any of these things would actually come to pass, and whether the public thinks they would come to pass, are different questions; in either case, both polls contain a fair number of items addressing public thinking on such matters.

A plurality of Caddell's respondents (47% of the total, or 55% of those with an opinion) *disagrees* with the statement that "requiring all handgun owners to be licensed is just the first step in confiscating all guns, including shotguns" (CADDELL 25). The comparable DMI item is somewhat different: in the personal survey, 51% *agreed* that "a national gun registration program might well eventually lead to the confiscation of all registered firearms by the government" (DMI 16). Obviously, the split in public thinking on this issue is so close to 50–50 that no certain statement about majority sentiment can be made; roughly one-half the population thinks that such measures might lead to confiscation of all weapons, and the other half does not. Reflecting the same ambivalence, 37% of Caddell's respondents think "it is possible to have effective controls on handguns without having controls on long guns," 40% think not, and the remainder are not sure (CADDELL 19). On the other hand, DMI finds a fairly sizable majority (62%) agreeing that "prohibiting private possession of handguns will *not* lead to prohibiting all types of guns" (DMI 21).

On the "larger issues," Caddell finds a clear majority (53% of the total, 59% of those with an opinion) *disagreeing* that "requiring all handgun owners to be licensed is just another step by government to interfere in people's lives and limit their freedom" (CADDELL 23). DMI has no comparably direct item; the closest it comes is its item 26, which asks people how they feel about the "loss of privacy" that might result if information on people's "credit ratings, income, gun ownership, or medical reports" was "kept in government computers." Most people, some 71%, would be "concerned" about all this. The quadruple-barreled nature of the question, however, renders it uninformative for our purposes, since we cannot tell from the item just what kinds of information-keeping people find objectionable.

The only remaining item that relates, even indirectly, to the topic at hand is Caddell's item 30: "The only way to control handguns is by Federal law; state laws which allow them to be purchased in some states but not others are ineffective." A large majority, 70%, agrees with this statement, but since the question is double-barreled, it is impossible to say precisely what the majority is agreeing to. One could, for example, readily agree with the second clause in the statement but disagree with the first, i.e., could believe that the solution to this problem is a set of state-level laws that are uniform across states (and, again, the parallel to regulation of automobiles might be appropriate).

CONCLUSIONS: WEAPONS AND THEIR CONTROL

Despite the occasionally sharp differences in emphasis and interpretation between the DMI and Caddell reports, the actual empirical findings from these two surveys are remarkably similar. Results from comparable (even roughly comparable) items rarely differ between the two surveys by more than 10 percentage points, well within "allowable" limits given the initial differences in sampling frame and the usual margin of survey error. The major difference between the two reports is not in the findings but in what is said about or concluded from the findings—what aspects of the evidence are emphasized or de-emphasized, what interpretation is given to a finding, and what implications are drawn from the findings about the need, or lack thereof, for stricter weapons controls. We thus conclude that the "anti-survey" hypothesis is not confirmed in this comparison; the two surveys differ in the aspects of public opinion they examine and in the conclusions they try to draw, but on virtually all points where a direct comparison is possible, the evidence from each survey says essentially the same thing.

What *does* the evidence say? First, large majorities favor any measure involving the registration or licensing of *handguns,* both for new purchases and for handguns presently owned.[15] The public would *not* favor such mea-

---

[15] Neither survey deals with the registration or licensing of long guns in any direct way; the standard "police permit" item suggests that most people would favor this as well.

sures if their costs were astronomical; likewise, there is substantial agreement that such measures would be effective only if they were uniform across states. There is very little popular support for an outright ban on private ownership of handguns, although the majority would favor a ban on the manufacture and sale of Saturday Night Specials. Large majorities believe that they have a right to own guns and that the Constitution guarantees that right. Most people also feel that a licensing requirement for handgun ownership would not violate that right. No more than about one-half the population feels that stricter controls would decrease the crime rate; many measures other than stricter weapons controls are thought to be more effective to this end. Virtually everyone agrees that criminals will always be able to acquire guns, no matter what laws are passed. Likewise, nearly everyone favors strict and mandatory sentences for persons using guns to commit crimes. Opinion is divided on the issue of whether handgun controls will eventually lead to control (or even confiscation) of all weapons; nonetheless the large majority favors such controls. There is little popular support for the idea that gun controls are somehow violations of Americans' basic freedoms.

So far as public opinion on such a complex issue can be summarized at all, the thrust of majority thinking on gun control seems to be that the government should be just as careful about who is allowed to own and use a firearm as it is about who is allowed to own and use automobiles or other potentially hazardous commodities. And just as licensing and registration of automobiles seem to have very little effect on reducing automobile accidents, so too do most people anticipate that stricter weapons controls would have little or no effect on crime. This, however, obviously does not prevent them from favoring at least some gun control measures. The underlying concept here seems to be that weapons, like automobiles, are *intrinsically* dangerous objects that governments ought to keep track of for that reason alone. Whether doing so would reduce the level of crime or violence in the society seems to be taken as a separate issue entirely.

TWELVE

REGULATING FIREARMS:
An Overview of Federal, State, and Local Practices

This chapter provides a brief overview of the history and provisions of existing weapons legislation in the United States at Federal, state, and local levels. It summarizes several much more detailed sources, which should be consulted for additional information on all points covered:

1. The Bureau of Alcohol, Tobacco, and Firearms (ATF) publication *Your Guide to Firearms Regulations* (1978). This source is fairly detailed on the provisions of existing Federal regulations, and somewhat less detailed on state and local regulations. The information on state and local regulations is derived from an annual postcard survey of local political jurisdictions with populations in excess of 25,000, asking whether any new regulations have been enacted in the past year. Thus, this publication provides no data for jurisdictions smaller than 25,000, and the data for larger jurisdictions are incomplete, since the response rate to the most recent survey was only 57%.[1]

2. The National Rifle Association's *Firearms and Laws Review* (1975). This publication contains brief and easy-to-understand summaries of applicable state regulations and of some local ordinances that are relevant to firearms users, especially hunters. It is especially useful for regulations involving the use of shoulder weapons (as opposed to handguns).

3. The three recent scholarly analyses of extant firearms regulations: Jones and Ray (1980) and Cook (1979a, 1980b). We have drawn liberally from the summaries provided in these sources, especially the first. Zimring's (1975) paper on the Gun Control Act of 1968 (GCA) is definitive on the history of Federal legislative efforts and on the intent of the GCA, and we have drawn heavily from it as well.

4. Finally, we present here some selected materials from our recent survey

---

[1] *The Federal Register* (1979), Vol 44, No. 119, Part II is the most recent Federal publication of state and local firearms regulations.

of weapons policies in a sample of U.S. police departments. The full report of this survey appears in Weber-Burdin et al. (1981).

The purpose of this chapter is descriptive, not evaluative. It discusses the kinds of laws that have been passed and, to some extent, their intended (or hoped-for) effects. The more specifically evaluative question—whether the laws achieved the intended, or any other, effects—is taken up in the next chapter.

In moments of polemical excess, advocates of stricter weapons regulations sometimes assert that the United States is virtually the only advanced civilized nation in the world that exercises no controls over the civilian ownership, possession, or use of firearms. In fact, there are about 20,000 firearms laws of one or another sort already on the books. These laws have been enacted at different times and places for different reasons, invoke different mechanisms of control, and have different intended effects. The problem, if indeed there is one, is clearly not that civilian ownership and use of firearms are unregulated, but that the extant regulations encompass a vast congeries of disparate Federal, state, and local laws, many of them working at direct cross-purposes with others. Furthermore, political jurisdictions with rather restrictive regulations often abut jurisdictions with barely any controls at all, an invitation to wide-spread law evasions. Proposals for a more uniform set of state laws, or a single overarching Federal law, date to at least the 1920's, but movement in this direction has been severely restricted by the Federal government's limited constitutional powers to regulate civilian arms.[2]

That criminal violence has, over the past two decades, risen dramatically in spite of the large numbers of gun laws on the books is taken in anti-control circles as evidence that gun laws "just don't work," and in pro-control circles as evidence that the wrong laws have been passed, or that enforcement has been indifferent or otherwise inadequate, or that the disparity in restrictions across jurisdictions means that no jurisdiction-specific law is going to reduce the availability of firearms for criminal purposes by very much. We have little to say about this debate in the present chapter. Our purpose here is merely to summarize the laws now on the books. In the following chapter, however, we do note that very few of the laws that have been passed seem to have had dramatic, or even noticeable, effects on criminal violence.

---

[2] Just what the Constitution does and does not allow the Federal government to do in this area is, of course, a hotly contested issue about which we can claim no expertise. Certainly, state-level firearms regulations pose no constitutional issues and, for this reason, state (and local) regulations frequently are far more strict than the corresponding Federal regulations, as the following review makes plain.

FEDERAL LEGISLATION

History

The GCA of 1968 was the first comprehensive piece of Federal legislation dealing specifically with firearms. Before that Act, Federal involvement and purview in regulating firearms was limited and minimally enforced.[3]

During the late 19th century and into the first decade of the 20th, there were isolated state and local attempts to control firearms, but no Federal efforts of importance. The first significant Federal involvement was a 10% manufacturers' excise tax on firearms that was part of the larger War Revenue Act of 1919. Although the tax was imposed largely for fiscal purposes, there are indications that it also reflected some concern with handguns as a public safety problem. The tax survived its emergency revenue-producing intent and still remains a part of Federal firearms policy. An important legacy of the Federal firearms excise tax is that the Federal agency empowered to collect the tax—the Department of the Treasury's Bureau of Internal Revenue— had administrative control over the enforcement of Federal firearms regulations. Not until 1972 was the Alcohol, Tobacco, and Firearms Division of the IRS constituted as a separate Bureau within the Department of Treasury (Zimring, 1975: 157).

With urban crime and gun use receiving increasing public attention, in 1927 debate was sparked on the Federal role in firearms regulations. In that year, Congress enacted a law prohibiting the mailing of concealable firearms to private individuals, in an attempt to support existing local and state legislation by stemming the flow of handguns into states with stricter controls. The law had limited impact because it was still legal to deliver firearms by private express companies. Throughout the 1920's, there was discussion about uniform state laws regulating possession and use of handguns, but no significant legislation was passed.

In the early 1930's, public concern over violence by organized crime resulted in two important pieces of legislation: the National Firearms Act of 1934 and the Federal Firearms Act of 1938. Both were precursors of the GCA of 1968.

The National Firearms Act (NFA) of 1934 curtailed civilian ownership of machine guns, sawed-off shotguns, silencers, and other forms of "gangster-type" weapons. Its regulatory mechanisms involved the imposition of a $200

---

[3] This historical summary of Federal involvement in regulating firearms is taken from Zimring's (1975) more detailed review.

tax per transfer of these types of weapons and provided for their registration with the Federal government. An NFA permit is still required for legal possession of such a weapon.

The Federal Firearms Act (FFA) of 1938 was the most significant attempt before the 1960's to impose Federal controls on the commerce and possession of firearms. The Act called for Federal licensing of all manufacturers, importers, and dealers involved in the shipping and receipt of guns in interstate commerce. Certain classes of individuals (some felons, fugitives from justice, persons under indictment, or those ineligible under state laws) were prohibited from obtaining licenses or purchasing guns. In addition, dealers were required to keep records of firearms transactions. The law, however, did not require dealers actually to verify the eligibility of customers, and the small cost of manufacturer's and dealer's licenses ($25 and $1, respectively) created a proliferation of firearms dealers (over 100,000 by the mid-1960's) (Zimring, 1975: 141). Consequently, it was impossible to monitor dealer compliance with the FFA effectively. The law also did not prohibit sales to individuals who crossed state lines to buy firearms in less restrictive states. For these reasons, as Zimring notes, the FFA was mainly "a symbolic denunciation of firearms in the hands of criminals, coupled with an inexpensive and ineffective regulatory scheme that did not inconvenience the American firearms industry or its customers" (1975: 143).

From 1939 to 1957, there was very little Federal or state legislative activity in this area. In 1958, new Federal regulations were adopted that extended the record-keeping period for dealers from 6 to 10 years after a firearm sales transaction and that required manufacturers' serial numbers on all firearms except .22 caliber rifles.

Present Legislation

For a number of reasons, among them outbreaks of urban unrest, ever-increasing crime rates, and sharply increased flows of foreign weapons into the domestic market, several new legislative proposals were introduced to the Congress in the period from 1963 to 1967. Most of them died in committee, and no new legislation was enacted. Many of these proposals, however, were incorporated into, and eventually passed as the Gun Control Act of 1968, after a bitter contest.

Although the legislative intent of the GCA is somewhat ambiguous, the major goals appear to have been:

1. To eliminate the interstate traffic in firearms, especially between less restrictive and more restrictive states.
2. To define certain classes of individuals as ineligible for legally purchasing firearms.

3. To end the importation of all surplus military firearms and all other guns unless they were "particularly suitable for . . . sporting purposes" (Zimring, 1975: 149).

The central element of this legislation was to ban interstate shipments to or from people who did not possess Federal licenses as dealers, manufacturers, importers, or collectors, and to make it illegal for any person except a licensee to engage in any firearms dealings, interstate or otherwise. Dealers were to be more strenuously regulated. Specifically, they were now obliged to obtain identification from a customer to verify state residency and age requirements, and to maintain records of firearms sales for periodic Federal inspection. Prohibitions against the receipt of firearms by certain classes of individuals were broadened to include (1) minors (under 18 for shotguns and rifles; under 21 for handguns); (2) convicted felons, fugitives from justice, and defendants under indictment; (3) adjudicated mental defectives or persons having been in mental institutions; (4) drug abusers; (5) people with dishonorable discharges from the Armed Forces; and (6) illegal aliens.

Concerning imports, the GCA prohibited the importation of guns not "suitable for sporting purposes," an obvious effort to reduce the availability of the low-priced Saturday Night Special. The IRS interpreted "sporting purposes" into a scoring system (termed "factoring criteria"), which excluded very small handguns and those without safety devices and which created standards of frame construction and handgun weight to qualify for import. Although these standards did reduce handgun *imports*, they did not stop domestic manufacturers from producing substitute guns (see Chapter 3). Indeed, because the GCA did not prohibit the importation of certain firearms *parts*, the result of the "sporting purposes" standard may have been to shift the assembly of such guns from Europe to the United States (Cook, 1979a).

Since enactment, several provisions of the GCA have proved difficult to enforce. The key issues appear to be the very large number of licensed dealers (who, because of their numbers, cannot be effectively monitored for compliance), the apparently sizable fraction of handgun transfers that take place between private individuals (which, for obvious reasons, are virtually impossible to monitor), and the limited enforcement budget given by Congress to ATF. For these and other reasons, several new Federal legislative efforts have been introduced to the Congress in the past 10 years, but none has been enacted. The 1968 GCA therefore remains the primary Federal firearms regulation.

STATE AND LOCAL REGULATIONS

State regulations of firearms focus more commonly on handguns than long guns. They concentrate on controlling handgun acquisition, transfer, and possession, and on defining the place and manner of legally carrying a handgun. Table 12-1 lists the types of handgun restrictions extant in each state and the District of Columbia as of 1978. Table 12-2 gives state restrictions on long guns.

Some states have no regulations on handguns beyond those contained in the GCA. However, cities in these states sometimes enact more stringent regulations. Many states delegate gun control legislation to municipalities, whereas other states specifically prohibit local legislatures from enacting handgun controls. State preemption may be partial or complete. California, Georgia, and Michigan, for example, partially preempt handgun control. Partial preemption may mean that (1) certain aspects of handgun control are not preempted; or (2) non-preempted aspects of handgun control are allowed to be more stringent at the local level. For instance, California preempts registration and licensing of commercially manufactured firearms but allows local ordinances to regulate licensing of firearms dealers and to define conditions under which concealable firearms may be carried. Maryland, on the other hand, completely preempts regulations of handguns; no city in Maryland has ordinances other than those already contained in state law. An overview of local regulations in 30 American cities is shown in Table 12-3.

Dealer Controls

1. Licensing. Twenty-five states and the District of Columbia require that firearms dealers be licensed. Investigation procedures for state dealer licenses are usually more extensive than those for federal licenses. The annual fees for dealer licenses range from $5 (Washington) to $100 (South Carolina). Some states (e.g., Virginia and New Jersey) require that employees of handgun dealers also be licensed by the state, subject to the same licensing criteria (and fees) as dealers.

2. Dealer record-keeping and report of sales. The District of Columbia and 30 states require that sales records be kept for all handgun transactions, including a description of the firearm sold, its serial number, and descriptive information on the purchaser. These record-keeping requirements are similar to those of Federal law. About 20 states require that a report of all handgun sales (usually a copy of the sales record) be sent within a certain time to the local police department or other enforcement agency. Three states (California, Massachusetts, and North Dakota) require that private handgun sales be reported.

Some localities go much further than their respective states in controlling handgun dealers. For example, Charlotte, North Carolina, requires separate licensing and fees to the city and to the county, as well as to state and

Federal governments. In Atlanta, Georgia, and Louisville, Kentucky, firearms dealers must take fingerprints of purchasers for inclusion in the sales record. Chicago levies a $400 annual fee for handgun dealers and requires additional record-keeping procedures. In the District of Columbia, annual license fees are also high ($300). In all cases, note that the local restrictions are in addition to any applicable state or Federal restrictions.

Acquisition and Transfer Controls

1. *License or permit to purchase.* Ten states require some form of permit to purchase handguns. The common procedure is for the handgun purchaser to apply for the permit at the local police department, filling out a form with information on address and criminal record, in addition to providing fingerprints and photograph, which are required in some states. The police department may then conduct an investigation to verify the information on the application form. In most cases, a permit is issued if the purchaser is not among the ineligible classes; in some states, such as New Jersey, applicants have to provide character references to establish good standing in the community. No state that requires a permit to purchase also requires the applicant to prove his or her need for a handgun, but some cities, such as Boston and Chicago, do. In Massachusetts, local police departments have interpretive discretion to decide whether handguns are purchased "for a proper purpose."

There is a waiting period of varying length before the permit is approved, some states setting statutory maxima of 30 days, after which the application is automatically approved. New Jersey requires a permit to purchase followed by a formal 7-day waiting period before an individual can purchase a handgun.

2. *Application to purchase.* Twelve states combine an application to purchase with a waiting period, which has an effect similar to policies that require a permit to purchase. The difference is that an application to purchase form is completed at the dealer's place of business and then forwarded to the police department, rather than being completed at the police department, as in the case of permits. After the form is forwarded, the department investigates the application during a formal waiting period. The department notifies the dealer of the approval or denial of the application, and the dealer in turn contacts the purchaser.

Most states requiring either permits or applications to obtain a handgun include *private* as well as dealer transactions under the legislation. However, on the basis of interviews with local authorities, Jones and Ray (1980) report that compliance with these permit systems by private parties is usually minimal.

Some differences between the permit to purchase and application to purchase systems are that (1) the application to purchase system usually has

TABLE 12-1A. *State handgun controls: Regulations on purchase and possession*

State	Dealer requirements			Acquisition and purchase requirements					Possession requirements		
	Dealer license	Handgun sales record	Sales report to police	Special ID card	Permit-to-purchase	Application-to-purchase	Registration	Police review	Certificate of registration	Special ID card	Permit for home/business
Alabama	x	x	x			x		x			
Alaska											
Arizona											
Arkansas											
California	x	x	x[a]			x		x			
Colorado		x									
Connecticut	x	x	x			x		x			
Delaware	x	x									
D. of C.	x	x				x[b]	x[b]	x	x		
Florida											
Georgia	x										
Hawaii	x				x		x	x	x		
Idaho											
Illinois		x		x				x		x	
Indiana											
Iowa	x	x	x		x			x			
Kansas											
Kentucky											
Louisiana											
Maine		x									
Maryland	x	x	x		x	x		x			
Massachusetts	x	x	x[a]	x	x			x			
Michigan		x	x		x[d]		x[c]	x	x	x	
Minnesota		x	x			x[d]		x			
Mississippi		x	x				x	x			
Missouri		x			x			x			

Montana							
Nebraska	x						
Nevada							
New Hampshire	x	x					
New Jersey	x	x	x			x	
New Mexico							x
New York	x		x[e]		x	x	
North Carolina	x		x			x	
North Dakota	x	x[a]	x[f]			x	
Ohio							
Oklahoma							
Oregon	x	x		x		x	
Pennsylvania	x	x		x		x	
Rhode Island	x			x		x	
South Carolina	x	x				x	
South Dakota	x	x		x		x	
Tennessee	x			x		x	
Texas	x						
Utah	x				x		
Vermont	x						
Virginia	x[g]		x[g]				
Washington	x	x		x		x	
West Virginia	x	x					
Wisconsin	x						
Wyoming							

[a] Includes private transactions.

[b] Only authorized purchasers are law enforcement and certain military agencies; 1977 law stipulates that only those handguns registered under 1968 law may be re-registered and only to the same owner. This law effectively prohibits all further purchases and transfers of handguns.

[c] Indirectly accomplished through mandatory safety inspections by police in order to possess handguns legally.

[d] Combines permit-to-purchase with application-to-purchase (see text).

[e] Prerequisite for permit-to-purchase is a license to possess or carry.

[f] Part of license-to-carry stipulation.

[g] Only in counties where population density exceeds 1000 per square mile.

Source: Adapted from Jones and Ray, 1980.

251

TABLE 12-1B. *State handgun controls: Carrying and motor vehicle requirements*

State	Carrying requirements					Motor vehicle requirements			
	Openly and concealed prohibited	Openly and concealed license required	Concealed prohibited	Concealed license required	License required	Unloaded	Securely encased	Not easily accessible	Not concealed
Alabama				x	x	x	x		
Alaska									
Arizona			x						
Arkansas[a]	x[b]					x			
California				x	x	x			x
Colorado				x					
Connecticut		x			x		x		
Delaware				x	x				
D. of C.				x	x	x	x	x	
Florida				x		x	x		x
Georgia	x	x[c]	x[d]		x				
Hawaii		x[e]			x	x	x		
Idaho				x					
Illinois			x						
Indiana		x[f]			x	x	x		x
Iowa					x	x	x		x
Kansas			x						
Kentucky			x						
Louisiana			x						
Maine				x					
Maryland			x		x				
Massachusetts		x			x				
Michigan		x		x	x	x	x		
Minnesota		x			x	x	x	x	
Mississippi			x[d]	x[d]			x	x	

Missouri			x					
Montana								
Nebraska			x					
Nevada								
New Hampshire	x[d]	x[d]	x[d]	x	x	x	x	x
New Jersey	x		x	x	x	x	x	x
New Mexico								
New York			x[g]	x	x			
North Carolina	x	x						
North Dakota	x		x	x	x	x		x
Ohio	x	x	x	x	x	x	x	x
Oklahoma	x				x			x
Oregon			x	x	x			
Pennsylvania			x	x	x	x		
Rhode Island	x	x	x	x	x	x		x
South Carolina	x	x			x	x		
South Dakota			x	x	x			
Tennessee	x[b]							
Texas	x							
Utah					x	x[h]		
Vermont	x[b]		x		x			
Virginia			x					
Washington			x	x	x	x		
West Virginia	x		x	x	x			
Wisconsin		x						
Wyoming			x					

253

[a] In Arkansas, it is illegal to carry a handgun in a motor vehicle with intent to use as a weapon.
[b] With intent to use as a weapon, to go armed, or to injure.
[c] Openly only.
[d] Except for classes of individuals exempted.
[e] Two licenses are issued: carrying openly only and concealed only.
[f] Two licenses are issued: "qualified" (for certain purposes) and "unlimited."
[g] An additional permit is required to carry in New York City.
[h] Applies to nonresident travelers only.
Source: Adapted from Jones and Ray, 1980.

TABLE 12-1C. *State handgun controls: Exemptions from carrying restrictions*[a]

State	Law enforcement officers	Military personnel	Shooting club members[d]	Licensed for game hunting[c]	Armed guards	Occupation: protecting $	Private investigators	Transporting firearm	Protection from imminent threat	Certain nonresidents	In compliance with motor vehicle regs.
Alabama	P	P	P					P[b]			P
Alaska	P										
Arizona	P										
Arkansas	P	P			P					P	
California	PR	PR	PR	PR	PR		R		R		P
Colorado											
Connecticut	P	P						P[b]			P
Delaware	LP										
D. of C.	P	P									
Florida	P	P	P	P	P			P[b]			P
Georgia	P	P						P[b]			
Hawaii	P	P			P			P[b]			P
Idaho	P										
Illinois	PR	PR	PR	PR	PR		PR	P[b]			
Indiana	P	P	P		P			P[b]			P
Iowa	L		P[b]	P[b]	L						P
Kansas	P	P		P	P		P				
Kentucky	P				P						
Louisiana	P				P						
Maine	P						P				
Maryland	PR	PR			PR		PR				
Massachusetts	P									P	
Michigan	PR	PR			L			P[b]			P
Minnesota	PR			P				P			

254

Mississippi	P	P		P						P	P
Missouri	P										P
Montana	P	P		P							
Nebraska	P	P		P			P				
Nevada	L	P									
New Hampshire	P	P	L	L		Pᵇ					P
New Jersey	P	P	Pᵇ	Pᵇ		Pᵇ					
New Mexico					LPR						
New York	LPR										
North Carolina	P										
North Dakota	P	P									
Ohio	PR	Pᵇ	Pᵇ	PR	PR	Pᵇ	PR		PR		P
Oklahoma	PR	PR	PR	PR	PR	Pᵇ					P
Oregon	PR	PR	PR	PR		Pᵇ					P
Pennsylvania	PR	PR	PR		L	Pᵇ					P
Rhode Island	LPR	Pᵇ	P	L	L	Pᵇ		P			P
South Carolina	LP	P	P	L	L						
South Dakota	P										
Tennessee	P	P								P	
Texas	P	P	P	P	P					Pᵇ	P
Utah	PR										
Vermont											
Virginia	P										
Washington	PR	PR	PR		L	Pᵇ	L		L		P
West Virginia	L	P	Pᵇ	P	L	Pᵇ					P
Wisconsin	P			P							
Wyoming	P				L						

a Key to symbols: L, specifically eligible for license to carry; P, exempt from carrying prohibition; R, exempt from "carrying in motor vehicle" restriction.

b Exemption applies if "carrying in motor vehicle" restrictions are obeyed.

c While engaged in sport.

Source: Jones and Ray, 1980.

255

TABLE 12-1D. *State handgun controls: Ineligible classes*[a]

State	Persons under age	Minimum age to possess	Drug abusers	Alcohol abusers	Mental patients	Juvenile delinquents	All felons	Violent felons	All misdemeanants
Alabama			P	PT				P	
Alaska							P		
Arizona								P	
Arkansas					P		P		
California		18	P			P			
Colorado								PC	
Connecticut							C		
Delaware			P		P			P	
D. of C.	21:PC	21	PC	BPTC	PC		C	P	
Florida	21:C						P		
Georgia	21:C				C		C		
Hawaii			PC		C		P	C	
Idaho									
Illinois		18	P		P	BPT	P		
Indiana				T				C	
Iowa									
Kansas			P	PT			P		
Kentucky							P		
Louisiana								PC	
Maine							P		
Maryland	18:B		P	BPT				P	
Massachusetts	18:PC	18	PC	BPT	P		PC		
Michigan	21:C	18			C		C		
Minnesota	21:C	18	PC	PC	PC			PC	
Mississippi		16					PC		
Missouri		M							
Montana									
Nebraska		18					P		
Nevada		14					P		
New Hampshire							P		
New Jersey	18:BP	18	PC	BC	PC		C	P	BC
New Mexico									
New York	21:P	21			PC		PC		
North Carolina							PC		
North Dakota		17	P	P	P			P	
Ohio			PC	BPTC	PC			BPTC	
Oklahoma							P		
Oregon		18					P		
Pennsylvania	18:B			T				P	
Rhode Island	21:C	15	PC	BPTC	PC			P	
South Carolina	21:P	21	P	BPT	P			P	
South Dakota								P	
Tennessee				BT				C	
Texas								P	
Utah		18	P		P			P	
Vermont		16							
Virginia									
Washington		14	C	BTC	C			PC	
West Virginia			C	C			C		
Wisconsin		M							
Wyoming									
United States (GCA)	21:T			BT	BPT			BPT	

256

TABLE 12-1D. (*continued*)

State	Violent misdemeanants	Fugitives from justice	Members of subversive orgs.	Aliens	Under influence of drugs	Under influence of alcohol	In "agitated" state of mind	Non-compliance purchase reqs.	Out-of-state residents
Alabama	PT								
Alaska	P				P	P			
Arizona	P								
Arkansas									
California								T	
Colorado					P	P			
Connecticut				TC					
Delaware	P					T			
D. of C.	BPT		C					T	
Florida									
Georgia	C								
Hawaii	PC	PC							
Idaho						PC			
Illinois								T	
Indiana	TC					T			
Iowa									
Kansas									
Kentucky									
Louisiana				P					
Maine									
Maryland	BPT	P			T	T		T	
Massachusetts				BPTC				T	
Michigan				BC	P	P			
Minnesota	PC								
Mississippi						T			
Missouri						T		T	
Montana									
Nebraska		P							
Nevada				P					
New Hampshire									
New Jersey	BP	PC						T	
New Mexico									
New York	BPC			BPC				T	
North Carolina								T	
North Dakota	P								
Ohio		PC			TC	TC		T	
Oklahoma					PTC	PTC	T		
Oregon									
Pennsylvania	P								
Rhode Island	PT	P		BPTC	C	C			
South Carolina	BPT	P	BPT					T	
South Dakota	PT							T	
Tennessee	BT			BT					
Texas					T	T			
Utah	P			P					
Vermont									
Virginia									
Washington	BPTC								
West Virginia				T					
Wisconsin									
Wyoming				P					
United States (GCA)		BT		BP				T	T

^a Key to symbols: B, ineligible to buy or receive; C, ineligible to carry; M, minor (age not defined); P, ineligible to possess; T, ineligible to sell or transfer to. For transfer (T) and receipt (B), only those state laws with more stringent requirements than the GCA are shown. For possession (P), *all* state-defined ineligibles are shown.

Source: Jones and Ray, 1980.

257

TABLE 12-2D. *State long gun controls: Dealer/acquisition or purchase controls*[a]

State	Dealer licensed	Permit/license-to-purchase	Application-to-purchase	Registration	Special ID card
Alabama					
Alaska					
Arizona					
Arkansas					
California					
Colorado					
Connecticut					
Delaware					
D. of C.			x	x	
Florida					
Georgia					
Hawaii	x			x	
Idaho					
Illinois			x		x
Indiana					
Iowa					
Kansas					
Kentucky					
Louisiana	x			x[b]	
Maine					
Maryland					
Massachusetts	x				x[b]
Michigan					
Minnesota					
Mississippi					
Missouri					
Montana					
Nebraska					
Nevada					
New Hampshire					
New Jersey	x				x
New Mexico					
New York	x				
North Carolina					
North Dakota					
Ohio					
Oklahoma					
Oregon					
Pennsylvania	x				
Rhode Island	x				
South Carolina					
South Dakota					
Tennessee	x				
Texas					
Utah					
Vermont					
Virginia					
Washington					
West Virginia		x[d]			
Wisconsin					
Wyoming					

[a] City exceptions indicated in NRA's *Firearms and Law Review:* Chicago (registration of all firearms), New York City (permit-to-purchase), and Philadelphia (license-to-purchase).
[b] If rifle barrel length is less than 16" or shotgun less than 20".
[c] Not required if person has a license to carry a handgun.
[d] Applies to "high-powered rifles."
Source: Adapted from Cook (1979a) for dealer licensing and from the NRA's *Firearms and Law Review* (1975) for remaining categories.

less restrictive provisions for eligibility requirements; (2) application to purchase systems do not require fees, whereas permit systems often do; and (3) in application to purchase systems, if the police do not specifically deny the application during the specified waiting period, the transfer is automatically approved.

State and city variations on permit to purchase and application to purchase systems usually involve different waiting periods (two days in Pennsylvania to a statutory maximum of 50 days in New Jersey). Cities such as Pittsburgh and Minneapolis circumvent time limits by providing written notification to the seller that the prospective purchaser may be ineligible. Permit to purchase systems usually take longer to process (up to 3 months) than application to purchase systems (usually about 2 weeks). Other variations exist also. In Dade County (Miami), Florida, a certificate that a handgun safety and firearms law course has been satisfied is required and serves as a purchase permit. In Cleveland, handgun owners must have a city-issued ID card, which serves as a purchase permit. In New York State, one must have either a license to possess or a license to carry a handgun to be eligible for handgun purchases. The holder of either type of license must go to the local police or sheriff's office and obtain a "purchase coupon" before purchasing a handgun.

Possession Controls

1. *License to possess.* In six states and one city (Cleveland), some certificate or license is required to possess a handgun, even if it is kept at home. As mentioned above, a New York State resident must have either a license to possess or a license to carry in order to purchase a handgun. In Hawaii and Mississippi, a certificate of registration is necessary for lawful possession of a handgun. Michigan requires that every handgun have a certificate of safety inspection for legal ownership. Massachusetts and Illinois have firearms identification cards, which are necessary for both lawful purchases and lawful possession. Each of these systems requires record-keeping that amounts to a form of registration of handgun owners and their handguns. All apply to handguns obtained privately as well as those obtained through dealers.

2. *Registration.* Two states (Hawaii and Mississippi) and the District of Columbia have formally labeled registration systems. In theory, registration focuses on firearms, not on owners, and does not serve as a screening system. In practice, registration is used to screen firearm owners when law enforcement officials check registrants against ineligible classes, usually by a criminal record check. The District of Columbia's 1977 handgun law contains the most stringent form of registration. It stipulates that only those handguns registered under the GCA may be reregistered and only to the same owners. This law

TABLE 12-3A. *Handgun controls in selected state and local jurisdictions: Regulations on purchase and possession*[a,b]

State/city	Dealer requirements			Acquisition and purchase requirements					Possession requirements		
	Dealer license	Handgun sales record	Sales report to police	Special ID card	Permit-to-purchase	Application-to-purchase	Registration	Police review	Certificate of registration	Special ID card	Permit for home/business
California	X	X	X				X		X			
Los Angeles	+	+	+				+		+			
Oakland	+	+	+				+		+			
San Diego	+	+	+				+		+			
San Francisco	+	+	+				+		+			
Colorado		X										
Denver		+	X[c]									
D. of C.	X	X						X	X	X		
Florida						X			X			
Dade County	X	X	X			X[d]						
Miami	X	X	X						X			
Georgia	X											
Atlanta	+	X										
Illinois		X	X		X						X	
Chicago	X	+			+			X[e]	X	X	+	
Kentucky								+	+			
Louisville	X	X	X[c]						X			
Louisiana	X						X		X			
New Orleans		X	X						X			
Maryland	X	X	X				X		X			
Baltimore	+	+	+				+		+			
Massachusetts	X	X	X[c]	X	X				X		X	
Boston	+	+	+	+	+				+		+	
Michigan		X	X			X		X[f]	X	X[f]		
Detroit		+	+			+		+	+	+		
Minnesota		X	X				X		X			
Minneapolis	+	X	X[c]				X		X			

Jurisdiction								
Missouri	X						X	X
Kansas City	+						+	+
St. Louis	+		X		+		+	+
New Jersey	X		X		X		X	X
Newark	+		+		+		+	+
New York	X		X	X	X	X	X	X
Buffalo	+		+	+	+	+	+	+
New York City	X		+[g]	X	+	+	+	+
North Carolina	X		X		X	X	X	X
Charlotte	+		+		+	+	+	+
Ohio	X							
Cincinnati	X	X	X		X	X		X
Cleveland	X	X	X	X	X	X	X	X
Oregon	X	X	X	X	X	X		X
Portland	+	+	+	+	+	+		+
Pennsylvania	X	X	X	X	X	X		X
Philadelphia	+	+	+	+	+	+		+
Pittsburgh	+		+	+	+	+		+
Texas	X							
Dallas	X							
Houston	+							
Washington	X		X	X	X	X		X
Seattle	+		+	+	+	+		+
Wisconsin								
Milwaukee	X		X	X	X	X		X

261

[a] Adapted from Jones and Ray (1980).

[b] Key to symbols: X, requirement originates in listed jurisdiction; +, local administration of a state statute.

[c] Includes private transfers.

[d] Purchasers must demonstrate knowledge of firearms laws and handgun safety.

[e] Because Chicago has stringent handgun regulations and high dealer license fees, Chicago dealers do not offer handguns for sale. Chicago residents who purchase handguns outside the city's limits must register their handguns within 10 days of bringing their handguns to Chicago.

[f] Registration is indirectly accomplished through mandatory safety inspections by police in order to legally possess handguns; safety inspection certificate must be kept with handgun at all times.

[g] A special New York City permit to carry or possess is a prerequisite for a permit-to-purchase.

TABLE 12-3B. Handgun controls in selected state and local jurisdictions: Carrying and motor vehicle requirements[a,b]

	Carrying requirements					Motor vehicle requirements			
	Openly and concealed prohibited	Openly and concealed license required	Concealed prohibited	Concealed license required	License required	Unloaded	Securely encased	Not easily accessible	Not concealed
California				X	X	X			X
Los Angeles				+	+	+			+
Oakland				+	+	+			+
San Diego				+	+	+			+
San Francisco				+		+			
Colorado				X					
Denver	X								
D. of C.				X	X	X	X	X	X
Florida				X		X	X		
Dade County				+		+	+		
Miami				+		+	+		
Georgia		X[c]			X				
Atlanta		+			+				
Illinois	X					X			X
Chicago					+	+		X	+
Kentucky			X						
Louisville			+						
Louisiana			X						
New Orleans			+						
Maryland		X			X				
Baltimore		+			+				
Massachusetts		X			X				
Boston		+			+				
Michigan				X	X	X	X	X	
Detroit				+	+	+	+	+	

Table (continuation) — states and cities with handgun regulation markings. Column headers appear on the preceding page; jurisdictions and their markings are reproduced below as read.

Jurisdiction	Markings
Minnesota	X + X +
Minneapolis	X +
Missouri	X +
Kansas City	X +
St. Louis	X +
New Jersey	X +
Newark	X X + X +
New York	X + X +
Buffalo	X +
New York City	+[d]
North Carolina	X +
Charlotte	X +
Ohio	X + X + X + X +
Cincinnati	+ + X + + +
Cleveland	X + + X + + + +
Oregon	X + X +
Portland	X +
Pennsylvania	X X + X + X X +
Philadelphia	X +
Pittsburgh	X +
Texas	X
Dallas	+
Houston	+
Washington	X X + X +
Seattle	X +
Wisconsin	X
Milwaukee	+

[a] Adapted from Jones and Ray, 1980.

[b] Key to symbols: X, requirement originates in listed jurisdiction; +, local administration of a state statute.

[c] In Georgia, carrying a handgun concealed is prohibited except for classes specifically exempted. Carrying a handgun openly is permitted with the appropriate license.

[d] A special New York City permit to carry a handgun is required.

263

TABLE 12-3C. *Handgun controls in selected state and local jurisdictions: Exemptions from carrying restrictions[a,b]*

	Law enforcement officers	Military personnel	Shooting club members[c]	Licensed for game hunting[c]	Armed guards	Occupation: protecting $	Private investigators	Transporting firearm	Protection from imminent threat	Certain non-residents	In compliance with motor vehicle regs.
California	PR	PR	PR	PR	PR		R		R		
Los Angeles											
Oakland											
San Diego											
San Francisco											
Colorado											
Denver	P	P	P[d]					P[d]			P[d]
D. of C.	LP	P						P[d]			
Florida	P	P	P	P	P			P[d]			P
Dade County											
Miami	P										
Georgia	P	P									
Atlanta											
Illinois	PR	PR	PR	PR	PR		PR				
Chicago	P	P	P	P	P		P	P[d]			
Kentucky	P				P						
Louisville											
Louisiana	P										
New Orleans											
Maryland	PR	PR			PR		PR				
Baltimore											
Massachusetts	P									P	
Boston					L						
Michigan	PR	PR						P[d]			
Detroit											P

264

Minnesota	PR						
Minneapolis					P		
Missouri	P						
Kansas City	P	Pᵈ	Pᵈ	P	P	P	P
St. Louis	Pᵈ	Pᵈ	P	P			
New Jersey	P	Pᵈ	Pᵈ	L	L		Pᵈ
Newark							P
New York	LPR			LPR			
Buffalo							
New York City							
North Carolina	P						
Charlotte	P			P			
Ohio	PR	PR	PR	PR	PR	PR	
Cincinnati							
Cleveland							
Oregon	PR	PR	PR				
Portland		PR					
Pennsylvania	PR	PR	PR	PR	PR	PR	Pᵈ
					P		
Philadelphia	R	R	R	R	R		
Pittsburgh	P	P	P	P	P	R	P
Texas	R						
Dallas	P						P
Houston							
Washington	PR	PR	PR	PR	L	L	Pᵈ
Seattle							P
Wisconsin	L						
Milwaukee							

ᵃ Adapted from Jones and Ray, 1980.

ᵇ Key to symbols: L, specifically eligible for license to carry; P, exempt from carrying prohibition; R, exempt from "carrying in motor vehicle" restriction. Note: State jurisdiction exemptions also apply to local levels, but they are not duplicated here. Local exemptions apply only to carrying restrictions required by local ordinance.

ᶜ While engaged in sport.

ᵈ Exemption applies if "carrying in motor vehicle" restrictions are obeyed.

265

TABLE 12-3D. *Handgun controls in selected state and local jurisdictions: Ineligible classes*[a,b]

	Persons under age	Minimum age to possess	Drug abusers	Alcohol abusers	Mental patients	Juvenile delinquents	All felons	Violent felons	Violent misdemeanants
California		18	P						
Los Angeles									
Oakland									
San Diego									
San Francisco									
Colorado								PC	
Denver									
D. of C.	21:PC	21	PC	BPTC	PC		C	P	
Florida	21:C						P		
Dade County									
Miami									
Georgia	21:C				C		C		
Atlanta									
Illinois		18	P		P	BPT	P		
Chicago	21:B								
Kentucky							P		
Louisville	21:BP	21		T	P				
Louisiana								PC	
New Orleans							P		
Maryland	18:B		P	BPT				P	
Baltimore									
Massachusetts	18:PC	18	PC	BPT	P		PC		
Boston									
Michigan	21:C	18		C			C		
Detroit									
Minnesota	21:C	18	PC	PC	PC			PC	
Minneapolis									
Missouri									
Kansas City									
St. Louis	17:P	17							
New Jersey	18:BP	18	PC	BC	PC		C	P	BC
Newark									
New York	21:P	21			PC		PC		
Buffalo									
New York City									
North Carolina							PC		
Charlotte									
Ohio			PC	BPTC	PC			BPTC	
Cincinnati		16							
Cleveland	21:PC	21					PC		BPTC
Oregon		18					P		
Portland									
Pennsylvania	18:B			T				P	
Philadelphia				B				BT	
Pittsburgh									
Texas								P	
Dallas									
Houston									
Washington		14	C	BTC	C			PC	
Seattle									
Wisconsin		M							
Milwaukee	18:B								
United States (GCA)	21:T		BT		BPT		BPT		

266

TABLE 12—3D. (*continued*)

	Violent misdemeanants	Fugitives from justice	Members of subversive orgs.	Aliens	Under influence of drugs	Under influence of alcohol	In "agitated" state of mind	Non-compliance purchase regs.	Out-of-state residents
California									
Los Angeles									
Oakland									
San Diego									
San Francisco									
Colorado					P	P			
Denver					T	T	T		
D. of C.	BPT	C						T	
Florida									
Dade County			T			PT	PT	T	
Miami			T			PT	PT		
Georgia	C								
Atlanta									
Illinois								T	
Chicago								T	
Kentucky									
Louisville	PT	P						T	
Louisiana				P					
New Orleans								T	
Maryland	BPT	P				T	T	T	
Baltimore									
Massachusetts				BPTC				T	
Boston									
Michigan				BC	PC	PC			
Detroit									
Minnesota	PC								
Minneapolis					PTC	PTC			
Missouri						T			
Kansas City									
St. Louis									
New Jersey	BP	PC						T	
Newark									
New York	BPC			BPC				T	
Buffalo									
New York City									
North Carolina								T	
Charlotte									
Ohio		PC			TC	TC		T	
Cincinnati				P					
Cleveland								T	
Oregon									
Portland									
Pennsylvania	P							T	
Philadelphia	BT							T	
Pittsburgh									
Texas					T	T			
Dallas									
Houston									
Washington	BPTC								
Seattle									
Wisconsin									
Milwaukee									
United States (GCA)		BT		BP				T	T

[a] Adapted from Jones and Ray, 1980.

[b] Key to symbols: B, ineligible to buy or receive; C, ineligible to carry; M, minor (age not defined); P, ineligible to possess; T, ineligible to sell or transfer to. Note: For transfer (T) and receipt (B), only those state or local laws with more stringent requirements than the GCA are shown. For possession (P), *all* state- and/or local-defined ineligibles are shown. Local ineligibility definitions that are identical to or less stringent than those defined by state law are excluded.

effectively prohibits all further purchases and transfers of handguns in the District, with the exception of those for law enforcement and some military personnel.

Provisions for Place and Manner of Carrying

There are many ways in which states and local jurisdictions regulate the carrying of handguns, concealed or openly, on the person or in motor vehicles. Some classes of individuals are exempted from carrying restrictions in all jurisdictions (e.g., police). Of all the forms of handgun restrictions, those on place and manner of carrying are the most numerous and varied. Although there are many kinds of carrying regulations, they can be grouped under two general headings: (1) those prohibiting the carrying of handguns on or about the person with exceptions and (2) those requiring that people wanting to carry handguns be licensed by state or local authorities. Most states require that people applying for licenses to carry concealed handguns show a need for the weapon in the course of their employment.

There is great variation in the fee for a carrying license. Michigan's fee for a 3-year license to carry a concealed handgun is $3, whereas Florida's annual license fee to carry a handgun openly or concealed is set by local authorities. In Miami, the initial fee is $300, followed by $150 for every year thereafter; in addition, individuals receiving the license must post a $100 bond conditional on lawful use of the weapon.

Penalties for the Use of Firearms in Crime

In 28 states, there are additional criminal sentences (sentence "enhancements") for people convicted of carrying or using a firearm while committing a felony. Some states (Florida, Maryland, Massachusetts, Minnesota, Missouri, and New York) have a mandatory minimum prison term for such offenders, allowing no possibility for suspended sentence. Massachusetts and New York have a mandatory 1-year prison term for people convicted of unlawfully carrying or possessing a handgun away from home or business, regardless of whether it was involved in a crime. Maryland also has a mandatory minimum sentence for violations of carrying restrictions, but the sentence is mandatory with the second offense. Mandatory sentencing for gun crimes is an increasingly popular control strategy, and so the above tallies will in all probability be quickly outdated.

Bans on Certain Handguns

Three states and three cities—Illinois, Minnesota, South Carolina, Dade County, Denver, and Cleveland—have provisions that forbid the manufacture, transfer, or possession of low-quality, inexpensive handguns, the so-called Saturday Night Specials. All three states and Denver use gun metal melting point as the primary criterion, whereas Dade County and Cleveland use barrel length (less than 3 inches) and caliber (.32 or less). Prohibitions in Denver and Illinois apply to firearms dealers; Denver prohibits transfer only, whereas Illinois prohibits manufacture and transfer. Minnesota prohibits manufacture by any person and transfer by dealers. The bans in Dade County and Cleveland apply to all people, including dealers. Dade County prohibits transfer only, whereas Cleveland's ban is the most inclusive, prohibiting manufacture, possession, receipt, and transfer of the Saturday Night Special.

COVERAGE OF EXISTING FIREARMS REGULATIONS

Cook (1979a, 1980b) has attempted to estimate the proportion of the U.S. population affected by firearms regulations. His analysis reveals that:

1. Twenty-two states have requirements that dealers be licensed; these states contain 57% of the U.S. population.

2. Twenty states have requirements that officials keep permanent records of handgun transactions; these states contain 51% of the U.S. population.

3. Twenty-three states have requirements that police be given the chance to check on buyers of handguns; these states contain 64% of the U.S. population.

4. The estimated percentage of the U.S. population 21 years and over that is ineligible from buying a handgun under GCA regulations is 25%, the largest ineligible classification being "users of illegal drugs" (21%), a category that includes users of marijuana, hashish, hallucinogens and cocaine, as well as heroin and other opiates (see Cook, 1980b: Table III-2 for the basis for these estimates).

Cook's analysis is based only on state laws and is therefore conservative. Some states lacking any of the above regulations nonetheless contain cities where such regulations are in force, as shown in Table 12-3. If we take the populations of cities that have such regulations in the states that do not, and add the figures to Cook's original state-level data, we get revised and slightly higher coverage figures. Specifically, adding in the city data shows that about 60% of the U.S. population are affected by state dealer licensing,

70% are affected by acquisition or purchase requirements, and 66% are subject to a police check before or after purchasing a handgun.

One portion of our Institute's national survey of local police and sheriff departments (Weber-Burdin *et al.*, 1981) dealt specifically with the responsibility of police departments for enforcing firearms regulations in their jurisdictions. Table 12-4 gives the responses to each of the regulation items. The proportions shown have been weighted by the size of the department, which correlates at 0.9 or higher with the size of the jurisdiction; for this reason, the numbers shown are the approximate equivalent of the proportion of the U.S. population presently covered by each regulation.

Several aspects of the table warrant comment. First, the proportions of the population covered by the various regulations are here higher than in Cook's original analysis and in the above amendment of that analysis. In these data, for example, 85% of the population reside in jurisdictions where firearms wholesalers are licensed (by the state or local community), and 89% reside in jurisdictions where retailers are similarly licensed. Likewise, 75% reside in jurisdictions that require a license or a permit to purchase or carry a firearm. In sum, the coverage revealed in these data (on all 15 regulatory measures asked about) is rather more widespread than any previous analysis has indicated. Most of the population of the United States, in short, already lives in jurisdictions that have relatively advanced policies for weapons regulation in effect.

Second, the data show that police undertake some regulatory activities in these areas even when they are not required to do so by law. Voluntary registration of weapons with the local police is especially common (about 15% of the population, that is, live in jurisdictions where the police register weapons even though the law does not require it).

Further analysis also shows, predictably, that there is regional variation in these matters, with the South and West tending to have fewer firearms restrictions.

IMPLEMENTATION OF GUN CONTROL LAWS

The ordinances and laws on the statute books of states and local jurisdictions may either be strictly enforced or barely observed in practice. The extent to which these statutes and ordinances are merely formal and not followed in practice is not known. In addition, there are many ways in which the laws may be evaded without transgressing. For example, Chicagoans who wish to purchase handguns can find legal sellers outside the city limits, a journey that need be no longer than 10 miles at the maximum. Widespread evasion of the law is evident, especially when the jurisdiction has very restrictive

TABLE 12·4. *Policing efforts in enforcing firearms regulations*[a]

Function	Required by law and done by		Not required by law but done by		Not done in jurisdiction (%)	Unsure (%)
	Your dept. (%)	Other agency (%)	Your dept. (%)	Other agency (%)		
Wholesalers/retailers						
Issue licenses to firearms wholesalers	11	71	0.1	0.9	15	2
Issue licenses to firearms retailers	22	64	0	1	11	2
Conduct investigations of persons applying to become firearms retailers	30	54	1	1	9	5
Firearms controls						
Issue permits to carry firearms openly	18	23	0.8	0.2	57	1
Issue permits to carry concealed firearms	38	33	0.5	0.5	28	0
Conduct investigations of persons who have applied for a permit to carry a firearm	52	18	1.8	0.2	27	1
Conduct investigations of persons applying for a license or permit to purchase or possess a firearm	44	26	3	1	25	1
Handgun controls						
Issue licenses, permits, or ID cards to purchase handguns	32	23	1.5	1.5	40	2
Issue licenses, permits, or ID cards to possess handguns	26	24	0.4	0.6	48	1
Handle registration of handguns	29	27	15	2	25	2
Long gun controls						
Issue licenses, permits, or ID cards to purchase long guns	14	17	1	2	63	3
Issue licenses, permits, or ID cards to possess long guns	12	13	1	1	71	2
Handle registration of long guns	9	17	16	3	53	2
Hunting controls						
Issue hunting licenses or permits	2	83	0.4	2.6	11	1
Ammunition controls						
Issue licenses or permits to sell ammunition	8	55	0	3	25	9

[a] Data from 1980 survey of a national sample of police and sheriff departments; see Weber-Burdin (1981) for details on questionnaire methodology and weighting of survey items by departmental size. Rows sum across to 100%, except for rounding error.

statutes or ordinances. Thus, there are very few valid New York City handgun permits at any time, but a fair proportion of New Yorkers own or possess handguns.

Precise estimates of the extent of law evasion are not available from the existing literature, although there are clear signs that such evasions are common. We have already mentioned some of the reasons for this condition, including the ease with which one may go to a less restrictive jurisdiction to obtain guns, the extent to which law enforcement agencies are not fully financed to implement the law in detail, and the difficulties in implementation when the law is vague, as, for example, in prohibiting sales to people with histories of mental health difficulties.

CONCLUSION

The major Federal weapons regulation policies are contained in the Gun Control Act of 1968 and are supplemented, literally, by tens of thousands of additional state and local laws. The lack of uniform laws across jurisdictions means, inevitably, that the laws in any particular jurisdiction will have no necessary implication for the availability of firearms for criminal purposes in that same jurisdiction. This fact, plus the evidence suggesting a rather substantial flow in criminal weaponry across jurisdictions, also implies that isolated jurisdictional laws will, in the normal course of things, have few or no dramatic crime-reductive effects. This topic is taken up in detail, and the above conclusion generally confirmed, in the following chapter.

THIRTEEN

WEAPONS CONTROL LEGISLATION AND EFFECTS ON VIOLENT CRIME

Although there is much disagreement on many of the empirical facts about the extent and distribution of firearms ownership in the United States, the level of accompanying emotionality seems almost to take the form of polite murmurings compared to the extent of disagreement and attendant feelings about legal control of weapons. Gun control legislation, existing and proposed, produces partisanship and fervor beyond any of the other issues surrounding weapons issues in the United States. The issues involved range in loftiness from constitutional questions—what does the Second Amendment really mean two centuries after its enactment?—to tricky technical research issues such as: do the trends in crime rates after the enactment of a gun control statute signify any impact on weapons-related crimes?

We shall leave the philosophical and constitutional issues of gun control legislation to scholars who have special competence to deal with them. This chapter reviews the technical issues involved in assessing the effectiveness of such legislation when enacted as well as some of the landmark studies that have attempted to estimate the direction and magnitude of such effects. Next, the chapter takes up some of the critical technical issues that arise in assessing the impact of legislation on an area of human behavior. The third section reviews the procedures and evaluates the findings of the major studies of impact assessment. Finally, we attempt to draw out the implications of preceding sections for future research on the effectiveness of gun control legislation.

ISSUES IN ASSESSING THE IMPACT OF GUN CONTROL LEGISLATION

The science and art of ascertaining the effects of the activities of government agencies and of legislation have grown considerably in sophistication over

273

the past two decades (Cook and Campbell, 1980; Cronbach, 1980; Rossi and Freeman, 1982). Although there have been attempts to make such assessments since the appearance of the social and behavioral sciences in the late nineteenth century, the development of this field received a considerable boost from the skepticism that accompanied the Great Society programs of the late 1960's. Whatever the reason, legislators and public officials then began to ask social scientists to estimate whether or not programs, such as Head Start or the Job Corps, were working. This interest in impact assessment also extended to legislation that was not accompanied by programs but that changed procedures, shifted sanctions, or otherwise changed the ways in which established government agencies operated.

The main problems involved in estimating the impact of a government action are well known. Solutions to these problems that are satisfactory to every skeptical reviewer are much more difficult to provide. All assessments of effectiveness are subject to question and hence vulnerable to more or less decisive criticisms.

Of the two main problems in assessment, the first is defining and measuring the intended effects of a governmental action. The preambles to legislation, which set forth legislative intent, tend to be stated in global and rather vague terms. For example, legislation authorizing housing subsidies for poor families may be described as intending to improve the "quality of life" of the intended beneficiaries. Although there may be very good reasons for the vagueness of legislative intent, it becomes difficult to decide upon specific evaluative measures that can index the success of the program in question. For instance, should an improvement in the "quality of life" be measured by changes in the levels of satisfaction with housing, or should one measure the extent to which housing fulfills criteria set forth by public health or housing specialists?

The second main problem is defining what is to be considered a sign of effectiveness. It is easy to define the effects of a program or legislation as changes that would not have occurred if the program or legislation had not been enacted, but then the problem becomes how best to compute what would have happened in the absent condition. There are many false signs of effectiveness; crime rates may decline after a gun control statute is enacted, but crime rates may have been declining anyway. For example, gun control legislation may have been enacted at the same time that penalty changes were introduced into the criminal code, and the effects of the latter may be mistaken for the effects of the gun control legislation. As we shall see in reviewing the studies on the effectiveness of gun control statutes, establishing the *ceteris paribus* conditions that will permit reasonable estimates of what would have happened without the gun control legislation is perhaps the most serious problem facing researchers who venture into this area.

How these and other problems manifest themselves in the assessment of gun control legislation is discussed in detail below.

Deciding on Possible Effects of Gun Control Legislation

The American gun manufacturing and distribution system and the patterns of gun ownership and use are not well known or understood. Yet legislation designed to alter the patterns of gun usage in crime must necessarily build on some implicit or explicit model of these systems and on some empirically based parameters concerning the size and distribution of household firearms stocks. More specifically, if a legislator were to decide that registration of all guns held by civilians and police should be required by law, that legislator should know how many such guns would need to be registered and how many new registrations or transfers of ownerships would be generated year to year. It would obviously make a considerable difference in the costs of running a registration system if the total stock of guns in the hands of civilians and the police was on the order of 120 or 200 million, or whether the annual new registrations and transfers amounted annually to 10 or 20 million. In addition, a registration system based on the assumption that all gun transfers occurred through the intermediary of a gun dealer would miss the apparently large number of transfers that take place among private citizens.

The implicit model or models of the system surrounding the distribution and use of guns also determine the kinds of consequences that one can anticipate from a particular legislative act. Thus, if one assumes that the use of guns in, say, robberies is largely premeditated (i.e., a person carries a gun and looks for a target after having decided to commit a robbery), then it might make some sense to raise the penalty for robberies in which guns are used in order to raise the potential costs to robbers. Alternatively, if one believes that gun owners engage in robbery when they are short of funds, then one might want to establish a criterion for permitted gun ownership that allows only people with steady employment or sources of legitimate income to own guns.[1]

Perhaps the main issue in what sort of model of gun distribution or of gun usage one should have in mind in drafting legislation centers around the reciprocal relationship between the level of crime and the stocks of guns in civilian hands. Those who believe that the number of guns in civilian hands affects either the amount of crime or the types of crimes committed are in

---

[1] The fact that this proposal would be unacceptable on many grounds is not the issue of concern at the moment.

favor of measures that would reduce the stock or change its distribution (i.e., keep guns out of the possession of people who would commit crimes). Those who believe otherwise are doubtful that any attempts at gun control would affect the level of crime; they may believe that changes in the stocks of guns or their distribution would lead to the substitution of alternative weapons in crimes. Indeed, the possibility of these "substitution" effects means that assessments of legislative impact should take them into account. A third position asserts that the stock in civilian hands is responsive to the crime level, that is, as crime rates rise, civilians arm themselves in response.

The main issue is further complicated by the fact that mixed models may be easily generated. For example, whereas income-producing crimes of certain kinds may be affected by the stock of weapons (e.g., bank or payroll robberies), "crimes of passion" (unpremeditated murders or assaults) may not be affected at all by the stocks of guns, assaulters and murderers using any weapons that may be at hand.[2]

The above discussion leads to a differentiation among three broad classes of anticipated effects of weapons legislation:

1. *Intermediate effects:* These are effects anticipated within the gun distribution system and in the patterns of gun distribution and usage.

2. *End effects:* These are anticipated effects that are more or less desired as the outcome of the legislation; the effectiveness of the legislation would be judged on the basis of them.

3. *Side effects:* These effects are not necessarily intended but are also a consequence of the legislation. Of course, a side effect could be beneficial or unwanted; the main point is that a specific governmental action can often have effects that were unintended and sometimes very much unwanted.

The distinguishing characteristics of intermediate effects are that they are intended to occur and constitute the mechanisms through which end effects are achieved. Thus, a gun control statute may have the desired end effect of reducing gun use in assaults, but its desired intermediate effect is to lower the availability of Saturday Night Specials. Of course, a given piece of legislation may be quite successful in producing its desired intermediate effect but not at all in achieving reasonable levels of success in its desired end effects. Conversely, desired end effects may appear without the desired intermediate effects, although this would be less likely.

The purpose in distinguishing among the three types of effects is to emphasize again that a given statute is built around a model of how the social system in general works and how the particular phenomenon in question

---

[2] The issue of how many murders start out as aggravated assaults and are transformed into murders by the availability of guns on the scene is also relevant; see Chapter 10.

proceeds, specifying instrumentalities (intermediate effects) for achieving a set of particular ends (desired end effects), ideally with no harmful side effects. This point also emphasizes the importance of some of the research discussed in previous chapters: an accurate and valid empirical understanding of the size, distribution, and uses of the stock of weapons held by American households is essential for the development of effective legislation aimed at controlling gun use in violent crime.

Table 13-1 lists some of the possible end, intermediate, and side effects that might be considered in an assessment of weapons legislation. Although the list is far from exhaustive, it suggests the wide variety of options available for choices among desired intermediate and end effects and the kinds of side effects that might accompany attempts to regulate the distribution and usage of firearms. Note that although this discussion is focused on firearms, easy modifications to restricted classes of firearms, e.g., handguns or certain types of handguns, can be made without loss of meaning. The inventory of

TABLE 13-1. *Inventory of desired end effects, intermediate effects, and side effects of potential gun control legislation*

I. Desired end effects
   A. Reduction in the use of weapons in crime
   B. Reduction in stock of weapons held by private households
   C. Reduction in accidental injuries, deaths, or suicides from weapons
   D. Reduction in stock held by "criminals"
   E. Reduction in stock of certain types of weapons (e.g., handguns, Saturday Night Specials)

II. Desired intermediate effects
   A. Regulating the weapons production system
      1. Restrictions on the manufacture of weapons
      2. Restrictions on the importation of weapons
   B. Regulating the distribution system
      1. Restrictions on the sale and transfer of weapons
   C. Regulating possession
      1. Restrictions on ownership
   D. Regulating usage
      1. Restrictions on carrying weapons
   E. Raising the costs of weapons ownership and use
   F. Raising the penalties for improper use

III. Possible side effects
   A. Substitution of other weapons for firearms in crime
   B. Creation of illegal manufacturing, distribution, and transfer systems
   C. Higher costs to the criminal justice system
   D. Higher costs to the administering agency
   E. Higher costs to weapons users
   F. Restrictions on legal uses of firearms for recreational purposes

desired effects includes some that are clearly outside the realm of current discussion and are included here mainly to provide a more complete set of policy alternatives. Only those falling within the current "policy space"—those proposals that are politically acceptable to significant portions of the decision-making elites—are actually likely to be considered.

An effective statute can be conceptualized as one that (1) specifies an intermediate effect that is administratively feasible, efficient, economical, and corresponds to an accurate understanding of the weapons distribution and usage systems, and (2) is directed toward an appropriate set of desired end effects. It is easy to think of statutes that would not fit the bill. For example, a statute that intends to reduce the stock of weapons held by criminals by regulating the manufacture and import of weapons may simply raise the cost of acquiring weapons for everyone. Such a statute ignores the difficulty of identifying the criminals and assumes that changing prices would affect criminals possibly more than other users of weapons.

Operational Measures of Effects on Crime

Although the major intent of most proposed and actual gun control legislation is to affect the criminal use of weapons, completely satisfactory measures of such improper usage are difficult to come by. Crime, as such, goes largely unmeasured: all that is ordinarily available are reports of crimes that have been detected by someone—victim or witness—who reports the event either to the police or to a survey interviewer. All the instances in which, for example, burglars carry weapons cannot be reported unless the burglar is actually seen by a witness and the weapon is visible in that encounter. Weapons may be carried and not used; witnesses may not be present to observe; and victims may not detect the commission of a crime or be willing to report the event either to the survey interviewer (in the case of victimization surveys) or to the police (in the case of police-generated statistics on crimes).

The defects of the *Uniform Crime Reports* (UCR) are too well known to bear repeating in this context (see Chapter 8). Victimization surveys correct some of the deficiencies of police-generated statistics, especially that of under-reporting, but create others. Victimization studies can contain many accounts of events that are either very trivial or only questionably crimes, and they are subject to the many defects of recall frailties. In addition, the national victimization surveys are usually taken too sparsely in any one jurisdiction to be useful, for instance, in studying the impact of gun control legislation in a single city, county, or state.

The problem with errors of measurement is that at best such errors tend to obscure the estimated effects and, at worst, may distort such estimations.

Thus, if the errors are random but extensive, small effects will be hard to distinguish from the ordinary "noise level" present in criminal justice statistics. If the errors are biased (e.g., systematic under- or overreporting of some types of events), then even genuine effects may be offset and impossible to detect. The most confounding situation is when the errors of measurement themselves are affected by the gun control legislation. For example, as we shall see in a later section, the Bartley-Fox Amendment enacted in Massachusetts appeared to increase the willingness of victims to report weapons-related crimes to the police, thereby creating an apparent rise in the number of such crimes and tending to obscure the effects of the Bartley-Fox Amendment itself.

Of course, very large effects—dramatic and drastic declines or increases in certain types of crimes—are likely to overcome the problem with errors of measurement, but such drastic and dramatic effects are unlikely to occur, least of all in the short run. If there is a single lesson to be learned from the past two or three decades of federal legislation addressed to social problems of various sorts, it is that *no* problem of any magnitude yields very dramatically to any one legislative effort or even to a broad program of legislation (such as the War on Poverty), and certainly not over a short period of time. A gun control bill that is designed to remove certain types of handguns from the privately owned stocks by prohibiting their manufacture, for example, may take years to manifest significant effects because the rate at which existing stocks are depleted may be quite low.

The Problem of Long-term Versus Short-term Effects

Some time can be expected to elapse before the effects of any statutory change are apparent, depending on the changes in existing administrative arrangements that the legislation requires. Thus, a gun registration law that requires the establishment of a new agency can manifest effects only after the agency has been set up, administrative regulations established, and the everyday procedures of administration worked out. Of course, some changes may require minimal adjustments and can be expected to show effects after a shorter period—for example, a statute that increased penalties for convictions on weapons-related felony charges. It may also take some time for side effects to appear. Increasing the length of prison sentences for people convicted of weapons-related crimes, for example, may produce the unwanted side effect of prison overcrowding, a potential source of pressure on prosecutors and judges to develop accommodations to the new statutes that would result in shorter prison sentences than prescribed in the statute.

For these reasons, careful consideration must be given to both long- and short-term effects of any gun control legislation that is enacted. Short-term effects may be more or less pronounced than long-term effects, depending on the ways in which a law affects various parts of the criminal justice system.

The Problem of Dosage

The problem of dosage is simply whether enough of the remedy prescribed in the statutes has been administered. Thus, it may well be that careful and conscientious monitoring of gun sales and transfers could interdict criminals from possessing weapons, but if insufficient funds are provided to monitor sales and transfers, conscientious and careful scrutiny of such transactions cannot be accomplished. Similarly, if penalties for weapons-related crimes are not raised enough, no deterrence effect may be shown. The issue of dosage looms large in the discussion of the effects of the 1968 Federal Gun Control Act (GCA) (Zimring, 1975). In this case, it is claimed that with inadequate funds for monitoring the dealer licensing system that was instituted, the legislation fell far short of interdicting cross-state weapons sales.

The dosage issue emphasizes the importance of careful analysis of the *implementation* of statutory changes. Dosage problems often show up quickly in the assessment of intermediate effects; thus, it was found very early that the 1968 GCA did not prevent the sales of weapons across state lines when the exporting state had less stringent requirements on gun ownership than the receiving state.

Establishing *Ceteris Paribus* Conditions

As discussed above, one of the main problems in evaluating the effects of any statute is to establish the proper conditions for estimating what would have occurred without the statute. The simplest and therefore most tempting solution is to consider before- and after-enactment comparisons of, say, weapons-related crime rates. The drawback is that many other things are happening at the same time that can affect the crime rates, either depressing or elevating them. Thus a comparison of crime rates before and after the enactment of the 1938 weapons legislation would have led to the naive conclusion that the statute was quite effective in lowering crime rates nationally. Trends in the 1930's and continuing into the 1940's consisted of a gradual decline in crime rates nationally. More careful consideration might have led to the likely conclusion that the trends were neither accelerated nor impeded by the passage of that legislation.

Before and after comparisons are reasonable only if the analyst is able to model the prevailing trends properly before enactment in order to make reasonable predictions about post-enactment levels of crime rates. The time-series analyses performed to assess the Massachusetts Bartley-Fox Amendment (Deutsch and Alt, 1977; Pierce and Bowers, 1979) are excellent illustrations of how this may be accomplished. Such techniques cannot simply be applied mechanically. On the contrary, time-series analyses depend very heavily on the selection of models that most appropriately characterize the existing before-enactment trends. The appropriateness of the models selected by Deutsch and Alt (1977) in their early analysis of Bartley-Fox was challenged by Hay and McCleary (1979). In addition, sometimes other changes that occur around the time that a statute is enacted may make it difficult to model appropriately what would have been expected in the absence of the statute. For example, the effects of a gun control statute that is enacted while changes are simultaneously being made in police practices will be confounded with those of the police reorganization, a double event that cannot be modeled easily.

Time-series analyses are perhaps the only way to estimate the effects of national statutory changes. When changes take place in some jurisdictions and not in others, comparisons across jurisdictions may provide another way of estimating what would have happened in the absence of the statute under scrutiny. The issue here is: What are appropriate comparison jurisdictions? The general principle is that a jurisdiction ought to be compared with others that are as nearly identical as possible. Since no two jurisdictions are exactly alike, comparability is always a matter of degree. Adjacent states in the same region are perhaps more comparable than more distant jurisdictions; nearby cities of comparable size and demographic composition are likely to be more comparable than more distant cities or ones of different size or composition. The choice of comparison jurisdictions is, of course, more a matter of art and judgment than science, and any choice is subject to dispute. Perhaps the best strategy is to use a number of comparison jurisdictions (see Pierce and Bowers, 1979): if most of the comparisons support a particular interpretation, the conclusions are considerably strengthened.

Under some special circumstances, it may be possible to conduct field experiments with gun control measures, especially ones that would test alternative means of implementation. The example that is closest to an experiment of this sort was an attempt to provide maximum administration of the 1968 GCA (as described in Zimring, 1975). In this case, licensed gun dealers in parts of Maryland and Virginia that were close to the District of Columbia were monitored carefully to detect sales to District residents, in violation of the 1968 Act. The impact of the "experimental" dosage level was measured by observing the trends in weapons-related crimes within the District.

Some General Observations on Impact Assessment

This discussion of impact assessment is designed primarily to alert the reader to some of the problems that face researchers who attempt to evaluate the effects of gun control statutes.[3] Perhaps the most important message is that such assessments cannot be made sensibly without intimate knowledge and understanding of how guns are distributed and used in the United States and in the particular jurisdictions in question. Such knowledge is useful in understanding how a given piece of legislation is intended to work and how it is likely to work—through what mechanisms and with what changes in the structure of incentives and sanctions for criminals, police, victims, courts, and other participants in the general criminal justice system.

Of course, such knowledge is agnostic a priori with respect to whether or not it is at all possible to achieve the desired amount of control and desired effects on crime. Indeed, one of the major motivations for increasing the depth and accuracy of our general knowledge about firearms and their distribution is to be able to make such predictions. This chapter assumes that gun control may be effective in achieving some ends, but that is simply a working assumption for this discussion.

Also of importance is the expectation that massive and dramatic effects on crime-reduction are unlikely outcomes of most contemplated gun control statutes. This expectation is founded on an understanding that crime rates are affected by many trends in the society, and consequently the contribution that gun control could make to changes in crime rates is probably relatively slight. The implication for evaluations of the effects of gun control measures is that such research efforts must be made carefully because the effects to be detected are likely to be slight and easily swamped by the noise level that ordinarily exists in the system. Another implication is that findings will usually be subject to dispute. Slight changes in the research models used to assess gun control legislation are likely to lead to changes in the estimated sizes or even the directions of effects.

LANDMARK EVALUATIONS OF GUN CONTROL EFFECTS

This section reviews some of the major attempts to assess the effectiveness of gun control legislation. The studies that are discussed were chosen because each has been cited repeatedly in the literature on gun control and because each represents a major approach to the problem posed by evaluation.

---

[3] More detailed and technical analyses of these problems can be found in the standard works on the evaluation of social programs, e.g., Cook and Campbell (1979), Cronbach et al. (1980), and Rossi and Freeman (1982).

The three major approaches, described in detail below, are (1) cross-sectional studies that attempt to estimate the effects of "natural variations" in gun control legislation by states or other political jurisdictions on weapons-related crimes, (2) time-series studies that examine the shifts in relevant crime rates accompanying the introduction of a change in gun control legislation, and (3) "process studies" that attempt to show how particular changes in gun control policies are implemented through intermediate effects.

Cross-Sectional Studies of "Natural Variation" in Gun Control

The 50 states and thousands of counties and municipalities in the United States provide considerable opportunity for "natural variation" to arise in the way in which particular political jurisdictions attempt to regulate the possession and use of weapons. Although state legislation ordinarily has priority over local ordinances and laws, states often delegate to localities the authority to enact additional regulations that go beyond what the state may require (see Chapter 12).[4] Generally, regulations tend to be more restrictive in states in the Northeast than in the South and the West, and more restrictive in larger cities and counties. Thus, among the most restrictive states are New York, Massachusetts, and New Jersey. Likewise, New York City, Boston, and Chicago are more restrictive than most cities in the country.

It would seem only sensible to attempt to trace out the implications of this natural variation for weapons-related crimes; indeed, two studies reviewed below attempt to do so for the 50 states.[5] The problem, of course, is that the 50 states are not comparable to each other, representing varying mixes of demographic, economic, and even historical factors that might conceivably affect crime rates independently of gun control legislation. Indeed, one might easily entertain the theory that the underlying conditions that induce legislators

[4] The extent to which such local variations exist may be seen in the results of the police department survey of Weber-Burdin et al. (1981) and in the survey of gun control regulations contained in Chapter 12.

[5] Other types of variation present even greater temptations, which most social scientists, at least, have resisted trying to analyze. Countries vary even more markedly in the restrictions placed on weapons possession, ranging from Switzerland (which virtually requires each adult male national to possess a weapon and ammunition as part of his service to the national militia) to England and Ireland (where ownership of handguns is virtually forbidden and severe controls are placed on the ownership of long guns). Some appreciation of the international variation in gun control can be attained from King (1973) as well as the Comptroller General (1978). Neither study attempts to draw conclusions from the cross-national comparisons presented except to note that crime rates and the restrictive or permissive nature of gun control cross-nationally seem scarcely to be related. On the problems of international comparisons, see also Bruce-Biggs (1976) and Chapter 7.

to enact gun control legislation are the same that produce state gun-related crime rates. Hence the assessment of the effects of gun control legislation depends for its plausibility on the researcher's ability to unravel the confounding effects of state socioeconomic, demographic, and political characteristics from legislative effects. The two studies described below take two different approaches, leading to markedly different conclusions about the effectiveness of gun control legislation.

Geisel et al. (1969),[6] using an inventory of state regulations in effect at the time, attempted to relate statistically a set of crime, accident, and suicide rates involving firearms to a combined gun control index formed from the state regulations. The index displayed in that article is one of several dozen ways in which numerical scores could be given to each state according to the particular configuration of gun regulations in effect. The scoring system that produced the highest relationship to the largest number of gun-related crime rates was selected for discussion in the article.

Recognizing that crime rates were also dependent on other characteristics of the states, the authors entered into a multiple regression model several state characteristics: average per capita income, median school years completed by adults, males per 100 females, police employees per 1000 residents, proportion black, population density, median age, and licensed hunters per capita. Multiple regression equations linking the dependent variables with the above, together with each state's numerical score on the regulations index, yielded sets of effect coefficients for all the independent variables. The coefficients for gun regulations tended to show for most dependent variables that the stricter the gun regulations in each state, the fewer the deaths, injuries, suicides, and crimes committed with guns. The authors further estimated that if each state brought its regulations up to the strictness of New Jersey, several hundred deaths from firearms would be averted nationally each year. Similar calculations were made for 129 cities, using state regulations in which the cities were located.

[6] Earlier studies conducted by Krug (1967, 1968a, 1968b) purported to show no relationship between gun control legislation and crime rates. However, because states were grouped into very large categories and socioeconomic and other relevant characteristics were not held constant, Krug's results have generally been heavily discounted in discussions of the effects of gun control legislation. Krug's studies received widespread publicity (they were published in the *Congressional Record*) and Geisel's research must be regarded as partly a response to Krug's analyses.

Another study (Seitz, 1972) may also be cited. Seitz attempted to model the effects of gun control on the availability of weapons across states and its subsequent effect on homicide rates. This study also suffers from insufficient attention to the processes that produce interstate variations in crime rates of all sorts. Among the least sensible statistics produced in this article is a correlation computed between the total homicide rate and the gun-homicide rate. Such a computation inflates the correlation coefficient perforce because gun-related homicide is included in all homicides, part–whole correlations generally being tautologically high (see Chapter 10).

The main problems with the analyses by Geisel *et al.* center around the statistical model used. As discussed above, establishing the *ceteris paribus* conditions in cross-sectional studies requires that the investigator have a fairly complete understanding of how the particular crime rates are generated. In this study, the variables entered into the equations as "controls" were largely ad hoc. Most are known correlates of crime rates, but they are not held together by any systematic theory of how crime rates are generated. For example, a theory of crime that weighed deterrence heavily might have led the investigators to include clearance rates, average sentences given out to persons convicted of gun-related offenses, or other similar variables as part of the analysis. Because the theoretical relevance of the control variables used was not explained (and hence cannot be evaluated), one can only suspect that the *ceteris paribus* conditions are not plausible. In other words, variables may be left out, causal relationships among variables may be wrongly specified, and some variables may be simply alternative proxies for the same underlying phenomenon. In short, the analysis presented is not very plausible just because it is not driven by a plausible or explicit theory about the dependent variable.

The Murray (*1975*) study can be contrasted with that of Geisel *et al.* (1969). It illustrates dramatically the effects of positing alternative statistical models in cross-sectional studies of the effects of gun control legislation. Murray used data from the 1970 Census to characterize each of the states in combination with UCR data from the same year. State regulations concerning guns were modeled as a set of dummy variables using information obtained from Bakal (1966), rather than summarized into an overall numerical index as done by Geisel *et al.*[7] In addition, certain variables were used in Murray's analysis that had not been employed by Geisel, including such factors as the log of total state population, percentage unemployed, percentage below the poverty line, and percentage of population who were interstate migrants. Thus, the implicit underlying theory of firearm violence employed by Murray is substantially different from the theory that appears in the report by Geisel *et al.* Murray, however, provides little rationale for or discussion of his model, either in general or in the specific ways in which it departs from the Geisel model.

The form of the statistical analysis employed by Murray was different in important ways from that employed by Geisel. Using a backward stepwise regression method, Murray "forced" all the independent variables (except the gun regulation dummies) into the equation, first allowing those variables

---

[7] Criticisms were raised by Jones (1980) that data were incorrectly transcribed by Murray from Bakal's state law inventory. Specifically, South Carolina was described by Murray as a strict gun control state, whereas Bakal shows that the laws in question had been repealed and that South Carolina was no longer a strict state by 1970.

to absorb as much variance in gun-related crimes as possible, and then adding the gun control dummies and allowing them to absorb any additional variance. Although this is a perfectly acceptable procedure for many purposes, it should be noted that its use implies a model that allocates any effects of the state characteristics that may be shared with the gun control legislation to the former. In other words, if legislators are more inclined to institute licenses to carry firearms in states that are outside the "Old South" because it is part of non-Southern culture to do so, any joint determination of crime rates by region and gun control legislation is allocated entirely to the regional variable in Murray's formulation.[8] This procedure, in short, stacks the deck against such effects as the gun legislation variables might otherwise produce.

Murray's analysis also includes data on handgun ownership obtained from Harris and Gallup polls. Since neither of these two surveys is based on samples large enough to permit state-by-state tabulations, only levels of gun ownership in four regions of the United States[9] were used, a decision that conceals potentially large variations from state to state within regions in the possession of guns by households (see Chapter 7).

Murray's analysis indicates that there are no significant effects of gun control legislation on the crime rates in question. These results are obtained for homicides, assaults, robbery, suicide, and gun accidents.

Murray's analyses are no more plausible than Geisel's. Taken together, the two studies confirm that cross-sectional studies of this sort are highly sensitive to alternative specification of the statistical models employed, and possibly to the analytical strategies employed as well. Cross-sectional studies that are not informed by reasonable theoretical models of how states, cities, or regions vary in crime rates can produce misleading and contradictory results. Until such theories are developed, little of substance can be concluded from studies of this type.[10]

---

[8] This statement does not imply that we accept the notion that there is a regional culture (see Chapter 6). All that we mean to suggest is that Murray's formulation implies that there is not. This and other features of the implicit theoretical structure underlying Murray's procedures are not clearly set out by him.

[9] Two states, Hawaii and Alaska, are ordinarily left out of the Harris and Gallup samples because each would be allocated only a very small number of very expensive interviews. However, these two states are somehow assigned to regions in Murray's analysis.

[10] On the other hand, the fact that alternative specifications of the underlying conditions that cause crime lead to entirely opposite research findings means certainly that the effects of state-level weapons control legislation are *not* sufficiently large to overpower specification errors. This implies that *if* state-by-state legislative variation has any effect at all on state-by-state variation in gun crime and gun violence, the effect can only be subtle at best. Assuming accurate measurement of the legislative variability, a truly powerful effect would be detectable in either Murray's or Geisel's data.

Longitudinal Studies of Gun Control Legislation

A much more promising strategy for examining the impact of gun control legislation is the before-and-after longitudinal study. States and other political jurisdictions shift in permissiveness whenever new gun legislation is enacted. These changes, under proper circumstances, obviate many of the difficulties in specifying *ceteris paribus* conditions because the jurisdictional experiences before the new legislation can be contrasted with those occurring after enactment. Of course, many caveats must be observed, since the legislative changes may be accompanied by other shifts that could also influence the anticipated outcome. For example, an urban disturbance occurring around the same time may increase gun possession, or a rise in unemployment among youth may increase the number of robberies. But the difficulties in studying such shifts in legislation are considerably fewer than those involved in the analysis and interpretation of cross-sectional differences.

One potentially very serious problem in any time-series analysis may be called the "timing" problem. Imagine a time-series data base that is tracking some variable of interest, such as the crime rate, unemployment, or worker productivity. In the normal course of things, because of the simultaneous effects of all other variables that influence the variable of interest, the time-series data bounce up and down between more and less desirable conditions. That is, troughs and peaks occur normally in the time series as part of its usual or customary behavior. The timing problem is simply that policy interventions tend, almost invariably, to be instituted during the troughs (that is, as the variable tends toward less desirable states) for the very simple reason that the inclination to do something about a problem sharply increases when it appears that the problem is getting worse. Because the normal behavior of the time series is to bounce, troughs tend to be followed by peaks. It is thus easy to see that the normal fluctuation of the time series can be easily mistaken for evidence of a positive program effect. The solution to the problem, of course, is to let the postenactment series run its course over a reasonable span of time before impact assessment is attempted. But legislators who want to know whether the program is working are seldom satisfied to hear that it will be several years before the question can be reasonably answered.

The major longitudinal studies can be roughly classified into two types, process studies and time-series analyses. The former are concerned mainly with the implementation of new legislation and less on the outcome in terms of the use of weapons in crime, whereas time-series analyses are more concerned with measuring the effects of legislation on various crime rates. Both types have value; process studies address the critical issue of the intermediate effects of such legislation, whereas time-series studies are concerned primarily with end effects.

A National Process Study: The 1968 Federal Gun Control Act (Zimring, 1975). Zimring's (1975) study is perhaps the most extensive examination of the latest major Federal legislative effort in the area of gun control. The 1968 Act contained a complex variety of measures aimed at eliminating interstate sales of guns (with the intention of preventing states with stronger gun controls from being undercut by dealers in more permissive states); prohibiting sales to certain classes of individuals, notably minors, persons convicted of felonies, mental defectives, and drug users; and limiting importation by prohibiting the import of surplus military firearms and restricting imports largely to weapons that could be used for sporting purposes.[11] Administrative responsibility for the Act was given to the Bureau of Alcohol, Tobacco, and Firearms (ATF) within the Treasury Department.

Zimring's account of the first 5 years of the operation of the 1968 Act was limited primarily to an analysis of the operating assumptions of the Act and a description of its administration.

Zimring notes that although the Act called for licensing of dealers who were to maintain records of their firearms transactions, very little was done to police the implementation of the licensing and transaction regulations. Although cases referred for prosecution increased considerably after the Act was passed, the sheer volume of transactions was such that almost any extensive policing of dealers would have been far beyond the capacity of ATF to undertake. The considerable task of investigating applications for dealers' licenses (there were about 160,000 licensed dealers in 1972) was simply more than could be expected of the relatively small number of Bureau agents. Inspecting dealer records for compliance with provisions of the Act, not to mention investigating whether dealers were complying with the exclusionary provisions of the Act, was completely beyond the capacity of the Bureau.

Much more success was achieved by the provisions that regulated the importation of certain types of guns. Aimed at the importation of Saturday Night Specials, the Act left it to the Bureau to find a specific definition. The Bureau came up with a quantitative "factoring" index that took into account, among other things, barrel length and weapon weight. The consequence of the introduction of this definition was to lower the number of handgun imports significantly during the first few years after the Act was passed. However, as Zimring was able to show, domestic production of handguns increased to fill at least part of the gap.[12]

---

[11] Thus, the GCA of 1968 is a classic example of a problem well-known in the evaluation literature. The Act is *not* a simple measure with a single intended outcome, but rather a large number of distinct measures, each with a different end purpose. Evaluating "the" effect of the 1968 GCA as a whole would obviously be a very difficult business.

[12] Some wide differences between Census and ATF import statistics make it ambiguous whether the trend toward lowering of imports continued through the end of 1975; see also Chapters 2–5.

Zimring attempts to show that reducing handgun imports had some impact on certain gun-related crimes, especially handgun homicides and firearm assaults. Although it is apparent that the rates of increase for such offenses began to decline after 1969, it is not at all convincing that the decline in importation produced the decline in rates. First, we do not know the price elasticity of weaponry for people who commit crimes. It may well be that doubling or even tripling the price of handguns on the legitimate and illegal markets would have no effect on their ownership for illicit purposes. Second, it is not at all clear that Saturday Night Specials are the weapons of choice for the commission of crimes (see Chapter 10). Finally, it may well be that the rate of increase in the relevant crime rates would have begun to decline in any event and that *the coincidence noted by Zimring may not indicate any causal link after all.*

Zimring also attempts to measure the ability of the Act to lower sales by dealers of handguns to people residing out of state. Since the local gun laws in Boston and New York are enforced strictly enough to essentially prevent sales of weapons within each city, weapons *perforce* have to be procured from out of the city and in most cases from out of the state. Trends in handgun homicides in the two cities, however, indicate no wiggles in the period after 1968 that would be consonant with the interpretation that the law was effective in reducing interstate sales. Indeed, if anything, it appeared that firearm assaults increased in New York and Boston more than in other places throughout the nation.

Zimring's analysis gives sharp emphasis to some of the points made earlier in this chapter about the importance of having a firm, empirically grounded understanding of the facts concerning gun use in crime before embarking on legislation. It is not entirely clear that Saturday Night Specials are the weapons of choice for criminals; rather, evidence is developing that such weapons are bought mainly by people who are not professional criminals. In addition, the pattern of interstate commerce in guns on the retail level was not well understood. Therefore, regulation of sales by dealers to out-of-state purchasers could not be adequately policed. Finally, a method of gun regulation that implied a considerable increase in ATF manpower should have been accompanied by such increases in order to achieve any effectiveness. Since the Act was based on little or no knowledge of the phenomena it was supposed to control, we should not be surprised that it produced few or none of the intended effects (the reduction of handgun imports possibly being the only major exception).

Although Zimring's analysis does not make any strong statements about the impact of the law on gun-related crimes (indeed, it could not do so), it is quite valuable because it investigated the important issues in administration as described above. For example, an import restriction that actually did not restrict imports could have no impact on weapon usage, nor could a registration system for sales have any impact without some efficient means for monitoring compliance. Hence such process studies prove to be of value even though they cannot (and should not) lead to estimates about end effects.

Local Process Studies of the Massachusetts Bartley-Fox Amendment (Beha, 1977; Rossman et al., 1979). In 1974 the Massachusetts legislature passed an amendment (known as the Bartley-Fox Amendment) to its gun control laws that expanded Massachusetts licensing procedures and made unlicensed carrying of firearms an offense with a mandatory sentence of one year. The Amendment prohibited the suspension of sentences, nonfiling of cases, plea bargaining, and other devices used by courts and prosecutors to avoid felony convictions.[13] The passage of the Bartley-Fox Amendment was accompanied by several months of widespread publicity before it became effective in April 1975.

In a very fine-grained study of process, Beha examined the facts of every arrest charge involving weapons that was processed through the courts of Suffolk County (Boston) in the period April through September 1975, as well as a parallel set of cases in a 6-month period in 1974. In addition, the analysis employed UCR and Boston Police Department arrest records, statistics on the issuance of firearms permits, and interviews with police, prosecutors, and defense attorneys.

Although Beha did undertake to assess the effectiveness of the Bartley-Fox Amendment in lowering firearms-related offenses, a major portion of his analysis centered on the ways in which the Suffolk County Courts handled such charges. Initially, there was some concern that the courts would resent the loss of discretion imposed by the Bartley-Fox Amendment and work out evasion tactics that would restore their ability to deal flexibly with cases of weapons-carrying violations. In addition, it was also believed that arresting police might be reluctant to enter a carrying charge because of the mandatory penalties carried in the Bartley-Fox Amendment.

Beha's study of court cases indicated widespread compliance with the provision of the Amendment that restricted judges' discretion. People charged with weapons-carrying violations were either acquitted or sentenced as the law required, whereas before enactment of the Amendment a fairly large proportion of such cases were given suspended sentences or kept on file for periods of time without sentencing.[14] In short, it appeared to Beha that,

[13] The publicity preceding the enforcement of the Bartley-Fox Amendment stressed possession as well as carrying, a theme that was not in fact true about the legislative change. People could still possess unlicensed weapons in their homes and places of business without violating the law, a provision of the law that was contradicted by its publicity.

[14] This is a Massachusetts device for achieving a "conviction" without creating a felony record for the accused. If the accused comes before the court again on a felony charge, the unfiled case is then activated and a sentence imposed. This device is used frequently for first offenders and for people who appear to the judge to be "ordinary" law-abiding citizens.

at least for the first 6 months, the law was being properly administered by the courts.

Inspection of the Boston police arrest records also led Beha to conclude that the Boston police were not reluctant to arrest on carrying charges. Although there was a drop in such arrests after Bartley-Fox, there was no evidence that this was due to arresting officer discretion. Rather, inspection of additional charges filed indicated that the association of carrying charges with other charges remained the same before and after Bartley-Fox.

Beha's study also indicated that the Bartley-Fox Amendment had little effect on other weapons-related charges. Thus, if a person was charged with armed robbery in which an unlicensed handgun was used, a weapons-carrying charge was ordinarily not filed as an additional charge. Indeed, the carrying charge carried with it under Bartley-Fox a much smaller mandatory sentence than that ordinarily given out for armed robbery and hence did not add much to the prosecution of the more serious weapons-related crimes.

Beha also made some comparisons of police reports of weapons-related crimes before and after Bartley-Fox. We shall not discuss those comparisons in detail because their meaning is ambiguous without careful specification of the *ceteris paribus* conditions.

This process analysis again shows the importance of working out and studying in detail the enforcement process in gun control legislation. There were several points at which the operation of the law could have been vitiated: police might have stopped entering carrying charges; prosecutors might have found ways in which to use the charges in plea bargaining with the accused; and judges could have avoided the mandatory sentencing provisions by dismissing more easily certain types of cases. Note that the issue here is not whether the end effects have been realized, but whether the cases of detected violations of carrying weapons are treated in the courts as the legislation apparently demands that they be treated.

Rossman *et al.* (1979) extended Beha's earlier study in several directions. Most important, the time period of analysis was extended beyond the first 6 months after Bartley-Fox came into operation. Moreover, the jurisdictions studied included Springfield and Worcester (in addition to Boston), and the data collected included systematic interviews with prosecutors, defense attorneys, policemen, judges, and clerks of the courts. In addition, a much more sophisticated before-and-after analysis of crime rates was undertaken (to be considered separately below).

Rossman and his colleagues found that there were differences in the accommodation of the criminal justice system to Bartley-Fox over time. In the year immediately following enactment, enforcement appeared to be pursued more vigorously than 2 years later. Arrests on carrying charges increased after enactment but then declined in the following year. Interviews with policemen indicated a widespread lack of clear understanding of the provisions of the law and its applicability, resolved in favor of enforcement in the first year and otherwise in the second year. Some of the courts systematically undercut the law by downgrading charges of carrying to possession, leading to the restoration of discretion to the courts that was intended to be reduced by the passage of Bartley-Fox.

Rossman *et al.* also noted that, after the passage of Bartley-Fox, convictions on carrying charges declined for those charged, indicating that judges and juries were less willing to convict on such charges, perhaps another type of evasion of the intent of Bartley-Fox. Indeed, the investigators conclude (very tentatively) that the Bartley-Fox Amendment led in Boston to only 40 more prison sentences for carrying charges over a year's period than would have been expected.[15]

The major importance of this study was to show that longer-term effects may be different from short-term effects. It apparently takes time for a complex, loosely coupled system such as the criminal justice system to absorb and assimilate a change such as that represented by the Bartley-Fox Amendment. Initial responses may not be the same as long-term responses; and the studies reviewed are hardly very long-term, extending only two years after enactment. Whether the trends seen by Rossman and his colleagues toward a reestablishment of the *status quo ante* continued or reversed in subsequent years is of course completely open.

Time-Series Analyses of the Bartley-Fox Amendment's Effects on Relevant Crime Rates (Deutsch and Alt, 1977; Pierce and Bowers, 1979).[16] Because crime statistics are collected and available on a fairly fine-grained time scale, it is possible to examine the effects of identified changes in the criminal justice system on crime rates in general and on specific types of crimes. The general logic of this approach is clear and simple even if the specific procedures employed are complicated and demanding. The general principle that underlies time-series analyses is that it is possible to estimate the behavior of a time series at a particular point in time through an analysis of trends in the data at previous points in time. This principle asserts that abrupt and dramatic changes are unlikely; the best way to predict how many crimes there will be in a given month is to analyze how long-term trends, seasonal

---

[15] The calculated number is based on a number of precarious assumptions and hence can be regarded only as providing some evidence that the number of convictions that could be attributed to Bartley-Fox was not large, beyond what would have been expected otherwise.

[16] Other investigators using time series to examine the effects of gun control include Deiner and Crandall (1979), who studied the effects on crime rates in Jamaica of a general crime control act that included gun control. The models used, however, are much more primitive than those in the studies reviewed here and cover a shorter period of time before and after the intervention.

trends, plus variability of an unstructured sort would lead one to predict a particular set of values for the month in question.

Deutsch and Alt, in an early article, applied sophisticated time-series modeling to investigating the effects of Bartley-Fox on gun assaults, homicides, and armed robbery in Boston for the 6-month period following the implementation of the Amendment. Using the estimation techniques of Box and Jenkins (1970), the investigators fitted an estimation formula to the monthly time series (1966 through 1974) for the three types of crimes, projected the series forward, and compared their estimates of what was to be expected with the rates of actual occurrence in each during 6 months after Bartley-Fox was implemented. Deutsch and Alt conclude that the Bartley-Fox Amendment affected crime rates for armed robbery and gun assaults but not for homicide.

It should be noted that these findings apply only to the city of Boston and only to the six months following the implementation of the law. The study also assumes that the Box-Jenkins model fitted was the best one among those available. This last qualification again emphasizes that theoretical models are critically important in assessing effectiveness.

In an article criticizing Deutsch and Alt, Hay, and McCleary (1979) dispute whether the time-series model used was appropriate. Asserting that another model was more appropriate, Hay and McCleary show that the use of their "better" model led to inconclusive findings in which the differences between predicted and actual crime rates for gun assault and armed robbery were not statistically significant. In a rejoining article, Deutsch (1979) disputes the criticisms of Hay and McCleary and asserts that the original Box-Jenkins (ARIMA) model was appropriate. We are not in a position to judge these claims and counterclaims, and the best we can do is to point to the clear implication that time-series analyses do not consist of applying a predetermined procedure but require the judicious selection among a variety of alternatives, a decision based on artful diagnoses of empirical data as well as matching models with theoretical understanding.

A much more extensive attempt to assess the effects of Bartley-Fox was undertaken by Pierce and Bowers (1979). These investigators enlarged the data to include a longer period of time after Bartley-Fox implementation, compared the trends in Massachusetts and Boston with other states and communities, and considered trends outside Boston as well as in Boston itself. Indeed, Pierce and Bowers achieve a more convincing analysis of the impact of Bartley-Fox because their several data bases strengthen each other considerably.

Trends for Massachusetts are compared with crime trends in nearby states, for the New England area as a whole, and for the Northeast region. In addition, trends in urbanized counties abutting on Massachusetts are compared with Boston and the state as a whole. Pierce and Bowers find that the incidence of gun assaults was deflected downward by the introduction of Bartley-Fox, with a compensatory increase in assaults in which guns were not used. Apparently, Bartley-Fox had both a deterrent and a displacement effect. For armed robberies, a moderate deterrent effect was detected, and a possibility was noted that guns were again beginning to be used two years after Bartley-Fox went into effect, particularly against victims in certain types of robberies. Finally, gun homicides showed a slight decline as a consequence of Bartley-Fox.

Note that it is not at all clear how the Bartley-Fox Amendment achieved these effects on the major gun crimes. The Amendment speaks directly to only one offense, namely, carrying an unlicensed firearm. It does not increase, decrease, or otherwise alter penalties for crimes in which guns are used. Bartley-Fox certainly increases the risk of carrying an unlicensed weapon, but evidence from the process studies does not seem to indicate much change among the police and the courts in their arresting and charge-processing behaviors, especially after the initial postimplementation period. If there is a deterrence effect, it is that Bartley-Fox deterred people from carrying unlicensed weapons, a side effect of which was to reduce the use of guns in connection with certain crimes. Of course, there is always the possibility that the Bartley-Fox Amendment was only imperfectly understood by the public as generally increasing the severity with which gun-related offenses would be treated by the police and the courts.[17]

In any event, it seems clear that the impact of such changes in the law must be studied in considerable detail, both for their effects on the criminal justice system and for their effects on the commission of crimes. We see from the studies reviewed that the system may have an initial reaction that differs from its long-run accommodation to the law. Crime rates may also be affected, but displacement and deterrent effects lead to a mixed set of outcomes. Perhaps it would be best if all assaults involved weapons other than firearms, but that conclusion is not totally obvious given that victims threatened with less deadly weapons might resist more vigorously and thus bring more harm to themselves.

The Washington, D.C. and Detroit laws (Jones, 1981; Loftin and McDowell, 1981). Two very recent studies, each focused on a widely publicized legislative change, also warrant review here. The first is a study of the effects of Washington D.C.'s Firearms Control Regulations Act of 1975 (Jones, 1981), sometimes said to be the toughest gun law in the nation. The second is a study of the

---

[17] Indeed, both Beha (1977) and Rossman et al. (1979) indicate that the major publicity campaign preceding implementation was quite misleading in claiming that weapons possession was also covered by the law.

impact of Detroit's recent (1976) mandatory sentencing law undertaken by Loftin and McDowell (1981).

Jones' (1981) paper is the latest in a series of rather embittered disputes over the effectiveness of Washington's new (as of 1976) gun laws, the provisions of which were described briefly in Chapter 12. The first widely publicized evaluation was sponsored by the United States Conference of Mayors (1980), which concluded that the new laws had successfully reduced both firearms crime in general, and handgun crime in particular, within the District. This study was immediately faulted on various methodological grounds, including the inappropriateness of the comparison jurisdictions and the failure of the evaluation model to take into account possible cyclical effects in the crime rate, both well-taken criticisms.

The passage of the 1975 Act illustrates the timing problem discussed earlier in this chapter. The Act was passed at a time when rates of violent crime had achieved all-time highs all over the nation (i.e., in the 1974–1975 era). In the years since, rates of violent crime have tended to decrease somewhat (an effect that many suspect is due to the changing age structure of the population and, in particular, to the passage of the post-war baby boom out of the years in the life cycle when criminality is at its highest peak, the 16- to 24-year-old category). The simple before–after comparison for legislation enacted in the peak years would, consequently, almost necessarily indicate some positive crime-reductive effects for the legislation in question. This is the essence of the criticism that the study by the U.S. Conference of Mayors was insensitive to the cyclical nature of the crime rate.

Jones (1981) presents before–after (1974–1976 and 1977–1979) data on "firearms incidents as a percentage of total incidents" for the United States as a whole, for Washington D.C., for nine other major American cities, and for eight Maryland and Virginia jurisdictions that are in the immediate area of the District (see his Table 1). The entries for the District show definite declines for both robbery and aggravated assault, but the entries elsewhere in the table show approximately similar declines in most other jurisdictions as well. Indeed, of the 38 entries in the table (19 jurisdictions times two crime rate indicators), 29 are negative in sign (that is, indicate declines in the proportion of either robberies or aggravated assaults that were committed with firearms). The declines in the District, although certainly present in the data, are in the whole neither more nor less substantial than the declines registered over the same period in most other cities for which data are presented.

A second tabulation in the Jones article compares handgun homicides in Washington, D.C. and Baltimore—which, because of its proximity, is perhaps the most appropriate comparison city. Both cities show a marked decline in handgun homicides between 1974 and 1978, but the Baltimore decline is clearly the more pronounced. Between the two years, the number of handgun homicides in Baltimore declined by 46% (from 193 to 104), whereas the number in the District declined by 36% (from 174 to 112). There were, however, some differences between the cities in the kinds of homicides that declined. In Washington, for example, within-family homicides did show a small percentage decline, whereas in Baltimore, within-family homicides increased. In contrast, crime-related murders increased in Washington but declined in Baltimore over the same period. It is thus possible that the 1975 Act in the District had some effect on the mix of crime types but, in general, not on the overall number.

In conclusion, it can be fairly said that none of the published evaluations of the Washington law shows an unambiguous crime-reductive effect. That violent crime decreased in the District (and elsewhere in the nation) in the few years immediately after the passage of the Act is clear in all data sources, but no persuasive evidence has yet been produced that this reduction was in any sense a result of the new legislative measure.

Loftin and McDowell's (1981) evaluation of the 1976 Detroit mandatory sentencing law is interesting in that it combines elements of both process and impact assessment studies. The nature of the law was to provide a mandatory 2-year add-on (or sentence enhancement) for felonies committed while in possession of a firearm. Similar in many respects to other sentencing enhancement policies, the general idea is that a felony committed with a gun results in some sentence for the felony *and* a mandatory add-on penalty for having used (or in this case possessed) a gun in the crime. The "process" question concerns how the mandatory add-on was implemented in the courts; the "impact" question is whether the add-on sentence provision had a detectable crime-reductive effect.

To examine the first question, Loftin and McDowell analyzed sentencing data from the Detroit Recorder's Court for three years (1976 through 1978) spanning the enactment of the new law ($N = 8414$ murder, armed robbery, or assault charges). These data suggest no observable change in sentencing practices for firearms homicides or armed robberies but some increase in the sentences for firearms assaults. The courts, apparently, were selective in applying the provisions of the new law. The interpretation given to this pattern is of some interest. Before enactment, typical sentences for assault convictions were relatively slight, and many cases were given suspended sentences or probation. Failure to add the mandatory 2 years would thus be highly visible in a typical assault case. In contrast, average pre-enactment sentences for homicide and robbery were rather stiff, and thus "the sentencing judge could simply shave a couple of years off the murder or robbery sentence, making the net sentence the same as it had always been" (Loftin and McDowell,

1981: 156). This is an interesting comment because it illustrates the subtle ways in which the criminal justice system modifies initial legislative intent through discretionary implementation of new measures, and it thus confirms once again the need for intelligent and sensitive implementation studies as a precondition for impact assessment.

An attempt to assess the impact of the Detroit law confronts the same timing problem discussed above in the case of the D.C. Act: the law was enacted when crime rates everywhere had reached all-time highs. Following the general pattern, rates for most violent crimes did decrease in Detroit after the new law was passed, sometimes quite dramatically, but the data suggest "several patterns that are inconsistent with the hypothesis that the gun law contributed to the decline" (Loftin and McDowell, 1981: 159). First, all the declines began several months *before* the law went into effect. Armed robbery declined sharply in the post-enactment period, but so did unarmed robbery. "For assaults the patterns are quite contrary to what would be expected if the gun law had a deterrent effect" (1981: 160). More refined statistical analyses confirm the conclusions derived from simple visual inspection of the data, "that the gun law did not significantly alter the number or type of violent offenses committed in Detroit" (1981: 162).

Sentence Enhancement for Gun-Related Crimes

The opponents of more restrictive policies on weapons ownership and use have frequently argued that trying to solve the problem of violent crime through such measures is to put the cart before the horse. Gun ownership among the population at large, they point out, is a right, not a crime. They argue that the proper strategy is therefore not to restrict that right but to punish those who abuse it. One solves the problem of violent crimes committed with firearms not by further restrictions on the legitimate ownership and use of firearms among the general population, but by quick and severe punishments of those who employ guns for illicit or criminal purposes. This argument directs attention to the criminal justice system, and the treatment of weapons offenders within it, as the nexus where the problem of criminal violence due to weapons may be most sensibly addressed.

Public opinion data reviewed in Chapter 11 show substantial (indeed, overwhelming) popular support for the concept of severe and mandatory prison sentences for those convicted of a violent crime involving the use of a weapon. Consonant with public thinking, several jurisdictions now have mandatory sentencing provisions for some firearms crimes and sentencing enhancements for crimes committed with weapons, among them Massachusetts, Detroit, and California (see Chapter 12 for a compilation of state weapons regulations and laws).

Measuring the effects of such laws on the rates of gun-related crimes is fraught with many of the difficulties outlined earlier in this chapter. Sentence enhancement provisions are intended to operate through a general deterrence effect, raising the costs to people contemplating criminal acts. As yet, no studies have appeared in the literature that attempt to make such estimates of effects on crime rates. However, there are studies of intermediate effects, some of which are reviewed below.

The study of intermediate effects is important because the sentence enhancement laws have to be implemented by law enforcement agencies and the courts. Police departments and criminal courts are organizations that have traditionally operated with wide discretionary powers. Police may or may not arrest a person accused of a crime, record one form of a charge or another, and make or not make recommendations to prosecuting attorney staffs or the courts. In turn, the prosecuting attorneys and courts also exercise considerable discretion. Prosecutors may dismiss a case, change the charges entered, or recommend to the courts and grand juries, and the courts, in turn, may or may not dismiss charges, move a case forward through the processing system, accept or not accept pleas of guilty, impose sentences, and so on. Although the discretionary powers of the police and courts are not ordinarily exercised arbitrarily or capriciously, such powers are used and are thought to be quite essential both in achieving justice and in making it possible for the police and the courts to function smoothly.

The importance of police and court discretion is that legislative intent to restrict the flexibility of the police and the courts in the treatment of offenders is often muted in the actual practices of the police and the courts. Thus it is alleged that the draconian punishments for drug offenses legislated a decade ago in New York State led to a decline in police arrests on drug-related charges because police were reluctant to impose harsh mandatory sentences on people they believed were guilty of only minor transgressions. In the case of the Massachusetts Bartley-Fox Amendment, the courts learned how to get around legislative intent by downgrading charges of illegal weapons possession (Pierce and Bowers, 1979). The implication for the present discussion is clear: one of the most important intermediate effects of sentence enhancement strategies is to change the sentencing practices of the courts. On this topic there is some research, which is reviewed below.

Research on sentencing practices of the courts has not been concerned very often with the effects of weapons usage in crime on the resulting sentences. There is a substantial literature on determinants of sentencing (see the bibliography compiled by Ferry and Kravitz, 1978), but the largest share of it has been concerned with what is called "sentencing disparity"—that is, whether certain classes of criminals, such as blacks, Hispanics, the lower classes, and women, are sentenced differently from other classes. In addition, the growing body of empirical work on the issues of prosecution and disposition of cases in the criminal justice system has also focused mainly on the questions of discrimination based on extra-legal factors. When there are any data available on weapons, most court studies include this factor simply as an additional control measure of the seriousness of the case or as an indication of the quality of evidence (for example, whether the weapon involved was recovered as evidence), and little attention is devoted to any weapons effect found (Bernstein et al., 1977b; LaFree, 1980; Lizotte, 1978; Nagel, Cardascia, and Ross, 1980). Since most court studies have directed attention to other questions, the effects of weapons use on case disposition have been largely unstudied (the exception is a study by Cook and Nagin [1979], which is discussed more fully below).

Systematic research on the arrest practices of the police in criminal cases is almost nonexistent. This situation is not for lack of interest in this topic but because arrests are so difficult to observe, occurring as they do on the streets and in private places. The few studies on police arrest behavior tend to be qualitative in character and often concerned mainly with differential treatment of alleged offenders according to race, socioeconomic status, age, or sex, and less concerned with the nature of the offense alleged. Indeed, we can safely report that there is almost nothing in the literature about how police handle cases in which firearms or other weapons have been employed in the offenses in question. Hence the remainder of this section is focused on the treatment of weapons offenses in the courts.

It has been well recognized, at least since the Wickersham Commission of 1931, that the popular image of the criminals courts—in which a defendant is initially charged, formally arraigned, goes to trial to be found innocent or guilty by a jury of peers, and, if guilty, is punished in some commensurate manner by the judge—is appropriate only to a very small percentage of all criminal cases that appear before the courts (see Blumberg, 1979; Brosi, 1979). Nearly all court cases (both misdemeanor and felony) are settled at some point in the criminal justice system before they reach the formal trial stage, either by outright dismissal or guilty pleas. The proportion of arrests initially charged as felonies that go to trial is on the order of 10% or less of all cases in many jurisdictions (Brosi, 1979: 4).

For this reason, to study the disposition of felony cases in the court system, one should conceptualize the court as a "case filtering" system consisting of a series of successively finer screens, with some proportion of the initial cases flowing out of the system at each stage. The significance of this view for the present discussion is simply that the factors influencing the case outcome may vary stage by stage, and, more important, the effects of weapons use on felony case dispositions may well be different at each point.

In a separate study arising from this project, we have analyzed the effects of weapons use on felony case dispositions in detail. Specifically, we focused on the ways in which felonies committed with a weapon were treated differently at all stages of the criminal court system. The project analyzed felony case dispositions made in the Los Angeles County Superior Court during 1977 and 1978. A more complete description of all of the findings of this study are presented in a separate report (Rossi, Weber-Burdin, and Chen, 1981). Only a brief summary highlighting the key findings is given here.

To give an impression of the full criminal court system, Figure 13-1 shows the ultimate fate of a sample of 5000 felony arrests[18] processed through the Los Angeles County Superior Court during 1977 and 1978. As the figure shows, slightly more than half the cases were dismissed at the initial screening by the prosecutor or were referred to a lower court for misdemeanor prosecution. About 40% of the cases eventually get to the preliminary hearing stage, whereupon an additional 10% are dismissed or referred to a lower court. Thus, only about one-third of the initial arrests presented to the Los Angeles prosecutors even make it as far as the felony arraignment stage, and of the cases that reach arraignment, the largest share are resolved by guilty pleas without a trial. Of the total felony cases in Los Angeles for this period, only 4.2% eventually were adjudicated by trial. This pattern of case flow in the Los Angeles courts in the late 1970's replicates patterns of court dispositions found by Mather (1979) and Greenwood et al. (1976) in the same court system in the early 1970's. Similar proportions of case dispositions are also reported in the 13-city comparison undertaken by Brosi (1979: 9) and in the in-depth study of the New York City courts (Vera Institute, 1977). Thus, although our analysis is based on data from only one city, it does not appear that the pattern of case dispositions here differs extensively from those found in other large, metropolitan court systems.

Our analysis of the effect of weapon use on felony case dispositions in

[18] A total of 79,885 felony cases were processed by the Los Angeles County Superior Court system between January 1977 and July 1978. Cases that were initially charged after this date were excluded from our analysis because many were still open—that is, they had not yet reached their final disposition.

The analysis of the disposition of cases is based on data from the Los Angeles PROMIS (Prosecutor's Management Information System), which provides a computerized record of both the case and defendant characteristics and the history of the case through the criminal courts (including such information as court events, multiple charges, and final disposition).

The analysis of the outcomes of each stage of the court process is based on a random sample of 5000 cases active at that stage. A more detailed description of data, sampling and analysis is found in the full report (Rossi, Weber-Burdin, and Chen, 1981).

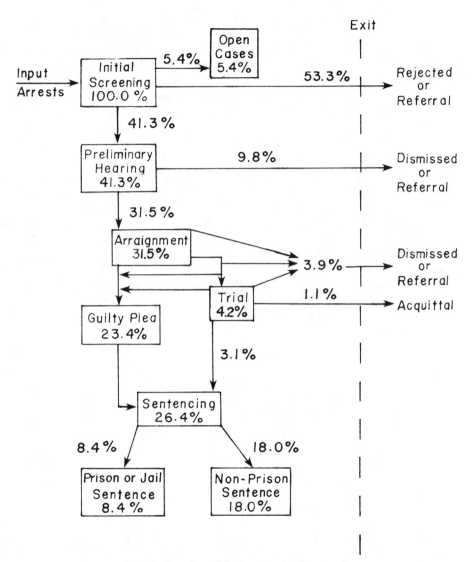

FIG. 13-1. Case flow of the Los Angeles Superior Court.

Los Angeles begins with the assumption that a large number of variables affect case outcomes at each stage. In particular, the nature and seriousness of the charge, the strength of the evidence, prior record of the defendant, characteristics of the defendant, the case load being managed by the prosecution, and the "convictability" of the case have all been shown to have an impact on case outcome. A unique feature of the Los Angeles data base (Prosecutor's Management Information System, or PROMIS) is that it contains enough detailed information on each case to allow one to model these various factors and to hold them constant in the empirical analysis. Thus, our estimates of the weapons effects are estimates *net of* the other many, potentially confounding, factors.

The major shortcoming of the Los Angeles PROMIS data for our research purposes is that the data on weapons are relatively crude, consisting of a single variable with four categories: gun involved in offense, other weapon involved, no weapon involved, or unknown. This information is gathered by the police at the time of the arrest and provided by them to the prosecutor's office. Thus, this variable is *independent* of any decision by the prosecutor concerning any specific weapons-related charges. For the sample of 5000 felony charges, the distribution of this weapon variable is as follows:

Gun involved in offense	13.9%
Other weapon involved	9.8
No weapon involved	60.4
Unknown	15.9
	100.0%

Notice that in roughly one-sixth of the cases information is missing on the involvement of a weapon.[19] Notice further that the data base does not contain additional weapons information that might be important in ascertaining the effect of weapon use on case disposition. For example, the data do not specify whether or not the weapon was fired during the incident, only brandished, or was merely possessed by the offender at the time; or is any information provided on the caliber or type of weapon. Given that this information is not available, the analysis is necessarily rather crude. However, the fact that the weapon variable is independent of the specific crime charged leads to a

---

[19] Because of the large amount of missing information (on the weapon variable and other variables such as employment of the defendant, prior record, etc.), we did not exclude "missing cases" but instead included them in the regressions as dummy variables. In the case of the weapon variable, three dummy variables were included in the regressions: (1) gun involved, (2) other weapon involved, and (3) missing information on weapon. The excluded category was, thus, those cases where it was known, for sure, that there was no weapon involved, and the "gun effect" is in comparison to this excluded category.

better description of any weapons effect than provided by studies that included such variables as "arrest charge includes possession of weapon charge" (Nagel, Cardascia, and Ross, 1980) or "weapon recovered" (LaFree, 1980).

It is important to emphasize that all the cases considered in this analysis are felony cases, that is, are relatively more serious crimes. Most of the weapons use represented in the data is use in the context of committing some other crime, such as robbery or assault, and not illegal possession or use of firearms charges, which constitute only 1.9% of the total charges.

Findings from our analysis of Los Angeles felony dispositions, stage by stage, are as follows. First, we find a statistically significant and positive effect for gun use at the stage of initial prosecution screening: with other relevant characteristics of case and defendant held constant, the probability that a case will be accepted for felony prosecution at initial screening is 34% higher for a case involving a gun than if no weapon was used. The effect for "other weapon" was insignificant at this stage. This weapon effect is independent of other measures of seriousness such as the charge itself and whether or not the victim was injured during the incident. This result is consistent with other court studies that have found that seriousness of the case is one of the strongest determinants of prosecution.

After a case has been accepted for prosecution as a felony, it goes to a preliminary hearing in which probable cause must be shown. Here too we find a positive and statistically significant gun effect. The probability of a case being accepted at the preliminary hearing is about 24% higher if a gun was involved in the offense than if no weapon was involved, regardless of the other case and defendant characteristics. Furthermore, the effect for "other weapon" was not significant at this stage.

If the case is accepted at the preliminary hearing stage, it goes to a formal felony arraignment in Superior Court. At arraignment, the case may be dismissed, the defendant may plead guilty, or the case may be sent to trial. We find that the probability of a dismissal at the arraignment stage is not significantly affected by the involvement of either a gun or of another weapon compared to cases with no weapon; all estimated coefficients are trivially small and not statistically different from zero. Given the large percentage of cases dismissed at the earlier court stages, the dismissals of cases at the arraignment stage are probably due to technical reasons (such as witness problems) or legal problems (for example, with evidence) and not related to case characteristics.

How does weapons use influence whether the case is resolved by a guilty plea or adjudication by trial? Our analysis finds that defendants in felony cases in which a gun was involved are *less* likely to plead guilty than offenders using no weapons, regardless of other case and defendant characteristics. The probability that the case went to trial after arraignment (rather than being pled guilty) is about 30% higher for cases involving a gun than for those involving no weapons. (Here again, the effect of "other weapon" is weak and statistically insignificant.)

Thus, in the Los Angeles criminal justice system, defendants who had a gun at the time of the offense (but not other weapons) are more likely to pass through initial screening to the preliminary hearing, more likely to pass from the preliminary hearing to formal felony arraignment, and less likely to plead guilty (as opposed to going to trial). How are trial outcomes affected by the presence of a weapon during the crime?

Trial outcomes, of course, are of two sorts: first, the finding as to guilt or innocence, and then, for the guilty, the sentence received for the convicted charge. Concerning the first, our analysis of Los Angeles felony trials finds no significant gun or other weapon effect on outcome: as it happens, gun offenders are about 19% more likely to be found guilty of the charge than are offenders using no weapons, but this effect does not quite pass the threshold of statistical significance.

Felons are judged guilty either by plea or by a trial finding; once judged guilty, they may receive a prison sentence or some other sentence not involving prison, such as a suspended sentence, probation, or fine. Among felons who pled guilty, the probability of a prison or jail sentence (of any length) is very much higher if a weapon was involved in the case than if not. Gun offenders (that is, those convicted of a crime in which a weapon was involved) are about 74% more likely to receive a prison sentence than offenders whose cases involved no weapons. Offenders whose cases involved other weapons are, likewise, about 45% more likely to be incarcerated than those with no weapon involvement.

Much the same is true for felons found guilty by trial. Among cases involving a gun, the probability of incarceration is about 67% higher than among offenders convicted at trial whose cases involved no weapon. For users of other weapons, the odds of doing time are about 33% higher. All effects of weapons on the probability of prison or jail sentence are statistically significant and are *net* of the other variables pertaining to the case and defendant.

Finally, we may inquire into the effects of weapons use on the length of sentence received. Among felons found guilty at trial, the gun effect is quite substantial: all else equal, the involvement of a gun in the felony increases the average sentence by close to 600 days for those sentenced to prison or jail. In contrast, the "extra time" for cases involving other weapons is only about 30 days (and not statistically significant). Both of these effects are in comparison to cases involving no weapons and are independent of the other case and defendant factors in the regression equation.

Among felons who pled guilty and were sentenced to prison, the gun effect is also quite substantial, although less so than for those found guilty at trial. The gun effect was about 400 extra days of sentence time. The effect for involvement of other weapon was also substantial and significant among those pleading guilty and sentenced, amounting to about 240 extra days compared to cases involving no weapons.

For both guilty pleas and guilty findings, then, it is apparent that substantially stiffer prison sentences were meted out to offenders convicted of felonies involving a gun than to offenders using no weapons, even with other potentially relevant factors held constant. The California Penal Code specifies sentence enhancements of 1 to 2 years for felonies committed with the use of a firearm, and this analysis confirms that the legislated sentence enhancements are being implemented by the courts.

At the earlier stages of the court process, it is also clear that the prosecutors in Los Angeles paid considerable attention to those cases in which a gun was involved. Gun offenders were more likely than non-gun offenders to pass through all of the stages in the criminal justice system, regardless of other factors that measure the seriousness of the case such as the charge and injury to the victim. The involvement of a gun in a felony case adds an additional element of seriousness to which the Los Angeles court system responds.

Whether the same weapons effect is also found in other jurisdictions is less obvious. Bernstein and her associates (1979) have analyzed the dispositions of about 3000 cases of persons arraigned for felonies or serious misdemeanors in the State Criminal or Supreme Court in New York during the winter of 1974–1975. Unfortunately, the data apparently do not contain any information on whether a gun (or other weapon) was present during the commission of each crime, but only a variable indicating whether the arrest charge included a charge of "illegal possession of weapon" (along with any other charges made in the case). The presence of an illegal possession charge had no significant effect on the probability of dismissal, but it had a slight positive effect on the probability of being imprisoned (see Bernstein, Cardascia, and Ross, 1979: 345). Because this study used a weapons charge variable (which the prosecutor has discretion to include or not), it is not surprising that no weapons effect was found on the probability of dismissal; those cases that were less serious and may have been more likely to be dismissed may also have been the ones to which the prosecutor did not bother to add the weapon possession charge.

Burr (1977) has produced some interesting information about the sentencing of gun-related felonies in his study in Florida. Florida courts, as stipulated in the Glisson Amendment, must give *mandatory* prison sentences for the use of a firearm in specific felony offenses. The length of the mandatory sentence is set between 3 years and life, according to judicial discretion. Burr's data consist of interviews with several hundred felony offenders who had used firearms in committing their convicted crimes.

One of Burr's questions asked whether offenders were aware of the mandatory sentence law at the time of their offense; 83% of the felons said that they were. About 73% said that they would continue carrying firearms when released from prison, despite the Amendment. More relevant to the issues of this chapter, Burr also inquired into the uniformity with which the Amendment was being applied by the judiciary throughout the state. Over roughly a 1-year period, Burr reports, about 525 felonies were committed in Florida that were apparently able to be prosecuted under the Glisson Amendment, of which only slightly more than one-half were actually given the mandatory add-on sentence. Burr concludes that "this information strongly suggests that the law is not being uniformly applied by members of the judiciary" (1977: 24).

The only other detailed evidence on the treatment of weapons offenders in the criminal court system is that reported by Cook and Nagin (1979) for the Washington, D.C. court system. As with the Los Angeles analysis summarized above, Cook and Nagin's research is based on data from PROMIS; also similar to Los Angeles, the Washington, D.C. prosecutor's office has an official "gun emphasis" policy.

Cook and Nagin note: "It is the announced policy of the Distict's prosecutor to give priority to weapons cases, and the District's Criminal Code specifies sentencing enhancements for such cases" (1979: 45). These statements, of course, are what may be called policies-in-principle. How these policies get implemented in the Washington, D.C. courts is an open empirical question to which the Cook and Nagin research is addressed.

Zero-order results in Washington, D.C. are similar to the results for Los Angeles described above. "For each of the four types of violent crime (murder, rape, robbery, and assault), a higher proportion of gun defendants are convicted than unarmed defendants. In addition, gun defendants are more likely to be incarcerated than those convicted of unarmed crimes of violence. Conviction and incarceration rates for defendants accused of violent crimes involving other weapons are in most crime categories quite close to conviction and incarceration rates for gun defendants" (Cook and Nagin, 1979: 45). The last finding contrasts sharply with the results from Los Angeles, where those using other weapons were rarely treated differently from those using no weapons at all.

It should be emphasized that Cook and Nagin's results are zero-order findings: none of the many variables other than weapons use that might affect case disposition was held constant. Thus, they are not adequate to determine the precise relationship between weapons choice and case disposition. No multivariate analyses are reported concerning rape, assault, or murder cases, but an extensive multivariate analysis of the robbery cases is presented.

The weapons effect apparent at the zero-order level also appears in the multivariate results for robbery cases, with some exceptions. First, given that a case has been accepted for prosecution, there are no statistically significant differences in the probabilities of conviction according to the type of weapon used after other relevant variables are held constant. This result was also found for all felony cases in the Los Angeles criminal courts. However, the probability of receiving a felony (versus a misdemeanor) conviction is significantly higher for armed than unarmed robberies; so too is the probability of a prison sentence, given that one has been convicted. Finally, armed robbers who receive prison sentences tend, on the average, to receive longer sentences than do unarmed robbers. The average sentence for armed robbers was 51 months, compared to an average of 29 months for unarmed robbers (Cook and Nagin, 1979: 57). The only sustained difference between these results and those from Los Angeles is that in Washington, D.C. defendants using weapons other than guns were treated virtually the same as gun-using defendants (opposite to the pattern observed in L.A.). It would thus appear that the Los Angeles prosecutor has a *gun*-emphasis policy that contrasts, perhaps in important respects, with the *weapons*-emphasis policy observed in Washington, D.C.

The handful of studies reviewed in this section lead to mixed conclusions about the implementation of sentence enhancement policies. The data from Los Angeles and Washington, D.C. indicate that legislative intents were fulfilled in those jurisdictions. The Florida data indicate the contrary. Because only a few jurisdictions were studied, it is not possible to state the conditions under which legislative intents concerning sentence enhancement are carried through in the courts. The best that can be said is that such conditions exist and hence are subject to study.

It must be emphasized that implementation of sentence enhancement is only a necessary condition for the effectiveness of this strategy in reducing weapons-related offenses. None of the studies reviewed addressed itself to the issue of how crime rates were affected by sentence enhancement laws.

ON THE EFFECTIVENESS OF GUN CONTROL LEGISLATION

The research reviewed in this chapter leads to no strong or certain conclusions about the ability of gun control legislation to affect changes in the criminal justice system or in rates of crime associated with the use of guns. In large part, the ambiguous character of the evidence has at its roots a lack of basic knowledge about the connections between crime and gun usage, the distribution system through which guns are circulated, and the ways in which criminal justice systems in this country operate.

The basic defects in gun control legislation stem from a lack of understanding about how the legislation will affect enforcing agencies and people who might commit crimes. Legislation for licensing gun dealers and regulating imports (as in the 1968 Gun Control Act) without too much thought for how to implement the law effectively simply leads to adjustments in the gun distribution system that restore the *status quo ante*. Similarly, gun control legislation that reduces judicial discretion may increase the use of discretion at other points in the criminal justice system. However, this discussion is not intended as an endorsement of more effective gun control legislation. We simply would emphasize that if effective legislation along these lines is desired, then considerable effort must be made to determine the most important points at which legislative control ought to be applied.

Similarly, gauging the effectiveness of legislation demands considerable thought in constructing the appropriate *ceteris paribus* conditions. Cross-sectional studies of natural variations across political jurisdictions appear to represent an approach that should be postponed until more is understood about how crime rates within jurisdictions are generated. Before-and-after studies are not as severely restricted but have problems of their own, as the efforts to estimate the impact of the Massachusetts Bartley-Fox Amendment indicate.

We come to the following conclusions:

First, any effort to estimate the effects of gun control legislation must be based on a thorough understanding of the phenomena intended to be affected and the institutional systems involved.

Second, although there is some evidence that the Massachusetts Bartley-Fox Amendment achieved at least an initial impact on gun-related crime, there is substantial reason to believe that long-range effects are not to be expected or will be considerably reduced in magnitude. In other words, there is some evidence that under some conditions gun-related crimes can be reduced through gun control legislation, but this outcome will be neither very common nor especially pronounced.

Third, sentence enhancement laws that increase punishment for crimes committed with weapons can be implemented in the courts, resulting in the desired additional periods of incarceration for convicted offenders. Whether such laws effectively act as deterrents to would-be offenders, however, is not known.

FOURTEEN

SOME POLICY IMPLICATIONS

The previous chapters have ranged rather widely and comprehensively over the research literature bearing on weapons, crime, and violence in America. Our principal aim has been to sort out from the vast array of claims and counterclaims those relative few that seem well-established on scientific grounds, and to note the many critical points that, in our view, have not been adequately researched. Ours has been, in short, a research agenda, not necessarily a policy agenda: our concern has been with what we know and what we do not know, and assuredly not with what the nation should do about the problems of weapons and violent crime.

In this chapter, we give free reign to our suppressed social policy interests (and some of our polemical urges as well) by drawing out from our analyses what we see as the main policy implications of the research. In the spirit of full disclosure, some information on the backgrounds of the senior authors are in order. When we began this project, both the senior authors would have favored stricter controls on the ownership and use of firearms. One of us (Wright) had earlier publications on the topic that reflect a fairly obvious pro-gun-control stance (see "The Demography of Gun Control" in *Nation,* 20 September 1975). At the same time, neither of us is a stranger to guns or to their use. One of us (Rossi) grew up in an urban neighborhood whose men hunted when they had the opportunity and in which hunting weapons were common household items. He is also a combat veteran of World War II and was familiar for a while with a variety of small arms. The other (Wright) grew up in a small Midwestern town, in a household where firearms of all sorts were always present and where hunting and shooting were favored leisure activities. Despite our both having been reared to some extent within the gun culture, neither of us presently owns any kind of firearm, nor have either of us even fired a gun in recent years. Both of us, however, count among our close friends people who do own and use guns, and we do not consider the gun owners we know to be either atavistic or morally suspicious.

THE CIVILIAN FIREARMS POLICY ISSUES

"Gun control" is itself an extraordinarily nebulous concept, one used to refer to an exceedingly wide range of policy initiatives ranging from simple registration or permit mechanisms through mandatory sentencing for people using firearms in committing a crime up to and including outright bans on the ownership, possession, or use of certain kinds of firearms. Thus, the policy space occupied by firearms issues is wide and multidimensional. To say that one "favors gun control," or that one does not, is thus to speak in ambiguities. "Gun control" means many different things to many different people, such that one of the major obstacles in writing a chapter such as this one is the multifaceted character of the central issues in the debate.

For many, the central issue is framed in Constitutional terms and involves interpretations of the intent of the Founding Fathers in drafting the Second Amendment (an issue on which we can claim no expertise whatever). From this viewpoint, access to firearms is guaranteed by the Constitution, and all other aspects of the issue are beside the point. As to the intent of the Founding Fathers, those who advocate this Constitutional interpretation will frequently emphasize that the Bill of Rights, including the Second Amendment, was first drafted by Thomas Jefferson, and that Jefferson was himself a tireless champion of the right of a free people to rise in armed revolution against an unjust government. In a famous letter to William Smith, written in 1787, Jefferson remarked, "And what country can preserve its liberties, if its rulers are not warned from time to time, that this people preserve the spirit of resistance. Let them take arms. The remedy is to set them right as to facts, pardon and pacify them. What signify a few lives lost in a century or two? The tree of liberty must be refreshed from time to time, with the blood of patriots and tyrants. It is its natural manure."

Many others believe that themes such as those enunciated in the Jefferson passage quoted above are completely anachronistic, and that the responsibility of the government to "insure domestic tranquility" and to "promote the general welfare" vastly overshadows such rights as the Second Amendment seems to guarantee. For people with these views, firearms are anathema per se, and the social harm done by the largely unrestricted access to firearms in this country is such that the complete disarmament of society is taken as a worthy—indeed, morally and socially essential—goal.

The extremes in the Great American Gun War are perhaps best illustrated by recently passed ordinances in two small American communities. Morton Grove, Illinois, has passed a law (now under appeal) that *forbids* the ownership of handguns; Kennesaw, Georgia, has recently passed a law (apparently in reaction to the Morton Grove ordinance) that *requires* every able-bodied male to possess a firearm—this for the common defense of the community!

As one moves away from these extremes, the relevant policy issues become less matters of unrestricted access versus complete disarmament, and more matters of *what kinds* of controls, targeted to *what kinds* of users, for *what kinds* of purposes, and dealing with *what kinds* of guns. Most observers would agree, certainly, that reasonable precaution is always in order, and, thus, that commodities as intrinsically hazardous as firearms must come under some sort of official purview. (For example, most would agree that the provisions of the National Firearms Act of 1938 concerning possession of "gangster-type" weapons are appropriate and reasonable, and no sensible person favors their repeal.) Here, away from the extremes of the debate, the controversial issues typically concern what kinds of measures will accomplish what kinds of aims, and at what social cost. Will a registration requirement actually make it easier for police to trace the firearms used in crime? Will a "waiting period" actually give people enough time to "cool off," or the police enough time to check up on an applicant? Will stiffer and mandatory sentences for gun use in crime actually cause criminals to "think twice" before they commit a crime?

Despite the wide and usually rancorous disagreement over policy issues and specific policy measures, there is little conflict over the desirable results of public policy in this area if achievable at an acceptable cost. All agree that the current level of incidents involving firearms is unacceptably high. Thirty thousand annual deaths and a quarter-million annual injuries, intentional or accidental, are shocking to all. The additional hundreds of thousands of annual incidents in which firearms are used to deprive people of their property, or to restrict personal freedom, or to frighten or intimidate are also unacceptable to nearly everyone. There is agreement that public policy ought to be directed at reducing the number of gun incidents experienced in our society: the disagreement centers around whether such aims can be achieved by any public policy and whether the costs of doing so are within acceptable ranges.

There are several important ways in which the findings of our research bear upon these issues, ranging from providing descriptive data on the role of firearms in American life to the direct testing of the efficacy of particular policies for controlling firearms. The remainder of this chapter takes up these points of contact between our research and public policy.

THE ROLE OF FIREARMS IN AMERICAN LIFE

Whether produced by advocates or by more "neutral" sources, all research on the household possession of firearms shows that around half of American households own some sort of firearms and that about one in four owns handguns. These statistics bear upon public policy in two ways: first, the widespread ownership of firearms means that the impact of gun control measures will be felt widely throughout American society, especially if such measures affect those who already possess firearms. Second, these figures reflect that firearms play an important role in some aspects of American life. Although ownership of televisions, telephones, and cars is more widespread than ownership of firearms, there are almost certainly more guns than typewriters or microcomputers in American homes. Indeed, it is sometimes claimed that with the exception of pairs of sneakers, firearms are the most commonly owned piece of sporting equipment in America today.

From the surveys that have been conducted on the prevalence of firearms, it is also fairly clear that the major use of firearms is recreational or sporting. Hunting and target shooting are widespread activities, apparently enjoyed by many. As we have remarked in an earlier chapter, it is somewhat strange that the surveys have not probed deeply enough to provide data on how frequent the participation is in such sports, the age and sex of the people involved, or, in short, to provide data on how important such activities are in household repertories of recreational activities. In addition, firearms also appear to be "collector's items" to many, objects to be owned for the sheer pleasure of possession. We also do not know such critical information as how many weapons are usable, how many households also possess ammunition, and how many households or their members know how to use firearms.

Evidence from a variety of sources indicates that the number of firearms in private hands has increased considerably in the last decade or so. At least some large part of this increase appears to be associated simply with a rise in the number of households in the United States, since the *proportion* of firearms-owning households has not increased. Also, rising real income has made it possible for more households to add firearms to their inventories of material possessions.

Some part of the increase in firearms ownership may have been generated by a sensed need for protection, as indicated by the fact that ownership of handguns has increased more rapidly than that of long guns. It is difficult, as we have shown, to pin down these trends with any precision. It is even more difficult to determine the extent to which firearms provide any realistic protection against the dangers involved. Nor is it possible to estimate the deterrence value of firearms ownership in general. Most of the relevant questions about the protective value of firearms remain unanswered.

The policy implications of these findings are as follows: First, the interests of millions of households in recreational activities involving firearms appear to be strong. Any policy that would encroach upon such interests most likely will meet opposition on those grounds. Second, the ownership of firearms in America is already so widespread that any attempt to control weapons now in private hands is going to be quite costly. The simple registration of all weapons privately held would be a fairly costly program even if the cost of each registration could be kept very low. Third, there is little evidence to suggest a "domestic arms race," even though there is some evidence that self-protection has been a motivating factor in many recent weapons purchases. Given the state of the evidence, one certainly cannot be definitive on such issues, but it appears that most of the recent "domestic arms build-up" has had relatively benign causes. At the minimum, it is clear that merely pointing at the recent trends is *not* a sufficient argument that stricter gun laws are needed.

It is *possible,* given the present state of knowledge, that private firearms ownership is a nontrivial crime deterrent. It is also possible, perhaps rather likely, that the major benefits of owning a gun for protection against crime are symbolic or psychological. But one cannot discount a benefit just because it is a symbolic one. If people feel safer because they own a gun, whether they actually are any safer or not, is pretty much beside the point. Given that no police force or other agency of social control can protect everyone against all forms of criminal victimization, any action taken by individuals that would lessen anxiety from this source is not to be dismissed lightly. Whatever limits society may want to place on how individuals choose to protect themselves would have to be justified in terms of, say, the potential harm from such actions.

VIOLENCE AND GUNS

The amount of death, injury, destruction, and generalized terror inflicted in the United States with firearms is a national disgrace—of that, there is no serious question. The serious question is whether the amount of death, injury, destruction, and generalized terror would be any less if fewer firearms were available. The world is full of objects that can be used to prey upon other human beings. Is the gun itself our national disgrace? Or is it the hatred and predation that sometimes involves guns? Thus, an important policy issue is if the availability of guns somehow enhances the probability that shameful incidents will occur, or, alternatively, if the use of guns per se is an ancillary and rather uninteresting by-product of acts that would be equally shameful (and equally destructive) whether firearms were involved or not. A closely related issue concerns the extent to which the use of guns in such incidents increases the negative consequences over and beyond the consequences that would ensue if guns were not available.

As we have shown in previous chapters, the evidence on both issues is far from clear. Homicides, assaults, robberies, rapes, and so on can obviously be carried out without the use of firearms, albeit perhaps less easily. How many assaults and other incidents are made possible simply by the presence of guns, or how many would fail to occur in the absence of guns, is not at all clear, or would it be an easy research task to find out. We can come reasonably close to estimating the number of incidents occurring each year that involve a gun, but this is clearly not the same as the number that would not occur if no guns were available. One finds throughout the literature reference to more or less apocryphal instances in which serious, often fatal, incidents occurred "just because the gun was there." These instances are useful for stereotyping the etiology of criminal violence, but they do not constitute useful evidence for anything. Whether these kinds of instances represent a large or small share of the total number of criminally violent acts is simply undetermined.

In short, assessing the damages, injuries, and trauma caused by firearms requires knowledge of the additional damages, injuries, and trauma occasioned by the use of guns over and above what would have happened in the absence of firearms. Certainly, some of the one million annual gun incidents would have been violent incidents in any event: the questions are how many would have occurred even without firearms and what damage would have resulted? Unfortunately, the existing literature provides virtually no firm answers to these questions.

Given what we have learned from the existing literature, it appears that a considerable advance in our knowledge about how guns are used might be made by distinguishing among three types of acts: (1) acts in which the use of a gun is absolutely essential, (2) acts in which gun usage mainly increases efficiency, and (3) acts in which the use of a gun is not at all essential. For example, it is unlikely that well-protected robbery targets (for example, banks and armored transfer trucks) can be successfully robbed ordinarily without the use of guns. However, strong-arm tactics will usually suffice to carry off a street robbery of a lone unarmed person. In contrast, brandishing a gun is somewhat superfluous in burgling an empty house. In attempting to control the use of guns in violent crimes, it is important to develop general models of the incentives for using firearms. Indeed, it is this system of incentives on which gun control policy should be attempting to act. It is upon such knowledge, now largely nonexistent, differentiated according to the class of violent act involved, that the design of an efficient and effective gun control policy should be based.

The policy implications of these considerations are as follows: First, the control of guns is *not* equivalent to the control of violence. Violent acts would undoubtedly continue even if a complete ban on possession of firearms were put into place and were effective. One might expect the form of violence to change, perhaps dramatically, in the face of such a ban. But people will continue to rob, assault, and otherwise prey upon each other whether they have firearms or not. Second, because the many roles that firearms may play in different forms of violence are not known very well, it is difficult to design a system of incentives and sanctions that would be acceptably effective and efficient. We do not know enough about why people arm themselves with guns in the first place to be very effective in getting them to stop it.

Both the above points cast some doubt on the ability of gun control measures to reduce effectively the million annual gun incidents. Without knowing why guns are used in some incidents, it is difficult to construct measures that would lower such gun use. Furthermore, since it is likely that the incentives for using guns vary according to the type of violent incident involved, any gun control system must be sensitive to such differences. Furthermore, even if guns were completely removed from use (an unlikely policy outcome), violence would still occur. Without knowing how much violence would be averted by each politically acceptable measure, it is impossible to evaluate such proposals comparatively.

THE CIRCULATION OF WEAPONS IN THE UNITED STATES

Fitting together various data, we arrive at an estimate of some 120 ± 20 million weapons in private hands, as of 1978. Firearms filter into the private market from a number of sources, among which American gun manufacturers are an important, but not the sole, supplier. A complicated set of marketing mechanisms holds the key to the circulation of weapons, including trade, sale, and barter among individual gun owners, black-market sales of stolen guns, sales by recognized dealers in firearms, sales or other dispositions by police departments and the military, and so on. Although some of these market mechanisms are known fairly well, what is not known is the share of the total circulation of weapons obtained by each. Furthermore, although we know that firearms are relatively durable goods, the average duration in use is not known, nor is the rate at which firearms are withdrawn from circulation.

The absence of good information on the circulation of weapons among civilians and between institutions and civilians strongly hinders the construction of effective measures designed to intervene in that circulation. For example, most firearms licensing laws ban the transfer of gun ownership to certain classes of individuals, defined by age, mental health condition, and felony record. Enforcing such restrictions is difficult when the definitions of the disqualifying condition are not clear (as in the case of the mentally ill) or when records are not ordinarily available (as in the case of previous felony convictions). Even age restrictions are easily circumvented, as the wholesale evasion of minimum-age drinking laws demonstrates. Furthermore, there are many hints that the barter or sale of weapons from one individual to another accounts for a large number of the total firearms transfers. If so, it is difficult to imagine how policy mechanisms that are not extravagantly expensive could intervene in or regulate such transactions.

Of course, policy interest centers around keeping firearms out of the hands of persons likely to contribute to the million annual incidents. Our survey of the literature is not very illuminating on whether such people can be identified in some easy way *ex ante* and whether they obtain their weapons in any characteristically different ways. For a while, a commonly held view was that inexpensive imported handguns were the weapons of choice among urban robbers and holdup men: Saturday Night Specials priced under $50 made it possible, it was said, for large numbers of young men to go into the robbery business with a minimal capital investment. Indeed, acting on this belief, the Gun Control Act of 1968 attempted to forbid the importation of such weapons. But several surveys of the characteristics of handguns confiscated by the police brought to light the fact that such guns were not predominantly the weapons used. Rather, confiscated guns tended to be relatively expensive weapons, and relatively new. It also appears that a fairly large proportion of such guns had been reported stolen from their purchasers and sold to their users on the black market.

The policy implications of these findings point mainly to the difficulty, in the absence of more detailed knowledge, of intervening in the distribution and circulation of firearms as a method of preventing their reaching the hands of people implicated in gun incidents. A circulation system in which merchants and brokers do not play exclusive roles but, rather, household-to-household sales and barter are primary appears to be difficult to control in precise (and democratic) ways. Similarly, we cannot be sure, on the basis of current knowledge, that the circulation of firearms for illegal purposes is distinctively different from the patterns that predominate for legitimate weapons. It is a great convenience to suppose that the society could devise some way to regulate the illicit firearms market while leaving the legitimate user more or less unaffected. This assumes that some sharp distinction exists between these two components of the market, an assumption that has not been adequately researched.

AN ASSESSMENT OF GUN CONTROL MEASURES

Various mechanisms have been proposed or enacted to control illegal and improper firearms usage, as summarized in Chapter 12. Every jurisdiction in the United States has some regulatory controls: at the minimum, federal laws governing manufacture and sale obtain. Ordinarily, state and local statutes impose additional conditions on the ownership, possession, and use of fire-arms. Such restrictions tend to be strongest in the Northeastern parts of the United States and weakest in the South and Southwest. Indeed, it is often a shock to those who are not aware of firearms regulatory legislation to learn that New York City has on the books one of the most restrictive set of statutes in the country governing the possession of handguns, one where virtually no one except municipal and private police can qualify for handgun permits. Likewise Chicago's gun control legislation is so restrictive that there are virtually no retail outlets that sell handguns within Cook County. The ownership, possession, and use of firearms are being regulated in the United States and have been under more or less strict statutory control for decades.

Can we learn anything from these attempts at control? There are several points that can be made on the basis of our review of the empirical studies of the effectiveness of gun control legislation already enacted. First, it is clear that gun legislation has become increasingly restrictive, especially concerning handguns, at the same time that the stock of handguns in the possession of civilians has increased drastically: the legislation has not been able to stem the tide of the past decade and a half. Second, studies that have examined the connections between state gun control legislation and state trends in gun incidents have not yielded consistent results. Some studies purport to show that gun homicides and gun assaults are relatively fewer in states that have very restrictive legislation, and other studies purport to show that there are no such trends. These differences among studies depend strongly on which characteristics of states are held constant in the statistical calculations, and all suffer from static formulations of the problems involved (as opposed to dynamic or time-related approaches). Third, before-and-after studies of the effects of changes in legislation, using sophisticated time-series analyses, have been able to find only modest effects for legislation that increased mandatory penalties for the illegal use of guns. None of these studies, however, has examined long-term effects, i.e., more than a year or two later, and even the findings of modest effects have been disputed.

It is a fair summary that the existing literature provides only very weak evidence for the effectiveness of gun control legislation that has been enacted in the United States. One may speculate why this is the case; indeed, many of the studies provide hints about why this should be the case.

One of the strongest points that can be made concerns the nature of guns themselves. The possession of a weapon is not an obvious or easily observable characteristic of a household: long guns can be kept in closets, in the basement, in the attic; handguns can be kept in a variety of places that effectively conceal their existence. Try asking friends and colleagues whose homes you think you know fairly well whether they own firearms, and you will be surprised at how many do. Because gun ownership is by no means always obvious, the registration of existing guns in the civilian stock is much more difficult to enforce than, say, the registration of vehicles or dogs, or enforcing requirements for building permits. Furthermore, most legislation exempts ownership and possession of guns that are kept strictly on home premises, apparently recognizing that to require the registration of all guns in possession is simply to invite widespread violation of the law. (Incidentally, those who contemplate outlawing the possession of all handguns must come to grips with the serious problems of enforcement under these conditions.)

Another characteristic of firearms is that they are not extremely expensive consumer goods. True, prices range widely: a well-made or rare hunting rifle can command almost as much on the market as a modest sports car, but a serviceable rifle can be purchased for under $100. Similar price ranges are encountered for handguns. A new police revolver retails for about $200–300; serviceable used weapons can be bought for even less; and black-market prices for stolen weapons are most likely even lower. In short, serviceable weapons can be purchased for less than color TVs and many other consumer goods.

The relative cheapness of firearms has certainly facilitated their widespread private ownership. At the same time, these market prices suggest a mechanism for gun control. If the price of weapons can be raised to a point beyond which it is no longer profitable to acquire weapons for use in illegal activities, then the number of gun incidents would certainly drop. Prices of new weapons can be easily affected by imposing taxes on their initial sale, an act that would also raise prices for used weapons, with which new weapons are in competition. On the other hand, such measures would also affect the price of weapons used for hunting and other sports, a move that would surely encroach upon the ability of many Americans to enjoy such uses of firearms. An even more serious obstacle facing the use of pricing strategies for firearms controls is that we do not know how high the price would have to go to lower illegal usage, and we also do not know whether such price levels would foster the growth of an extensive smuggling industry, encourage the theft of firearms for resale in black markets, or otherwise encourage evasions of the pricing strategy.

Much existing legislation that requires permits for the purchase, possession, or use of firearms prohibits certain classes of individuals from holding permits. As mentioned earlier, without extensive investigation, such regulations are impossible to enforce thoroughly. For example, many of the weapons confiscated by New York and Boston police because they were used in crimes were traced to gun retailers in Southern seaboard states, despite the federal legislation that prohibits sales to residents of other states. Intermediary purchasers probably were able to furnish proof of residence and then to sell at a mark-up legally purchased firearms illegally transported across state lines to Boston and New York residents. In short, where there is a strong enough demand, entrepreneurs will apparently furnish the desired goods and services. Demand creates its own supply.

A weak point in gun permit and registration legislation is the cost and difficulty of enforcement. Requiring retailers to adhere to police prohibitions against classes of owners and users is only to invite widespread violation. To set up separate agencies or to require the police or other existing agencies to enforce such regulations is also to invite widespread violation, especially if the full cost of conducting thorough investigations is not underwritten.

One promising strategy appears to be to raise the costs of illegal gun usages. Statutes that require mandatory sentences on conviction of gun registration or permit violations are one tactical maneuver. Another is to require increased penalties for crimes in which guns are used, so-called sentence enhancements for felonious gun use. The main weakness in these approaches is that agencies given the responsibility for enforcement use their discretionary powers to facilitate the flow of their work as much as to serve the cause of justice. Thus a police officer may slap on a charge to increase his productivity, knowing that a district attorney will remove the charge in return for a guilty plea to a lesser charge. Judges may suspend sentences or place a convicted offender on probation because the prisons or jails are overcrowded or for other reasons that are related more to the problems of processing charged persons than to the administration or intent of mandated sentences. In short, legislative intent may often be distorted by the criminal justice system's systemic imperatives.

These considerations cast some doubt on whether the appropriate mechanisms for effective gun control have ever been developed. First, federal laws are needed to iron out the differences among jurisdictions, to prevent easy evasion in a period of ready transportation and widespread mobility. Second, attempts to prevent certain classes of people from obtaining guns appear difficult and expensive to administer effectively. Finally, a system of strong deterrents for the illegal use of guns must be integrated carefully with the needs of the criminal justice system.

A CONCLUDING POLEMIC

The progressive's indictment of American firearms policy is well known and is one that both the senior authors of this study once shared. This indictment includes the following particulars: (1) Guns are involved in an astonishing number of crimes in this country. (2) In other countries with stricter firearms laws and fewer guns in private hands, gun crime is rare. (3) Most of the firearms involved in crime are cheap Saturday Night Specials, for which no legitimate use or need exists. (4) Many families acquire such a gun because they feel the need to protect themselves; eventually, they end up shooting one another. (5) If there were fewer guns around, there would obviously be less crime. (6) Most of the public also believes this and has favored stricter gun control laws for as long as anyone has asked the question. (7) Only the gun lobby prevents us from embarking on the road to a safer and more civilized society.

The more deeply we have explored the empirical implications of this indictment, the less plausible it has become. We wonder, first, given the number of firearms presently available in the United States, whether the time to "do something" about them has not long since passed. If we take the highest plausible value for the total number of gun incidents in any given year—1,000,000—and the lowest plausible value for the total number of firearms now in private hands—100,000,000—we see rather quickly that the guns now owned exceed the annual incident count by a factor of at least 100. This means that the existing stock is adequate to supply all conceivable criminal purposes for at least the entire next century, even if the worldwide manufacture of new guns were halted today and if each presently owned firearm were used criminally once and only once. Short of an outright house-to-house search and seizure mission, just how are we going to achieve some significant reduction in the number of firearms available?

The figures given above can be considered in another way. Suppose that, as a society, we did embark on a program of firearms confiscation, with the ultimate aim of achieving the Edenic "no guns, therefore no gun crime" condition. We would have to confiscate at least 100 guns to get just one that, in any given year, would have otherwise been involved in some sort of unfortunate firearms incident. We would have to round up several hundred to get just one that, in any given year, would have otherwise been involved in a chargeable crime, and several thousand to get just one that, in any given year, would have otherwise been used to bring about someone's death. And even these counts are unduly optimistic, since they assume that the probability of a successful confiscation is the same for all firearms. A more reasonable assumption is that the criminally abused fraction of a percentage would be the *last* firearms touched by any sort of gun control program.

One of the NRA's favorite aphorisms is that "if guns are outlawed, only outlaws will have guns." There is more truth to this point than the sophisticated liberal is usually willing to admit. It follows by definition that laws are obeyed only by the law-abiding! If we were to outlaw, say, the ownership of handguns, millions of law-abiding handgun owners would no doubt turn theirs in—most of them people who would never even contemplate, much less commit, a criminally violent act. But would we expect a person who owns a handgun for illicit reasons to turn his in? Anything illicit that this person might be contemplating is *already* against the law. Can we expect him to abide by a gun law when he routinely ignores our other laws anyway? It is assuredly not in the interest of progressive causes that we be foolish about such things.

A related point is that even the rather Draconian proposals that periodically surface, for example, an outright ban on the ownership of handguns, make an exception for handguns to be used by the military and by the police, as indeed they should. This means that even under the most restrictive imaginable legislation, handguns will continue to be manufactured, and so long as they are being manufactured, they will remain available *at some price.* That price may be well above what the average citizen is willing to pay, but even an exceptionally high price is not likely to provide much of a deterrent to the person intent on acquiring a firearm for illicit reasons. (To be sure, the price elasticity of the criminal firearms demand is a seriously understudied topic.)

One could, of course, take things to the logically extreme case: an immediate and strictly enforced ban on both the ownership and manufacture of all firearms of every sort. Let us even assume perfect compliance with this law— that we actually rounded up and disposed of all 120 million guns now in circulation, that every legitimate manufacturing establishment was permanently shut down, and that all sources of imported firearms were permanently closed off. What we would then have is the firearms equivalent of Prohibition, with (one strongly suspects) much the same consequences. A black market in guns, run by organized crime (much to their profit, no doubt), would spring up to service the now-illegal demand. It is, after all, not much more difficult to manufacture a serviceable firearm in one's basement than to brew up a batch of home-made gin. Afghanistani tribesmen, using wood fires and metal-working equipment that is much inferior to what can be ordered through a Sears catalog, hand-craft rifles that fire the Russian AK-47 cartridge. Do we anticipate a lesser ability from American do-it-yourselfers or the Mafia?

Even if we were somehow able to remove all firearms from civilian possession, it is not at all clear that a substantial reduction in interpersonal violence would follow. Certainly, the violence that results from hard-core and predatory criminality would not abate by very much. Even the most ardent proponents of stricter gun laws no longer expect such laws to solve the hard-core crime problem, or even to make much of a dent in it. There is also reason to doubt whether the "soft-core" violence, the so-called crimes of passion, would decline by very much. Stated simply, these crimes occur because some people have come to hate others, and they will continue to occur in one form or another as long as hatred persists. It is possible, to be sure, that many of these incidents would involve different consequences if no firearms were available, but it is also possible that the consequences would be exactly the same. The existing empirical literature provides no firm basis for choosing one of these possibilities over the other. Restating the point, *if* we could solve the problem of interpersonal hatred, it may not matter very much what we did about guns, and *unless* we solve the problem of interpersonal hatred, it may not matter very much what we do about guns. There are simply too many other objects in the world that can serve the purpose of inflicting harm on another human being.

Many recent gun control proposals have focused explicitly on the handgun, for rather straightforward reasons. To those who themselves are more or less alien to the use of guns, it appears obvious that handguns have, at best, extremely limited sport or recreational applications. And given the number of crimes committed with handguns, it appears equally obvious that the handgun is the preferred crime firearm. Legislating specifically against the handgun therefore addresses the worst part of the gun crime problem and poses minimal encumbrances to the legitimate firearms owner. In fact, this line of argument has two main defects. First, as a quick perusal of any of the dozens of gun magazines makes clear, handguns *are* used in a variety of legitimate sport and recreational ways. Even the cheap, low-caliber, light-weight, short-barreled handgun has at least some recreational application, as our discussion of so-called trail guns makes clear (see Chapter 5). No matter what we do to control even the handgun, we are going to infringe in some way on the rights and prerogatives of at least some legitimate firearms users. This, assuredly, is *not* an argument that we should simply not try to regulate such guns, which is a separate matter entirely. It *is* an argument that we have to be realistic about the costs and consequences of such regulations.

Second, although it is true that under current conditions the large majority of gun crimes are committed with handguns (on the order, perhaps, of 70–75% of them), it definitely does *not* follow that, in the complete absence of handguns, crimes now committed with handguns would not be committed! The more plausible expectation is that they would be committed with other weaponry. Just what other weaponry would be used is extremely uncertain, as the relevant research has not been done. It is possible that much of the crime now done with handguns would be done instead with knives, but the consequences of this sort of "substitution" are not at all clear-cut, as our earlier discussions have indicated. It is also possible that much of the crime now done with handguns would, in their absence, be committed with shoulder weapons (suitably modified to make them concealable, if need be). In this vein, we would do well to remember that there are already some three or four times more shoulder weapons than handguns in circulation in the United States, and that, on the average, they are much deadlier than handguns. If someone intends to open fire on the authors of this study, our *strong* preference is that they open fire with a handgun, and the junkier the handgun, the better. The possibility that even a fraction of the predators who now walk the streets armed with handguns would, in the face of a handgun ban, prowl with sawed-off shotguns instead, causes one to tremble. It can be taken as a given that some people will continue shooting at one another as long as there are *any* guns around. This being the case, we have to muster the courage to ask whether we wouldn't be just as happy if they shot at one another with handguns.

Although it is often claimed that the United States is virtually the only advanced nation that exercises no rational control over firearms, the fact is that there are perhaps 20,000 gun laws now in effect in this country. That these laws have had limited or no effect on the rate of violent crime is reasonably transparent. Whether a national gun control program, one that got around the existing patchwork of jurisdictionally-specific laws (and the attendant easy violation of them), would work any better in reducing crime is very much an open question. Certainly, it is possible that it would. On the other hand, the knowledge base on which such policies would have to be designed is not very firm, or such is the principal conclusion of our research. As we have stated earlier, we do not yet know enough about why criminals carry guns to design a policy that would effectively prevent that practice. We do not know enough about the characteristics of the illicit firearms market to intervene effectively within it. And we do not know enough about the systemic prerequisites of the criminal justice system to be certain that the intention of new gun laws would not be subverted at the point of policy implementation. As we learn more about the role that guns play in both legal and illegal activities, we may find that an equitable, efficient, and effective gun control mechanism can be devised. In the meantime, hasty and ill-considered attempts to control guns are likely to foster widespread evasions and noncompliance by citizens, by the police, and by other criminal justice agencies. Laws that cannot be enforced, or that violate what citizens perceive to be their rights, or that invite widespread noncompliance, cannot help but undermine the foundations of a society attempting, sometimes fitfully, to exist under the rule of law.

There are several strands of evidence uncovered in our review to support the assertion that a strong subcultural theme in American life centers around the ownership and use of guns. The correlation between parents' and childrens' gun ownership is one of those evidential strands, suggesting that the familiarity with and liking for guns and their use in sport and recreation are matters of early childhood socialization, especially for males. In much of small town and rural America, the rites of passage from childhood to adulthood may include that a father train his son in the use and lore of small arms.

To members of the gun subculture who have been around guns all their lives and have owned and used guns as long as it has been legal for them to do so, the indictments of gun control advocates must appear to be incomprehensible, if not simply demeaning. We should not be surprised to learn that they may resent being depicted as irresponsible, nervous, potentially dangerous, prone to accidental or careless firearms handling, or as using their firearms to bolster sagging masculine self–images. Of course, from their viewpoints, they have none of these characteristics and in all likelihood resent being depicted as a demented and bloodthirsty lot when they are only guilty of embracing a set of rather traditional, rural, and masculine values. Indeed, one can only begin to understand the virulence with which gun control initiative are opposed in these quarters when one realizes that what may be at stake is a way of life.

American progressivism has always taken a strong and justifiable pride in its cultural pluralism, its belief that minority or "deviant" cultures and values have intrinsic legitimacy and are therefore to be at least tolerated if not nourished, and certainly not be suppressed. Progressives have embraced the legitimacy of many subcultures in the past, including tolerance for a vast heterogeneity of religious beliefs, regional diversities, a belated recognition of the rights of American Indians, and tolerance for immigrant peoples. And more recently, progressives have hastened to affirm the legitimacy of black culture, Hispanic culture, youth culture, homosexuals (and, for that matter, nearly every other subculture that has pressed its claim for recognition).

A critical issue in modern America is whether the doctrine of cultural pluralism should or should not be extended to cover the members of the gun subculture. Is this cultural pattern akin to the segregationism of the South that was broken up in the interest of the public good? Or, is it more akin to those subcultures that we have recognized as legitimate and benign forms of self-expression?

BIBLIOGRAPHY

Alviani, Joseph D., and Drake, William R. (1975). *Handgun Control: Issues and Alternatives.* Washington, DC: United States Conference of Mayors.

Askrant, Albert P., and Joliet, Paul V. (1968). *Accidents and Homicide.* Cambridge, MA: Harvard University Press.

Bakal, Carl (1966). *The Right to Bear Arms.* New York: McGraw Hill.

Beha, James A. (1977). "And *Nobody* Can Get You Out": The impact of a mandatory prison sentence for the illegal carrying of a firearm on the use of firearms and on the administration of criminal justice in Boston," Parts I and II. *Boston University Law Review* **57** (1, January), 96–146; and **57** (2, March), 289–333.

Berelson, Bernard, Lazarsfeld, Paul, and McPhee, William (1954). *Voting.* Chicago: University of Chicago Press.

Bergman, S., Bunten, E., and Klaus, P. (1977). *LEAA Police Equipment Survey of 1972. Volume V: Handguns and Handgun Ammunition.* Washington, DC: U.S. Government Printing Office.

Berkowitz, Leonard (1968). Impulse, aggression, and the gun. *Psychology Today* **2**, 19–22.

Berkowitz, Leonard, and LePage, Anthony (1967). Weapons as aggression-eliciting stimuli. *Journal of Personality and Social Psychology* **7**, 202–207.

Bernstein, Ilene, Kelley, W., and Doyle, P. (1977a). Societal reaction to deviants: The case of criminal defendants. *American Sociological Review* **47**, 743–755.

Bernstein, Ilene N., Kick, Edward, Leung, Jan T., and Schulz, Barbara (1977b). Charge reduction: An intermediary stage in the process of labelling criminal defendants. *Social Forces* **56** (2, December), 362–384.

Bernstein, Ilene N., Cardascia, John, and Ross, Catherine E. (1979). Defendant's sex and criminal court decisions. In *"Discrimination in Organizations"* (R. Alvarez, K. Lutterman, and Associates, eds.), pp. 329–354. San Francisco: Jossey Bass.

Biderman, Albert, Johnson, Louise, McIntyre, Tennie, and Weir, Adrienne (1967). *Report on a Pilot Study in the District of Columbia on Victimization and Attitudes toward Law Enforcement. Field Surveys I.* Washington, DC: U.S. Government Printing Office.

Black, Donald (1970). Production of crime rates. *American Sociological Review* **35** (4), 733–748.

Block, Richard (1977a). *Violent Crime.* Lexington, MA: Lexington Books.

Block, Richard (1977b). Homicide in Chicago: A ten-year study (1965–1974). Unpublished paper, University of Chicago: Center for Studies in Criminal Justice.

Blumberg, Abraham S. (1979). *Criminal Justice: Issues and Ironies,* 2nd ed. New York: New Viewpoints.

Bordua, David J., and Lizotte, Alan J. (1979). Patterns of legal firearms ownership: A cultural and situational analysis of Illinois counties. *Law and Policy Quarterly* 1 (2, April), 147–175.

Box, G. E. P., and Jenkins, G. M. (1970). *Time Series Analysis: Forecasting and Control.* San Francisco: Holden Day.

Brill, Steven (1977). *Firearms Abuse.* Washington, DC: The Police Foundation.

Brosi, Kathleen B. (1979). *A Cross-City Comparison of Felony Case Processing.* Washington, DC: Institute for Law and Social Research.

Brownmiller, Susan (1975). *Against Our Will: Men, Women, and Rape.* New York: Simon and Schuster.

Bruce-Biggs, B. (1976). The great American gun war. *The Public Interest* **45**, 37–62.

Burnham, David (1970). Few police told about spray use. *New York Times,* 22 February, 88.

Burr, D. E. S. (1977). *Handgun Regulation.* Orlando, FL: Florida Bureau of Criminal Justice Planning and Assistance.

Buss, Arnold H., Booker, Ann, and Buss, Edith (1972). Firing a weapon and aggression. *Journal of Personality and Social Psychology* **22**, 296–302.

Caetano, Donald F. (1979). The domestic arms race. *Journal of Communication* **29** (2, Spring), 39–46.

Cambridge Reports, Inc. (1978). *An Analysis of Public Attitudes Towards Handgun Control.* Cambridge, MA.

Campbell, Angus, Converse, Phillip, Miller, Warren, and Stokes, Donald (1956). *The American Voter.* New York: John Wiley.

Cash, W. J. (1940). *The Mind of the South.* New York: Alfred Knopf.

Clotfelter, Charles T. (1977). Crime, disorders and the demand for handguns: An empirical analysis. Unpublished paper, Duke University, Durham, NC.

Coles, Robert (1966). America amok: Is the gun-ridden USA a violent nation? *New Republic* **155** (27, August), 12–15.

Comptroller General of the United States (1978). *Handgun Control: Effectiveness and Costs.* Washington, DC: General Accounting Office.

Conklin, John E. (1972). *Robbery and the Criminal Justice System.* Philadelphia: Lippincott.

Cook, Philip J. (1976). A strategic choice analysis of robbery. In *Sample Surveys of the Victims of Crime* (W. Skogan, ed.), pp. 173–187. Cambridge, MA: Ballinger.

Cook, Philip J. (1978). The effect of gun availability on robbery and robbery murder: A cross-section study of 50 cities. In *Hearings before the Subcommittee on Crime of the Committee on the Judiciary, House of Representatives, May 4 and 18.* pp. 281–311. Washington, DC: U.S. Government Printing Office.

Cook, Philip J. (1979a). The Saturday Night Special: An assessment of alternative definitions from a policy perspective. Unpublished paper, Duke University Center for the Study of Policy Analysis. Duke University, Durham, NC.

Cook, Philip J. (1979b). An overview of federal, state and local firearms regulations. Unpublished paper, Duke University Center for the Study of Policy Analysis, Duke University, Durham, NC.

Cook, Philip J. (1979c). The effect of gun availability on robbery and robbery murder: A cross-section study of fifty cities. In *Policy Studies Review Annual* (Robert Haveman and B. Bruce Zellner, eds.), Vol. III, pp. 743–781. Beverly Hills, CA: Sage Publications.

Cook, Philip J. (1980a). Reducing injury and death rates in robbery. *Policy Analysis* **6** (1, Winter), 21–45.

Cook, Philip J. (1980b). Regulating handgun transfers: Current state and Federal procedures, and an assessment of the feasibility and cost of the proposed procedures in the Handgun Crime Control Act of 1979. Unpublished paper, Duke University: Center for the Study of Policy Analysis, Duke University, Durham, NC.

Cook, Philip J. (1981). The effect of gun availability on violent crime patterns. *Annals of the American Academy of Political and Social Sciences* **455** (May), 63–79.

Cook, Philip J. and Blose, James (1981). State programs for screening handgun buyers. *Annals of the American Academy of Political and Social Sciences* **455** (May) 80–91.

Cook, Philip J., and Nagin, Daniel (1979). *Does the Weapon Matter?* Washington, DC: Institute for Law and Social Research.

Cook, Thomas, and Campbell, Donald T. (1980). *Quasi-experimentation.* Chicago: Rand McNally.

Cramer, Harry L., and Scott, Gregory L. (1978). The command car and total response concept. *The Police Chief,* October, 66–69.

Cronbach, Lee (1980). *Toward Reform of Program Evaluation.* San Francisco: Jossey Bass.

Curtis, Lynn A. (1974). *Criminal Violence: National Patterns and Behavior.* Lexington, MA: D. C. Heath.

Daniels, D. N., Gilula, M. F., and Ochberg, F. M. (eds.) (1970). *Violence and the Struggle for Existence.* Boston: Little Brown.

Decision-Making Information, Inc. (1978). *Attitudes of the American Electorate Toward Gun Control.* Santa Ana, CA.

DeFronzo, James (1979). Fear of crime and handgun ownership. *Criminology* **17** (3, November), 331–339.

Deiner, Edward, and Crandall, Rick (1979). An evaluation of the Jamaican anticrime program. *Journal of Applied Psychology,* March, 129–140.

Deiner, Edward, and Kerber, Kenneth W. (1979). Personality characteristics of American gun owners. *The Journal of Social Psychology* **107,** 227–238.

Delaney, Paul (1977). Special tactics units of the police are frequently idle in the suburbs. *New York Times,* 2 May, 20.

Department of Health, Education, and Welfare (1977). *Vital Statistics of the U.S., 1975.* Washington, DC: U.S. Government Printing Office.

Department of Health, Education, and Welfare (1979). *Healthy People.* DHEW (PHS) Publ. E79-55071. Washington, DC: U.S. Government Printing Office.

Deutsch, Stephen Jay (1979). Lies, damn lies, and statistics: A rejoinder to the comment by Hay and McCleary. *Evaluation Quarterly* **3** (2, May), 315–328.

Deutsch, Stephen Jay, and Alt, Francis B. (1977). The effect of Massachusetts gun control law on gun-related crimes in the city of Boston. *Evaluation Quarterly* **1** (March), 543–568.

DiMaio, Vincent, Jones, J. Allen, Caruth, W. W., Anderson, Louie L., and Petty, Charles S. (1974). A comparison of the wounding effects of commercially available handgun ammunition suitable for police use. *FBI Law Enforcement Bulletin* **43** (12, December), 3–8.

Douglas, Jack (1967). *The Social Meaning of Suicide.* Princeton, NJ: Princeton University Press.

Eastman, George D. (ed.) (1969). *Municipal Police Administration.* Washington, DC: International City Management Association.

Ellis, D. P., Weiner, P., and Miller, L. (1971). Does the trigger pull the finger? An experimental test of weapons as aggression-eliciting stimuli. *Sociometry* **34,** 453–465.

Ennis, Phillip (1967). *Criminal Victimization in the United States: A Report of a National Survey. Field Surveys II.* Washington, DC: U.S. Government Printing Office.

Erlanger, Howard S. (1975). Is there a subculture of violence in the South? *Journal of Criminal Law and Criminology* **66** (December), 483–490.

Erlich, Isaac (1973). Participation in illegitimate activities: A theoretical and empirical investigation. *Journal of Political Economy* **81,** 521–565.

Erskine, Hazel (1972). The polls: Gun control. *Public Opinion Quarterly* **36** (3, Fall), 455–469.

Farberow, Norman L., and Schneidman, Edwin S. (1961). Statistical comparisons between attempted and committed suicides. In *Cry for Help* (Norman L. Farberow and Edwin S. Schneidman, eds.), pp. 19–47. New York: McGraw Hill.

Ferry, John, and Kravitz, Marjorie (1978). *Issues in Sentencing.* Washington, DC: National Institute of Law Enforcement and Criminal Justice.

Fischer, D., Kelm, J., and Rose, A. (1969). Knives as aggression-eliciting stimuli. *Psychological Reports* **24,** 755–760.

Fisher, Joseph C. (1976). Homicide in Detroit: The role of firearms. *Criminology* **14** (November), 387–400.

Fordi, A. (1973). The effects of exposure to aggression-eliciting and aggression-inhibiting stimuli on subsequent aggression. *Goteburg Psychological Reports* **3** (8).

Garofalo, James (1979). Victimization and the fear of crime. *Journal of Research in Crime and Delinquency* **16**, 80–97.

Gastil, Raymond D. (1971). Homicide and a regional culture of violence. *American Sociological Review* **36** (June), 412–427.

Geisel, Martin S., Roll, Richard, and Wettick, R. Stanton (1969). The effectiveness of state and local regulation of handguns: A statistical analysis. *Duke University Law Journal* **4** (August), 647–676.

Gelles, Richard (1974). *The Violent Home.* Beverly Hills, CA: Sage Publications.

Gil, D. G. (1971). Violence against children. *Journal of Marriage and the Family* **33**, 637–648.

Giuffrida, Louis O., Moorman, Charles B., and Roth, Jordan T. (1978). Service sidearm retention: A matter of life or death. *The Police Chief,* October, 50–52,

Greenwood, Peter W., Wildhorn, Sorrel, Poggio, Eugene C., Strumwasser, Michael J., and DeLeon, Peter (1976). *Prosecution of Adult Felony Defendants.* Lexington, MA: Lexington Books.

Hackney, Sheldon (1969). Southern violence. In *The History of Violence in America* (H. Graham and T. Gurr, eds.), pp. 505–527. New York: Bantam.

Hamill, Pete (1970). The revolt of the white lower middle class. In *The White Majority* (Louise Kapp Howe, ed.), pp. 10–22. New York: Vintage.

Hamilton, Claud (1979). Pack a trail gun. *Gun World,* December, 38–41.

Hamilton, Richard F. (1972). *Class and Politics in the United States.* New York: John Wiley.

Hare, G. B., Klaus, P., and Bunten, E. D. (1977). *LEAA Police Equipment Survey of 1972. Volume VI. Body Armor and Confiscated Weapons.* Washington, DC: U.S. Government Printing Office.

Harries, Keith D. (1974). *The Geography of Crime and Justice.* New York: McGraw Hill.

Hay, Richard, and McCleary, Richard (1979). Box-Tiao time series models for impact assessment: A comment on the recent work of Deutsch and Alt. *Evaluation Quarterly* **3** (2, May), 277–314.

Heaphy, John F. (1978). *Police Practices.* Washington, DC: The Police Foundation.

Hindelang, Michael (1976). *Criminal Victimization in Eight American Cities: A Descriptive Analysis of Theft and Assault.* Cambridge, MA: Ballinger.

Hindelang, Michael (1979). Sex differences in criminal activity. *Social Problems* **27** (2), 143–156.

Hindelang, Michael, Gottfredson, Michael R., and Garofalo, James, (1978). *Victims of Personal Crime: An Empirical Foundation for a Theory of Personal Victimization.* Cambridge, MA: Ballinger.

Hirsch, C. S., Rushford, N. B., Ford, A. B., and Adelson, L. (1973). Homicide and suicide in a metropolitan county: Long-term trends. *Journal of the American Medical Association* **223**, 900–905.

Hofstadter, Richard (1970). America as a gun culture. *American Heritage* **21** (October), pp. 4 ff.

Inciardi, James, and Pottinger, Anne (1978). *Violent Crime: Historical and Contemporary Issues.* Beverly Hills, CA: Sage Publications.

Jones, David A. (1979). *Crime Without Punishment.* Lexington, MA: Lexington Books.

Jones, Edward D. (1980). Handguns, gun control laws, and firearm violence: A comment. Unpublished paper.

Jones, Edward D., III (1981). The District of Columbia's 'Firearms Control Regulations Act of 1975': The toughest handgun control law in the United States—Or is it? *Annals of the American Academy of Political and Social Sciences* **455** (May), 138–149.

Jones, Edward D., and Ray, Marla Wilson (1980). Handgun control: Strategies, enforcement, and effectiveness." Unpublished paper, U.S. Department of Justice.

Kakalik, James S., and Wildhorn, Sorrel (1971). *Private Police in the United States: Findings and Recommendations.* Santa Monica, CA: The Rand Corporation.

Kates, Donald B. (1978). Some remarks on the prohibition of handguns. *St. Louis University Law Journal* **23** (11), 11–34.

Kates, Don B. (1982). Brief filed in the United States Court of Appeals for the Seventh District in the case of Reichert and Metler v. Village of Morton Grove, Illinois.

Kellert, Stephen R. (1978). Hunting Survey. Washington, DC: U.S. Fish and Wildlife Survey.

Kennett, Lee, and Anderson, James L. (1976). *The Gun in America: The Origins of a National Dilemma.* Westport, CT: Greenwood Press.

King, Daniel P. (1973). Firearms and crime. *The Criminologist* **8** (Spring), 50–58.

Kleck, Gary (1979a). Capital punishment, gun ownership, and homicide. *American Journal of Sociology* **84** (4, January), 882–910.

Kleck, Gary (1979b). Guns, homicide, and gun control: Some assumptions and some evidence. Paper read at the annual meetings of the Midwest Sociological Society, Minneapolis, MN.

Kleck, Gary (1982). "The relationship between gun ownership levels and rates of violence in the United States." In *Firearms and Violence: Issues of Regulation* (D. Kates, ed.), in press. New York: Ballinger.

Krug, Alan S. (1967). The relationship between firearms licensing laws and crime rates. *Congressional Record* **113** (July), 200060–64.

Krug, Alan S. (1968a). The relationship between firearms ownership and crime rates. *Congressional Record* **114** (January), 1496–98.

Krug, Alan S. (1968b). The misuse of firearms in crime. *Congressional Record* **114** (April), 8585–88.

LaFree, Gary D. (1980). The effect of sexual stratification by race on official reactions to rape. *American Sociological Review* **45** (5), 842–854.

Landauer, Jerry (1971). Gunmaking booms in the U.S. . . . *The Wall Street Journal,* 8 June, 40 ff.

Leynes, J. P., and Parke, R. D. (1975). Aggressive slides can induce a weapons effect. *European Journal of Social Psychology* **5,** 229–236.

Light, R. J. (1974). Abused and neglected children in America: A study of alternative policies. *Harvard Educational Review* **43,** 556–598.

Lizotte, Alan J. (1978). Extra-legal factors in Chicago's criminal courts: Testing the conflict model of criminal justice. *Social Problems* **25** (5), 564–580.

Lizotte, Alan J., and Bordua, David J. (1980). Firearms ownership for sport and protection: Two divergent models. *American Sociological Review* **45** (2, April), 229–244.

Lizotte, Alan J., and Bordua, David J. Military socialization, childhood socialization, and current situation: veterans' firearms ownership. *Journal of Political and Military Sociology,* in press.

Lizotte, Alan J., Bordua, David, and White, Carolyn S. (1981). Firearms ownership for sport and protection: Two not so divergent models. *American Sociological Review* **46** (4, August), 499–503.

Loftin, Colin, and Hill, Robert H. (1974). Regional subculture and homicide: An examination of the Gastil-Hackney thesis. *American Sociological Review* **39** (5, October), 714–724.

Loftin, Colin, and McDowell, David (1981). "One with a gun gets you two": Mandatory sentencing and firearms violence in Detroit. *Annals of American Academy of Political and Social Sciences* **455** (May), 150–168.

Marks, Alan, and Stokes, C. Shannon (1976). Socialization, firearms, and suicide. *Social Problems* **23** (5, June), 622–629.

Marlow, Paul (1977). Design evolution of the Detonics .45 ACP. *The Police Chief,* October, 30–34.

Massachusetts Council on Crime and Correction, Inc. (1974). *A Shooting Gallery Called America.* Boston, MA.

Mather, Lynn (1979). *Plea Bargaining or Trial.* Lexington, MA: Lexington Books.

Montreal Star (1971). Ratio of homicides a startling 100 to 3 in Detroit, Windsor. 8 April.

Moorman, Charles B. (1976). The use of semi-automatic sidearms in California. *The Police Chief,* October, 274–275.

Munford, Robert, Kazer, Ross, Feldman, Roger, and Stivers, Robert (1976). Homicide trends in Atlanta. *Criminology* **14** (2), 213–232.

Murray, Douglas R. (1975). Handguns, gun control laws, and firearms violence. *Social Problems* **23** (1, October), 81–93.

Nagel, Ilene, Cardascia, John, and Ross, Catherine E. (1980). Sex differences in the processing of criminal defendants. Paper to appear in *Women and the Law in the Social Historical Perspective* (D. Kelly Weisberg, ed.), to be published. New York: Schenkman Pub. Co.

National Advisory Committee on Criminal Justice Standards and Goals (1976). *Private Security: Report of the Task Force on Private Security.* Washington, DC: Law Enforcement Assistance Administration.

National Center for Health Statistics (1967a). Suicide in the United States: 1950–1964. *Vital and Health Statistics,* Series 20, No. 5. Washington, DC: U.S. Government Printing Office.

National Center for Health Statistics (1967b). Persons injured and disability days by detailed type and class of accident: 1959–1961. *Vital and Health Statistics,* Series 10. Washington, DC: U.S. Government Printing Office.

National Center for Health Statistics (1976a). Persons injured and disability days by detailed type and class of accident, 1971–1972. *Vital and Health Statistics,* Series 10, No. 105. Washington, DC: U.S. Government Printing Office.

National Center for Health Statistics (1976b). Current estimates from the Health Interview Survey, 1975. *Vital and Health Statistics,* Series 10, No. 115. Washington, DC: U.S. Government Printing Office.

National Center for Health Statistics (1977). Instruction manual, data preparation, Part 5: Data preparation of the Current Mortality Sample. Washington, DC: U.S. Government Printing Office.

National Center for Health Statistics (1978). Current estimates from the Health Interview Survey, 1977. *Vital and Health Statistics,* Series 10, No. 126. Washington, DC: U.S. Government Printing Office.

National Rifle Association (1975). *Firearms and Laws Review.* Denver, CO.

National Safety Council (1975–79). *Accident Facts.* Chicago, IL.

Newsweek (1974). The dumdum debate. 9 September: 53–54.

Newton, George D., and Zimring, Franklin E. (1969). *Firearms and Violence in American Life: A Staff Report to the National Commission on the Causes and Prevention of Violence.* Washington, DC: U.S. Government Printing Office.

New York Times (1974). To stop or kill? Editorial for 11 November, 28.

New York Times (1975). States and cities seeking to ban police use of dumdum bullets. 16 January, 21.

New York Times (1975). U.S. report urges more powerful police bullet. 9 August, 21.

New York Times (1977). The idle SWAT squads. 8 May, Section IV: 7.

Nordheimer, Jon (1975). Tough elite police units useful but controversial. *New York Times:* 14 July, 1 ff.

Normandeau, Andre (1968). *Trends and Patterns in Crimes of Robbery.* Unpublished Ph.D. Dissertation, University of Pennsylvania, Philadelphia, Pennsylvania.

Northwood, Lawrence, K., Westgard, Richard, and Barb, Charles E. (1978). Law abiding one-man armies. *Society* **16** (1, November–December), 69–74.

O'Connor, James F. and Lizotte, Alan J. (1978). The 'Southern subculture of violence' thesis and patterns of gun ownership. *Social Problems* **25** (4, April), 420–429.

O'Neill, Michael T. (1979). Gun retention. *FBI Law Enforcement Bulletin* **48** (9, September), 20–23.

Page, David, and O'Neal, Edgard (1977). "Weapon effect" without demand characteristics. *Psychological Reports* **11,** 29–30.

Page, Monte M., and Scheidt, Rick J. (1971). The elusive weapons effect: Demand awareness, evaluation apprehension, and slightly sophisticated subjects. *Journal of Personality and Social Psychology* **20,** 304–315.

Parsonage, William (1979). *Perspectives on Criminology.* Beverly Hills, CA: Sage Publications.

Phillips, Llad, and Votey, Harold (1976). Handguns and homicide: Minimizing losses and the costs of control. *Journal of Legal Studies* **5** (June), 463–478.

Pierce, Glenn L., and Bowers, William J. (1979). The impact of the Bartley-Fox gun law on crime in Massachusetts. Unpublished paper, Northeastern University: Center for Applied Social Research.

Pinto, Vince (1971). Weapons for the home front. In *Police on the Homefront* (National Action/Research on the Military Industrial Complex, ed.), pp. 74–89. Philadelphia, PA.

Pittman, David J., and Handy, William (1964). Patterns in criminal aggravated assault. *Journal of Criminal Law, Criminology, and Police Science* **55** (4), 462–470.

Police Foundation (1977). *Domestic Violence and the Police: Studies in Detroit and Kansas City.* Washington, DC: The Police Foundation.

President's Commission on Law Enforcement and Administration of Justice (1967). *Task Force Report: Crime and Its Impact—An Assessment.* Washington, DC: U.S. Government Printing Office.

Reed, John Shelton (1971). To live—and die—in Dixie: A contribution to the study of Southern violence. *Political Science Quarterly* **86** (September), 429–443.

Reiss, Albert (1967). Measurement of the nature and amount of crime. *Studies in Crime and Law Enforcement in Major Metropolitan Areas. Volume I: Field Surveys III,* pp. 1–182. Washington, DC: U.S. Government Printing Office.

Rossi, Peter H., and Freeman, Howard E. (1982). *Evaluation: A Systematic Approach,* 2nd ed., Beverly Hills, CA: Sage Publications.

Rossi, Peter H., Weber-Burdin, E., and Chen, H. (1981). Effects of weapons use on felony case disposition: An analysis of evidence from the Los Angeles PROMIS system. Unpublished paper, Social and Demographic Research Institute, University of Massachusetts, Amherst.

Rossman, David, Froyd, Paul, Pierce, Glen L., McDevitt, John, and Bowers, William (1979). *The Impact of the Mandatory Gun Law in Massachusetts.* Boston University School of Law: Center for Criminal Justice.

Schuman, Howard, and Presser, Stanley (1977–1978). Attitude measurement and the gun control paradox. *Public Opinion Quarterly* **41** (4, Winter), 427–438.

Search Group, Inc. (1976). *Gun Tracing Systems Study Report.* Technical Report 15. Sacramento, CA.

Seitz, Stephen T. (1972). Firearms, homicides, and gun control effectiveness. *Law and Society Review* **6** (May), 595–614.

Sellin, Thorsten, and Wolfgang, Marvin (1964). *The Measures of Delinquency.* New York: John Wiley.

Sherrill, Robert (1973). *The Saturday Night Special.* New York: Charterhouse.

Skogan, Wesley (1974). The validity of official crime statistics: An empirical investigation. *Social Science Quarterly* **55** (1), 25–58.

Skogan, Wesley (1976a). Citizen reporting of crime: Some national panel data. *Criminology* **13**, 535–549.

Skogan, Wesley (1976b). Crime and crime rates. In *Sample Surveys of the Victims of Crime* (Wesley Skogan, ed.), pp. 105–119. Cambridge, MA: Ballinger.

Skogan, Wesley (ed.) (1976c). *Sample Surveys of the Victims of Crime.* Cambridge, MA: Ballinger.

Smart, Carol, and Smart, Barry (1978). "Accounting for rape: Reality and myth in press reporting." In *Women, Sexuality and Social Control* (C. Smart and B. Smart, eds.), pp. 89–103. London: Routledge and Kegan Paul.

Smith, Howard (1979). Scenes. *The Village Voice,* 22 January.

Spiegler, Jeffrey H., and Sweeney, John J. (1975). *Gun Abuse in Ohio.* Cleveland, OH: Governmental Research Institute.

Steele, Kevin E. (1979). Heckler and Koch: A new leader in the police arms race? *Guns Magazine,* December, 33 ff.

Stickney, S. B. (1967): Hunting. In *Motivations in Play, Games, and Sports* (R. Slovenko and J. A. Knight, eds.), pp. 582–596. Springfield, IL: Thomas.

Stinchcombe, Arthur L., Adams, Rebecca, Heimer, Carol, Scheppele, Kim, Smith, Tom W., and Garth Taylor, D. (1980). *Crime and Punishment: Changing Attitudes in America.* San Francisco: Jossey Bass.

Sullivan, Ronald (1977). High-power arms debated by police. *New York Times,* 27 March, Section XI, p. 1 ff.

Taylor, R. (1973). Gunshot wounds of the abdomen. *Annals of Surgery* **177**, 174–175.

Tittle, Charles R. (1969). Crime rates and legal sanctions. *Social Problems* **16**, 409–423.

Turner, Charles W. and Simons, Lynn (1974). Effects of subject sophistication and evaluation apprehension on aggressive responses to weapons. *Journal of Personality and Social Psychology* **30**, 341–348.

United States Bureau of Alcohol, Tobacco and Firearms (1976a). *Project Identification: A Study of Handguns Used in Crime.* Washington, DC: BATF.

United States Bureau of Alcohol, Tobacco and Firearms (1976b). *Project 300.* Washington, DC: Public Affairs Office, BATF.

United States Bureau of Alcohol, Tobacco and Firearms (1978). *Your Guide to Firearms Regulations.* Washington, DC: BATF.

United States Bureau of Alcohol, Tobacco and Firearms (n.d.). *Concentrated Urban Enforcement (CUE).* Washington, DC: BATF.

United States Bureau of the Census (1977). Current population reports: Estimates of the population of the U.S. by age, sex, and race, July 1, 1974–1976. Series P-25, No. 643. Washington, DC: U.S. Government Printing Office.

United States Bureau of the Census (1979a). *Current Population Reports. Population Characteristics, 1978* (#336), April. Washington, DC: U.S. Government Printing Office.

United States Bureau of the Census (1979b). *1979 Census of Manufactures. Industry Series: Small Arms (SIC 3484). Preliminary Report #MC77-I-34E-3(P).* Washington, DC: U.S. Government Printing Office.

United States Bureau of the Census (1970–1980). *Statistical Abstract of the United States.* (Annual publ.) Washington, DC: U.S. Government Printing Office.

United States Department of Commerce, National Bureau of Standards (1977). LEAA Police Equipment Survey of 1972, Vol. VI: Body Armor and Confiscated Weapons. NBS Special Publications, pp. 480–486.

United States Department of Justice, Federal Bureau of Investigation (1960–1978). *Crime in the United States (Uniform Crime Reports).* (Annual publ.) Washington, DC: U.S. Government Printing Office.

United States Department of Justice (1973–1976) *Criminal Victimization in the United States.* Washington, DC: U.S. Government Printing Office.

United States Department of Justice (1977–1979). *Sourcebook of Criminal Justice Statistics.* Washington, DC: Law Enforcement Assistance Administration.

Vera Institute of Justice (1977). *Felony Arrests: Their Prosecution and Disposition in New York City's Court.* New York: The Vera Institute of Justice.

Vinson, T. (1974). Gun and knife attacks. *Australian Journal of Forensic Science* **7** (2, December), 76–83.

Weber-Burdin, Eleanor, Rossi, P. H., Wright, J. D., and Daly, K. (1981). Weapons policies: A survey of police department practices concerning weapons and related issues. Unpublished paper, Social and Demographic Research Institute, University of Massachusetts, Amherst.

Williams, J. Sherwood, and McGrath, John H. (1976). Why people own guns. *Journal of Communication* **26** (4, Autumn), 22–30.

Wolfgang, Marvin (1958). *Patterns in Criminal Homicide.* Philadelphia: University of Pennsylvania Press.

Wolfgang, Marvin (ed.) (1967). *Studies in Homicide.* New York: Harper and Row.

Wolfgang, Marvin, and Franco Ferracuti (1967). *The SubCulture of Violence: Towards an Integrated Theory in Criminology.* London: Tavistock.

Wright, James D. (1981). Public opinion and gun control: A comparison of results from two recent national surveys. *Annals of the American Academy of Political and Social Science* **455** (May), 24–39.

Wright, James D. (1982). The ownership of firearms for reasons of self-defense. In *Firearms and Violence: Issues of Regulation* (D. Kates, ed.), in press. New York: Ballinger.

Wright, James D., and Marston, Linda (1975). The ownership of the means of destruction: Weapons in the United States. *Social Problems* **23** (1, October), 93–107.

Wright, James D., Rossi, Peter H. and Juravitch, Thomas (1980). Survey Research. In *Harvard Encyclopedia of American Ethnic Groups* (Stephan Thernstrom, ed.), pp. 954–971. Cambridge, MA: Harvard University Press.

Wright, James D., Rossi, Peter, Wright, Sonia R., and Weber-Burdin, Eleanor (1979). *After the Cleanup: Long Term Effects of Natural Disasters.* Beverly Hills, CA: Sage Publications.

Yeager, Matthew G., Alviani, Joseph D., and Loving, Nancy (1976). *How Well Does the Handgun Protect You and Your Family?* Washington, DC: United States Conference of Mayors.

Zimring, Franklin E. (1968a). Is gun control likely to reduce violent killings? *The University of Chicago Law Review* **35**, 721–737.

Zimring, Franklin E. (1968b). Games with guns and statistics. *Wisconsin Law Review* **4**, 1113–1126.

Zimring, Franklin E. (1972). The medium is the message: Firearm caliber as a determinant of death from assault. *Journal of Legal Studies* **1** (1), 97–123.

Zimring, Franklin E. (1975). Firearms and Federal law: The Gun Control Act of 1968. *Journal of Legal Studies* **4** (1), 133–198.

Zimring, Franklin E. (1976). Street crime and new guns: Some implications for firearms control. *Journal of Criminal Justice* **4**, 95–107.

Zimring, Franklin E. (1977). Determinants of the death rate from robbery: A Detroit time study. *Journal of Legal Studies* **6**, 317–332.

INDEX

A

Accident Facts, 168, 169
Accidents, with guns. *See* Gun accidents
Aggravated assault. *See* Assault, aggravated, with guns
Alt, Francis B., 281, 292–294
Alcohol, tobacco, and firearms. *See* Bureau of Alcohol, Tobacco, and Firearms
Alviani, Joseph D., 81, 107, 134, 138–141, 145, 148
American Civil Liberties Union, 79
American Firearms Industry Magazine, 34
Ammunition, of U.S. police. *See* Policemen, United States, ammunition used by
Anderson, James L., 109
Annals of the American Academy of Political and Social Science, 215
Armed robbery. *See* Robbery
Assault, aggravated, with guns, 2, 14, 141, 153, 162–166, 313–314
    Trends in, 159, 160

B

Bakal, Carl, 2, 285
Barb, Charles E., 81, 100, 108, 109, 128
Bartley-Fox Amendment (Massachusetts), 22, 235, 279, 281, 298, 308
    Evaluation studies of, 290–294
Beha, James A., 22, 290–291
Berelson, Bernard, 112

Berkowitz, Leonard, 202
Bernstein (Nagel), Ilene, 299, 303, 305
Biderman, Albert, 160
Black, Donald, 154, 155
Block, Richard, 156, 157, 193, 195, 208
Blose, James, 232
Blumberg, Abraham S., 299
Booker, Ann, 202
Bordua, David, 12, 100, 101, 103, 104, 107–109, 115–120, 128, 136, 237
Bowers, William J., 281, 292–294, 298
Box-Jenkins (time series models), 293
Brill, Stephen, 17, 175, 177–181
Brosi, Kathleen B., 299, 300
Bruce-Biggs, B., 4, 25, 35, 60, 125, 283
Bureau of Alcohol, Tobacco, and Firearms, 27, 46–48, 175, 177–181, 182, 243, 245, 288
Bureau of the Census, 46, 48, 160
Burr, D. E. S., 107, 108, 118, 119, 129, 176, 183–187, 305, 306
Buss, Arnold H., 202
Buss, Edith, 202

C

Caddell, Patrick, 142–145, 147, 215–241
    Handgun attitude poll, 142–147, 215–241
Caetano, Donald F., 99, 115
California Penal Code, 305
Cambridge Reports, Inc., 142, 215–241
Campbell, Angus, 112

335

Campbell, Donald T., 274, 282
Cardascia, John, 299, 303, 305
Cash, W. J., 109
Census, Bureau of the. See Bureau of the Census
Center for the Study and Prevention of Handgun Violence, 20, 142, 216
Chen, Huey T., 300
City size, effects on gun ownership. See Gun ownership, by city size
Civil disorders, 101, 131
    Effect of, on gun sales. See Fear and loathing hypothesis
Clotfelter, Charles T., 49, 101
Coles, Robert, 121
Collectors. See Gun collectors
Comptroller General of the United States, 27, 47, 98, 283
Conference of U.S. Mayors, 295
Congressional Record, The, 284
Conklin, John E., 208
Cook, Philip J., 19, 44, 46, 62, 136, 139, 140, 205, 206–212, 232, 243, 269, 299, 306, 307
Cook, Thomas, 274, 282
Cramer, Harry L., 72
Crandall, Rick, 292
Crime. See also individual crime types
    Cause of gun ownership, 81–101, 128, 129
    Fear of, 98, 100, 116, 117, 120, 128
    Guns as a cause of. See Guns, as a cause of crime
    Guns used in, 16–18, 175–188
        Compared to legitimate guns, 183–187, 188
        Penalties for, 268
    Motivations to commit, 18, 19, 189–212
    Theories of, 7, 8, 19, 21
    Trends in, 14, 15, 153–174
    Victimization by, 5, 14, 15, 99, 100, 117, 120, 128, 129, 140, 141, 143–145, 153
    Surveys of, 160–166, 278
"Crimes of Passion," 130, 156, 192, 196
Criminal Victimization in the United States, 162–164, 172
Criminal victimization surveys. See Crime, victimization by, surveys of
Cronbach, Lee J., 274, 282
Culture, of guns. See Gun culture

Current Mortality Sample, 166
Current Population Survey, 219, 220
Curtis, Lynn, 2, 19, 192, 193, 195, 198, 200–203

D

Daniels, D. N., 120
Decision-Making Information, Inc. (DMI), 39, 40, 56–58, 60–62, 95–98, 119, 142, 145–148, 215–241
Deer Hunter, The (movie), 196
DeFronzo, James, 100, 120, 128
Deiner, Edward, 104, 114, 118, 121, 292
Demand-side estimates, of gun prevalence. See Gun prevalence, methods of estimation
Department of Treasury
    Bureau of Alcohol, Tobacco, and Firearms. See Bureau of Alcohol, Tobacco, and Firearms
    Bureau of Internal Revenue, 245
Detroit, crime in. See Zimring, Franklin E.
Detroit gun law. See Loftin, Colin
Deutsch, Stephen J., 281, 292–294
DiMaio, Vincent, 78
DMI. See Decision-Making Information, Inc.
Domestic production of guns. See Guns, supply of
Douglas, Jack, 166
Drake, William R., 81, 107, 134

E

Eastman, George D., 69
Eisenhower, Milton, 216
Ellis, D. P., 202
Ennis, Phillip, 160
Erlanger, Howard S., 110
Erlich, Isaac, 139
Erskine, Hazel, 34, 104, 106, 118, 221
Exportation of guns. See Guns, exportation of

F

Farberow, Norman L., 168
FBI Law Enforcement Bulletin, 69, 75, 78

FBI Uniform Crime Reports. See Uniform Crime Reports

"Fear and loathing" hypothesis, 49, 81–101
    Studies of, 93–101

Fear of crime. *See* Crime, fear of

Federal Firearms Act of 1938, 245, 246, 311

Federal gun laws. *See* Gun Control Act of 1968

Federal Register, The, 243

Ferracuti, Franco, 201

Ferry, John, 298

Field and Stream, 58

Firearms. *See* Guns

Firearms and Laws Review, 243

Firearms Control Regulation Act of 1975 (Washington DC), 294

Fischer, D., 202

Fisher, Joseph C., 135

Florida handgun study. *See* Burr, D. E. S.

Ford, Gerald, 28

Fordi, A., 202

Freeman, Howard, 274, 282

Fromm, "Squeaky," 28

Frotto, Nicholas, 77

G

Gallup Organization, The (American Institute for Public Opinion), 34–37, 39, 55, 84, 87, 91, 220, 221, 232, 234, 286

Garofalo, James, 100, 155

Gastil, Raymond D., 109–111

Geisel, Martin S., 284–285, 286

General Social Surveys. *See* National Opinion Research Center

GIGO (Garbage In, Garbage Out), 38

Gilula, M. F., 120

Glisson Amendment (Florida), 184–186, 306

Gottfredson, Michael R., 155

"Great American Gun War." *See* Bruce-Biggs, B.

Greenwood, Peter W., 300

Guiffrida, Louis O., 76

Gun accidents, 15, 131, 132, 140–145, 147, 311
    Estimates of, 172–175
    Trends in, 166–170

Gun collectors, 61, 62, 97, 186, 312

Gun control, public opinion concerning, 20, 215–241
    Measurement issues, 216–217
    Robustness of, 217
    Survey comparisons, 221–241

Gun Control Act of 1968, 21–22, 46, 47, 243, 245, 246, 272, 280, 281, 288–290, 308, 316
    Effects of, 47–49
    Implementation of, 288–290
    Provisions of, 246, 247

Gun control legislation, 21, 22, 44, 47–49. *See also* Gun control policies

Gun control policies, 21, 22, 43, 44, 82–84, 243–272, 315–317. *See also* Bartley-Fox Amendment; Federal Firearms Control Act of 1938; Firearms Control Act of 1975; Glisson Amendment; Gun Control Act of 1968; National Firearm Act of 1934
    Buy-back laws, 233
    Coverage of US population by, 269, 270
    Dealer licensing laws, 248, 249
    Effectiveness of, 316–319
    Effects on crime rates, 273–308
    Enforcement and implementation of, 270–272, 290–294
    Evaluation studies of, 273–308
    Goals of, 275–278
    Handgun bans, 269
    History of, in US, 245–247
    Implications of this study for, 309–324
    Interstate comparisons of, 283–286
    Issues in measuring impact of, 273–275
    License or permit
        To possess (guns), 259–268
        To purchase (guns), 249–259
    Penalty provisions of, 268
    Place and manner of carrying laws, 268
    Public opinion about, 215–241
    Registration and licensing, 20, 44
    Sentence enhancements for gun crimes, 297–300, 319
    Short- versus long-term effects of, 279, 280
    Side effects of, 276, 277
    Similarity to automobile licensing laws, 232, 233, 318
    Time-series studies of, 287, 297
    Use of controls in study of, 280–282, 285

Gun culture, 1, 2, 11, 13, 22, 86, 112–120, 309, 313, 323–324
Gun market, 275, 315, 316
    Barter and trade, 118, 119
    For guns used for crime, 181–183
    Interstate commerce in, 178, 183, 187, 247
Gun owners, characteristics of, 11, 103–122, 220. See also Gun ownership
    City size, 104–107
    Personality characteristics of, 120, 121
    Race, 107–109
    Region, 104–107
    Religion, 107–109
    Sex, 107–109
    Social class, 107–109
    Socialization of, 111, 112–120
    Veteran's status, 114, 115, 118, 142
Gun ownership, 103–122
    Among veterans, 114, 115, 118, 142
    By city size, 86, 87, 104–107
    By personality characteristics, 120, 121
    By region, 104–107
    By social characteristics, 86–90
    Personal versus household ownership, 103
Gun prevalence, 25–44, 311, 312
    By type of gun, 52
    In England and Ireland, 283
    In Israel, 1
    In Norway, 1
    In Switzerland, 1, 283
    In the United States, 8, 9, 25–44
    Methods of estimation, 26, 31, 36–38
    Trends in, in United States, 45–101
Guns
    As catalysts of violence, 130, 202, 203
        Experimental studies of, 202, 203
    As cause of crime, 123–149, 129–138, 189–212
        Public opinion about, 235–237
    As crime deterrent, 13, 14, 123, 124, 138–149. See also Self-protection, by guns
    As symbols, 8, 120
    Average number owned, 25–44, 85
    Confiscations by police, 175–183, 187, 188
        Age of confiscated guns, 179, 188
    Exportation of, 34, 51
    Illegal sales of. See Gun market
        Public opinion concerning illegal sales, 215–241

Guns (continued)
    Lethality of, 6, 190–193, 198, 200, 203, 208, 209
        By caliber, 203
    Lifetime of, 28, 31–34
        Of police guns, 70
    Military, 27
    Number of. See Gun prevalence
    Police, 27, 65–72
    Prices of, 59, 60, 180, 187, 318
    Reasons for owning, 94–96, 103, 104, 312
    Sport and recreational use of, 45–63, 82, 83, 94, 96, 97, 103–105, 112, 113, 116, 117, 128, 185, 186, 312. See also Hunting; Gun usage; Gun collectors
    Sports shooting, 61, 312
    Supply of, 25–44
        Domestic production, 28–31, 43, 46–48, 79
            By caliber (handguns), 43
        Imports, 30, 31, 46–48
    Theft of, 178, 179, 181, 182, 184, 185, 187
Guns and Ammo, 58
Guns Magazine, 75, 76
Gun usage, 9, 10, 12. See also Guns, sport and recreational use of; Self-protection, by guns; Gun owners, characteristics of
    Models of, 314, 315
    By police, 10, 65–79
    Regional patterns, 13, 106, 107, 109–112
Gun use, in crime. See Crime, guns used in
    Socialization into, 111, 112–120
Gun World, 58

H

Hackney, Sheldon, 109–111
Hamill, Pete, 81
Hamilton, Claud, 58
Hamilton, Richard F., 104
Handgun control. See Gun control policies
Handgun Control, Inc., 216
Handguns. See Guns; various subcategories; Saturday Night Special
Handy, William, 202
Harries, Keith, 109

Hay, Richard, 281, 293
Heaphy, John F., 68, 70
Hill, Robert H., 110, 111, 127
Hindelang, Michael, 155
Hirsch, C. S., 157
Hofstadter, Richard, 1, 112
Homicide, with guns, 2, 14, 107, 110, 111, 127, 133, 137, 153, 190–200, 311, 313, 314
    Among acquaintances, 194–196, 203, 204
    Domestic, 193 ff
    Of policemen, 170–172
    Relationship to gun prevalence, 3, 189–212
    Trends in, 156, 157
Homicide, with knives, 197–200
Homicide rates, international, 2, 125
Households, increase in number in United States, 50–53
Hunting, 53–63, 96, 97, 104, 106, 186, 196, 312

I

Importation, of guns. See Guns, supply of
International Association of Chiefs of Police, 76
Interstate comparisons, of gun laws. See Gun control policies, interstate comparisons of
Interstate market, in guns. See Gun market; Crime, guns used in

J

Jefferson, Thomas, 310
Jones, Edward D., 243, 249, 261, 263, 265, 267, 294–296
Juravich, Thomas, 109

K

Kakalik, James S., 66
Kates, Don, 136, 197, 199
Kellert, Stephen R., 59
Kelm, J., 202
Kennesaw (Georgia), 310

Kennett, Lee, 109
Kerber, Kenneth W., 104, 114, 118, 121
King, Daniel P., 283
Kleck, Gary, 14, 35, 39, 135, 136, 139, 141, 193, 198, 202, 203
Kravitz, Marjorie, 298
Krug, Alan S., 284

L

LaFree, Gary, 299, 303
Landauer, Jerry, 49
Law Enforcement Assistance Administration, 66, 75, 78, 153, 160, 176
Law Enforcement Bulletin, FBI. See FBI Law Enforcement Bulletin
Lazarsfeld, Paul, 112
Leynes, J. P., 202
LePage, Anthony, 202
Lethality of guns. See Guns, lethality of
Liddy, G. Gordon, 49
Lifetime of guns. See Guns, lifetime of
Lizotte, Alan J., 12, 100, 101, 103, 104, 107–109, 111, 115–118, 120, 128, 136, 237, 299
Loftin, Colin, 110, 111, 127, 294, 296, 297
Louis Harris and Associates, 34–40, 119, 221, 286
Loving, Nancy, 138–141, 145, 148

M

McCleary, Richard, 281, 293
McDowell, David, 294, 296, 297
McGrath, John H., 99, 120
McPhee, William, 112
Mandatory sentencing laws, for gun use. See Gun control policies, sentence enhancements for gun crimes
Marks, Alan, 109, 113, 114
Marlow, Paul, 69
Marston, Linda L., 25, 44, 98; 99, 104–108, 120, 128, 220
Massachusetts Council on Crime and Corrections, 3, 81, 134
Massachusetts gun law. See Bartley-Fox Amendment
Massachusetts Research Center, 76

Mather, Lynn, 300
Military guns. See Guns, military
Miller, L., 202
Moorman, Charles B., 76, 77
Morton Grove (Illinois), 310
Munford, Robert, 157
Murder. See Homicide
Murray, Douglas, 135, 285, 286

N

Nagin, Daniel, 208, 299, 306, 307
Nation, The, 309
National Advisory Committee on Criminal
    Justice Standards and Goals, 66
National Bureau of Standards, 78, 175–177
National Center for Health Statistics, 166,
    167, 170, 172
National Commission on the Causes and Pre-
    vention of Violence, 25, 35
National Crime Survey, 160, 161
National Firearms Act of 1934, 245
National Health Survey, 15, 166, 169, 170
National Opinion Research Center (General
    Social Survey), 34, 84, 87, 91, 94–99,
    100, 104, 105, 108, 109, 111, 118, 120,
    136, 145, 221
National Rifle Association, 4, 20, 39, 57, 118,
    142, 170, 216, 243, 320
National Safety Council, 168, 169, 172
Newsweek, 76
Newton, George D., 2, 3, 10, 13, 25–29, 31,
    32–39, 41–46, 50, 52, 53, 55, 60, 81,
    93–99, 104, 106, 107, 109, 118, 119,
    123, 127, 130–135, 137–140, 170
New York Times, The, 75–79, 205
NORC. See National Opinion Research Cen-
    ter
Northwood, Lawrence K., 81, 100
Number of guns, in United States. See Gun
    prevalence

O

Ochberg, F. M., 120
O'Connor, James F., 107, 108, 111
O'Neal, Edward, 202
O'Neill, Michael T., 69
Outdoor recreation, trends in, 54

P

Page, David, 202
Page, Monte M., 202
Parke, R. D., 202
Phillips, Llad, 135
Pierce, Glenn L., 281, 292–294, 298
Pinto, Vince, 72
Pittman, David J., 202
Police Chief, The, 68, 69, 72, 74–76
Police Equipment Survey of 1972 (PES72),
    67, 68, 70, 77, 78
Police Foundation, The, 68–70, 193
Policemen, United States
    Ammunition used by, 77–79
    Arms policies of US police, 72–79
    Assaults on, 170–172
    Confiscation of guns. See Guns, confisca-
        tions by police
    Guns. See Guns, police
    Number of, 67
    Personnel trends, 66–72
    Slayings
        By, 170–172
        Of, 170–172
Policy, gun control. See Gun control policies
President's Commission on Law Enforce-
    ment and Criminal Justice, 155, 160
Presser, Stanley, 221
Prices of guns. See Guns, prices of
Private security forces, 66
Project CUE (Concentrated Urban Enforce-
    ment), 175, 180, 182, 183, 187, 188
Project Identification (ATF), 175, 177–181,
    183
Project 300 (ATF), 175, 181, 182
PROMIS (Prosecutor's Management Infor-
    mation System), 301
Protection, with guns. See Guns, reasons for
    owning; Self-protection, by guns
Public opinion about guns. See Gun control
    policies, public opinion about

R

Rape, 140, 153, 162–166, 313, 314
    Trends in, 157–158
Ray, Marla Wilson, 243, 249, 261, 263, 265,
    267

Reasons for owning guns. *See* Guns, reasons for owning
Reed, John Shelton, 109
Region, effects on gun ownership. *See* Gun ownership, by region
Registration, of guns. *See* Gun control policies, registration and licensing
Regression analysis, 90–92
Reiss, Albert J., 160, 161
Religion, effects on gun ownership. *See* Gun ownership, by religion
Reporter, The, 25
Rifles. *See* Guns
Robbery, 2, 14, 137, 138–141, 153, 162–166, 205–212, 313, 314
  Death and injury from, 210, 211
  "Strategic choice" analysis of, 206–209
  Trends in, 158, 159
Rose, A., 202
Ross, Catherine E., 299, 303, 305
Rossi, Peter H., 109, 274, 282, 300, 309
Rossman, David, 290–294
Roth, Jordan T., 76

S

Saturday Night Special, 17, 58, 62, 178, 180, 182, 188, 196, 203, 234, 241, 247, 276, 277, 288, 289, 316, 319
  Bans on, 269
Scheidt, Rick J., 202
Schneidman, Edwin S., 168
Schuman, Howard, 221
Scott, Gregory L., 72
Search Group, Inc., 176, 180
Second Amendment, 273, 310
  Public opinion concerning, 238–240
Seitz, Stephen T., 135, 204, 205, 284
Self-defense. *See* Self-protection, by guns
Self-protection, by guns, 10, 11, 12, 14, 42, 49, 57, 94–96, 103, 104, 116, 117, 123, 128, 129, 138–149, 184, 186, 312. *See also* Guns, as crime deterrent
  Public opinion about, 238
Sentence enhancements. *See* Gun control policies, sentence enhancements for gun crimes
Sherrill, Robert, 1, 25, 120, 121
Shields, Nelson T., 216

Shotgun News, 119
Shotguns. *See* Guns
Simons, Lynn, 202
Skogan, Wesley, 154, 155
Smith, Howard, 1
Smith, William, 310
Social class, effects on gun ownership. *See* Gun owners, by social class
Socialization, to gun use. *See* Gun use, socialization into
Sourcebook of Criminal Justice Statistics, 75, 164–166
Special Weapons and Tactics (SWAT), 77, 79
Spiegler, Jeffrey H., 25, 27, 29, 41–43, 52, 81, 83, 97, 98
Sport and recreation with guns. *See* Guns, sport and recreational use of
Sports Illustrated, 59
Statistical Abstract of the United States, 29, 30, 48, 51, 53, 54, 56, 67, 167, 171
Steele, Kevin, 73, 75
Stickney, S. B., 120
Stinchcombe, Arthur L., 221
Stokes, C. Shannon, 109, 113, 114
Stolen guns. *See* Guns, theft of
Substitution effects, 189–212, 322
  In homicide, 190–206
  In robbery, 206–212
Suicide, with guns, 15, 132, 133, 311
  Trends in, 15, 166–170
Supply of guns. *See* Guns, supply of
Supply-side estimates, of gun prevalence. *See* Gun prevalence, methods of estimation
SWAT. *See* Special Weapons and Tactics
Sweeney, John J., 25, 27, 29, 41–43, 52, 81, 83, 97, 98

T

Taylor, R., 197
Theft of guns. *See* Guns, theft of
Thompson, Hunter S., 49
Time-series studies. *See* Gun control policies, time-series studies of
Tittle, Charles R., 139
"Trail guns," 58
Turner, Charles W., 202

U

Uniform Crime Reports (FBI), 5, 14, 15, 66,
    67, 101, 153, 154, 156–159, 161, 170–
    172, 208, 278, 285
    Limitations of, 154–156
United States Census of Manufacturers, 79
United States Conference of Mayors, 295
United States Department of Commerce,
    175, 176, 180
United States Fish and Wildlife Service, 59

V

Vera Institute, 300
Victimization by Crime. *See* Crime, Victim-
    ization by
Victim-offender relationships, in homicide
    and assault, 192–194
Vietnam, 73, 77
Vinson, T., 195, 198
Violence, subculture of, 108
    In the South, 109–112
Violence-proneness, 209
Violent crime. *See also* Various categories
    of violent crime.
    City and county comparisons of crime
        rates, 126, 128, 134, 136
    Estimates of, 172–174
    Guns used in, 175–188
    Incidence of, in United States, 153–173
    International comparisons of rates of, 125,
        126
    Regional and state comparisons of rates
        of, 126, 127, 135
    Relationship to gun ownership, 123–149
    Trends in, 154–166

Vital Statistics of the United States, 166, 167,
    170, 171
Votey, Harold, 135

W

War Revenue Act of 1919, 245
Washington, DC gun law, 294
Weber-Burdin, Eleanor, 244, 270, 271, 283,
    300
Weiner, P., 202
Westgard, Richard, 81, 100
White, Carolyn S., 117
Whitman, Charles, 121
Wickersham Commission, 299
Wildhorn, Sorrel, 66
Williams, J. Sherwood, 99, 120, 128
Wolfgang, Marvin, 190, 201, 204, 205, 206
Wright, James D., 25, 34, 44, 98, 99, 104–
    109, 120, 128, 138, 140, 196, 215, 220,
    309

Y

Yeager, Matthew G., 138–141, 145, 148
Your Guide to Firearms Regulations, 243

Z

Zimring, Franklin E., 2, 3, 10, 13, 21, 25–
    29, 31–39, 41–43, 45–48, 50, 52, 53,
    55, 60, 81, 93–99, 104, 106, 107, 109,
    118, 119, 123, 127, 130–135, 137–140,
    170, 175, 191–201, 203, 204, 207, 243,
    245–247, 280, 281, 288–290